Arizona

50 miles

50 km

www.insight

INSIGHT GUIDES

ARIZONA & THE
GRAND CANYON

APA PUBLICATIONS

Part of the Langenscheidt Publishing Group

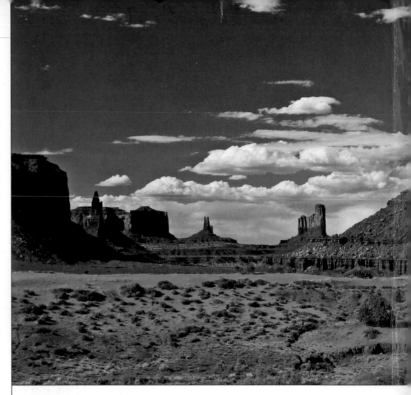

☀ **INSIGHT GUIDE**

ARIZONA

Editorial
Project Editor
John Gattuso
Picture Manager
Steven Lawrence
Series Manager
Rachel Fox

Distribution
North America
Langenscheidt Publishers, Inc.
36–36 33rd Street, 4th Floor
Long Island City, New York 11106
orders@langenscheidt.com

UK & Ireland
GeoCenter International Ltd
Meridian House, Churchill Way West
Basingstoke, Hampshire RG21 6YR
sales@geocenter.co.uk

Australia
Universal Publishers
1 Waterloo Road
Macquarie Park, NSW 2113
sales@universalpublishers.com.au

New Zealand
Hema Maps New Zealand Ltd (HNZ)
Unit 2, 10 Cryers Road
East Tamaki, Auckland 2013
sales.hema@clear.net.nz

Worldwide
Apa Publications GmbH & Co.
Verlag KG (Singapore branch)
7030 Ang Mo Kio Avenue 5
08-65 Northstar @ AMK
Singapore 569880
apasin@singnet.com.sg

Printing
CTPS - China

©2009 Apa Publications GmbH & Co.
Verlag KG (Singapore branch)
All Rights Reserved

First Edition 2002
Second Edition 2009
Reprinted 2010

CONTACTING THE EDITORS
We would appreciate it if readers
would alert us to errors or out-
dated information by writing to:
Insight Guides, P.O. Box 7910,
London SE1 1WE, England.
insight@apaguide.co.uk
NO part of this book may be reproduced,
stored in a retrieval system or transmitted in any form or means electronic,
mechanical, photocopying, recording
or otherwise, without prior written per-
~~mission~~ of *Apa Publications*. Brief
~~quo~~tations with use of
~~photograp~~hs are exempted for book
~~review purp~~oses only. Information has
~~been obtained~~ from sources believed
~~to be reliable, b~~ut its accuracy and
~~completeness, a~~nd the opinions based
~~thereon, are no~~t guaranteed.

~~www.insight~~guides.com

ABOUT THIS BOOK

The first Insight Guide pioneered the use of creative full-color photography in travel guides in 1970. Since then, we have ex-panded our range to cater to our readers' need not only for reliable information about their chosen des-tination but also for a real under-standing of the culture and workings of that destination. Now, when the internet can supply inexhaustible (but not always reliable) facts, our books marry text and pictures to provide those much more elusive qualities: knowledge and discernment.

How to use this book

Insight Guide: Arizona is structured to convey an understanding of the state and its people as well as to guide readers through its attractions:
◆ The **Features** section, indicated by a pink bar at the top of each page, covers the natural and cultural history of the region as well as illu-minating essays on outdoor adven-ture, cowboy lore, and exploring ghost towns and Indian ruins.
◆ The main **Places** section, indi-cated by a blue bar, is a complete guide to all the sights and areas worth visiting. Places of special interest are coordinated by number with the maps.
◆ The **Travel Tips** listings section, with a yellow bar, provides full infor-mation on transportation, hotels, activities from culture and shopping to sports, and an A–Z section of essential practical information. An easy-to-find contents list for Travel Tips is printed on the back flap, which also serves as a bookmark.

The contributors

This thoroughly updated and redesigned edition was managed by **John Gattuso**, a veteran Insight

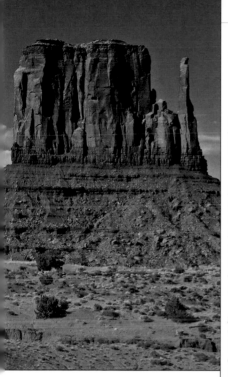

LEFT: Monument Valley.

often for *Arizona Highways* and is the author of many books on the Southwest, including a guide to the region's national parks.

Nora Burba Trulsson has lived in Arizona long enough to see golf courses outnumber dude ranches. She writes about both in "The Arizona Cowboy" and "Golfer's Paradise." She is a contributor to *Sunset* and *Phoenix* magazines and co-author of *Living Home*, a book on sustainable architecture.

Santa Fe writer **Richard Mahler** guides readers to "Arizona's West Coast," a stretch of the Colorado River on the state's western border. Mahler is a columnist for *Desert Exposure* and the author of 11 books.

With more than 30 years' experience as an editor and writer at newspapers in the New York area, **Edward A. Jardim** knows how to transform a complex story into a concise narrative. Here he condenses four centuries of history into an engaging chronicle of Arizona's founding and development.

The spectacular photography in this book is the work of some of the most distinguished photographers in the Southwest. The two principal photographers are **Richard Nowitz**, a frequent Insight Guide contributor whose recent assignments include guides to China, Peru, and Florida, and **Kerrick James**, a Phoenix-based photographer whose work has appeared in publications such as *National Geographic Adventure*, *Arizona Highways*, *Sunset*, *Islands*, and many others.

Isobel McLean indexed the book. The map editor was **Zoë Goodwin**.

Guide editor and writer whose earlier books include guides to the national parks, American Indian cultures, and several western states.

Updating her work from the original edition of this book was **Nicky Leach**, an award-winning travel writer and long-time Insight Guide contributor whose work appears in guides to New Mexico, Utah, Colorado, Florida, and numerous other destinations. Leach covers a host of Arizona topics, from geology and archaeology to ghost towns and cultural history, then leads readers into every corner of the state, from the saguaro-studded Sonoran Desert to the lonely expanses of the Arizona Strip.

Arizona writer **Rose Houk** covers familiar territory – the Grand Canyon, where she worked as a park ranger before embarking on a writing career, and Flagstaff, her home for more than 15 years. She writes

Map Legend

Symbol	Meaning
– ∙ – ∙	International Boundary
▬▬	State Boundary
– – – –	County Boundary
⊖	Border Crossing
– ∙ –	National Park/Reserve
✈ ✈	Airport: International/Regional
🚌	Bus Station
❶	Tourist Information
⛪ † ⸸	Church/Ruins
†	Monastery
☾	Mosque
✡	Synagogue
🏰	Castle/Ruins
∴	Archaeological Site
∩	Cave
🛉	Statue/Monument
★	Place of Interest
🏠	Mansion

The main places of interest in the Places section are coordinated by number with a full-colour map (e.g. ❶), and a symbol at the top of every right-hand page tells you where to find the map.

Contents

LEFT: Mather Point, Grand Canyon National Park.

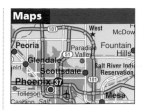

THE BEST OF ARIZONA: TOP ATTRACTIONS

Spectacular scenery, thrilling adventures, a mix of Native American, Hispanic, and Anglo cultures, plus more than 300 days of sunshine a year, make Arizona a classic Southwestern destination

△ Check into one of Arizona's famously plush **resorts** and pamper yourself with spa treatments, healing massages, fine cuisine, and long hours lounging by the pool. For the adventurous, **dude ranches** are a uniquely western experience, ranging from working cattle ranches to elaborate "resorts with horses." *Pages 116, 275–6, 278, 338–40*

▽ The backdrop of countless western movies, **Monument Valley** is one of the iconic landscapes of the American West and an epicenter of traditional Navajo culture. *Pages 181–2*

△ Words can't easily express the scale and grandeur of the **Grand Canyon**, one of the world's natural wonders, millions of years in the making. *Pages 131–47*

△ Set within stunning red-rock formations, **Sedona** has a lively arts scene, lots of shopping and dining, and a reputation for New Age vibrations. *Pages 229–39*

◁ On the **Havasupai Reservation** deep within the Grand Canyon is a hidden world of waterfalls and pools of blue-green water. *Pages 143–4*

△ Boaters can explore more than a million acres of sandstone wilderness on **Lake Powell**, created by the flooding of Glen Canyon. *Pages 164–5*

△ In the heart of the Navajo Nation is **Canyon de Chelly**, a spectacular gorge where Navajo sheepherders tend flocks and fields and ancient pueblos are perched on cliffs. *Pages 185–6*

△ The most thrilling way to experience the Grand Canyon is **whitewater rafting on the Colorado River**, a multiday journey on one of the mightiest waterways in the western US. *Pages 151–9*

◁ Sun-baked Arizonans escape to the **White Mountains**, where cool forests, leaping streams, and an abundance of outdoor recreation offer a welcome break from the desert heat. *Pages 251–65*

▷ Native American art and culture are interpreted with intelligence and sensitivity at the **Heard Museum**, site of the annual Indian Fair and Market. *Pages 286–7*

THE BEST OF ARIZONA: EDITOR'S CHOICE

Awe-inspiring landscapes including the Grand Canyon, Sedona's red rocks, and the Sonoran Desert, plus outdoor adventures, ancient Indian ruins, plush resorts, and hip urban centers ... here, at a glance, are our top recommendations for a visit

BEST SCENERY

● **Grand Canyon National Park.** One of the must-see wonders of the world, the "Big Ditch" delivers sublime scenery and glimpses of 2 billion years of earth history. *See page 131.*

● **Kartchner Caverns State Park.** A wet, living cave system in the Whetstone Mountains, the beautiful caverns below this former ranch make it Arizona's top state park. *See page 316.*

● **Monument Valley Navajo Tribal Park.** The wind-sculpted buttes and mesas in this park on the Arizona-Utah border have sheltered Ancestral Pueblo and Navajo people for millennia and inspired movie Westerns since the 1930s. *See page 181.*

● **Petrified Forest National Park.** Moody badlands and petrified tree trunks with mysterious gem-laden centers created during the Age of the Dinosaurs spread below the Hopi Mesas of northern Arizona. *See page 252.*

● **Saguaro National Park.** Like Jolly Green Giants, these one-ton cacti march across southern Arizona's Sonoran Desert hills in likeable profusion and provide photo ops in two different park units. *See page 302.*

● **Sedona.** These eroded red sandstone mesas are a magnet for outdoor-lovers, artists, and New Age spirits drawn by the rocks' famous healing energies. *See page 229.*

BEST FAMILY ATTRACTIONS

● **Arizona Science Center.** With an IMAX theater, planetarium, and over 300 hands-on exhibitions, this vibrant science center in an Antoine Predock-designed building next to Heritage Square is a must for hyperactive kids. *See page 272.*

● **Challenger Space Center.** Fly simulated space flight missions as a flight crew, mission controller, or scientist at this educational space center affiliated with the Smithsonian Institution in Peoria, near Phoenix. *See page 304.*

● **Grand Canyon Railway.** Ride a steam train and experience a shootout on the way home on the historic railroad between Williams and the Grand Canyon. *See page 136.*

● **Lowell Observatory.** Walk through a recreation of the solar system, look at the stars through a telescope, play with interactive exhibits, and take part in special presentations at this nationally known planetarium in Flagstaff. *See page 195.*

● **Phoenix Zoo.** The annual ZooLights holiday display and the chance to view 1,200 animals, from white rhinos to desert tortoises, make this private zoo the top-rated kid's destination in Arizona. *See page 277.*

LEFT: Grand Canyon. **ABOVE:** Arizona Science Center.

BEST WILDLIFE VIEWING

● **Grand Canyon condors.** Restored populations of endangered California condors regularly visit the South Rim to pose for pictures on the guard rail. *See page 90.*
● **Kofa National Wildlife Refuge.** Relict California palm trees, stranded during the Ice Age, and even rarer desert bighorn sheep inhabit this primitive refuge near Phoenix. *See page 223.*

ABOVE: bighorn sheep.

● **Chiricahua Mountains.** Apache fox squirrels, Chihuahua and Apache pines, and neon-hued neotropical migratory birds like the rare elegant trogon live crosscultural lives amid southern Arizona's "sky islands." *See page 311.*
● **San Pedro Riparian National Conservation Area.** This river corridor on the US-Mexico border is a layover for an astonishing 4-10 million migratory birds each year. *See page 317.*
● **White Water Draw, Willcox.** Birders flock to flooded Willcox Playa each winter to view the spectacular landings and takeoffs of over 10,000 migrating sandhill cranes, Canada, and snow geese. *See page 316.*

ABOVE: the internationally minded Phoenix Art Museum.

ART AND CULTURE

● **ASU Gammage Auditorium, Tempe** This building designed by Frank Lloyd Wright offers a full roster of performing arts events in up-and-coming Tempe. *See page 344.*
● **Grand Canyon Chamber Music.** The South Rim is a musical mecca for a month every September with world-class chamber music and the occasional jazz and blues concert by professional musicians. *See page 346.*
● **Sedona International Film Festival.** This month-long February event draws

A-list celebrities and movie fans to celebrate independent films in a stunning setting. *See page 344.*
● **Tempe Center for the Arts.** This beautifully designed, state-of-the-art community center houses two theaters, an art gallery, a restaurant with a view of the restored downtown Salt River, and a pleasant riverwalk with a sculpture garden. *See pages 344.*

RIGHT: squash blossom necklace, Heard Museum.

MUST-SEE MUSEUMS

● **Arizona-Sonora Desert Museum.** Not really a museum but a huge zoo in Tucson celebrating animals of the Sonoran Desert, which are housed in naturalistic enclosures and star in well-conceived presentations. *See page 303.*
● **Heard Museum.** The perfect introduction to Arizona's Indian cultures through an award-winning multimedia presentation, special collections, contemporary exhibits, and Indian arts and crafts festivals, all in a historic setting in Phoenix. *See pages 274 and 286.*
● **Museum of Northern Arizona.** Founded in Flagstaff by archaeologist Harold Colton, MNA is

the major repository for artifacts unearthed at nearby Wupatki Pueblo and other archaeological digs and has exhibits on northern Arizona's geology, history, and cultures, as well as juried Indian art shows. *See page 197.*
● **Phoenix Art Museum.** After undergoing a huge expansion to double its size, PAM has become a major venue for international traveling art exhibits as well as displaying art from around the world. *See page 273.*
● **Titan Missile Museum.** This missile silo is the only site in the US with a (disarmed) nuclear missile still on its underground launch pad. Guides lead one-hour tours of the subterranean museum and control center. *See page 305.*

BEST HISTORIC SITES

● **Bisbee.** Visit underground and open-pit mines of old, take a historic walking tour of Bisbee's steep streets, and visit museums, art galleries, retro restaurants, and quaint hotels in old (and sometimes haunted) buildings. *See page 313.*

● **Hubbell Trading Post National Historic Site.** A restored working trading post in Ganado, complete with store, bullpen, rug room, and craft demonstrations, shows trading life on the Navajo Reservation over the last century. *See page 185.*

● **Pipe Spring National Monument.** A preserved 1870s Mormon fort, cattle ranch, Ancestral Pueblo settlement, and cultural remains from the adjoining Kaibab Paiute Reservation all tell a fascinating history on the lonely Arizona Strip situated north of the Grand Canyon. *See page 169.*

● **Presidio Historic District, Tucson.** Visit a series of restored buildings housing museums, restaurants, B&Bs, and businesses in Tucson's downtown to experience its lively Mexican and Territorial American past. *See page 294.*

● **Taliesin West.** A visit to Frank Lloyd Wright's Scottsdale home and school is de rigueur for fans of the master's organic architecture. *See page 277.*

● **Tumacacori National Historical Park and San Xavier Del Bac Mission.** One of several missions founded by Father Kino, the ruined Tumacacori mission was built near the Spanish presidio of Tubac, an early American boomtown and now an arts center. San Xavier Del Bac church, near Tucson, still serves the San Xavier Reservation and has a beautiful white-carved facade. *See pages 319 and 320.*

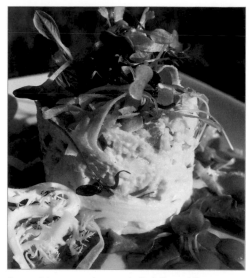

ABOVE: Arizona resorts promote their fine cuisine.

BEST WINING AND DINING

● **Brix Wine Bar and Restaurant, Flagstaff.** This charming fine-dining restaurant in an old carriage house mesmerizes with its locally sourced Mediterranean cuisine and exceptional wines. *See page 204.*

● **Café Poca Cosa, Tucson.** Susana Davila's vibrant café offers a taste of Mexico City in downtown Tucson, with imaginative tamales, mole sauces, and daily specials. *See page 306.*

● **Canela Southwestern Bistro, Sonoita.** The location may be rural but the European-inspired dishes created by the chef-owners of this backcountry bistro are world class – a perfect marriage of local foods and wines, sophisticated culinary techniques, hard work, and passion. *See page 324.*

● **Kai, Sheraton Wild Horse Pass Resort, Chandler.** Phoenix's top fine-dining restaurant leads the pack by reimagining traditional Native American cuisine for the 21st century, sourcing foods locally, executing dishes perfectly, and creating a beautiful setting in which to enjoy them. *See page 283.*

● **Turquoise Room, La Posada, Winslow.** English-born John Sharpe's foods play on local ingredients and cross-cultural dishes to magnificent effect in his attractive restaurant inside Winslow's historic La Posada. *See page 265.*

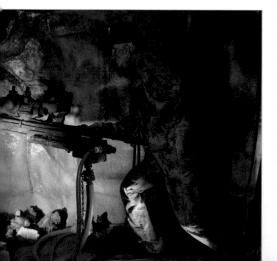

LEFT: a mining exhibit, one of Bisbee's attractions.

OFF THE BEATEN TRACK

● **Biosphere 2.** This experiment in futuristic living inside a 3-acre building is now a research center managed by the University of Arizona. *See page 305.*

● **Grand Canyon Skywalk.** A 75-ft-long (23-meter) Plexiglass viewing platform, 4,000ft (1,200 meters) above the Colorado River on the Hualapai Indian Reservation, offers vertiginous views of the western Grand Canyon. *See page 219.*

● **Greer.** This remote Mormon village in the White Mountains has rustic cabins, top-rated B&Bs, hearty ranch food, hiking, fishing, downhill skiing on the Apache reservation, and one-of-a-kind history museums. *See page 256.*

● **Hopi Mesas.** Hopi farmers and craftspeople live in 12 villages on or below isolated mesas surrounded by the Navajo Nation. Second Mesa has a cultural center, restaurant, and examples of each mesa's pottery, katsinas, and jewelry. *See page 186.*

● **Patagonia.** A favorite Tucson getaway, this laid-back former mining community offers backroads for biking, top bird-watching, art galleries, historic B&Bs, great little eateries, wine tastings, and healing retreats. *See page 318.*

ABOVE: the much photographed Antelope Canyon.

OUTDOOR ADVENTURE

● **Antelope Canyon.** Hike northern Arizona's most alluring slot canyon with Navajo guides, then enjoy a gourmet meal at the Antelope Marina on Lake Powell, whose architecture and water-front dining facilities showcase Navajo culture. *See page 165.*

● **Grand Canyon rafting and hiking.** Guides offer trips highlighting the quintessential Grand Canyon experience: paddling the Colorado River. Hikes into side canyons are a bonus; rim-top hikers will enjoy the North Rim's cooler, forested trails. *See pages 151 and 139.*

● **Havasu Falls, Havasupai Reservation.** Whether hiking down from the rim or up from the river to the homeland of the People of the Blue Green Water, a swim in idyllic Havasu Falls is the reward at the end of the hike. *See page 143.*

● **Lake Powell house-boating.** Its waters are gradually evaporating, but Lake Powell is still a mecca for boaters of all stripes, including laid-back houseboaters and more active kayakers. *See page 164.*

ABOVE: Biosphere 2, center for an unusual experiment.

MONEY-SAVING TIPS

● **America the Beautiful Federal Lands Pass:** If you plan to visit more than a couple of US national parks, national forests, or BLM sites in the next year, be sure to buy an annual federal lands pass, which offers admission for one vehicle containing four passengers to sites across the country for $80.

● **National parks on the Navajo Reservation:** Entrance to the spectacular Canyon de Chelly and Navajo national monuments in northern Arizona is free.

● **Flagstaff Festival of Science:** Lectures, star-gazing, hands-on archaeological digs, hikes to local pueblos, and other events are free for the whole family at Flagstaff's annual 10-day celebration of science.

● **Camping in national forests.** Primitive camping is free on national forest lands, if you're willing to do without any amenities and bring your own food, water, supplies, and practice No Trace camping ethics.

● **Summer rates at resorts.** Locals flock to southern Arizona's swankiest resorts, when summer temperatures hit the low 100s, and enjoy all the amenities for a fraction of the high-season rates.

● **Weekend wine tastings.** Arizona's up-and-coming wineries offer free wine tastings year-round in Elgin, near Sonoita, and the Verde and Chino Valleys, south and west of Flagstaff.

THE GRAND CANYON STATE

One of the world's great natural treasures,
the Grand Canyon is just the first of
Arizona's many wonders

V isiting the Grand Canyon in 1903, Theodore Roosevelt delivered a speech that would become a classic summation of conservation principles. "Leave it as it is," he declared. "You cannot improve on it. The ages have been at work on it, and man can only mar it. What you can do is keep it for your children, your children's children, and for all who come after you, as the one great sight which every American… should see."

Five years later, he declared the Grand Canyon a national monument to prevent it from being "improved upon" by human hands, And though a clutch of hotels and parking lots now stand on the rims, and the Colorado River has been restrained by dams, the canyon remains an emblem of the grandeur of the American West, its protection a watershed in the history of environmental stewardship.

Today, almost 4½ million visitors a year journey to view this natural wonder – "the Big Ditch," as locals call it. Most arrive at the easily accessed South Rim, via the gateway community of Tusayun, where hotels, restaurants, and services are abundant. At Mather Point, the first overlook into the canyon, some fall into awed silence. Some are moved to tears. Others lapse into poetry. And still others, like World War II Allied Supreme Commander Ferdinand Foch, stare at the canyon, then, unable to take it all in, simply say, "How about a cup of coffee?"

Monoliths and malls

Even more wondrous is that the Grand Canyon is just one of Arizona's many natural treasures. From the sandstone monoliths of Monument Valley and the soaring walls of Canyon de Chelly to the trees-turned-to-stone of the Petrified Forest and the giant saguaros of the Sonoran Desert, the state is a catalog of wonder.

The human imprint is just as fascinating and, despite the proliferation of strip malls, tract housing, and other modern developments, surprisingly

PRECEDING PAGES: Havasu Canyon; aspens in the San Francisco Peaks; Chiricahua National Monument. **LEFT:** Monument Valley. **ABOVE LEFT:** Arizona Biltmore Resort and Spa, Scottsdale. **ABOVE RIGHT:** Thomas Moran's *Chasm of the Colorado*, 1873–74.

ancient. The mesa-top villages of the Hopi include the oldest continuously inhabited town in the United States (since AD 1150), and their culture is filled with echoes of the long-vanished Sinagua and Ancestral Puebloans, or Anasazi, whose ruins are strewn throughout the northern canyons.

The Navajo and Apache, both descendants of Athabascan nomads who migrated into the Southwest six centuries ago, integrate traditional values into their modern lives, as do the descendants of the Spanish and Mexican immigrants who settled the missions and ranchos of the south. Cowboys still ride the range in remote corners of the state, and a few lone prospectors scratch a living from played-out mines. Even Phoenix, the country's sixth-largest city and a prime example of the New West, sits atop an ancient Hohokam settlement, whose elaborate irrigation system, once used to water fields of maize and melon, now serves corporate towers and shopping malls.

Iconic landscapes

For many people, a visit to the Navajo and Hopi Reservations, east of Flagstaff, is the highlight of their trip to northern Arizona. Time seems to stand still in this epic landscape, whose stone landmarks and secret canyons are sacred to the people who have called this home for centuries. The 29,817-sq mile (77,226-sq km) Navajo Nation is the largest Indian reservation in the country. The crown jewel in the Navajo tribal park system is undoubtedly Monument Valley, instantly familiar to everyone who has seen classic John Ford movies such as *Stagecoach, She Wore a Yellow Ribbon, The Searchers, Sergeant Rutledge*, and *Cheyenne Autumn*.

A number of Navajo families live inside the boundaries of the parks, on traditional homesteads usually consisting of a frame house, a hogan (log and earth hut), a shady *ramada* (shelter), a nearby sweat lodge, and livestock corrals for sheep, goats, and horses. Many local Navajos are licensed to offer horseback and Jeep tours of their homeland. Almost every family makes turquoise and silver jewelry, rugs, baskets, sand paintings, and folk art, and the seasonal income from tourists is their principal means of support.

The big picture

Travelers with a taste for creature comforts will find no lack of plush resorts and trendy restaurants in Arizona, and enough golf courses to keep them swinging for years. But those who venture beyond the usual tourist trails will discover that the state, like its best-known feature, is a place of uncommon depth. Seeing the big picture can be overwhelming at first. Only by descending beneath the rim, exploring the state layer by layer, is its true nature revealed. ❏

TOP RIGHT: palm-shaded beach at Lake Havasu City. **ABOVE LEFT:** underground mine tour, Bisbee. **RIGHT:** a rock climber clings to a limestone cliff south of Flagstaff.

THE CULTURAL LANDSCAPE

A colorful combination of Indian, Hispanic, and Anglo cultures is enriched by immigrants from all over the world

Early in 1856, an eastbound stagecoach arrived in a cloud of dust in Tucson, then a Spanish-speaking adobe village. Arizona had passed from Spanish to Mexican rule in 1821, and just two years before, as part of the 1854 Gadsden Purchase ending the Mexican War, become American territory. Papers signed thousands of miles away had little impact on residents of northern Mexico and southern Arizona, then as now united by a shared landscape and ancient cultural ties. Not until the arrival of the railroad in 1880 and the end of the Apache Wars in 1886 would Arizona Territory attract the flood of white settlers that dominate the state ethnically today. Statehood, granted in 1912, was still 56 years away.

Aboard that stagecoach in 1856 was one of Tucson's first Anglo immigrants. Sam Hughes, a 28-year-old Welshman, had been working in a bakery in a California gold-rush town. He was dying of tuberculosis and, in a last-ditch attempt to save his life, started making his way to Texas, hoping the warm, dry air would improve his health. The stage driver didn't share his faith. Expecting the sickly foreigner with the sing-song accent to

Indian gaming rakes in about $800 million annually. In the coming years the figure is expected to exceed $1.3 billion – nearly a sixth of the state government's yearly budget.

expire at any moment, he dumped him in Tucson. Of the 500 or so residents, Hughes was assured, five spoke English.

PRECEDING PAGES: White Mountain Apache rodeo princess. **LEFT:** Mexican dancers at Tumacacori National Historic Site. **RIGHT:** San Xavier del Bac Mission.

Founding father

Hughes didn't die. Just the opposite. Like the thousands who would later come here for their health, he was cured by the Arizona desert. Grit and determination made up for formal education in frontier Tucson, a town where, as journalist J. Ross Browne observed in 1864, "Every man went armed to the teeth, and street-fights and bloody affrays were of daily occurrence."

Hughes's weapons were a steel will and a capacity for hard work. He made friends with his Mexican neighbors, learned their language, married a young Sonoran girl, and had successful careers in ranching, real estate, and politics. By the time he died, at the age of 88, he was considered one of Tucson's founding fathers.

At about the same time, in the opposite end of the state, Mormon colonists, recently settled in Utah, were now setting their sights on Arizona. In 1858, Mormon missionary Jacob Hamblin traveled across the Arizona Strip to the Hopi Mesas in search of Indian converts and new farmland along the Little Colorado River. He was warmly welcomed at Moenkopi by Hopi chief Tuva, who became the first of many Hopis to convert to Christianity. Hamblin's trip laid the groundwork for settlements in the 1870s, when government persecution in Utah led Mormons to establish communities all the way down to St David in the San Pedro River Valley. In one of the odd twists of

ico to travel north to Arizona and begin trading some 3,000 years ago. They mingled with Archaic hunter-gatherers in the Sonoran Desert and shared information about farming, pottery, and religion that would be passed along to tribes throughout the state. Without this exchange among cultures, it's unlikely the Mogollon, Hohokam, and Ancestral Pueblo would ever have come to dominate the prehistoric Southwest.

It must have been opportunity, too, that lured nomadic Athabascans – today's Navajo and Apache – from northwest Canada between the 12th and 15th centuries. Around the same time, Shoshoneans and the Utes and Paiutes were also

history that seem to abound in this state, the Mormons were convinced that the Hopi spoke Welsh, and Hamblin brought with him a Welsh-speaking translator. Had they met, the translator and Hughes would undoubtedly have enjoyed the joke.

Opportunity knocks

For immigrants, Arizona has always been a land where dreams could come true, a "blank slate on which they could etch their visions of the future," according to historian Thomas Sheridan. Nor is this a recent phenomenon. Opportunity undoubtedly spurred the very first paleo-hunters to venture into Arizona's game-rich grasslands after the retreat of the Ice Age glaciers 12,000 years ago. It may have been what motivated people from Mex-

moving in from the Great Basin. In the 1600s it was the promise of gold and silver, timber and fertile land that lured first Spaniards and Mexicans, then Anglos and other immigrants to the state. Though they didn't always find what they were looking for, pioneers of every race stayed and made a life for themselves.

The trend continues. Arizona is the second-fastest growing state in the country, posting a growth rate of 40 percent between 1990 and 2000. It has an ethnic diversity rare even in the West. Of the state's 5.1 million residents, Hispanics constitute 25 percent, American Indians 5 percent, African Americans 3 percent. Most of the others are white people of various nationalities and religions. The result isn't so much a melting pot, in which ethnic groups are boiled down to a bland homogeneity, but a tossed salad in which distinct groups coexist and occasionally come into conflict.

The first Arizonans

Though American Indians are a relatively small minority, no other group is more closely identified with the state or, ironically, more misunderstood. For starters, there is no one over-arching Indian culture. Each of the 21 tribes in Arizona has its own history, traditions, and language, though almost all now speak English and many hold jobs off their reservations. While some tribal members have chosen to maintain traditional ways of life,

nos, resort developments, and other businesses on Indian reservations have let tribes get ahead economically but may also represent a compromise of traditional values.

Ironically, one of the keys to sustaining cultural values has been embracing positive change. Every tribe has borrowed cultural traits from its neighbors, creating dynamic societies that not only survive but, surprisingly, thrive in the face of change. Navajo kids use computers to learn their native tongue. Indian youth go away to law school, then return to the reservation to represent their tribes in centuries-old disputes over land and water rights, housing, subsistence hunting and gathering, and

the influence of modern culture is unavoidable and often produces unexpected and calamitous results.

Introduced diseases, substance abuse, and domestic violence – while not uniquely Indian problems – have devastated many tribes already struggling to hold onto cultural identities after years of government-sponsored re-education, land reallocation and, during the 19th century, extermination. Tribal councils, introduced in the early 1900s, are frequently at odds with themselves or mired in the long debates that Indian people have traditionally employed to reach consensus. Casi-

access to public lands for traditional religious uses. Reservation doctors and nurses combine modern medicine and traditional healing in the treatment of diabetes and other modern ailments.

The trick for most tribes is to engage the outside world without being overwhelmed by it. As more tribes take over the management of their institutions and natural resources, and encourage the development of tribal businesses, there is a shift in decision-making from federal policy-makers to tribal governments.

The Navajo

The 210,000-strong Navajo Nation, the largest in the country, grapples with this issue daily. The Navajo, or *Diné*, as they call themselves, live on

FAR LEFT: A Navajo dancer, *c.*1904.
NEAR LEFT: Apache men, *c.*1909. **ABOVE:** a
Navajo silversmith works inside a hogan, 1915.

a 29,000-sq-mile (47,000-sq-km) reservation that encompasses the mesas, canyons, black lava promontories, and high-desert grasslands of northeastern Arizona, northwestern New Mexico, and a sliver of southern Utah. A matriarchal society, where women own all the property and men move in with the wife's family, Navajo life is governed by complex clan relationships and the pursuit of traditional religious beliefs, often referred to as the Beauty Path. Modern Navajos still strive for *hozho*, a state of harmony with all things, taught by the Holy People who created First Man and First Woman, and later, Changing Woman, the ideal Navajo woman whose spirit is evoked in the

kinaalda, a puberty ritual observed by Navajo girls.

The ancestors of the Navajo were Athabascan nomads who migrated into the Southwest from Canada perhaps as early as the 12th century. In addition to hunting and gathering, they raided Pueblo settlements, a practice that intensified after they acquired Spanish horses in the 1600s. But they also saw the merits of Pueblo agriculture and, during times of peace, intermarried, traded, learned weaving, and adapted some aspects of Pueblo religion. They were such proficient corn farmers that the Pueblo called them *Navajú*, a Tewa word meaning "great fields." Corn remains central to Navajo rituals, and corn pollen is used in all blessing ceremonies.

Culture and conflict

Though relations between Navajo and Pueblo people are cordial in most day-to-day interactions, tensions have simmered over the years – particularly between the Navajo and Hopi. In 1680, the Navajo united with Pueblo people in a revolt against the Spanish and, for a time, lived with them in small defensive *pueblitos* in New Mexico. But in 1868, after the Navajo's four-year incarceration at Fort Sumner, relations between the Navajo and Hopi soured fast. The reservation created for the Navajo was rapidly expanded to accommodate a rebounding Navajo population and its hungry livestock. Eventually, Navajo grazing lands surrounded the compact cornfields and villages of the much smaller Hopi Reservation. A long and complex land dispute over boundaries and the relocation of families in some joint-use areas is still being adjudicated today, and there are ongoing concerns about how overgrazing of fragile desert grasslands by Navajo sheep and goats

NAVAJO CODE TALKERS

Navajos have fought bravely in every major American military engagement in the last century, but their most important contribution came during World War II, when 400 Navajo Code Talkers served with the US Marine Corps throughout the Pacific, sending and receiving messages in a disguised version of their native language. The code, which was never broken by the Japanese, is now recognized as having been one of the keys to victories at Iwo Jima and other major battles.

It was the brainchild of Philip Johnston, a white missionary's son who had grown up on the Navajo Reservation and spoke the language fluently. In 1942, Navajo recruits at Camp Pendleton, California, devised their own code, using three Navajo words for each letter – e.g., ant, ax, and apple

for A, or badger, bear, and barrel for B.

So secret was their work, Code Talkers didn't receive national recognition until 1982, when President Ronald Reagan proclaimed August 14 National Navajo Code Talkers Day. In 1999, President Bill Clinton visited the reservation and gave a speech that included a few words in Navajo code. For Navajos, the symbolism of that speech lay not so much in a recognition of their people's patriotism but in the use of a language that, for years, the US government actively worked to stamp out as un-American.

continues to exacerbate erosion on Navajo land.

What we now regard as traditional Navajo culture was also profoundly influenced by Europeans. The Spanish introduced not only horses but sheepherding, rug weaving, and silversmithing. After the Long Walk, the Navajo adopted a version of the tiered Mother Hubbard dress they saw army wives wearing at Fort Sumner and developed a taste for flour, canned goods, and other consumer products. This created opportunities for merchants, who opened trading posts on the reservation in the 1870s. Early entrepreneurs like Lorenzo Hubbell in Ganado befriended the Navajo, became intermediaries between the tribe

in the mountains of Arizona. Historically, there were five groups of Western Apache. The four territorial bands of the San Carlos Apache inhabited the rolling high desert surrounding the Pinal, Apache, Mescal, and Catalina Mountains. The Eastern and Western bands of the White Mountain group occupied the area from the Pinaleno Mountains to the high plateau north and east of the White Mountains. The Cibecue, Southern Tonto, and Northern Tonto groups lived in the high country from the Salt River north to present-day Flagstaff. Though they shared resources and recognized ties to each other, the bands owed no political allegiance to the larger group. Conflicts

and federal government, and developed a market for Navajo weaving by suggesting improvements and selling finished rugs to eastern buyers. Rugs woven by women (and several men) all over the reservation now command top prices. Not far behind is the beautiful silver jewelry made by Navajo artisans, along with pottery, kachina dolls, and other crafts learned from the Pueblo people.

The Western Apache

The *Indé*, or Western Apache, are descended from the same Athabaskan stock as the Navajo and live

LEFT: a young Apache woman is painted with clay during a puberty rite known as the Sunrise Ceremony.
ABOVE: White Mountain Apache Rodeo.

with white settlers in the 1850s and 1860s led to the establishment of Fort Apache in the White Mountains in 1868. The White Mountain and Cibecue Apache allied with whites and served as scouts in the wars against the Tonto, Chiricahua, and Pai groups. Beginning in 1874, the federal government forced Apaches from four reservations to walk to the San Carlos Reservation, where tensions eventually arose between the 20 independent bands. In 1886, Victorio and Geronimo escaped with their bands of Chiricahua Apache and hid out in the Chiricahua Mountains and Mexico's Sierra Madre. They were forced to surrender in 1886 and were shipped to Florida. Most never returned to Arizona. Eventually, the White Mountain, Cibecue, and Tonto groups were allowed to return to their own reservations. The Tonto Apache population was much reduced, however, and merged with the Yavapai in the Verde Valley. Some members of the Eastern White Mountain band stayed on the San Carlos Apache Reservation, while others returned to the Fort Apache (now White Mountain) Reservation. The Cibecue group merged with the White Mountain Apache.

Today, Arizona's Apache live on three reservations and maintain strong links with the land. The White Mountain Apache Reservation has 10,000 members and operates a successful logging and recreation economy. The adjoining San Carlos

Tonto lost most of their land to white settlers. Today, Cliff Castle Casino is the tribe's main source of income.

Like the Navajo, the Western Apache believe the world was made by the Creator, or Sun, and that it was first inhabited by animals and monsters. Central to Apache belief are the *Gaan*, Mountain Spirit people who live beneath sacred mountains. They serve as protectors, teachers, and role models. At special ceremonies, *Gaan* dancers with elaborate headdresses appear in groups of five – four *Gaan* representing each of the sacred directions and a messenger who communicates with them.

Reservation is slightly larger, at 1.8 million acres (730,000 hectares), and has 8,000 residents. The San Carlos Reservation is known for its cattle and cowboys, a tradition that dates to the 1870s, when people accumulated their weekly allotments of beef to obtain a live steer. By the 1880s, the Indian agency was encouraging a cattle industry at San Carlos, which has grown to 20,000 head managed by five cattle associations. The reservation produces more cowboys than any area of comparable size in Texas or Oklahoma. The San Carlos Rodeo is one of the highlights of the year.

The Tonto Apache are now officially known as the Yavapai Apache Tribe and inhabit a small reservation in the Verde Valley. While they were on the San Carlos Reservation in the 1870s, the

The Hopi

The Navajo and Western Apache are newcomers compared with the Hopi, whose ancestors – the *Hisatsinom* or Ancestral Puebloans – have lived on the Colorado Plateau for millennia. The Hopi moved to these stone villages atop the Hopi Mesas in the 1100s. Each village was founded separately during a period of contraction that saw many Pueblo clans seeking refuge in larger, more easily defended sites. Hopis identify primarily with their village rather than with a single tribe. People in different villages speak different languages but have an overarching Pueblo culture centered on agriculture, seasonal ceremonies, and the making of pottery, basketry, jewelry, and kachinas. Many Hopi have embraced education and professional jobs, but frequently stick to traditional dress, which, like so many aspects of Pueblo culture, have strong symbolic meaning.

Tohono and Akimel O'odham

If the Tohono O'odham (Desert People) and Akimel O'odham (Water People), who live on reservations in southern Arizona, are indeed descended from the ancient canal-building Hohokam, they rival the Hopi for ancient origins. We may never know. The Hohokam disappeared around 1400 and the O'odham encountered by the Spanish were hunter-gatherers who knew nothing

The Akimel O'odham, or Pima, who live on the Gila Indian Reservation with the Maricopa, south of Phoenix, were highly successful irrigation farmers along the Salt and Gila rivers. They became the first agricultural entrepreneurs in Arizona during the US–Mexico War, when they traded flour and other goods with the US Army, and later supplied gold miners headed for California. They too saw their farms wither as white settlers dug canals and diverted water. By the late 1800s, the people who had once fed a whole state found themselves poverty-stricken and in need of aid.

Coolidge Dam, built in 1924, was designed to

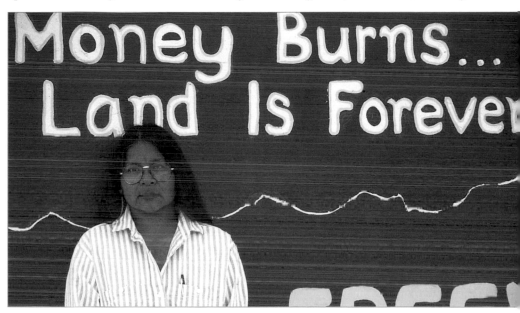

of pottery making, city building, and the construction of canals. In historic times, Tohono O'odham, or Papago, farmers relied on irrigation from the Santa Cruz River and dry farming at the base of *bajadas*, or mountain slopes. In the early 1900s, non-Indian settlers dug channels from the Santa Cruz River to intercept the water table, destroying O'odham agriculture in the process. Lawsuits filed by the tribe finally led to settlements in the 1980s that require the City of Tucson to negotiate with the O'odham on returning some of the water.

LEFT: San Carlos Apache Gaan dancer. **ABOVE:** a Pima activist protests freeway construction on the edge of the Salt River Indian Reservation.

return water to the Akimel O'odham but was an expensive failure. Built during a long drought, its reservoir not only never filled but prevented seasonal flooding, one of the last viable means of agriculture on the reservation. Today, the Akimel O'odham are farming again, and in 2003 they opened a multimillion-dollar resort, the Sheraton Wild Horse Pass, on their land.

The Colorado River Yumans

The struggle for access and control of the Colorado River was also at the root of fighting between Quechan Indians and Spanish and later Anglo settlers. The Quechan, who had historically manned the ferry crossing at Yuma, were forced to cede control to Americans in the mid-1800s, after the construction of Fort Yuma. In the late 1800s, irrigation projects brought Anglo farmers to the desert and forced the Yumans to share newly created reservations with refugees from the Navajo, Hopi, and other tribes.

The Yumans' ancestors covered their bodies in elaborate tattoos, wore shells in their ears, and made beautiful painted effigy pottery. They were guided by powerful dreams about every aspect of daily life, including institutionalized warfare. The most important battle waged by the Colorado River Tribes in recent times has been a legal one in the 1980s over zoning of tribal lands – a fight they won handily.

world with a large-scale resort and airport. The Yavapai merged with the Tonto Apache in the Verde Valley. Both groups are known for fine basketry.

The Southern Paiute

The Southern Paiute are also superb basket makers. When encountered by John Wesley Powell during his 1869 and 1871 surveys of the area around the Colorado River, they were still hunting and gathering seasonally on the North Rim and using tightly woven burden baskets for collecting seeds and plants, winnowing, and headgear. Only the San Juan Paiute Tribe keeps the tradition alive today. They do a lively trade in Navajo wedding

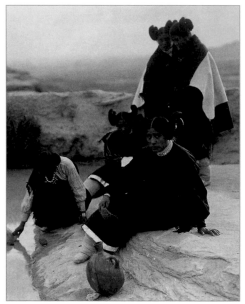

The Pai

The Yavapai, Havasupai, and Hualapai tribes were nomads who once occupied nearly a third of northern and central Arizona. They speak closely related languages. Hualapai means Pine Tree People, Havasupai means People of the Blue Green Water, and Yavapai means People of the Sun. They believe themselves to be "the only true human beings on earth."

The Havasupai live in the western Grand Canyon in one of the most beautiful and remote settings in the Southwest. Access to the village of Supai is by foot or mule from the rim of the canyon, or by boat. The Havasupai receive provisions by mule but also farm in the canyons. Their neighbors, the Hualapai, live atop the rim and have embraced the modern

baskets, an essential part of Navajo nuptials. Arizona's Kaibab Paiute tribe lives on a very small reservation, north of the Grand Canyon, and is embracing cultural tourism as its main means of support, next to Pipe Spring National Park.

Spanish legacy

Unlike New Mexico, which became the headquarters of Spanish government in the north in the 1600s, Arizona was never dominated by New Spain. The earliest explorers were mainly interested in finding the fabled Seven Cities of Gold. There were no such places in arid, overheated southern Arizona, only abandoned Hohokam towns melting back into the caliche soil. Poor Pimas and Papagos (today's O'odham people) wandered around the Sonoran Desert, hunting and gathering and sleeping in makeshift shelters. Warlike Yumans repelled the foreigners in the Mohave Desert along the Colorado River, and bands of Apache warriors hid in every corner of the mountains and staged lightning raids on livestock. To the north, there seemed to be nothing but mountains, mesas, and the impenetrable Grand Canyon.

The *conquistadores* did not stick around. They hurried northeast to what is now New Mexico, where Spanish culture would change New Mexican pueblos forever, a fate that never befell Arizona's fiercely independent Hopi on their remote mesas in northern Arizona.

His respect for the Indians was largely undone by the Franciscan priests who replaced Jesuit missionaries in the 1700s. These priests taught Indians livestock ranching, farming, Old World construction techniques, and the rituals, paraphernalia, and icons of a paternalistic new religion.

But this hardly mattered when the Indians were dying in huge numbers from introduced diseases and driven to exhaustion by the incessant demands of Spanish priests, soldiers, and land grantees who expected the *encomienda*, or tribute, promised them by the Spanish Crown. Pima rebellions occurred twice, but even worse, Apache raiding constantly posed a serious threat to the missions,

The mission era

Spanish missionaries returning to Arizona 150 years after the first Spanish explorers also found their work cut out for them. That Indian missions at Tumacacori and San Xavier del Bac in the Santa Cruz River valley south of Tucson were established in the 1690s was entirely due to the charisma of Father Eusebio Kino, an Italian-born Jesuit, who was warmly received in Indian communities throughout Sonora and southern Arizona.

FAR LEFT: an O'odham boy at the O'odham Tash parade. **NEAR LEFT:** Hopi girls gather water, 1906. Their whorl hairstyles indicate that they are unmarried. **ABOVE:** Holy Trinity Monastery, St David. Catholicism has a long tenure in southern Arizona.

even when garrisons were built to protect them.

In the end, Arizona proved too full of recalcitrant Indians and too wild a place for Spanish colonial efforts. When Mexico won its independence from Spain in 1821, the aristocrats who had sought their fortunes there headed home. Three hundred years after Spanish conquest, Mexico had become a country of Spanish-speaking Catholic Indians. It is this Mexican culture that pervades southern Arizona today.

Mexican influences

Ironically, Mexicans did not begin to filter up into Arizona until the land passed into American hands and US soldiers were dispatched to defend settlers from marauding Apaches. People from

Sonora, many of them Yaqui Indians, now felt safe heading north to find new lands to farm, ranch, and mine. The strong Sonoran influences that still pervade Tucson culture began during the early territorial period. Extended families lived in cool, thick-walled adobe compounds with saguaro and ocotillo rib ceilings, dirt floors, courtyards, and shade ramadas like those preserved in downtown's colorful historic districts. People of all races socialized with each other, two-stepped to Norteña music played by mariachi bands, and ate *carne asada* (barbecued beef) and other typically Sonoran dishes made with beef raised on the huge Spanish land grants along the border.

At the center of Mexican life was a deep Catholic faith, which, after being introduced by the Spanish, had taken permanent root with the miracle of the Virgin of Guadalupe, the dark-skinned madonna who appeared to an Indian man, Juan Diego, in 1531. The Virgin of Guadalupe is a ubiquitous presence throughout southern Arizona, in colorful murals, shrines, and dedicated churches. The miracle of Guadalupe is celebrated every December 12 with food, music, prayer, and a midnight Mass.

Most families still celebrate a daughter's *quinceañera*, the traditional puberty observance that probably dates back to Indian "coming of age" ceremonies not unlike those of the Navajo and Apache tribes. Another pre-Columbian ritual that remains popular is the Day of the Dead, held around November 1, All Souls Day. Celebrants honor the deceased, celebrate life, and acknowledge death by lighting candles, decorating graves, and offering food at altars, along with sugar representations of skulls. Other important festivities in Hispanic culture include Cinco de Mayo, the Fifth of May, which commemorates the Battle of Puebla, and Mexican Independence Day, or Fiestas Patrias, observed on September 16, the day in 1810 when Padre Miguel Hidalgo y Costilla called on Mexicans to throw off Spanish rule.

Unlike the Mexican peasants and laborers attracted to the agricultural fields of Phoenix, those who came to Tucson were often from ambitious, upper-class Sonoran families. One such immigrant was Federico Ronstadt, the son of a Sonoran mother and German father, who had trained as an engineer in his native land. Ronstadt opened a successful coach works in Tucson and,

A TASTE OF MEXICO

It's a balmy summer night at El Charro, Tucson's oldest Mexican restaurant. Waiters move through the old adobe bearing warm tortilla chips, guacamole, and salsa – a piquant blend of chopped tomatoes, onions, jalapeño peppers, and cilantro. Diners are tucking into platters of meat- and cheese-filled tacos, enchiladas, tamales, flautas, burritos, and chiles rellenos, accompanied by rice, beans, flour tortillas, and sopaipillas, doughy deep-fried puffs doused with honey. The more adventurous are trying the house specialty, carne seca – sundried beef simmered with onions and peppers – and flan, a creamy custard.

Ranch-style, Sonoran beef dishes have been a staple since Arizona was part of Mexico. Chile colorado and chile verde (red and green chile beef stew) are longtime favorites. But other Mexican regional dishes are increasingly popular: huachinango à la Veracruzana, fish simmered in a sauce of garlic, tomatoes, capers, and nutmeg from Veracruz; pan de cazon, a kind of shark-and-bean sandwich from the Yucatan; birria, a goat pot roast from Guadalajara.

At the heart of most dishes is the alpha and omega of Mexican spices: the chile pepper, which has been grown by Indians in Central America for thousands of years. Ranging from incendiary orange Habañeros to mild Anaheims, chiles add complexity to dishes that bring the tastebuds alive.

like Sam Hughes, became one of Tucson's founding fathers. Future generations of Ronstadts went on to fame and fortune, too. Federico's daughter was an opera singer with an international reputation. His great-granddaughter is the pop singer Linda Ronstadt.

Worldwide appeal

Arizona attracted a great variety of other immigrants as well, some seeking refuge, others seeking fortune or adventure in the far West. Even before the Civil War, African-Americans were escaping to Arizona to find a new life. Wiley Box and his wife came to Tucson from Louisiana in the

ico to chase Pancho Villa. Their physique and character impressed the Apache, who called them "buffalo soldiers." The 24th and 25th Infantry regiments, and 9th and 10th Cavalry regiments, were all stationed at Fort Huachuca, as was the first black graduate of West Point, Henry O. Flipper. Until the 1890s, blacks constituted 20 percent of all cavalry forces on the American frontier.

The promise of overnight riches drew prospectors from all over the world, making mining one of the most multicultural occupations in the West. A gold rush along Arizona's Gila River in the 1850s lured many hopefuls from California, including Chinese cooks, laundry workers, and

1850s. A runaway slave named Ben McClendon found gold in the Superstition Mountains in 1862.

In territorial times, as many as a quarter of Arizona's cowboys were black. They included John Swain of Tombstone, who rode with Cochise Sheriff "Texas" John Slaughter; Nat Love, who claimed to be Deadwood Dick, the fictitious hero of 33 dime novels; and Isom Dart, a black cowboy who was shot dead in 1903 for cattle rustling. Black soldiers were deployed by the US Army during the Apache Wars and were also used by General George Pershing when he rode into Mex-

LEFT: a mural in Tucson's historic El Presidio district depicts the Virgin of Guadalupe. **ABOVE:** mariachi band at St Augustine Cathedral, Tucson.

miners as well as Jewish traders, who set up shop in the boomtown of Gila City. A 1918 survey in the copper-mining town of Jerome found that foreign-born mine workers outnumbered Americans by more than two to one. The nationalities listed on the report included 401 Mexicans, 393 Americans, 96 Slavs, 98 Spaniards, 60 Austrians, 57 Italians, 53 Irish, and 32 Serbs. The ethnic makeup of Bisbee in southeastern Arizona was equally diverse.

Immigrants continue to pour into Arizona, some illegally, smuggled over the Mexican border by "coyotes" in order to labor namelessly in the underground economy, others attracted by high-tech jobs with executive salaries. Either way, it's a typically American story. Where opportunity lies, diversity is not far behind. ❑

DECISIVE DATES

PREHISTORIC CULTURES

circa 10000 BC

Paleo-Indians enter the region, hunting big game such as woolly mammoth and giant ground sloth with stone-tipped spears.

AD 1

The earliest evidence of pottery dates to this period. Living in pithouses, people of the Cochise culture sustain themselves by hunting, gathering, and farming.

AD 50

Hohokam begin building irrigation canals near present-day Phoenix.

1064

Sunset Crater erupts. Sinagua farmers return to the region attracted by increased rainfall and moisture-retaining, ash-covered soil.

1250

Ancestral Puebloans, or Anasazi, begin construction of Betatakin and Keet Seel in Tsegi Canyon, now part of Navajo National Monument.

1250–1450

Settlements in the Southwest are abandoned due possibly to drought, disease or overuse of resources.

1250–1450

Athabascans migrate from the north, later diverge into Navajo and Apache tribes.

EUROPEAN ARRIVALS

1540

Coronado expedition extends Spanish domain to the Southwest in futile search for reputed cities of gold.

1582

Antonio de Espejo finds some of the silver and copper deposits that would yield immense riches three centuries later.

1598

Juan de Oñate crosses Arizona and establishes the first European settlement in the Southwest, near Santa Fe, New Mexico.

1680

A sudden rebellion by Pueblo Indians costs the lives of more than 400 settlers in Arizona and New Mexico.

1687

Father Eusebio Francisco Kino begins the wide-ranging efforts that make this "Padre on Horseback" and founder of Tumacacori and San Xavier del Bac the most celebrated of the Spanish missionaries.

1751

Pima Revolt leads to establishment of a presidio at

Tubac – which was moved to Tucson in 1776 – to protect missionaries and settlers from Indian attack.

1805
A Spanish military expedition into Canyon de Chelly results in the massacre of 115 Navajo, virtually all of them women, children and old men.

1821
Mexico wins independence from Spain, thereby ruling Arizona.

AMERICAN TAKEOVER

1848
The United States, victorious in war with Mexico, takes over most of Arizona.

LEFT TOP: Hopi priest, c.1910. LEFT MIDDLE: Sinagua pueblo ruins at Tuzigoot National Monument. LEFT BOTTOM: San Xavier del Bac, founded by Father Eusebio Francisco Kino in 1700. ABOVE: Thomas Moran's impression of the Grand Canyon, *Chasm of the Colorado*, 1873-74. RIGHT: Fort Defiance was an Army outpost on the Navajo Reservation.

1854
The southern strip of Arizona is acquired from Mexico in the Gadsden Purchase.

1858
Discovery of gold nuggets in a prospector's pan on the Gila River gives rise to Gila City, first of many Arizona mining boomtowns.

1859
The first of Arizona's Indian reservations is established at Gila River. The greatest of all will be the Navajo Nation, covering nearly 16 million acres (7 million hectares), the largest reservation in the United States.

1863
President Abraham Lincoln signs a statute recognizing Arizona as a territory separate from New Mexico.

1869
Civil War veteran Major John Wesley Powell leads a pathfinding three-boat expedition down the Colorado River through the Grand Canyon.

Queen, tap into a rich vein in Bisbee, one of many deposits that will produce vast fortunes and make Arizona famous as one of the world's greatest sources of copper.

1885
University of Arizona established.

1886
Surrender of Apache warrior Geronimo marks the end of Indian resistance.

1877
Arizona enters the era of transcontinental railroading with erection of a bridge over the Colorado River at Yuma for the Southern Pacific. Three years later, the line's arrival in Tucson sets off a grand celebration.

1881
Wyatt Earp, two of his brothers and Doc Holliday survive shootout at the O.K. Corral in Tombstone that becomes a Western legend.

1884
Two mining companies, Phelps Dodge and Copper

1889
Phoenix becomes Arizona's state capital.

MODERN TIMES

1911
Dedication of Roosevelt Dam is first step in a federal irrigation project in the Salt River Valley that spurs development of the region.

1912
Arizona becomes the 48th state in the Union.

1917
About 1,200 striking copper miners and their supporters are removed from Bisbee by

train and deposited in a desert hundreds of miles away as labor-management conflict intensifies.

1919
Grand Canyon National Park established.

1937
Frank Lloyd Wright, consultant on the spectacular Arizona Biltmore Hotel in Phoenix, establishes a

home and studio, Taliesin West, where he works until his death in 1959.

1941
The nation's entry into World War II makes Arizona

stone, makes the reservoir area the most popular tourist attraction after the Grand Canyon.

2000
Arizona's population reaches 5.1 million, an increase of 40 percent in 10 years; it is second only to Nevada as the fastest-growing in the nation.

2005
Grand Canyon's El Tovar hotel observes its centennial on January 14, 2005.

2006
Forests around Sedona are struck by severe fires that force many residents to evacuate.

2006–08
Volunteer groups known as Minutemen protest illegal immigration and organize patrols of the US–Mexico border in Arizona and other western states.

2008
Arizona Senator John McCain loses the race for president to Senator Barack Obama.

a busy location for defense purposes, stimulating population growth and transforming the state's socioeconomic character.

1960
Sun City, a new community near Phoenix equipped with golf course and shopping center for "active" senior citizens, puts five model homes on display on January 1 and is besieged by thousands of prospective buyers.

1963
Arizona's claim to a major portion of the water from the Colorado River is upheld by the United States Supreme Court.

1968
Congress approves the Central Arizona Project, a large-scale effort to deliver water

to the state's most populous region.

1983
Governor Babbitt calls out the National Guard after strikers shut down the Phelps Dodge mine in Morenci. The company eventually sells part of the mine and closes operations in Ajo and Douglas.

1990
London Bridge is rebuilt at Lake Havasu in western Arizona. The improbable import, rebuilt stone by

LEFT TOP: a popular melodrama in 1907 romanticized frontier life. LEFT MIDDLE: Geronimo, c.1886. LEFT BOTTOM: mining town of Bisbee, 1916. ABOVE: completed in 1911, the Roosevelt Dam impounds the Salt River. RIGHT: A protester voices his opinion about illegal immigration at a Border Patrol Station in Naco, Arizona.

NATIVE HERITAGE

Archaeologists studying Arizona's prehistoric peoples
find evidence of complex societies engaged in an
ever-shifting network of cultural exchange and conflict

People have lived in Arizona for at least 11,000 years, perhaps longer. In southern Arizona are remnants of hunting camps, cave shelters, bones of extinct megafauna, and stone tools from paleo and archaic times, as well as Hohokam pithouses, great houses atop platform mounds, and 1,000-year-old irrigation systems. To the north, colorful sandstone canyons and high-desert knolls are the settings for pithouses, multi-story cliff dwellings, and granaries that blend so seamlessly with their settings that they seem more like natural outcroppings than man-made structures.

In between, atop and below central Arizona's Mogollon Rim and along the Colorado River, are the remnants of the Mogollon, Salado, and Hakataya cultures, influenced by the powerful Pueblo and Desert cultures yet different enough to keep everyone guessing about who they were, where they came from, and where they went. Far from being monocultural, prehistoric Arizona was a melting pot of highly adapted cultures interacting with each other through trade, marriage, warfare, and overlapping territorial boundaries.

> *The Hohokam traded for seashells from the Pacific Coast, which they etched with fermented saguaro juice, strung into bracelets and necklaces, or decorated with a mosaic of semiprecious stones.*

This fact was lost on early 20th-century archaeologists. Impressed by the beautifully built pueblos discovered at Mesa Verde in Colorado

LEFT: White House Ruins was inhabited by Ancient Puebloans from AD 1040 to 1275. **RIGHT:** potsherds at Homolovi Ruins, a 14th-century Indian pueblo.

and Chaco Canyon in New Mexico, they came to believe that a single, evolving culture migrating through different environments and developmental stages was responsible for the ruins of the Southwest. They spent time among the Hopi and other contemporary pueblo tribes and used them as a basis for understanding prehistoric pueblo people, forgetting that modern pueblos have also undergone a great deal of cultural change over the past four centuries.

By the late 1940s, the single-culture model was out of favor, and the prehistoric picture in the Southwest was beginning to look far more complex. It remains so today, as archaeologists continue to identify distinct and shared traits among the Southwest's cultures.

Prehistoric Cultures

Ancestral Puebloan (Anasazi)
Hakataya
Sinagua
Hohokam
Salado
Mogollon
Cochise

Monument Valley
Keet Seel Ruin
Kayenta
Betatakin Ruin
Page
Navajo National Monument
Canyon de Chelly National Monument
Mummy Cave Ruins
Antelope House Ruins
White House Ruins
Kinlichee Ruins
Tusayan Ruin and Museum
Wupatki National Monument
Homolovi Ruins State Park
Flagstaff
Petrified Forest National Park
Kingman
Walnut Canyon National Monument
Holbrook
Tuzigoot National Monument
Camp Verde
Montezuma Well
Montezuma Castle National Monument
Raven Site Ruins
Casa Malpais Archaeological Park
Kinishba Ruins
Tonto National Monument
Pueblo Grande
Phoenix
Besh-Ba-Gowah Archaeological Park
Snaketown
Casa Grande Ruins National Monument
Yuma
Ventana Cave
Tucson
Benson
Murray Springs Clovis Site
Nogales

Lake Powell
Lake Mead
Colorado
Little Colorado
Verde
Salt
Gila
San Pedro
Gila

0   50 miles
0   50 km

Ancient hunters

The earliest people in Arizona were paleo-hunters at the end of the last Ice Age, when the climate was cooler and big game lumbered across grasslands and forests in what are deserts today. These ancient hunters trapped mammoths and other prey in marshy areas or drove them off cliffs, making their kills using percussion-flaked Clovis arrowheads attached to spears. They butchered their prey on the spot, leaving behind tools and bones that have been uncovered at the Murray Springs Clovis Site in the San Pedro River Valley and in the recesses of Ventana Cave on the Tohono O'odham Indian Reservation, both in southern Arizona.

they killed using spear-throwers known as atlatls. Artifacts from this period include chipped stone tools and debris and occasionally sleeping circles and cleared areas.

In southwestern Arizona, the San Dieguito I period of the Archaic is represented in the Barry Goldwater Bombing Range (north of Cabeza Prieta National Wildlife Refuge), which preserves evidence of mortar holes in rocks, where stone and wooden pestles were used to grind seeds and bean pods into flour. In northern Arizona, split-twig willow figurines, thought to be hunting fetishes, were secreted in caves high above the Grand Canyon.

The big-game bonanza didn't last. Eventually, overhunting and a drier climate doomed the woolly mammoth, ground sloth, and other large mammals to extinction.

With the loss of their main prey, paleo-hunters were forced into a different lifestyle. The Southwestern Archaic period (8,500 BC–AD 300) was a widespread hunting-gathering adaptation to the changing climate. The Archaic people were autonomous groups with defined territories. They moved around seasonally, taking advantage of a wide range of wild plants and small game, which

ABOVE: petroglyphs adorn the Vermillion Cliffs in northern Arizona. Evidence of human habitation in the region stretches back more than 10,000 years.

Cochise culture

In southeastern Arizona, University of Arizona archaeologist Emily Haury dubbed people of this Archaic period the Cochise culture and divided them into three phases: Sulphur Springs, Chiricahua, and San Pedro. As the culture advanced technologically, such artifacts as stemmed points, storage pits, and heavy millstones indicate that farming became an influential factor in the subsistence of the culture. Irrigated and dry farming of squash and teosinte, a Mexican grass that later developed into corn, produced reliable food supplies and resulted in permanent settlements.

About 2,000 years ago, the introduction of pottery from Mexico offered desert dwellers a new technology, allowing for storage of water and dried food.

By the final San Pedro phase, Cochise people were living in small pithouses. It is believed that the San Pedro phase of the Cochise culture evolved into the Mogollon tradition of the central highlands.

The Mogollon

The Mogollon people lived in the mountains along the Arizona–New Mexico border and south into Mexico from 100 BC to the AD 1400s. Considered the least complex of the three main cultures that came to dominate the prehistoric Southwest, the Mogollon were farming and making pottery earlier than any other group in the region. Perhaps it was merely their isolation in rugged mountains

Mexico. It featured human-like figures, lizards, birds, and scenes that depict trade in tropical birds. It is believed that the merged Pueblo and Mogollon culture contributed to the cultural background of the Hopi, Zuni, and Acoma pueblos and the Tarahumara Indians of Mexico.

The Hohokam

In the Sonoran Desert, around 300 BC, Archaic people were evolving into the Hohokam, a Pima word for "all used up," proposed by archaeologist Jesse Fewkes in 1910, while he was excavating the Hohokam "great house" of Casa Grande, south of Phoenix. Like other archaeologists of his day,

that prevented the mobility and exchange of ideas that allowed other cultures to advance.

Sometime between AD 900 and 1100, the Mogollon culture merged with that of the Ancestral Puebloans (formerly known as the Anasazi) to the north and ceased to exist as a separate entity. The Mogollon began constructing multistory pueblos but continued to favor rectangular kivas (ceremonial chambers), such as the great kiva found at Casa Malpais in Springerville, Arizona, built in AD 1277. In New Mexico, around the same time, they built the unusual Gila Cliff Dwellings beneath canyon overhangs.

Their basic red pottery also evolved into beautiful black-on-white vessels, perfected by a branch of the culture living on the Mimbres River of New

Fewkes made no cultural distinction between the Hohokam and the Pueblo people to the north, believing that the same culture had built all the ruins.

All that changed in the late 1920s, when Harold Gladwin, a Wall Street financier and archaeology enthusiast, financed the excavation of sites in the Sonoran Desert. The breakthrough for Gladwin and his research organization, the Gila Pueblo Foundation, came in 1935, during the huge Snaketown dig. Project archaeologist Emil Haury and his team used new dating techniques and comparisons of building styles, pottery, and burial practices to establish the Hohokam as a distinct prehistoric culture. In the 1930s, and during a second major excavation of Snaketown in the 1960s, Haury refined the Hohokam cultural sequence, consisting of four main phases: Pioneer (300 BC–AD 550), Colonial (AD 550–900), Sedentary (AD 900–1100), and Classic (AD 1100–1450).

Hohokam dwellings were single-story oval or rectangular huts built over shallow pits using a framework of poles, brush, and reeds, covered with caliche mud. They included entryways, living areas with basin-shaped firepits, and storage space for single families. An outdoor shade structure, or ramada, protected residents from the sun. More than 60 pithouses were uncovered at Snaketown, a site in use for almost the whole of the Hohokam period. Pithouse dwellings have been found in Organ Pipe Cactus National Monument and as far

prized artworks for red argillite and other resources. Macaw feathers, pyrite mirrors and copper bells, probably used in rituals, were imported from tribes in Mexico and distributed throughout the Southwest.

More than 200 Mesoamerican-style ball courts have been found at Hohokam sites. Introduced in the 700s (Casa Grande has the earliest known ball court) and aligned to the cardinal directions, ball courts were probably used for games that involved keeping a heavy rubber ball in play without using hands or feet. Ball games provided an opportunity to interact with neighboring villages, arrange marriages, exchange goods, and mediate disputes,

north as Montezuma Well in the Verde Valley.

The Hohokam specialized in a distinctive red-on-buff micaceous pottery, coiled on an anvil support and smoothed with a wooden paddle. Large storage jars, flat-bottomed dishes, jars with narrow openings, and legged containers such as incense burners were covered with geometric designs, curved motifs, and animal or human figures.

The Hohokam also invented a process for etching shell imported from the Gulf of California, using fermented cactus juice and wax to create lizard, toad and other motifs; they traded these

LEFT: O'odham women in the early 20th century harvested cactus fruit and used baskets much as the Hohokam did. **ABOVE:** a Pueblo Grande ball court.

but they probably also had a symbolic aspect: the movements of the ball and players reenacted the annual passage of the sun, moon, and planets around the heavens and ensured cosmological harmony.

The importance of astronomy to desert farmers may also account for the introduction of multistory adobe structures atop platform mounds during the final Classic period. The four-story Casa Grande building, the only great house to survive, is 35ft (11 meters) high and contains 11 rooms. The existence of window alignments has suggested that such structures may have been inhabited by ritual specialists who tracked the movements of celestial bodies and predicted rainfall, the desert's most precious commodity, during times of increased drought.

Platform mounds like the one at Casa Grande

have been linked to the Hohokam's sophisticated canal irrigation system and may have played a part in regulating water use along the Gila and Salt Rivers. More than 85 miles (135km) of irrigation canals have been mapped at Casa Grande, with many more lying beneath the freeways, buildings, and modern canals of Phoenix. These canals were undoubtedly the key to supporting the estimated 24,000 people who eventually concentrated in the Salt-Gila River Basin in the early 1300s – a remarkable population for such an arid region. It may have been the collapse of this irrigation system, perhaps during a major flood, that spelled the end for the Hohokam. When the Span-

ish arrived in the 1500s, they encountered Akimel O'odham (Pima, or Water People) and Tohono O'odham (Papago, or Desert People), probable descendants of the Hohokam who had reverted to a simpler life of hunting and gathering.

The Puebloans

It's not hard to understand the appeal of the Pueblo people's dramatic stone villages for 19th-century archaeologists, who perhaps interpreted the move from simple pithouses to high-rise "apartments" as an orderly progression in the rise of civilization. But, like the Hohokam and Mogollon, the Pueblo people started out as hunter-gath-

THE ABANDONMENT

They built great cities of stone, became successful traders, and reached heights of aesthetic brilliance. Then, between AD 1300 and 1450, the major cultures of prehistoric Arizona simply disappeared. What happened?

The straw that broke the camel's back seems to have been a severe drought between AD 1276 and 1299. Crop failures would have been a disaster for civilizations that had risen to power during times of plenty, specialization of labor, and adequate leisure time to create trade goods. Now it was every man for himself. The hilltop pueblo of Tuzigoot shows clear signs of battening down the hatches. The cliff dwellings at Navajo National Monument hide in plain sight in their alcoves. Add to this the environmental havoc caused

by overuse of resources, the subsequent social breakdown, and you get the picture. Time to move on.

Where did they go? Clan by clan, the Ancestral Puebloans migrated to the Hopi Mesas and the 19 pueblos strung along the Rio Grande. The Hohokam probably never left. When the Spanish arrived in the mid-1500s, the O'odham claimed to know nothing of their predecessors, yet lived in houses that resembled 1,000-year-old Hohokam dwellings. A coincidence? Archaeologists doubt it. The old way of life was simply, as the O'odham say, *hohokam*, "all used up."

erers during the long Archaic period and gradually evolved into farmers.

Around the start of the Christian era, ancestors of the Puebloans were living in scattered pithouse villages and making baskets, which led "cowboy" archaeologist Richard Wetherill to name them Basketmakers. By the Pueblo I period, between AD 700 and 900, people living in small hamlets of multistory dwellings had incorporated earlier pithouses as underground ceremonial chambers, known as *kivas*. They were now hunting with bows and arrows and farming more extensively.

During the Pueblo II (AD 900–1100) and Pueblo III phases (AD 1100–1300), larger towns appeared

New Mexico, which may have functioned as a kind of redistribution center orchestrated by "priests" whose understanding of astronomy allowed them to predict favorable planting and harvesting times.

At the height of Pueblo civilization, the fertile bottomlands of the Colorado, Little Colorado, San Juan, and Virgin Rivers quickly filled up with farmers. The Tsegi Canyon-Marsh Pass area near Monument Valley, on today's Navajo reservation, was occupied for centuries by Kayenta Anasazi people, a western branch of the Pueblo culture. The Kayenta were less celebrated for their architecture than the Chacoans or Mesa Verdeans to the east and north but were distinguished by their resourcefulness,

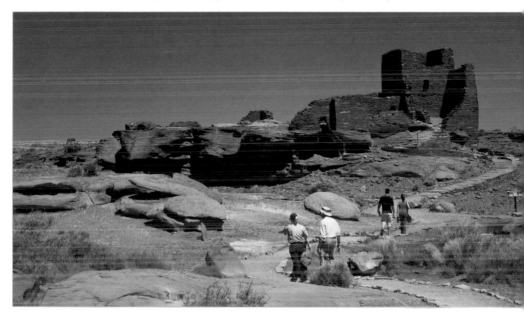

and, in the 1200s, the cliff dwellings that spark our fascination today. Pueblo civilization seems to have benefited from coalescence and the exchange of goods and ideas. Each community began to have its specialties and to reach new heights of invention, building more sophisticated structures, creating beautiful baskets, weaving fine cotton cloth, firing distinctive pottery, and refining tools. Centralized towns could stockpile and share food with surrounding villages during times of shortage and demand tribute and manual labor in return. This may have led to the rise of the Chaco Canyon site in

adaptability during hard times, and fine polychrome pottery. In the mid-1200s, increasing drought and shrinking resources forced families to engineer the impressive Betatakin and Keet Seel sites of Navajo National Monument. Nearby Canyon de Chelly and Monument Valley also contain Kayenta Anasazi ruins, while the Arizona Strip, on the border with Utah, was the domain of the Virgin River Anasazi. Perhaps an offshoot of the Kayenta, the Virgin River people built pueblos and grew corn, a skill they taught the incoming Southern Paiute, who claim links to these early Puebloans today.

TOP LEFT AND ABOVE: Wupatki National Monument encompasses several Sinagua pueblos. **LEFT:** a doorway leads into a Sinagua indian ruin near Sedona.

The Sinagua

The Sinagua ("without water" in Spanish) were dry-land farmers living in the Flagstaff area of northern Arizona a thousand years ago. They built the lovely but lonely pueblos of Wupatki National Monument between the San Francisco Peaks and the Painted Desert, and cliff dwellings at Walnut Canyon that look surprisingly like those constructed by the Mogollon above the Gila River in New Mexico. First investigated by Harold Colton, founder of the Museum of Northern Arizona, the Sinagua straddled the frontier between Anasazi, Hohokam, and Mogollon territories, apparently absorbing aspects of each culture. They began as pithouse dwellers near Sunset Crater around AD 500, but were forced to flee south to the Verde Valley following the 1065

development of Wupatki Pueblo, near Flagstaff, which contains Chaco-style masonry and over-scaled public architecture. The pueblo also has a Hohokam-style ball court, the northernmost ball court in North America and the only one lined with masonry.

Also noticeable is the loosely mortared, blocky style of Kayenta Anasazi construction in the many small outlying pueblos and field houses scattered between the main pueblo and the Little Colorado River. Ceremonial burials of high-status leaders and the presence of Mexican macaws and other imported items suggest that Wupatki may have functioned as an important

eruption of the volcano. While in the Verde Valley, contacts with the Hohokam and other tribes exposed the Sinagua to new ideas and influences. The large Tuzigoot Pueblo, built on a defensible knoll above the Verde River in AD 1000, is Sinaguan, as are nearby Montezuma Castle and the multistory cliff dwellings around Sedona's picturesque red-rock country.

Land rush

When Sunset Crater Volcano stopped erupting, a prehistoric land rush seems to have occurred in northern Arizona, attracting the Sinagua and other tribes eager to take advantage of the fertile volcanic soil and increased rainfall. This combination of cultures may have been responsible for

trade and ritual center following the abandonment of the Chaco Canyon pueblos. By AD 1250, after just a century of use, the Sinagua had abandoned Wupatki and Walnut Canyon. They probably resettled on the Hopi Mesas to the east and at Zuni and other pueblos along the Rio Grande in New Mexico, where their descendants still live.

Prehistoric puzzles

Similarly enigmatic in their origins and disappearance is the Salado ("salty" in Spanish), a name given the tribe by Padre Eusebio Kino when he discovered its people living along the Salt River in the late 1600s. Known for their beautiful cotton cloth and polychrome pottery, the Salado originated in Pueblo territory, along the Little Colorado River, and settled in the Salt River Basin, picking up Mogollon traits along the way. Filling a niche between the Mogollon to the east and the Hohokam to the west, the Salado seem to have influenced the Hohokam during the Classic period, from about AD 1300 to 1450. They built the multistory cliff dwelling of Tonto National Monument and the large pueblo of Besh-ba-Gowah in the city of Globe, which has yielded large quantities of pottery.

The Sinagua and the Salado weren't the only tribes that didn't quite fit the emerging picture of prehistoric cultures. In the late 1940s, new

and Havasupai of the western Grand Canyon, the Yavapai of west-central Arizona, and the Quechan, Chemuevi, and Mojave desert people of the lower Colorado River.

Athabascan immigrants

The cultural picture was complicated further by the arrival of Athabascan hunter-gatherers from western Canada possibly as early as the 12th century. The Athabascans diverged into two groups: the Navajo, who settled in the plateau country of northern Arizona, and the Apache, who roamed southern Arizona and New Mexico.

The Navajo were deeply influenced by their

research and dating techniques revealed many local deviations in cultural traits, especially in the area where the Colorado Plateau meets the Colorado River valley and adjacent low deserts.

This group of cultures, dubbed the Hakataya, after a Yuman word for the Colorado River, included the Cohonina, south of the Grand Canyon; the Cerbat, who lived along the Colorado River where it emerges from the Grand Canyon; the Prescott, living in the verdant areas of west-central Arizona; and the Laquish of the lower Colorado River. Modern descendants include the Hualapai

Pueblo neighbors, taking up corn farming, weaving, and various aspects of Pueblo religion, and later by the Spanish, from whom they adopted sheepherding and silversmithing. The Apache, on the other hand, remained hunter-gatherers and broke up into wide-ranging bands. The Apache acquired horses from the Spanish in the 1700s and some bands, like the Jicarilla of northern New Mexico, took on some of the cultural traits of the Plains tribes.

The best-known group, however, was the Chiricahua. Led by warriors such as Cochise and Geronimo, they were the last Indians in the Southwest to be pacified by yet another wave of immigrants – the white, English-speaking invaders from the East. ❑

LEFT: Sinagua ruins are tucked into isolated Walnut Canyon near Flagstaff. **ABOVE:** Tuzigoot was inhabited from about AD 1000 to 1400.

THE SPANISH ERA

Seeking mythical cities of gold and pagan souls,
the Spanish planted the seeds of European
culture throughout the Southwest

A new chapter in Arizona's history began to unfold on February 22, 1540. Its main character was a young and by all reports dashing Spaniard named Francisco Vásquez de Coronado. He was leading an expedition of some 1,300 men and two or three women – Spaniards, Indians, and Africans – heading north from Mexico.

Coronado, governor of New Galicia in western Mexico, hoped to find the "Seven Cities of Gold." He was one of the *conquistadores* who followed in the wake of Columbus in that swashbuckling age sometimes known as the Spanish Century, their names once familiar to every Iberian schoolboy: Balboa, discoverer of the Pacific Ocean; Cortés, who wrested control of the Aztec empire in Mexico from Montezuma; Pizarro, the harsh ruler of Peru who exacted an immense ransom before killing off the Inca emperor; de Soto, whose own expedition traipsed across the American Southeast from Florida as far west as Oklahoma between 1539 and 1542.

Coronado had been born into a wealthy family in the old university town of Salamanca about 1510. He became an assistant to the viceroy of New Spain, António de Mendoza, and married into one of Mex-

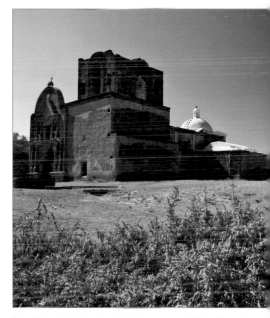

Spanish colonials, but their interest could be piqued by any reports suggesting that the otherwise unpromising El Norte might turn out to be an El Dorado brimming with precious metals.

Cities of Gold

The notion of Seven Cities of Gold persisted in the imagination of those times. There were variations on the theme, but one basic Iberian legend involved Seven Bishops who fled the peninsula to escape persecution by Moorish infidels, crossed the Sea of Darkness, and wound up on an island named Antilia that was blessed with gold. One of those who helped keep that legend alive was Alvar Nuñez Cabeza de Vaca.

Sailing from Florida in 1528 after having sur-

> *Cárdenas, the first European to see the Grand Canyon, discovered a basic truth about the chasm: it's bigger than it looks. Failing to reach the bottom, he reported "what seemed easy from above was not so, but instead very ... difficult."*

ico's wealthiest and most powerful families. It was Mendoza who picked him to head the expedition to the north. That region never held much appeal for

LEFT: St Augustine Cathedral, Tucson. **RIGHT:** Tumacacori was founded in 1691 by Father Eusebio Francisco Kino.

vived one great shipwreck, Cabeza de Vaca became shipwrecked again in the Gulf of Mexico, off the land that would become Texas. He and three surviving companions were taken in by Indians before embarking on a long trek across Texas into the New Mexico–Arizona region. When, after eight long years, they met up again with Spaniards, Cabeza de Vaca and his companions had become very knowledgeable about Indians and recounted stories of supposedly great Indian kingdoms to the north.

The stories got back to Mendoza, who, before sending forth Coronado, dispatched two men on a reconnaissance mission. One was a Franciscan friar, Marcos de Niza. The other, as guide, was Esteban,

that was larger than Mexico City, and his glowing report stirred new interest in the legend of the seven great cities. It was his report that prompted Mendoza to mount the ambitious Coronado expedition of 1540, plus two additional ships commanded by Hernando de Alarcón – a venture that resulted in the discovery of the mouth of the Colorado River.

And so Coronado set forth, amid much fanfare, a large financial investment by several parties and great expectations of a rich reward. After a public pledge of allegiance to Coronado, the expedition proceeded from southern Nayarit up the coast of the Gulf of California. It reached the Sonora River and followed it, then crossed the Gila River to

a North African slave who had accompanied Cabeza de Vaca. They set out in March 1539, traveling up the west coast of northern Mexico. Esteban, going ahead of the friar, crossed into southeastern Arizona, probably through the San Rafael Valley, and followed what is now the Arizona–New Mexico border. But his luck soon ran out. The Zuñi Indians he was now encountering were less pacific than those of the south, and they found much of Esteban's behavior – including his appetite for their women – objectionable and swiftly cut him to pieces.

Great expectations

Friar Marcos continued on and, according to his much exaggerated account, came upon the Zuñi pueblo of Cíbola. He described it as a dazzling place

Cíbola, in what is now western New Mexico.

Unfortunately, there was nothing imposing about Cíbola, which turned out to be a plain Zuñi pueblo. Coronado determined that Marcos de Niza had lied, and in disgrace the friar was ordered to return to Mexico City. The mission was deemed a fiasco. In actuality, it was the first systematic exploration of the Southwest and extended Spain's empire into North America. The expedition traveled as far into the interior as the land that would become central Kansas.

Coronado sent one of his lieutenants, García López de Cárdenas, and 25 comrades to search for a great river to the west that had been described by the Hopi Indians, and they became the first Europeans to encounter one of the world's great natural wonders – the Grand Canyon. For three days Cárdenas and his men tried to descend into that great abyss to reach the Colorado River, but the effort was futile and they turned back.

They also encountered herds of buffalo for the first time, to which the Spaniards were directed by a Pawnee Indian guide they called El Turco. And there was another, though far more tragic, precedent – the first of many battles that would pit Indians against whites in what is now the United States was fought on July 7, 1540, in New Mexico.

El Turco spun a tale of a great city of gold called Quivira that also turned out to be illusory – it seems that Indians were finding it convenient to tell the Spanish intruders what they wanted to hear – and his mendacity cost him his life. Then, on December 7, 1541, Coronado was thrown from his horse during a race with one of his lieutenants and badly injured. Struck on the head by the horse's hoof, he was never the same again. The expedition returned home in 1542, without precious metals, and Coronado died 12 years later in Mexico City.

It would be 40 years before another exploration was undertaken. In 1582, Antonio de Espejo led a party of nine soldier-prospectors and a hundred or so Zuñi Indians up the Rio Grande to what is now New Mexico in search of three missionary priests – they had been killed, as it turned out – and deposits of precious minerals. His party visited Hopi villages as Coronado's group had done four decades earlier, and the territory was officially claimed for Spain's King Philip II. Silver and copper deposits were discovered in the area that came to be known as Jerome, east of modern-day Prescott. Three centuries later Jerome would be the site of a copper bonanza.

Spanish colonization of the Southwest began in earnest in 1598 under Juan de Oñate, a wealthy Mexican-born miner with important connections – his wife was a descendant of both the *conquistador* Hernán Cortés and Montezuma, the Aztec emperor. Oñate, who had received a contract from Philip II, led 130 families, 270 single men, and several thousand head of cattle up the Rio Grande to San Juan Pueblo, just north of present-day Santa Fe, New Mexico. This was probably the first European settlement in the Southwest. The settlers were mostly Mexicans and *mestizos* (of

European and Amerindian racial descent) who had come in search of a new life.

Oñate traveled across Arizona and got as far east as Kansas, where he fought an unsuccessful battle against Indians. Meanwhile, a small troop of men under the command of one of his officers, Captain Marcos Farfán de los Godos, found a rich deposit of silver ore near present-day Prescott.

Heavy metal

Farfán and his eight companions, in addition to some Hopi guides, headed into the timberland of the Mogollon Rim. They encountered Jumana Indians who led them to the Verde River valley.

Farfán's group came close upon the mineral deposits that had been discovered years earlier by Espejo and that were being mined by the Indians themselves. It was the Europeans' introduction to Arizona's mineral wealth. Farfán returned in 1604 with another expedition, and over the next two years the locations of much of the area's mineral deposits were found.

Oñate's achievement was to solidify Spanish control over a vast area that encompassed Arizona, New Mexico, Texas, Colorado, Nevada, Oklahoma, and Kansas. He has been called the Last Conquistador. After him, and for much of the 17th century, a missionary fervor took hold in the Americas, which sought to bring natives into the Christian fold through spiritual persuasion and peaceful means.

LEFT: Indians bring gold to conquistadores in this 17th-century depiction of Spain's New World conquest.
RIGHT: the Hopi resisted Spanish dominance.

Indian revolt

Three religious orders become dominant – Franciscans, Dominicans, and Jesuits. The Franciscans came first, reaching Arizona about 20 years after Oñate's visit. Arriving at the Hopi villages in 1629, they established the first permanent structures erected for use by whites in Arizona.

Colonization was enhanced by the Catholic priests, their missions, and their peaceable ways. But among some native tribes, such as the Hopi, resentment simmered. A major rebellion erupted in 1680 in the Pueblo Revolt, owing mainly to unhappiness over Spanish inability to protect the tribes against guerrilla attacks by nomadic Apache and Navajo warriors. The leader of the revolt, Popé, was determined to drive the Spaniards entirely out of northern New Spain. In a surprise, well-planned attack, Pueblo Indians in Arizona and New Mexico arose. Some 400 settlers, including 22 priests, were slain, and the remainder were driven all the way back south to El Paso.

The most famous of the missionaries was Father Eusebio Francisco Kino, an Italian-born Jesuit who became legendary as the tireless "Padre on Horseback." He arrived in Mexico in 1681, established his first mission six years later in Sonora, and first visited Indian villages in Ari-

THE CROSSING OF THE FATHERS

Missionaries did a lot of traveling in the old days. A case in point is the journey made in 1776 by the intrepid Franciscan priests Silvestre Valez de Escalante and Atanasio Dominguez, who hoped to find a good route from Santa Fe to California. The priests journeyed north from New Mexico into Colorado and then over to Utah but failed to find their way to the Pacific.

Disappointed, they headed for home, whereupon they became the first white men to encounter one of the few places along the 1,500-mile (2,400-km) Colorado River where it could be crossed on horseback. It is in northern Arizona, at Lake Powell, and known today as the Crossing of the Fathers – *El Vado de Los Padres.*

zona (part of the Spanish region known as Pimería Alta) in 1691. Father Kino rode thousands of miles in the course of introducing European crops and teaching Indians how to farm and raise livestock, exploring and map-making in addition to tending to spiritual needs. By his death in 1711 he had started 25 missions, three of them between Tucson and Nogales in Arizona – including the future sites of the architecturally renowned San Xavier del Bac and San Jose de Tumacácori.

There were other major outbreaks of native violence. In 1700 Hopis killed priests and sacked Awatovi, ending Spanish colonization of northern Arizona. The Apache and Pima resisted the gradual entry of miners and farmers in Santa Cruz Valley. In 1751 a revolt by Pima warriors resulted in the death of a hundred or so people and the destruction of missions and farms. Spanish soldiers caught up to, and defeated, the Pima in the Santa Catalina Mountains north of Tucson.

Holy mission

The Jesuit era in Arizona ended in 1767 when the powerful order was expelled by Spain's King Carlos III. Taking their place in the Southwest missions were the Franciscans, and the priest assigned to the Arizona missions was Francisco Tomás Garcés. Like Kino, he proved to be a tireless presence who established a strong rapport with the natives. He sought to establish a link with the mis-

Indian ways so intimately was martyred in the great Yuma Revolt of 1781 in which Quechan Indians rebelled against their Spanish oppressors. The revolt shut the land route to California via Arizona, at the strategic Yuma Crossing for four decades.

Tucson was chosen as the site for one of 15 presidios along a route stretching west from San Antonio, Texas. Construction began in 1775. Seven years later the fort was attacked by a large war party of Apaches. Under the able Don Pedro Allande, the presidio withstood the attack.

Apaches were always especially troublesome, but a Spanish policy initiated in 1784 by Viceroy Bernardo de Galvez took a new tack that sought to

sions newly founded in California by another Franciscan who would become equally renowned, Father Junípero Serra.

Garcés accompanied Captain Juan Bautista de Anza on two major expeditions to California in the mid-1770s. Garcés explored the westernmost reaches of the Grand Canyon and named the great river that coursed through it Río Colorado ("ruddy-colored"). He then headed east and reached the Hopi villages. His journey lasted 11 months and covered about 2,000 miles (3,200km). Sadly, this popular priest who came to know

pacify them and all other tribes. Indians were now encouraged to settle near trading posts, amply supplied with alcoholic beverages, and generally reduced to dependency on Spanish largesse. It was an effective, if cynical, strategy.

Nonetheless, the Spanish colonial phase was nearing an end. At the peak of its power, as historian David J. Weber observed, Spain claimed an area in North America alone, from ocean to ocean, that was larger than all of Western Europe. Now the tide was receding. And as political problems mounted for the Spanish governors in Mexico City, less attention could be paid to the outermost reaches of the empire. Shifts in power were looming that would reconfigure the political map of the American Southwest. ❑

LEFT: Navajo petroglyphs at Canyon de Chelly depict the coming of Spanish soldiers.
ABOVE: the interior of Mission San Xavier del Bac.

COWBOYS, INDIANS, AND MINERS

Spurred on by nationalism and the promise of
mineral wealth, Americans take possession
of a harsh and violent land

The 19th century brought a major change of identity for Arizona and the Southwest. What had long been a Spanish colonial outpost would now become an Anglo-American homeland. The old order of Iberian *conquistadores*, missionaries, and remote bureaucrats yielded to an influx of North American gringos – the so-called mountain men at first, then miners and merchants, farmers and ranchers – driven by an imperative of materialism and Manifest Destiny.

Behind the transformation were such main historic currents as Anglo expansion and Iberian decline, an American self-confidence imbued with revolutionary fervor, even the nationalist sentiment of the tumultuous Napoleonic period. Those same nationalist winds of change that swept over all of Latin America were felt by Mexicans, who rebelled against their Spanish overlords in 1810 and achieved independence by 1821.

Oddly enough, the last years of Spanish rule in the Southwest had been relatively peaceful and productive. There had been good relations with the Pima. Farming and ranching activities were prospering, especially in the Santa Cruz Valley of

Mexican independence

This era of good feelings lasted about a quarter of a century, starting to dissipate about the time Mexicans began agitating for independence. When it was achieved, Arizona became Mexican territory. Ironically, the break with Spain helped open the Southwest to the gringos, who were at first welcome to enter the region. Mexico's regime, unlike the aloof and suspicious Spaniards, favored not only commercial relations with the Americans but settlement as well.

In pre-independence Texas, for example, large tracts of land were made available   as long as prospective settlers swore fealty to Mexican rule and Catholic belief. For their part, what the Mexicans sought were large numbers of homestead-

> *Territorial governor Anson P. K. Safford returned all but $5,000 of a $25,000 bribe intended to secure a land grant for the Southern Pacific Railroad; the briber apparently over-estimated the legislature's price.*

southern Arizona. Minerals were discovered and missions erected – San Xavier del Bac was completed in 1797, San José de Tumacácori dedicated in 1822.

LEFT: A Hopi man ascends a kiva ladder, *c.*1897.
RIGHT: Christopher "Kit" Carson.

ers whose presence would mitigate the threat of depredations by Apache, Comanche, and other hostile Indians.

Anglos, disposed to free trade and commerce, began trickling into the territory. Many were trappers – beaver fur was profitable at a time when men generally wore that type of hat. The basic trade route, the Santa Fe Trail, became an American landmark. It stretched from Independence, Missouri, to Santa Fe, New Mexico, where it picked up the Chihuahuan Trail south to Mexico City. Some trappers added California to their itinerary, as did Christopher "Kit" Carson, who became a renowned frontier guide and Indian

agent and served as a Union general in the Civil War. Traders came, mated – many with Mexican brides – and settled, laying down a foundation for a different Arizona that emerged after mid-century.

American takeover

The turning point came when war erupted in 1846. Mexicans had become unnerved by all the Americans they had once welcomed, and Texas was already lost. War was declared and the US Government sent troops, including the Army of the West headed by General Stephen Watts Kearny. Kearny seized Las Vegas, a village on the Santa Fe Trail, and announced on September 22, 1846, that henceforth New Mexico and Arizona were US territory.

Kearny was assigned the task of opening up a wagon route across the Arizona wilderness to California, and the work was carried out efficiently by a specially formed unit of Mormon volunteers. Traveling more than 1,000 miles (1,600km) in just 102 days, the Mormon Battalion of 340 men and a few women hacked out a road from Santa Fe through Tucson and on to San Diego. Some of the Mormons settled in Arizona, largely as farmers and ranchers.

Mexico lost a lot of ground – nearly half of her land – when the Treaty of Guadalupe Hidalgo ended hostilities on February 2, 1848. The lost acreage included Arizona north of the Gila River. Six years later, the Gadsden Purchase brought all of the Arizona territory under US control. James Gadsden, a railroad promoter serving as American minister to Mexico, purchased on behalf of the United States some 29 million acres in southern New Mexico and Arizona south of the Gila River.

ONE HUMP OR TWO?

The US Army once had its own Camel Corps. It got started in 1855 when Congress agreed that camels would be useful in exploring arid lands. So 33 were shipped to Texas, with another 44 to follow. All were the one-humped dromedary type, as opposed to the 20 bactrians (two humps) later imported by mine owners in Nevada.

The camels could haul heavier loads than mules, were fast, and could go for long periods without water. They came in handy when the Army opened a road across the Arizona territory to the Colorado River. But, alas, these large, shaggy creatures also had a way of startling horses and mules, not to mention people, and cavalrymen disliked them. The camel drivers imported to handle them proved to be inept, although one of them achieved prominence – Hadji Ali, a Syrian known as Hi Jolly who was honored following his death in Arizona in 1902 with a grave monument at Quartzsite *(right)*. The camels were generally mistreated and malnourished. The Civil War caused the War Department to lose interest and the camels were auctioned off, many relegated to a nomadic existence.

The cost: $10 million. The land was wanted, mostly, for a southern railroad route to California, but the project was never carried through.

Gold diggers

What really stimulated traffic across the Arizona territory was the gold rush, that frenzy which seemed to lure half the world to California after James Marshall found some bright metal in a stream at Sutter's Mill on January 24, 1848. The quest for mineral wealth attracted settlers to Arizona. Transportation was by wagon, stagecoach, and even, on the Colorado River, steamboat. Tracks were laid by the Southern Pacific and the Atlantic

protect travelers from attack by hostile Indians.

Most of the Anglos who were settling in Arizona were Southerners. With the outbreak of the Civil War, Confederate leaders noted that the territory was poorly defended by federal troops and sought to take advantage of that fact. Citizens of Tucson voted to join the secessionist cause, and Confederate troops occupied the town in February 1862. They withdrew, however, when Union forces from California arrived.

Most of the entire western half of the New Mexico territory was controlled by Indians, and they were not thrilled by the wave of fortune-seekers intruding on their land like a plague of

and Pacific (later called Santa Fe) Railroads, and direct connection with the California coast was made in 1883, at San Diego. Arizona became inextricably linked to the rest of the United States.

Settlement remained sparse in the 1850s. In southern Arizona there were some mining communities but only two military posts (Fort Buchanan and Fort Breckinridge). The beginning of American occupation of the lower Colorado Valley occurred in February 1852, with the establishment of Fort Yuma on the California side of the Colorado River. More military forts would be constructed to

LEFT TOP: Indian scouts pursue Geronimo in a *Harper's Weekly* illustration by Frederic Remington, 1886. **ABOVE:** a stylized depiction of an Apache raid.

locusts. Before the Forty-niner fever ran its course, the region would be visited by an estimated 50,000 gold diggers and tradespeople.

Indian relations with settlers had waxed and waned ever since the Spanish arrival. The chaotic period that followed Mexican independence in 1821 brought a breakdown in relations, especially with Apaches. They made assaults on farms and ranches in Mexico's Sonora region and in southern Arizona, running off herds of horses and dislocating commerce and agriculture. There would be many notorious incidents. One of them, in 1837, involved a group of Mexicans led by an Anglo settler, John Johnson, who abruptly ended two days of peace talks by suddenly gunning down their Apache counterparts, about 20 in all.

Apaches, who conducted their raids from mountain strongholds, had waged an especially fierce resistance against all invaders. To a Spanish missionary writing in 1630, they were "fiery and bellicose and very crafty in war," and so they appeared to the Anglo-Americans who inherited the territory and with it Indian hostility.

Apaches were greatly skilled in handling the horse – a once-native species, which was reintroduced to the New World by Spaniards – and were accustomed to moving about freely. Now, however, their way of life was threatened – miners were a particular nuisance – and they struck back.

Hostilities worsened in the 1860s. Bounties were paid for Indian scalps, and Arizona's territorial legislature called on the federal Department of War to carry out a policy of extermination. The request denied, a citizens' mob took it upon itself to slaughter 75 unarmed Apache women and children near Tucson.

Massacre of innocents

A more notorious incident occurred in the Camp Grant Massacre of April 1871. A posse organized in Tucson to avenge Indian raids rode 60 miles (95km) northeast to the abandoned military camp, where Aravaipa Apaches were confined. The posse attacked at dawn, when most of the Apache men

A GRAND RIDE THROUGH THE CANYON

Exactly 100 years before Neil Armstrong became the first earthling to step on the Moon, a one-armed Civil War veteran was making his own fantastic voyage down the Colorado River. Major John Wesley Powell, 35, and his boating expedition traveled 900 miles (1,450km) from Green River, Wyoming, through the Grand Canyon in Arizona in 1869. It was a grueling, dangerous journey that had been considered impossible, even by Native Americans. Indeed, the expedition was given up as lost before Powell and five comrades emerged from the mouth of the Virgin River 3 months later. The date was August 30, 1869. Four men had dropped out along the way, three of them

killed by Indians in apparent retaliation, wrongfully, for the murder of an Indian woman.

Powell's right arm had been amputated after he was wounded at Shiloh, but he remained in active service on the condition that his bride, Emma, accompany him. After the war, she became the first woman to climb Pike's Peak, as part of an expedition headed by her husband. Powell, a geology professor, explored the Green and Colorado rivers again in 1870–71. He took up the frustrating duties of a government official, founding and directing the US Geological Survey and later the Bureau of Ethnology, a post he held until he died in 1902.

were out hunting, and caused as many as 100 deaths. Virtually all of the victims were women and children. The raiders were tried for murder in Tucson but acquitted. Bent on revenge, Apaches launched their own raids and ambushes against settlers and soldiers, with terrible atrocities committed.

In 1864, Colonel Kit Carson headed an army operation that rounded up some 9,000 Navajo at Canyon de Chelly in Arizona and forced them on an infamous 300-mile (500-km) "long walk" to a desolate area in New Mexico known as Bosque Redondo, where they were incarcerated for 4 years. Seven years later, President Ulysses S. Grant sent General George Crook to Arizona. He

and the subjugation of their people, though it was a struggle doomed to failure.

Mangas Coloradas ("Red Sleeves"), a giant of a man at 6½ft (2 meters) tall, had conducted campaigns against Mexicans and even offered to help General Kearny when they met in 1846. Turning in later years against Anglo-Americans, Mangas Coloradas attacked a 126-man army unit at Apache Pass in the Chiricahua Mountains and was wounded by gunfire. Captured in January 1863, he was imprisoned at an abandoned fort in New Mexico and gunned down by soldiers when he resisted being taunted with heated bayonets.

Cochise, who married a daughter of Mangas

proved adept at reining in roving bands of Apache marauders while at the same time winning greater Indian acceptance of the reservation concept.

The so-called Indian Wars in effect tied down America's military establishment before subjugation of Native Americans was completed by 1890. Three names are particularly prominent in most accounts of Indian leaders at this period in Arizona's history: Mangas Coloradas, Cochise, and Geronimo. All were Chiricahua Apaches who fought fiercely against the takeover of their land

ABOVE: Geronimo (fourth from left) discusses surrender with Gen. George Crook (second from right), 1886. **LEFT TOP:** Navajo men. **LEFT:** John Wesley Powell confers with a Paiute scout.

Coloradas, was captured in 1861 at Apache Pass by an army lieutenant named George Bascom who had pretended to be friendly. The notorious Bascom Affair involved the abduction of a 12-year-old boy from a ranch for which Cochise was wrongfully accused. Cochise escaped, but hostages on both sides were killed, including his brother and two nephews. Apaches took 150 lives in two months, and hostilities raged until 1872, exacting 4,000 casualties and causing entire settlements to be abandoned.

Geronimo was the last Indian to surrender to the United States, in 1886. Earlier in his life his mother, wife, and children were killed in an attack by Mexican soldiers on an Apache camp. In 1877 he was arrested and confined to a reservation in

Arizona. He broke free with a band of followers and for five years conducted raids that harassed army troops and terrorized southeastern Arizona and neighboring areas in Mexico and New Mexico.

General Crook pursued Geronimo and his Apache force and twice attempted to negotiate the terms of a surrender. A compromise allowing a return to the Arizona reservation was overruled by President Grover Cleveland, who suggested that Geronimo be hanged. The Apache warrior slipped away again. With his fourth and final surrender, this time to a less sympathetic General Nelson Miles, harsh terms were imposed on the Apache warrior and his cohort. They were shipped in chains

a few years earlier had made prospecting a popular activity in the region, and western Arizona was one of the nearby areas being searched.

Spaniards had made discoveries as far back as the 16th century, but the means of taking out the ore were limited. There were silver mines at Alamos, Zacatecas, Guanajuato, and other places in New Spain. In 1736, a rich lode of silver was found about 25 miles (40km) southwest of what is now Nogales, Arizona, by a Spaniard who was guided to the site by a Yaqui Indian. Thousands of pounds of silver were mined.

One of the first of the latter-day Arizona miners to hit pay dirt was Charles D. Poston, a Kentuck-

to a prison camp in Florida, and later to Alabama.

Late in life Geronimo performed in Wild West shows, took part in President Theodore Roosevelt's inaugural parade in 1905, dictated his memoirs for a biography published in 1906, and died three years later of pneumonia, still a prisoner of war, at Fort Sill, Oklahoma.

Mining bonanza

If the Anglo-American takeover was Arizona's most important development in the 19th century, not far behind was the fact that the territory turned out to be so rich in precious metals – gold, silver, and copper. Mining activity on a serious scale got under way right after the Gadsden Purchase fixed boundaries in 1854. The gold strike in California

ian who came to be known as the "father of Arizona." Poston went to California about 1850 and four years later visited southern Arizona, taking ore samples at Tubac and Ajo. With him was Herman Ehrenberg, a German-born mining engineer he had met.

The high quality of the ore led to creation of the Sonora Exploring and Mining Company, excavation near the old Spanish presidio at Tubac, and a booming business in silver. About $3,000 worth was extracted daily before the start of the Civil War in 1861 necessitated the removal of federal troops from the Santa Cruz area and, with no protection against hostile Indians, shutdown of the mines.

Poston pushed for territorial status for Arizona,

going to Washington in 1862 to lobby. The territory and the name "Arizona" became official on February 24, 1863, and Poston was elected its first delegate to Congress. Whatever profit he accrued was dissipated by the time of his death in 1902.

Another silver miner and Arizona promoter was Sylvester Mowry, an ex-soldier who built a thriving business in the late 1850s. He kept it operating despite the removal of troops at the start of the Civil War and in the face of harassment by Apaches. The Mowry Mine was one of the nation's richest silver producers early on, but wartime complications deprived its founder of any lasting fortune.

Arizona was found to have ample deposits of million worth of gold being taken there before it too ran dry. The richest discovery was made in 1863 near what is now Congress Junction when in just three months more than a quarter of a million dollars in placer gold was found.

Rich copper deposits

There were many other gold and silver strikes worth millions of dollars in the latter years of the 19th century, but the precious metal that became Arizona's most valuable resource was copper. The first substantial effort at open pit mining was undertaken at Ajo in 1854 by the American Mining and Trading Company – the ore was shipped

both placer gold, the surface kind easy to get at, and lode gold, which requires a large-scale mining enterprise. Placer gold became scarce after a relatively short period, and serious mining was left to the big companies. The territory's first gold rush occurred in 1858 when rich deposits of placer gold were discovered by Jake Snively, a Texan, about 20 miles (32km) beyond the junction of the Gila and Colorado Rivers.

A boomtown known as Gila City arose, but by 1864 the site was virtually cleaned out. Another rich strike was made in 1862 at La Paz, some $8

ABOVE: the town of Clifton (shown here in 1909), together with nearby Morenci, was part of one of the richest copper-mining districts in the country.

via Cape Horn all the way to Wales for smelting. Other large mining operations would be established at Bisbee, Clifton, Globe, Morenci, Bagdad, Tucson, and other places.

Bisbee, in southeastern Arizona, turned out to be one of the richest copper areas in the world. Here the Copper Queen company began mining in 1880. The site had been chanced upon by an army scout from nearby Fort Bowie, and ownership eventually passed to a San Francisco group of financiers. They formed the Copper Queen Mining Company, a huge deposit of rich ore was unearthed, and thus was born the boomtown of Bisbee, which took its name from the company's attorney, who never set foot in the place.

Now entering the picture was Phelps, Dodge &

Company, a small metal-importing firm based in New York that had been urged to set up mining operations in southern Arizona. It bought out Copper Queen and reaped a fortune. By 1908 copper totaling 730 million pounds (330 million kg) and worth millions of dollars was mined. Phelps Dodge became one of the nation's "Big Three" copper interests, the others being Anaconda and Kennecott. It has been estimated that by 1975 the Bisbee area alone produced gold, silver, copper, lead, and zinc worth over $6 billion.

Fortunes were made. James Douglas, the assayer-consultant who steered Phelps Dodge to Arizona and became president of Copper Queen Consoli-

dated, was worth $20 million at his death in 1918. Douglas and Phelps Dodge did, however, miss out on one opportunity: a mine operation in Jerome that became the prodigious United Verde company.

Its principal figure was New York financier Eugene Jerome, whose offer to sell for $300,000 was met by the Montana mining tycoon and politician William A. Clark after Douglas held off one day too many. Clark eventually took in more than $100 million from United Verde. The company was bought by Phelps Dodge in 1935 for $21 million.

The town too tough to die

Most famous of all the boomtowns that grew out of the mining bonanza was Tombstone. Ed Schieffelin, who arrived in Arizona in 1876 with nothing to show after 20 years of prospecting, hit it rich in 1877. He discovered rich silver deposits in the San Pedro Valley about 70 miles (110km) southeast of Tucson. Joining him in the enterprise was his brother Albert and Dick Gird, an assayer who realized the value of the ore. Schieffelin was warned that the territory was Apache country and "all you'll find will be your tombstone." The name stuck.

With support from Eastern investors, the Tombstone Mining District was established. By 1888, some $30 million worth of silver had been taken out. At least 50 mines were lodged in the hills around Tombstone by 1886, and they employed hundreds of teamsters, millworkers, and a host of other laborers in addition to miners.

Schieffelin and his brother Albert sold their claims for a half million dollars each in 1880, and Gird, too, cashed in handsomely the next year. Ed Schieffelin kept trying his luck over the years in various places, including Alaska. He died in a

THE ENIGMA OF TOMBSTONE

Hero? Villain? None of the above? Wyatt Earp is a hard man to pin down – buffalo hunter, gambler, gold-digger, sometime lawman who, craving excitement, lit out for Arizona and enduring notoriety. But one thing is certain: he had a knack for survival. He alone emerged unscathed in that bloody shootout near the O.K. Corral and then beat the rap – getting away with murder, as some people saw it – along with brothers Virgil and Morgan and their hot-tempered friend Doc Holliday. Then, when Morgan was mysteriously dispatched by a bullet while shooting pool, a second one went sailing by Wyatt. In another shooting, Virgil's arm was crippled. And in 1900, younger brother Warren was terminated by a bullet in an Arizona bar.

Wyatt outlasted all of his eight siblings. He and Josie Marcus, the showgirl who became his lifetime companion, knocked about mining camps in Colorado. They joined the Idaho gold rush in 1884, and ran a saloon in San Diego. In 1896, Earp took to the boxing ring in San Francisco to officiate at a match between heavyweights Bob Fitzsimmons and Tom Sharkey – in the process exposing the .45 Colt he packed under his frock coat. Then it was off to the Alaska gold rush and a profitable saloon-gambling venture. After further prospecting, Wyatt and Josie settled in Los Angeles, where he died in 1929, an 80-year-old Western legend. Among the pallbearers were film cowboy stars Tom Mix and William S. Hart.

shack in Oregon and is buried in Arizona near the site of one of his strikes, a monument 25ft (8 meters) tall towering over his grave. Tombstone's mines started to flood in 1883 and were shut down completely by 1909.

Frontier boomtowns like Tombstone attracted a variety of people, many with rough edges. Its population soared to 15,000 in a short time and the town acquired a notorious reputation – indeed, President Chester A. Arthur once threatened to impose martial law in the entire territory. Most notably, this was the heyday of the cowboy, that Anglo version of the *vaquero* character Spaniards introduced to the American West. Pulp fiction and

Gang, and made political friends and enemies: Virgil Earp was appointed town marshal. Differences with the Clantons, a rowdy family of small ranchers and cattle rustlers, simmered into a poisonous enmity that finally exploded in a deadly shootout.

It happened near the O.K. Corral in Tombstone on the night of October 25, 1881. When it was over, three members of the Clanton faction lay dead, Earp's brothers Virgil and Morgan were wounded, and Holliday was creased by a bullet. Wyatt Earp was unhurt. The gunfight lasted less than 30 seconds but the legend has endured. Virgil later was wounded in an ambush and Morgan shot to death while shooting pool in a saloon.

Hollywood fantasy would tranform the drab, proletarian cowboy into a mythical hero-gunfighter.

Wyatt Earp is a good example. Born in Illinois in 1848, he worked at various jobs in the West, hunting buffalo, fighting Indians and occasionally running afoul of the law. In 1876 he was a deputy policeman in Dodge City, the wild and woolly Kansas cattle town. Here he met some characters now equally well known in Western lore – Doc Holliday, Luke Short, and Bat Masterson.

They, Earp, and his four brothers gravitated to Tombstone, became known as the Dodge City

Bloodier yet was the Graham-Tewksbury feud that raged for six years between cattlemen and sheepmen in Pleasant Valley, in the Tonto Basin, starting in 1886. It exploded when sheep by the thousands were allowed to graze in the valley despite a strict prohibition. Ambushes, shootouts, and other violence left dozens of casualties, some of them innocent victims. One woman lost a husband and four sons.

Hollywood burnished the myth on screen in a steady flow of shoot-'em-ups – *Fort Apache, Arizona Kid, Broken Arrow,* and, of course, *Gunfight at the O.K. Corral.* But the times were a-changin' for Tombstone and Bisbee and all the get-richquick boomtowns as another century dawned over Arizona Territory. ❏

LEFT: staged in 1907, the drama *An Arizona Cowboy* romanticized the rigors of frontier life. **ABOVE:** gallows at the county courthouse in Tombstone.

BIRTH AND REBIRTH

Reclamation projects, wartime industry, and a cool
new invention called air-conditioning powered
Arizona through the 20th century

Gunfire flared in Arizona on St. Valentine's Day in 1912, but it wasn't triggering any Chicago-style gangland massacre, nor was it a resurgence of frontier lawlessness. It was a celebration of something happening in far-off Washington, D.C. A proclamation admitting Arizona to full-fledged membership in the Union was being signed there by President William Howard Taft.

After half a century as a territory, it was becoming the 48th and last of the continental United States. Taft's ceremonial signing was a good photo-op, as we say nowadays, so a motion-picture camera was on hand to film the historic moment. And who could blame the armed citizenry back in Arizona for being fired up? They had waited a long time. There were too many Democrats out there to suit the Republican gatekeepers in Congress, who had voted "Nay" on statehood in 1906, and who even considered wrapping Arizona and New Mexico together and labeling the package "Montezuma."

Taft had his own reservations about some progressive features in Arizona's new constitution.

> *George Warren lost his claim to the Copper Queen Mine in a drunken bet that he could outrun a man on horseback. It later became one of the most productive mines in the history of the West.*

But the day finally arrived and the old territory became the so-called "Baby State." It was a new chapter in the Arizona story, and there would be

LEFT: miners at work in a Bisbee tunnel.
RIGHT: workers inspect a diversion tunnel during the construction of Hoover Dam, 1934.

more transforming moments ahead as this hot, dry desert started blossoming into a modern-day El Dorado for sun-seekers and fun-seekers who came and stayed in increasing numbers.

Bringing up baby

A year before admission to the Union, another important event occurred. Taft's predecessor as president, Theodore Roosevelt, came to Arizona to dedicate a great dam named in his honor. Roosevelt, champion of conservation, had been a vital force behind the Reclamation Act of 1902 authorizing the federal government to build reservoirs and stimulate irrigation projects in the West. The first major effort was the Salt River Project in Arizona. It was the same area in which Hohokam

Indians a couple of thousand years earlier had carried out their own irrigation project, building an extensive canal system to bring water to their fields of corn, beans, and squash.

Roosevelt Dam was built on the Salt River about 90 miles (145km) upstream of Phoenix. Work began in 1905, and the dam was dedicated on March 18, 1911. It is the world's tallest masonry dam at 280ft (85 meters), and it cost $10 million to build on rough terrain where it could get hotter than hell. It allowed for water to be stored, floodwaters controlled, arid land turned into an agricultural oasis, and Phoenix to bloom into a big city. Three more dams would

In 1968 Congress approved the Central Arizona Project, a grand federal undertaking to funnel water from the Colorado River to the state's populous central region, which includes Phoenix and Tucson. Total cost for the canal system? About $4 billion.

Prosperity and conflict

Railroads unified the state and stimulated its development starting in the late 19th century. North-south tracks were put down to connect the transcontinental lines – the Southern Pacific in Arizona's south, the Santa Fe in the northern part, where it was the dominant economic force. The

Deportation of 1... July 12, 1917.

MARCHING PAST LOWELL.

be built along the Salt River and two on its major tributary, the Verde, storing water to irrigate vast acres of cotton, citrus, vegetables, and other crops. The dams helped to spur farm acreage in the state by almost 400 percent between 1910 and 1920.

Also harnessed was the Southwest's mightiest waterway, the 1,450-mile-long (2,330-km) Colorado River, with the construction of Boulder, Glen Canyon, Parker, and Davis Dams. Arizona is one of seven states served by Boulder Dam, which was dedicated by President Franklin D. Roosevelt in 1935 and renamed Hoover Dam in 1947 (the name changed back and forth for years). Arizona's claim to a major share of Colorado River water was affirmed by the US Supreme Court in 1963.

powerful copper interests, faced with the need to transport larger ore extractions, built their own connections when necessary, as Phelps Dodge did when it fought over terms with the transcontinental companies.

The livestock industry prospered as large ranches were established, their chief customer being the army forts. Mining companies thrived but were beset with labor problems – a shortage of manpower early on; ethnic and racial antagonisms involving Anglos, Mexicans, Chinese, Italians, and others; union militancy. That militancy usually brought a harsh response from mine owners. When, for example, Mexican and Italian workers went on strike in 1903 at the Clifton-Morenci mines, Arizona's governor was enlisted to call out both the National Guard and the Arizona Rangers.

There were many labor-management conflicts in Arizona's mining areas during the early decades of the 19th century. Patriotic fervor during World War I engendered a fear of industrial sabotage and a hatred for militants like the "Wobblies"– the radical agitators, real or alleged, popularly associated with the Industrial Workers of the World.

The most notorious incident, known as the Bisbee Deportation, occurred in July 1917. As many as 1,200 people were rounded up by 2,000 "sheriff's deputies" and armed citizens, herded like cattle into railroad cars, shipped to Columbus, New

but revenues now fell sharply. The cattle industry was hurt as well. Some of the copper mines were shut down, the communities they had spawned turning into ghost towns.

Wartime stimulus

Despite a reputation for rugged individualism, Arizona traditionally has benefited from a good deal of federal largesse – settlers were protected from hostile Indians by army troops, farmland was irrigated, floodwaters restrained, cotton growers subsidized. And it was the federal government once again that played a prominent role in the state's phenomenal development, which started

Mexico, and unloaded in the dark of night.

More copper was produced in Arizona than in any other state in the Roaring Twenties, its mines supplying half of the total demand in the nation. The most productive year was 1929, when extractions totaled more than $155 million. Only a fraction of that was realized a few years later when the industry was hit hard by the Great Depression. The economic downturn affected Arizona as severely as it hurt other places. Cotton had been the state's leading crop,

LEFT: striking miners are forced out of Bisbee during the "deportation" of 1917. ABOVE: Arizona, New Mexico, and Oklahoma wait for their stars, signifying statehood, in a 1911 political cartoon.

with the onset of the World War II period.

The war itself was a major stimulant. Defense plants and research laboratories launched operations in Arizona that created jobs and brought prosperity. Air bases and other military installations were established in the state out of fears for security posed by its location near the West Coast. (The federal government is the largest landowner in the state, possessing a major portion of its 113,642 sq miles/294,331 sq km.)

After the war, veterans returned to settle and start families. Homes went up, and businesses attracted by the labor pool opened plants, among them electronics giants like General Electric and Motorola. Mining production was revitalized in the war years.

Even before the war there were factors in play that opened Arizona to outsiders and made it the "Grand Canyon State." Railroad construction was at its peak from 1880 to 1920 and brought many visitors. The automobile had an even greater impact, stimulating road-building. Great vistas and spectacular scenery, once the preserve of explorers and then the privileged class, began attracting masses of ordinary people.

Theodore Roosevelt had created Grand Canyon National Monument in 1908, seven years after a passenger train first brought tourists there. It became Grand Canyon National Park in 1919, drew 56,000 tourists the following year and three times that number within a decade (currently the park receives some 5 million visitors). Other national parks and monuments established in the 1906–08 period were Petrified Forest, Montezuma Castle, Tonto, and Tumacácori.

Birth of the cool

Arizona was once regarded as so forbidding that General William Tecumseh Sherman recommended starting another war with Mexico to "make her take it back." But during the first two decades of the 20th century, the state began attracting people suffering from tuberculosis and other respiratory ailments. The dry climate had

MR CONSERVATIVE

He was either a plain-speaking hero or a loose cannon in scary nuclear times. Such were the depictions of Barry Goldwater (1909–98), grandson of a Russian Jewish emigrant, who became the champion of an effort to outduel Soviet communism, revive American conservatism, and save Western Civilization. Goldwater gave up a career managing the family business in favor of public service. Starting out on the Phoenix City Council, he rose to become the Republican standard-bearer for president in 1964. He was defeated handily, returned to the US Senate, and ultimately won the public's admiration for his steadfast conviction as "Mr Conservative."

been sought out as early as the mid-1800s by a few health-seekers. But now churches and other groups, especially in Phoenix and Tucson, were starting facilities that cared for the afflicted. The state's climate was giving southern Arizona a national reputation as a health haven.

Great change also came with the advent of air-conditioning. In the 1930s, attempts were made to provide relief from the searing heat by evaporative devices. These so-called "swamp coolers" began appearing in windows and on roofs, and Phoenix billed itself as the "Air Conditioned Capital of the World." The city was a leading center for production of the artificial coolers, which were later replaced by the superior technique of refrigeration cooling. Air-conditioning made work conditions more pleasant and were an inducement for out-of-staters to relocate to southern Arizona.

One man attracted to Phoenix for health reasons played a major role in the Arizona transformation. Del Webb was born in California and moved to Phoenix in 1927. Forming the Del Webb Corporation, he entered the housing field and won fame and fortune by designing Sun City, a vast community of homes for retired people and a model for similar developments throughout the Southwest.

Encompassing 30,000 acres (12,000 hectares), it offered ranch-style houses with carports, golf courses, swimming pools, shopping centers, and other attractions. All were tailored to the needs of active senior citizens eager to enjoy the rewards of their "golden years" (a term popularized by Webb) and possessing the resources to do so. It was a major innovation in the American social landscape.

Arizona was being transformed once again, propelled by an explosive growth in population that began intensifying in the 1950s and keeps on spiraling upward. The population ballooned from 335,000 in 1920 to 3.6 million in 1990, and a decade later it exceeded 5 million. In just seven years (1990–97) it grew by 24.3 percent.

The most exceptional growth has been experienced by Phoenix, which did not exist until 1867 and now has more than 1.5 million inhabitants. Its founding came as part of an effort to clean out the old Hohokam canals, an action seen as breathing new life into an ancient settlement, hence the adaptation of the name of the mythical Egyptian bird that rose from the ashes.

Phoenix, the capital since 1889, surpassed Tucson as Arizona's largest city in 1920. Both are among the fastest growing in the nation. And both are burdened with helter-skelter urban development and suburban sprawl as well as the traffic congestion and smog that arise from a near-exclusive reliance on the automobile for transportation.

In the public spotlight

Several latter-day Arizonans achieved national reputations in the political realm. Barry Goldwa-

LEFT: suburbs sprawl around downtown Phoenix, now the sixth-largest city in the United States.
RIGHT: frequent traffic jams are one result of the state's exuberant growth.

ter, a longtime US senator and 1964 Republican presidential nominee, became the leading voice for American conservatism. Stewart Udall, scion of a pioneer Mormon family, was Secretary of the Interior in the Kennedy administration after he served in Congress, as did his equally liberal brother, Morris. Also highly regarded is Bruce Babbitt, a two-term governor from Flagstaff who became Secretary of the Interior in the Clinton administration. Senator John McCain, who endured a long and harrowing captivity after his plane was shot down during the Vietnam War, was a favorite among many Republicans, independents, and even Democrats during the presidential

election of 2000 and was the GOP standard-bearer in 2008.

No one played a more enduring role in Arizona's development, however, than Carl Hayden. He was present at the state's creation in 1912, when voters chose him to be the new state's first representative in Congress. He went off to Washington at the age of 34, and 56 years later he was still on the job. Hayden served in both the House and Senate, his long career capped by congressional approval of the Central Arizona Project in 1968.

His life stretched from the Indian Wars to the Vietnam War, and the family's history stretches as far back as 1858, when his father, Charles, settled in Tucson and became a prominent merchant and civic leader. ❑

THE NAKED EARTH

Arizona bares its geological bones in some of
the West's most spectacular landscapes

For Arizona's Indian tribes, the state's mountains, mesas, and eroded formations aren't just rocks; they are sacred touchstones. The Tohono O'odham believe their creator god lives on Baboquivari Peak near Tucson. Traditional Navajo rarely feel at home beyond the boundaries of the four sacred mountains that encircle their homeland and view rock formations as petrified gods, monsters, or the settings of creation myths and legendary battles. Hopi dances honor the kachinas, spirit helpers whose summer home is the San Francisco Peaks near Flagstaff and whose intercession with the creator spirit ensures good crops and survival. The Paiute learn the song of every rock in the territory they "own" and act as caretakers of the natural world.

You don't have to be an Indian to feel the drama of this desert landscape. Thousands make pilgrimages to Sedona each year seeking to be healed by mud, crystals, and the powerful vortexes said to vibrate out of the red rocks. Geologists make their own pilgrimages to view the world's oldest and best-preserved rock formations in the Grand Canyon. Miners continue to risk their lives to

Though restrained by Glen Canyon and Hoover dams, the Colorado River continues to rasp away at the Grand Canyon, transporting an average of half a million tons of sand and silt per day.

extract precious minerals from within the earth. A caver shines his headlamp through a tiny open-

PRECEDING PAGES: a backpacker peers into the Grand Canyon from the South Kaibab Trail. **LEFT:** Matkatamiba Canyon, Grand Canyon National Park. **RIGHT:** Vishnu schist is the oldest rock in the Inner Canyon.

ing deep beneath the Whetstone Mountains, discovers an elaborate, untouched limestone cave system laid out in front of him, and spends 14 years fighting to protect it, as if it were his first-born child.

A tale of two regions

Arizona's extraordinary geology can be explained partly by its geographic location between the faults that created the Rocky Mountains and Sierra Nevada, its diverse topography (a 12,000-ft/3,700-meter elevation span), and its dry climate, which leads to unvegetated rocks that clearly show what's going on in the ground beneath our feet. The state divides neatly into two broad geological provinces: the basin-and-range country of southern Arizona's deserts and northern Arizona's Colorado Plateau region.

The Colorado Plateau, the dramatically carved sandstone country of the north, covers 130,000 sq miles (340,000 sq km) of Arizona, Utah, Colorado, and New Mexico. A relatively stable, monolithic landmass a mile high and rising, it began to be pushed up about 75 million years ago, when the collision of the Pacific and North American Plates on which the continent sits reverberated east. This caused movement in faults that forced up the modern Rocky Mountains, a process known as the Laramide Orogeny. Localized uplifts split the region into distinct highland areas known

ley Powell, the first man to run the Colorado River through the Grand Canyon and explore the region in 1869.

Carving the canyon

The Grand Canyon, centerpiece of the Colorado Plateau, is not geologically ancient – it was carved by the Colorado River within the past 4.7 million to 1.7 million years. The ancestral Colorado flowed south into Arizona from Utah, staying east of the Kaibab Upwarp. Another stream flowed west of the Kaibab Upwarp, cut back into the plateau, and "captured" the Colorado, which turned westward to its present

as the Coconino, Kaibab, Kanab, Shivwits, Kaibito, Defiance, and Paria Plateaus.

The area has been subject to continued volcanism, visible as lava flows in the western Grand Canyon, along the southern edge of the plateau at the 2,000-ft-high (600-meter) Mogollon Rim, and as volcanic necks, dikes, and other magma-intruded rocks and upwarps across the Navajo and Hopi Reservations. At Flagstaff, hundreds of cinder cones were thrown up in the large San Francisco Volcanic Field. The state's highest point, 12,633-ft (3,850-meter) Humphreys Peak, is part of the San Francisco Peaks, an ancient collapsed stratovolcano. To the east, Sunset Crater Volcano, which erupted between AD 1064 and 1065, was given its evocative name by geologist John Wes-

position through the newer, steeper route.

At this point, sediment-heavy waters began to carve the Grand Canyon in earnest, deepening the chasm to its present mile depth. The Colorado, the "Red River" in Spanish, churned tawny and soupy with sediments that it carried all the way to the Gulf of California. Downcutting has slowed now that the river has reached resistant schists at the bottom of the canyon and its erosive force has been tamed by the construction of Glen Canyon Dam.

Different types of erosion – tributary streams, flashfloods, rockfalls, rain, ice, dust, wind, animal movements – have been responsible for widening the canyon to its 10-mile (16-km) width. Differential erosion of rocks of various composition, thickness and hardness have created ledges, cliffs, dramatic mesas, buttes, totems, spires, and other features.

Little rivers

The Little Colorado River now runs along the ancestral course of the Colorado, which it joins within the canyon. The Little Colorado is today a major river on the Navajo Reservation, winding through the Painted Desert and tumbling over Grand Falls during heavy spring snowmelt. It has carved its own beautiful gorge, visible just west of Cameron. The Paria River, on the Utah–Arizona border, has also gouged out a dis-

and cement them to the rock; others believe that a purely chemical reaction occurs between the iron, manganese, and water. New evidence points to a combination of both.

Layer upon layer

Almost half of the earth's 4.5-billion-year history is contained within the horizontal layer cake of sedimentary rocks found in the Grand Canyon. The 1.7-billion-year-old Vishnu Schist in the Inner Canyon was laid down as sandstone, shale and limestone, interleafed with lava flows, in a sea that washed onto a shore at the western edge of the continent. These rocks were buried up to

tinctive course for itself through a uniform bed of sandstone, creating a picturesque 2,000-ft-deep (600-meter) slot canyon barely 30ft (9 meters) wide, in which sunlight rarely reaches the sandy floor.

Sandstone is frequently stained with desert varnish, a shiny dark brown or black coating made up of manganese oxides (black) and iron oxides (reddish brown). It is unclear how the manganese and iron, which are derived from sources outside the rock, are bonded to the rock surface. Many geologists now believe that the process involves bacteria that oxidize minerals

ABOVE: the ruddy, water-sculpted walls of Oak Creek Canyon rise above the surrounding forest.

12 miles (19km) deep, then uplifted and folded into a mountain chain, injected with veins of molten rock, eroded to their roots, redeposited, and then uplifted and folded again. This created strata that are today banded and contorted in some places, and platey and shiny in others. The earliest fossils are found here – large mats of algae known as stromatolites.

Resting directly on top of the Vishnu Schist are sandstones that are only 545 million years old. What happened to the intervening 1.2 billion years of rocks? Were none deposited? Were they laid down and then eroded away? The Great Unconformity, as it is called, is one of the mysteries of the Grand Canyon.

These 500-million-year-old layers of sandstone

were deposited at the start of the Paleozoic era, at the edge of a Cambrian sea. The Tapeats Sandstone, Bright Angel Shale, and Muav and Temple Butte Limestones contain fossil sponges, brachiopods, mollusks, corals, crinoids, and trilobites up to 3ins (8cm) in size – the first organisms on the planet to have developed a skeleton.

Ancient seas

During the Devonian Period (408–360 million years ago), the North American continent, which was slowly moving north, straddled the equator, and a tropical sea covered much of the present-day Southwest. Fish with armored heads began to

appear during this time, which has led geologists to call the Devonian the Age of Fishes.

The Redwall Limestone, formed in Mississippian times (365–330 million years ago), contains small invertebrate creatures known as crinoids, related to sand dollars and sea urchins, that looked like plants, with a base, a stem, and a flowerlike top. It is a gray rock stained red by iron deposits in overlying Supai rocks, a group of siltstones and sandstones produced in a low, swampy environment, and the Hermit Shale, which was deposited about 280 million years ago.

Near the rim of the canyon is the yellow, cross-bedded Coconino Sandstone, which was deposited in a desert filled with large sand dunes. The Toroweap and Kaibab Formations, laid down in Permian times (286–245 million years ago), make up the rim of the canyon. The fossil-rich Kaibab forms terraces that are cloaked with ponderosa pine forests across much of northern Arizona.

Where dinosaurs walked

Younger rocks of the warm, tropical Triassic era (245–208 million years ago) dominate the Navajo Reservation. The soft, banded Moenkopi Formation was born in a delta, when stream sediments mixed with limy marine deposits. It is barely distinguishable from the colorful overlying Chinle Formation, which is well exposed near Canyon de Chelly. A crumbly purple, yellow, and brown formation, the Chinle contains large quantities of uranium, produced from groundwater and likely leached out of volcanic ash. Certain plants, such as yellow feathery princes plume and milkvetches, are a good indication that uranium is present in soil.

The Chinle also preserves a lot of petrified

TRIASSIC PARK

Her name is Gertie, and she is one of the oldest dinosaurs known to science. When her bones were found eroding out of the crumbling hills of Petrified Forest National Park in 1984, she had been resting silently beneath the Painted Desert for 220 million years.

Gertie was a chindosaur – a small, fast-moving dinosaur that ate flesh and walked on two feet – and she represented a world in transition, from gentle herbivores like the heavily armored aetosaur to the giant carnivores whose bones thrill museum-goers to this day. Even the 30-ft-long (9-meter) crocodile-like phytosaur, which patiently stalked its prey in the swamps, could not compete. Gertie, and descendants such as the three-toed,

10-ft-tall (3-meter) dilophosaurs, whose tracks are preserved in the red sandstone west of Tuba City, ruled the world for another 150 million years.

The park's Rainbow Forest Museum and the Museum of Northern Arizona in Flagstaff have exhibits of dinosaur skeletons and eggs. Arizona's southern deserts have also yielded their share of dinosaur remains. The 97 million-year-old *Sonorasaurus thompsoni*, a new species of brachiosaur, was recently found in the Sonoran Desert and will be displayed at the Arizona-Sonora Desert Museum. Mesa Southwest Museum, near Phoenix, is also worth a visit. It has one of the largest exhibits of dinosaur skeletons in the West.

wood, formed in a process similar to that of uranium, but with groundwater that was silica-rich, creating quartz. During this era, the first dinosaurs and mammals appeared. Fossilized dinosaur skeletons are often found preserved in the Chinle Formation, while dinosaur tracks are nearly always found in the red Kayenta Formation, a rock that was laid down in damp, interdunal areas as the climate dried and desert sand dunes started piling up.

Deserts at the end of the Permian era, 260 million years ago, formed the De Chelly and Wingate Sandstones that make up the buttes, totems, and mesas in Monument Valley. A significant period of

and seeps that undermine the sandstone, causing it to peel away like an onion.

Water-loving plants are attracted to these seeps, where they form hanging gardens of moss, maidenhair fern, monkeyflower, and columbines, which also contribute to the destabilization of overlying rocks.

Volcanic remnants

Igneous intrusions of hot molten lava (magma) along faults beneath heavy layers of sandstone have pushed up and deformed much of the area in and around Monument Valley into anticlines (upwarps), monoclines (dropping on one side),

desertification also took place during the Jurassic period (208–144 million years ago), when a Sahara-like desert of 3,000-ft-high (900-meter) sand dunes covered 150,000 sq miles (390,000 sq km) of the West, eventually hardening into the beautiful pink Navajo Sandstone. Dune-formed sandstones have been eroded into distinctive shapes by the "exfoliation" process that occurs in porous sandstone. Groundwater passes easily through the rock and, when it encounters the impervious layers below, exits as dripping springs

LEFT: lava fields and a cinder cone at Sunset Crater Volcano National Monument north of Flagstaff.
ABOVE: spring runoff sends a torrent of muddy water over the Grand Falls of the Little Colorado River.

and synclines (downwarps). Also clearly visible on the horizon are laccolithic ranges like Navajo Mountain, where magma has risen along a zone of weakness, spread laterally between sedimentary layers, pushed them up into a dome, and eventually been uncovered by erosion.

A San Juan River trip, from Mexican Hat to Clay Hills Crossing, offers an indispensable opportunity to view these rock strata and float through the Goosenecks of the San Juan, technically an entrenched meander, where uplift of the Colorado Plateau has caused an older river to cut down several thousand feet into its Cedar Mesa Sandstone course and form hairpin bends. Rivers won't meander for long without seeking a more direct route past obstacles in their way. In this case, the grinding action of the river currents punches a hole in a meander wall, widens it, and eventually leaves behind a natural bridge like those at nearby Natural Bridges and Rainbow Bridge National Monuments. Natural bridges are water formed; arches are formed by erosion along joints in sandstone, forming linear fins and eventually arches.

Basin and range

Southern Arizona's basin-and-range country is much younger and more mobile than the Colorado Plateau and largely the result of pulling apart, not pushing up. Starting about 20 million years ago,

One of southeastern Arizona's most violent volcanic events occurred 27 million years ago, when six ash flows shot out of Turkey Creek Caldera near present-day Chiricahua National Monument, producing a 2,000-ft-thick (600 meter) layer of dark volcanic rock, known as rhyolite. Subsequent erosion by water, ice, and wind sculpted the rhyolite into columns, balanced rocks, and hoodoos. Five to 13 million years later, lava and ash spewed out of a volcano in the southwestern part of the state. The light and dark rocks make up the Ajo and Bates Mountains of Organ Pipe Cactus National Monument.

Volcanic action along a northwest-southeast

the Earth's crust beneath these deserts began to extend, stretch thin, overheat, and crack along a roughly north-south trend. The mountains in this region have been described as a swarm of "giant caterpillars marching northwest," so linear are these volcanic ranges.

Some blocks of earth started to break and tilt, forcing huge chunks of land to rise and others to drop. The ones that dropped formed the basins and began to fill with sediments washing down in huge alluvial fans called *bajadas* from the Huachucas, Chiricahuas, Dragoons, and other sky island ranges. Some basins contain 15,000ft (4,600 meters) of fill and rubble. Movements of the Earth's crust along these faults continue to the present day.

trend within sedimentary rocks, such as limestones, is thought to be the reason Arizona has such huge deposits of porphyry copper. One theory is that the continent drifted northwest over a hot spot in the Earth's mantle. Copper ores may have been the last substances to crystallize out of the magma. Prior to crystallization, the copper-bearing minerals dissolved in the hot water that permeates most magma, making them able to penetrate narrow fissures and fractures in the channels of adjacent rocks.

Most significant copper deposits were injected by a molten granite batholith, or deep igneous intrusion, into nearby limestone rocks, such as the Mule Mountains around Bisbee, where beautiful turquoise malachite deposits have been found. ❑

Arizona Volcanoes

Spectacular eruptions have occurred at various periods in the geological formation of the Southwest's extraordinary landscapes

When hot, molten rock, or magma, rises along vents and erupts at the Earth's surface, an extrusive mountain, or volcano, is created. Volcanoes that erupt violently and shower ash and lava over a large area are called composite, or strato, volcanoes and have a classic cone shape. Volcanoes that erupt in slow-moving lava flows and build up gradually are known as shield volcanoes.

Cinder cones erupt along side vents, which explains why they seem to cluster in chorus lines around the mother volcano. Magma that never reaches the surface forms an intrusive, domed mountain, or laccolith. Laccoliths are common on the Arizona–Utah border, at places like Navajo Mountain on the Navajo Reservation, where sedimentary layers are thick and hard to break through. Dark, jagged volcanic "necks" or "plugs" provide additional evidence of older volcanism on the Colorado Plateau. Erosion has uncovered the volcanic cores inside the sediments at places like Agathla Peak in Monument Valley, Church Rock in nearby Kayenta, and the Hopi Mesas.

Volcanic activity is greatest at the southern margin of the Colorado Plateau and may indicate that volatile basin and range activity in the southern part of the state is beginning to affect the relatively stable plateau along the Mogollon Rim, the 2,000-ft-high (600-meter) dividing line between the low deserts and the high country. Arizona's highest mountains are all found here. The highest, 12,633-ft (3,850-meter) Humphreys Peak, one of the San Francisco Peaks outside Flagstaff, is a stratovolcano that was built of lava and ash over a period of 1½ million years.

The Peaks stopped erupting about 400,000 years ago, but they are skirted by a 2,300-sq-mile (6,000-sq-km) volcanic field – the largest in the US – with more than 400 younger cinder cones. The best known is 1,000-ft-high (305-meter) Sunset Crater. It was one of the last volcanoes to erupt, some 900 years ago, leaving behind lava flows that were used

LEFT: erosion exposes bands of colorful sediments in Coal Canyon on the Navajo Reservation.
RIGHT: cinder cones near the San Francisco Peaks.

by the Sinagua Indians as mulch for their crops.

The state's second highest mountain, 11,403-ft (3,476-meter) Baldy Peak, is at the center of the White Mountain Volcanic Field, which erupted 8 million years ago. The nearby 1,158-sq-mile (3,000-sq-km) Springerville Volcanic Field is the third largest in the continental United States and contains 405 vents, craters, and shield volcanoes, which began erupting 3 million years ago. The state's third highest mountain, 10,912-ft (3,326-meter) Escudilla Mountain, is found here.

Just below the Mogollon Rim, 10,720-ft-high (3,270-meter) Mount Graham, the tallest of the Pinaleno Mountains, towers 8,000ft (2,400-meter)

above the cottonfields of Safford – the greatest vertical rise in Arizona. The most violent volcanic episode in southern Arizona's geological history, the eruption of Turkey Creek Caldera, occurred nearby about 27 million years ago. Ash covered a large area and settled as rhyolite, which eroded into the strange totems and balanced rocks of the Chiricahua Mountains.

The Earth's crust is undergoing far more heating, extension, and deformation here than anywhere else in the state. The result is younger and craggier mountains, rising as "sky islands" from flat desert basins. The clarity of the desert air has attracted astronomers, perhaps since ancient times. Powerful telescopes are found atop Kitt Peak in the Baboquivari Mountains, Whipple Observatory in the Santa Ritas, and Mount Graham in the Pinalenos. ❑

DESERT LIFE

Though Arizona's deserts may at first seem stark and lifeless, they sustain a fascinating array of plants and animals adapted to extreme heat and aridity

Spanning 118,000 sq miles (306,000 sq km), and with elevations ranging from 70ft (21 meters) above sea level at Yuma to 12,643ft (3,854 meters) at Humphreys Peak near Flagstaff, Arizona is much more than the searingly hot desert flats, saguaro cacti, and howling coyotes of popular myth. In fact, it is the most biologically diverse state in the American Southwest, with 137 species of mammals, 434 different species of birds, 48 snake species, 41 lizard species, 22 types of amphibians, thousands of arthropods, and a stunning 3,370 species of plants.

Such diversity can be attributed to the state's wide range of habitats, which include four converging deserts – the Sonoran, Chihuahuan, Great Basin, and Mohave – basin-and-range topography, and unusual ecozones, from lava flows to caves, where species have had to make special adaptations. In addition, a large number of plants and animals have migrated permanently north of the US–Mexico border to occupy protected niches in riparian corridors.

This is remarkable because when one thinks about Arizona, one instantly thinks of aridity. The Sonoran Desert of southern Arizona is found at

Only one of Arizona's 30 scorpion species, the bark scorpion, is considered life-threatening, though no deaths have been attributed to the species in the state for more than 30 years.

the 30th parallel north of the equator, which creates atmospheric circulation patterns that affect world climate and lead to desertification. Another

LEFT: poppies bloom in the Sonoran Desert.
RIGHT: rattlesnakes are often found under rocks, logs, and other protected places.

leading factor is that Arizona is a long way from the coast, too far to benefit from moisture. Moreover, any coastal moisture it might have received is effectively blocked by California's 14,000-ft (4,300-meter) Sierra Nevada, placing the Grand Canyon State in a rain shadow. Even high-elevation areas often receive less than 15 inches (38cm) of precipitation a year – the high desert range.

Precious water

Finding and holding on to water is what life is all about here, especially for those plants and animals that, unlike people, birds, and larger predators such as wide-ranging coyotes and mountain lions, cannot leave. Desert plants and animals have evolved a variety of strategies for survival, many so strange one can only marvel at nature's ingenuity. The kangaroo rat gets all its water from seeds. Spadefoot toads encase themselves in slime in the bottom of dried-up potholes, or *tinajas*, and wait months for heavy rains. Cacti gave up leaves in favor of protective spines and large water-saving waxy trunks that also help them photosynthesize food.

"In the desert ... the very fauna and flora proclaim that one can have a great deal of certain things while having very little of others," observed naturalist Joseph Wood Krutch in *The Desert Year*. "[T]hat one kind of scarcity is compatible with, perhaps even a necessary condition of, another

utaries. In between, at 3,500 to 5,000ft (1,100–1,500 meters), are sweeping grasslands around the fast-growing communities of central Arizona's Payson and Prescott and the US–Mexico border around Patagonia (Arizona's historic cattle country), transitioning to pinyon-juniper dwarf forest between 5,500 and 7,000ft (1,700–2,100 meters) in areas like Sedona on the Mogollon Rim.

Most of southern Arizona is in the Sonoran Desert, at 10,000 years old a relatively young desert, averaging 3,000ft (900 meters) in elevation, that slices diagonally from the southwest quarter of Arizona down to the Sea of Cortez in Sonora, Mexico, as far as the Sierra Madre in the

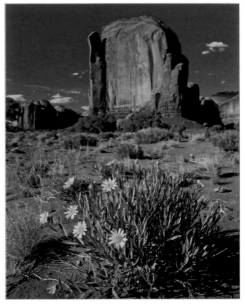

kind of plenty ... that plenty of light and plenty of space may go with a scarcity of water."

The lay of the land

The southern part of the state is "basin and range," a land of craggy, young volcanic mountains that form verdant "sky islands" above huge desert basins and ephemeral "playa" wetlands, such as those around Willcox, that attract thousands of migratory waterfowl each winter. By contrast, northern Arizona's Colorado Plateau soars from 5,000 to 12,000ft (1,500–3,600 meters) in a sprawling high country of volcanic peaks and uplifted plateaus, expansive ponderosa pine forest, glittering lakes, alpine meadows, and sandstone canyons carved by the Colorado River and its trib-

east and the lower southeast corner of California on the west. Because of its location, the Sonoran receives moisture twice a year – summer "monsoons," as they are dubbed (incorrectly), from July to September, and winter storms – making it the greenest of the West's deserts.

In the drier west deserts, around Organ Pipe Cactus National Monument, dominant plants include foothill paloverde, saguaro, cholla, and ironwood; in areas with more moisture, such as the Arizona Uplands around Tucson, add to the mix blue paloverde, mesquite, catclaw, desert willow, and desert hackberry, and shrubs such as bursage, creosote, jojoba, and brittlebush. When previous summer and early winter rains have been adequate, the Sonoran no longer seems a desert but a flower garden, with poppies, brittlebush, desert marigolds, lupines, fairyduster, fleabane, and other beauties blooming in waves, beginning in February.

A lush desert

More than 100 species of cactus call the Sonoran home, including organ pipe, Mexican senita, cholla, pricklypear, beavertail, pincushion, claret cup, hedgehog, and the symbol of the Sonoran Desert: the many-limbed saguaro. Cacti like these are the most successfully adapted of all desert plants. They take advantage of infrequent but hard rains by employing shallow root networks to suck up water, which is then conserved, accordion-like,

the Sonoran Desert and include the topknotted Gambel's quail, roadrunner (the state bird), mourning dove, phainopepla, and birds that carve out cool nests in saguaro trunks, such as the Gila woodpecker, northern flicker, cactus wren, curved-bill thrasher, and elf owl. Birds of prey and other avian species that can move easily from shade to sun are visible in daytime desert skies soaring on thermals. Often spotted are Harris's and red-tailed hawks, peregrine falcons, and golden eagles on the lookout for darting jackrabbits, cottontails, or ground squirrels.

Be careful where you walk and put your hands during daytime hikes. Mottle-skinned rattlesnakes,

in the gelatinous tissues of their waxy trunks. Cacti use their broad trunks to photosynthesize sunlight for food and have modified leaves into spines, which are much more useful as protection.

Three-quarters of desert animals are nocturnal. Your best chance of sighting a javelina, coati, kit fox, raccoon, bobcat, badger, coyote or a rare desert bighorn sheep is to visit a water hole in the cool dusk or dawn hours, or pay a visit to the Arizona-Sonora Desert Museum, west of Tucson, to view desert creatures in naturally landscaped enclosures. More than 400 species of birds live in

brightly hued collared lizards, whiptails, chuckwallas and the impressive-looking Gila monster, North America's only venomous lizard, keep cool under rocks and bushes during the day and don't become active until twilight, when they can regulate body temperature more comfortably. Lizards have a variety of strategies to evade capture, including detaching their tails when caught and later growing a new one. Gila monsters can live for several years on fat stored in their tails.

An unforgiving environment

Parts of southeastern Arizona are in the Chihuahuan Desert, two-thirds of which is found in Mexico. At a mean elevation of 3,500 to 5,000ft (1,100–1,500 meters), this desert has relatively

ABOVE: desert plants employ such formidable defenses as spines and bitter-tasting or bladelike leaves, but their blossoms are often large and brightly colored.

long, chilly winters, with occasional snowfalls that melt quickly. As with the Sonoran Desert, summer temperatures in the Chihuahuan exceed 100°F (38°C) but are cooled by violent summer monsoons, which drop 8–12ins (20–31cm) of annual rainfall in places like Bisbee, Tombstone, and the Willcox Playa area. Limestone caverns, such as those at Kartchner Caverns State Park near Benson, are found in this area, which was inundated by a Permian Sea 250 million years ago. Ocotillo, pricklypear, and cholla cactus do well in these calcium-rich soils. The signature vegetation of the desert is the lechuguilla agave, which has thick spikes rising from a rosette of fleshy, swordlike "leaves." After exiting the Mule Mountains tunnel, north of Bisbee, watch as the Chihuahuan Desert starts to blend with the Sonoran, with ocotillo and agave neighboring with saguaro.

Mohave and Great Basin

The Mohave Desert extends into Arizona along the Colorado River on Arizona's western border. The least colorful and most overheated of all the deserts in summer, the Mohave can transform overnight into a wildflower extravaganza with enough rainfall. Ironwood, desert holly, creosote, blackbrush, and bursage are spaced evenly to take advantage of available moisture. The indicator

SAGUAROS: GIANTS OF THE DESERT

The many-armed saguaro cactus seems as timeless as the Sonoran Desert it inhabits. Indeed, saguaros may live for more than 150 years, given warm southern exposures and sufficient rain on mountain slopes, or bajadas. They don't even begin to grow their appendages until they are 75 years old. Their shallow roots suck up moisture into barrel-like torsos that swell like an accordion, storing as much as 200 gallons (750 liters).

Saguaros take summer highs in excess of 100°F (38°C) and freezing winter temperatures in their stride. Spines protect them from intruders, trap cool air, provide shade, and along with the cacti's waxy coating, protect them from

dehydration. Unlike leafy plants, saguaros photosynthesize food along their arms and trunks, the latter often reaching 35–40ft (11–12 meters) in height. In spring, saguaros sprout white blossoms that attract visiting Mexican long-nosed bats, which pollinate the cactus with their wings as they sip nectar. In late summer, saguaros sport ruby-red fruit that, for centuries, have been made into syrup and jelly by the Tohono O'odham. Their ancestors made shelters from saguaro ribs, glue from the flowers, and treated arthritis with saguaro poultices. Urban sprawl, pollution, and vandalism threaten saguaros. Millions are protected in Saguaro National Park, outside Tucson.

species here is the shaggy Joshua tree, a giant yucca named by Bible-minded Mormons passing through in the 1800s. Relict palm trees have found a niche in a canyon in the Kofa Mountains, along with a thriving population of endangered desert bighorn sheep. A herd of about 500 bighorns lives in Cabeza Prieta National Wildlife Refuge, on the US–Mexico border. Every June, as temperatures soar, volunteers count the sheep – the true calling of "desert rats."

The northwestern corner of Arizona is primarily Great Basin desert, which extends all the way to eastern Utah and Oregon. A cool desert, found at elevations of 4,000ft (1,200 meters) or higher,

Animal magnetism

Arizona's southern desert "sky islands," with their higher elevations and thick stands of evergreen-deciduous forest, are a powerful magnet for living things trying to escape the heat of the desert. For every 1,000ft (300 meters) gain in elevation, the temperature drops 4°F (2°C) and precipitation increases about 4 inches (10cm). In the sheltered canyons of the Chiricahua and Huachuca Mountains, near the Mexican border, Arizona cypress and alligator juniper mingle with Mexican natives like Chihuahua and Apache pine, while at higher elevations, Douglas fir, aspen, and ponderosa pine provide browse for white-tailed deer and cover

the Great Basin was once dominated by lush, tall native bunchgrasses such as Indian rice grass, sideoats, and blue grama. Today, most of these native grasses have given way to disturbance species such as sagebrush, saltbush, snakeweed, rabbitbrush, and the ubiquitous cheatgrass after more than a century of grazing by cattle and sheep. Grasslands in protected parcels of southern Arizona like Las Cienegas National Conservation Area are beginning to recover.

LEFT: the common raven, the subject of much Native American folklore, is extremely intelligent and displays complex social behavior.
ABOVE: Oak Creek supports a lush growth of reeds, grasses, and other water-loving plants.

for sulphur-bellied flycatchers, Mexican chicadees, and long-tailed elegant trogons, which nest here every spring.

Wildlife (and human residents) in the desert borderlands are particularly drawn to cool riparian areas, where perennial streams offer that most precious of gifts: reliable water. Southeast of Tucson, places like Ramsey Canyon in the Huachucas and Madera Canyon in the Santa Ritas are oases, attracting 14 of 19 hummingbird species that winter in Mexico and nest in the huge sycamores, maples, and oaks that line the creeks.

San Pedro River is one of the country's most important waterways, protecting cottonwood-willow bosques for hundreds of resident birds and literally millions of migratory waterfowl, such as sandhill cranes and snow and Canada geese, which also use flooded desert basins, or playas, in Sulphur Springs Valley, near Willcox in southeastern Arizona. In northern Arizona, bald eagles are often found wintering on alpine lakes and reservoirs near Flagstaff, where cold-water fish are plentiful.

Northern uplands

Glorious though southern Arizona's desert mountains are, the most spectacular area of Arizona is the canyon country of the Colorado Plateau, the uplifted region north of the Mogollon Rim that takes in the White Mountains, the San Francisco Peaks, and the Coconino and Kaibab Plateaus of

responding changes in temperature, moisture, soil type, slope angle, and exposure to sun and wind.

The bottom of the Grand Canyon is as torrid as the Lower Sonoran Desert in summer, with temperatures exceeding 100°F (38°C). Life concentrates along the river, where willow and tamarisk form bowers for large numbers of songbirds, including the endangered Southwest willow flycatcher. Small canyon wrens flit around the rocks, their presence announced by their haunting descending songs.

It's a different story on the rims. Huge, airy forests of ponderosa pine and Gambel oak sweep across the Coconino and Kaibab Plateaus, forming the largest ponderosa forest in the continental

the South and North Rims of the Grand Canyon. The largely sedimentary layers of the monolithic Colorado Plateau began to be pushed up by faulting in the mid-Cretaceous period, some 75 million years ago. The area continues to rise and has been further uplifted and sculpted by local faulting into breathtaking high peaks and plateaus.

Even more extraordinary, the Colorado River has carved deep canyons through the uplifted plateaus creating the Grand Canyon, a vast abyss that drops from an elevation of 8,200ft (2,500 meters) at the North Rim to 1,300ft (400 meters) at the Colorado River. This kind of sudden elevation change has created a unique situation for wildlife, which has had to adapt to vastly different environments, from desert to montane, and cor-

United States. The forests are home to noisy Steller's jays, mule deer and two species of related tassel-eared squirrels, the Aberts of the South Rim and Kaibab of the North Rim, whose destinies diverged millennia ago, when the Grand Canyon separated them. In high country, black bear are common, though grizzlies no longer roam the peaks. The last grizzly, nicknamed Bigfoot, was sighted on Escudilla Mountain near Springerville, in the White Mountains, in the 1930s.

Return from the brink

A number of endangered species are now once again roaming their natural habitats in Arizona. California condors were successfully introduced to the Arizona Strip area, 30 miles (48km) north of the

Grand Canyon, in 1996, after a 10-year captive breeding and release program guided by the Arizona Game and Fish Department, federal wildlife and land management agencies, and private conservation groups. California condors are the largest land birds in North America, with a wingspan of more than 9ft (3 meters) and weighing up to 22 pounds (10kg). Members of the vulture family, they are opportunistic scavengers, feeding exclusively on carrion, traveling 100 miles (160km) or more per day in search of food. The birds managed to maintain a strong population until the settlement of the West, when shooting, poisoning from lead and DDT, egg collecting, and general habitat degra-

dation began to take a toll. Today, they may often be seen soaring over Marble Canyon and House Rock Valley in northern Arizona.

The reintroduction of another endangered species, the Mexican wolf, remains controversial. Mexican wolves once ranged from central Mexico to West Texas, southern New Mexico, and central Arizona, but by the mid-1900s had been virtually eliminated from the wild by ranchers concerned about livestock predation. Since March 1998, six packs of radio-collared wolves have been released

Above Left: endangered California condors have been reintroduced to northern Arizona and are occasionally seen at the Grand Canyon. **Above Right:** coyotes prey mostly on small animals but will eat just about anything.

into Apache-Sitgreaves National Forest in eastern Arizona, after being bred in more than 40 zoos, then acclimated in large pens in Sevilleta National Wildlife Refuge and on Ted Turner's Ladder Ranch in southwestern New Mexico. There are currently about 30 wolves in the wild.

Although the program is going as planned, local reaction remains mixed, and some wide-ranging animals have been hit and killed by vehicles, several have been shot, and some pups have not survived.

Other reintroduction efforts include a black-footed ferret breed-and-release program in the Aubrey Valley, in northwestern Arizona, and the release of endangered Sonoran pronghorn ante-

lope in the Buenos Aires National Wildlife Refuge, southwest of Tucson.

The jaguar, the largest cat in the western hemisphere, was listed as endangered in the United States in 1997. Jaguars have historically ranged from Central America's tropical forests into the arid oak-pine woodland corridors on the US–Mexico border, where they prey on javelina, deer, and a variety of smaller animals. If jaguars can make it into the United States without being shot in western Mexico, they stand a good chance of survival. Recent sightings in the Huachuca, Baboquivari, and Chiricahua Mountains are cause for cautious optimism. ❏

● *For more information, contact the Northern Jaguar Project in Tucson; tel: 520-623-9653 extension 5.*

OUTDOOR ADVENTURE

Arizona offers great opportunities for backpacking,
rock climbing, mountain biking, river running,
and even skiing – but you need to be prepared

The first thing to remember when contem-
plating an outdoor adventure is that "adventure" is a relative term. Look at the pictures
on these pages. How do they make you feel?
Excited? Curious? If so, you probably have what
psychologists call a high tolerance for risk. When it
comes to exploring the outdoors, you're inclined to
challenge yourself physically, find out what you're
made of, test your mettle against the elements.

If, on the other hand, the pictures make you feel
a little queasy, or you're more interested in the
composition of the rock than the predicament of
the people, then you may prefer an adventure that
emphasizes personal discovery instead of physical
challenge. You're probably more interested in getting close to nature, exploring new places, and
opening yourself up to novel experiences

A good start

Either way, the opportunities for adventure travel
in Arizona are more abundant than ever, and it's
never been easier to get started. Schools and clubs
are available that will teach you the basics of
wilderness travel as well as adventure sports such

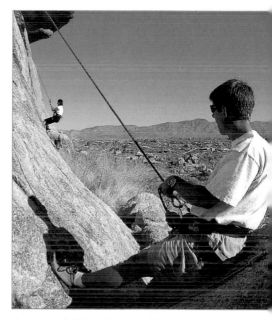

*Even clear streams can harbor parasites that cause
severe gastro-intestinal illness. All water from wild
sources should be boiled for at least a minute, treated
with iodine, or passed through a portable filter.*

as rock climbing and kayaking. There are also a
growing number of tour companies that specialize
in "light adventures" for people who want to expe-

LEFT: a camper enjoys the view from Toroweap Point
on the North Rim of the Grand Canyon.
RIGHT: a climbing guide teaches beginners the basics.

rience the thrill and beauty of the outdoors without committing themselves to months of training
or the hassles of planning a trip.

If you're a few years (or several pounds) past
your prime, don't despair. Though the ads in outdoor magazines may lead you to believe otherwise, you don't need to be a latte-swilling
20-something with washboard abs and chiseled
features. A minimal level of fitness may be
required, but in most pursuits good judgment and
a willing spirit count for more than brawn and
bravado. Which is not to say you'll be dangling by
your fingertips or wheeling down a mountainside
on your first day out. Making an honest assess-
ment of your limitations – including your tolerance for danger – is an essential first step in any

adventure, as is learning to say no when more experienced companions try to pressure you into situations that exceed your abilities.

A walk in the park

For some, hiking is adventure enough. They owe no apologies. A walk in the desert is not to be taken lightly, and even a short jaunt can turn ugly if you're not properly prepared.

What gets most people into trouble isn't snakebite, flash floods, or falling off cliffs but the far more mundane risk of dehydration – a critical loss of moisture due to extreme heat and aridity. The condition is particularly insidious

Coupled with the symptoms of mild dehydration – fatigue, light-headedness, disorientation – losing your way can quickly spiral into a life-threatening situation. Carry high-energy food and a map and compass (or GPS unit) and know how to use them, and leave a travel plan with someone at home, so they know when and where to start looking if you don't turn up at the expected time.

Other basics you'll need to take with you are a hat, sunglasses, and sunscreen with a high SPF. The Arizona sun is unrelenting, and shade is scarce. Left unprotected, your skin and eyes will be fried in no time.

because in the desert even mild exertion, like hiking, can cause the body to lose moisture faster than the brain can generate an urge to drink. In other words, you become dehydrated before you feel thirsty.

Prevention is simple enough. Carry plenty of water and drink it at regular intervals, whether or not you feel thirsty. The rule of thumb is one gallon (4 liters) per person per day, but it's best to take more than you think you'll need just in case you want to extend your trip or you lose your way. Getting lost is notoriously easy to do in the desert, where the absence of trees and other landmarks leaves you with few reference points and the abundance of bare ground makes it easy to stray from even a well-marked trail.

Foot notes

As a hiker, you will rely almost entirely on your feet, so keep them in good shape with the best hiking boots you can afford. Gone are the days of heavy leather clunkers that took forever to break in. Modern boots are lightweight but sturdy enough to protect your feet from cactus and thorny underbrush and need little or no breaking in, which helps avoid painful blisters. Wearing polypropylene liner socks under a thick pair of poly-wool outer socks will wick moisture away from your feet and prevent blisters. Avoid cotton socks, which soak up moisture and tend to be rough. If a hot spot develops, cover the area with moleskin (available at most camping supply shops) or white athletic tape and allow yourself extra time to rest.

Overnight trips are naturally more complicated to plan and require a rather daunting list of additional equipment, including a backpack, sleeping bag, tent, water-purifying kit, and camping stove. The design and quality of camping gear has never been better, though choices (and prices) can quickly become overwhelming. Unless you have an experienced friend to show you the ropes, the best advice is to start by doing a little research in books and magazines and on the Web, then go to a reputable camping-supply retailer and work with a salesperson who's willing to take the time you need to make the right decisions.

Remember: comfort is key. Roughing it in the

ning a successful trip. A summer hike into the Grand Canyon may seem like a good idea when you're enjoying a cool breeze on the South Rim, but it's another story when, a few hours later, your strength is sapped by the searing heat of the inner canyon and you're facing a long steep slog back to the top.

The best approach is to let your interests be your guide. Do you enjoy hiking in forests? Consider a trip through the aspen groves of the San Francisco Peaks or among stands of juniper and ponderosa pine on the Mogollon Rim. Have an interest in birding? More than 350 avian species, including a dazzling variety of hummingbirds, have been re-

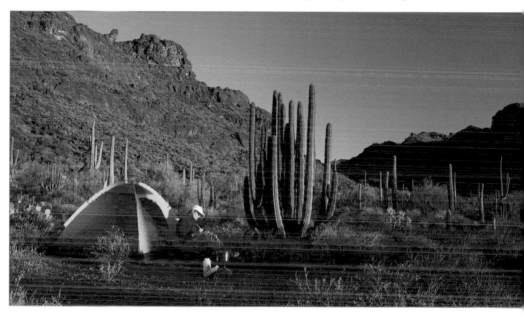

outdoors shouldn't be rough at all. The idea is to simplify your life, unload stress, and enjoy the place, people, and moment, not aggravate yourself with ill-fiting or poor-quality equipment that leaves you cold, hungry, achy, and generally miserable.

Now that you're properly equipped, you can begin making the tough decisions about where to go. Trail conditions, topography, and weather vary widely in Arizona, so gathering accurate information about a destination – the length and difficulty of your route, the availability of water, the location of facilities – is essential for plan-

LEFT: exploring a slot canyon outside Page in northern Arizona. **ABOVE:** camping In Organ Pipe Cactus National Monument.

corded at Madera and Ramsey Canyons in Coronado National Forest south of Tucson. Red-rock country? Explore the swirling sandstone formations of Paria Canyon-Vermilion Cliffs Wilderness. Fly-fishing? Pull on your waders and cast a line into Oak Creek just north of Sedona in one of the state's most picturesque canyons.

Pedal power

The possibilities become even more enticing when you consider alternate modes of transportation such as mountain biking or rafting, which usually free you from the burden of lugging a backpack and open up territory that may have been unreachable on foot. Advances in the technology and design of mountain bikes, for example, make it

Golfer's Paradise

Arizona is an above-par place for the sport, which has been a growth industry since the first official round was played in 1908

Golf isn't usually considered an adventure sport, but in Arizona you can make it so. At the annual Cowboy Golf tournament in Springerville, a rural community in the White Mountains, you can play nine holes on a working cattle

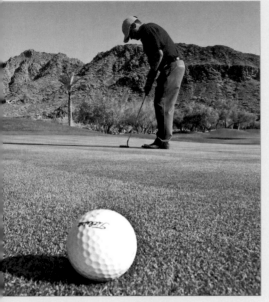

ranch. You ride horseback between holes and use cowpies as tees. There's the risk of having your "cart" gallop off while you're in mid-swing or twisting an ankle in a tumbleweed-filled arroyo.

In Apache Junction, east of Phoenix, there's a true desert course. The "greens" are sand (doused with recycled french-fry oil to keep the dust down), and golfers must make their way between creosote bushes and cacti. When you're done playing a hole, you have to drag a piece of carpet across the sand to erase your footprints.

Want more adventure? Book a tee time in Phoenix or Tucson at midday in July, when temperatures frequently reach 110°F (43°C) or higher.

For those who prefer the sport in its more traditional form, Arizona is a golfer's nirvana. The first official round of golf in the state was played in

1908, and it's been a growth industry ever since. There are 338 courses statewide, and most are public. Couple that with more than 300 days of sunshine a year and mild weather between October and May, and you have plenty of opportunities to hit the links. Courses are active even in summer, with golfers booking tee times between dawn and 7am and driving golf carts rigged with giant ice-water jugs.

Golf courses are as varied as the terrain. Phoenix and Tucson feature dramatic courses set at the base of desert mountains, with greens surrounded by massive granite boulders and towering saguaro cacti. In the mountainous communities of northern Arizona, such as Flagstaff, Payson, Prescott, and Pinetop, courses are surrounded by pine and juniper trees and cooled by mountain breezes. Still other courses are decidedly urban (and suburban), with office buildings or housing developments as backdrops. Older courses are lush with mature trees, such as the San Marcos course in Chandler, near Phoenix, which was established in 1912. The state's most challenging public course is said to be Las Sendas in Mesa, which has a rating of 73.8 and a 149 slope.

The cost to play 18 holes also varies, ranging from about $20 for a municipal course to $240 for Scottsdale's tony courses. If you want to learn golf or improve your game, there are plenty of golf schools and pros willing to help you sharpen your skills.

For some people, golf is strictly a spectator sport, and in Arizona, there are plenty of tournaments to watch. The three biggest tournaments are played in metro Phoenix during peak golf season. The PGA's Phoenix Open, held in late January, draws the nation's top golfers as well as more than 400,000 enthusiastic spectators, who come as much for the party atmosphere as the great game. In March, it's the women's turn with the LPGA's Standard Register Ping tournament, followed in April by the august members of the Senior PGA, who tee up for The Tradition.

There are still a few more ways to turn golfing into an adventure. Heli-golfing involves a chopper picking up a foursome in one town, dropping them off in an exotic locale, and returning in time for cocktails at the clubhouse. Then there's night golfing, which includes fluorescent golf balls and lighted fairways. But perhaps the most adventurous of all is encountering one of the state's wild residents on a green – a javelina, a coyote ... maybe even a rattlesnake. ❑

● *For more information about golf in Arizona, contact the nonprofit Arizona Golf Association at 602-944-3035 or www.azgolf.org*

easier and safer than ever to get started. The clunky, inflexible contraptions of 20 years ago have evolved into sleek and rugged riding machines designed to handle terrain that would reduce an ordinary bike to scrap metal. The advantages are obvious in a place like Arizona, where much of the backcountry is crosshatched with logging and mining roads. You'll cover more ground on wheels than on foot, and, unlike motorized travel, biking is great exercise, is easy on the environment (so long as you stay on prescribed trails), and lets the landscape unfold at a speed that's more akin to hiking than driving.

While it can take months to master the subtleties ows of the White Mountains, the stark desert ranges of Organ Pipe Cactus National Monument, the slickrock trails of Sedona, the volcanic highlands of Coconino National Forest, and the "high, wide and lonesome" backroads of the Kaibab Plateau to little-known overlooks of the Grand Canyon and Colorado River.

Many of the same safety issues pertain to biking as to other wilderness travel. Bring plenty of water and nutritious food, keep abreast of weather conditions, and don't overtax your skills or endurance. Carry a repair and first-aid kit, and be courteous to jeeps, horseback riders, and hikers who may be sharing the trail. Be particularly wary

of the sport, the basics aren't all that different from riding a garden-variety road bike. As long as you steer clear of extremely steep, tortuous or rocky routes and technically demanding single tracks (trails just wide enough for one bike), beginners shouldn't encounter too many difficulties.

Best of all, opportunities for mountain biking in Arizona are virtually endless. Even business travelers confined to offices in downtown Phoenix or Tucson will find good biking in classic Sonoran landscapes only a short drive from downtown. Farther afield, bikers can explore the alpine mead-

LEFT: a golfer lines up a putt at a Scottsdale resort. ABOVE: hikers view the Colorado River from the rim of the Grand Canyon.

of logging trucks, which often barrel down backroads at breakneck speed, kicking up a giant plume of dust in their wake. Truckers may not be able to see you and probably can't stop in time if they do. Don't let your last thought be: "Funny, I didn't see that truck a moment ago."

Wet behind the ears

If, as naturalist Loren Eiseley wrote, there's magic in water, then the rivers of Arizona are truly a miracle. They bring life to sun-blasted deserts, sculpt rock into breathtaking canyons, and serve as natural corridors for travelers and wildlife.

The premier river trip in Arizona – and arguably in all of North America – is a whitewater rafting trip through the Grand Canyon on the Colorado

River. The full journey takes about two weeks (although motorized rafts take about half as long) and is filled with wild rides through heart-stopping rapids, long peaceful paddles between soaring canyon walls, and hikes into enchanting side canyons where ancient Indian ruins are sheltered by rocky alcoves, waterfalls plunge into aqua pools, and seeping springs sustain gardens of maidenhair fern and crimson monkeyflower.

The real beauty of the experience is that just about anyone can do it. Outfitters authorized by the Park Service handle all provisioning and navigation. About all you have to do – aside from paying the (very substantial) bill – is show up.

technical skill and strength are paramount, the opportunities for beginners are expanding. Not too many years ago, the only practical way to learn rock climbing was to tag along with experienced climbers. Today, it's much more common for newcomers to hone their skills at climbing gyms before they actually put flesh to rock. "We can usually get people climbing within 20 or 30 minutes," says Eric Eaglstun, manager of the Phoenix Rock Gym in Tempe, although "there's only so much you can learn without being out on the rock." For that, he suggests contacting organizations like the Arizona Mountaineering Club, which runs a two-week course for novices that

River running elsewhere in the state can be quite good depending on the season and ranges from boat-bashing whitewater to long stretches of calm water that can be floated in an inner tube. The Verde, Salt and Gila Rivers promise solitude, scenery and glimpses of desert wildlife, though water levels are often too low to boat. Flatwater enthusiasts can explore the countless red-rock gorges that feed into man-made Lake Powell, the watery caves and canyons of the lower Colorado River near Lake Havasu City and, farther south, the rich bird habitats of Imperial and Cibola National Wildlife Refuges.

Climbing the walls

The learning curve is far more precipitous for rock climbing, although even in this sport, in which

covers the fundamentals of climbing techniques, equipment and, above all, safety.

Climbing skills are also being used by a new breed of adventurers known as canyoneers, who combine hiking, rappelling, and rock climbing to explore some of the least accessible canyons in the Southwest.

Much less technical but still challenging are the hundreds of peaks that rise from desert ranges scattered throughout the state. The degree of difficulty varies considerably from one mountain to another, but most require no special skills or equipment and can be climbed in a single day. Those with little or no experience may want to set their sights on a modest goal – say, the 2,608-ft (795-meter) summit of Squaw Peak in

Phoenix, one of the most popular hikes in the state. On the opposite end of the scale is the lung-searing trek to the top of 12,643-ft (3,854-meter) Humphreys Peak north of Flagstaff, where climbers will find the only patch of alpine tundra in Arizona.

Powder to the people

Arizona isn't particularly well known for skiing. In fact, most people – including quite a few Arizonans – are surprised to learn that a place known for its eyebrow-singeing temperatures has skiing at all. Thanks largely to its basin-and-range geography, Arizona is one of the rare as much as 250 inches (635cm) or more a year.

The possibilities for cross-country skiing are even more extensive, with miles of trails at such facilities as the Flagstaff Nordic Ski Center and Mormon Lake Ski Touring Center, both in northern Arizona. For those who want to break their own trails, there are countless acres of snow-covered backcountry in Apache-Sitgreaves, Coconino, and Kaibab National Forests, including wilderness treks to the North Rim of the Grand Canyon for those with sufficient stamina and logistical know-how to make the 45-mile (72-km) journey from Jacob Lake, the nearest town with year-round access.

places where you can spend the morning schussing through fresh powder and the afternoon sunbathing at poolside.

Arizona has four ski areas – the Arizona Snowbowl and Williams Ski Area outside Flagstaff, the Mount Lemmon Ski Valley in the Santa Catalina Mountains near Tucson (the southernmost ski resort in the United States), and the Sunrise Ski Resort in the White Mountains. None has snowmaking capabilities, so they're entirely dependent on the whims of weather which, when generous, deliver mounds of dry, fluffy powder –

FAR LEFT: a rock climber in the Santa Catalina Mountains. **NEAR LEFT:** Lake Powell kayaking. **ABOVE:** meditating in Paria Canyon.

Elbow room

In the end, the deepest rewards of adventuring come not from mastering a particular sport but from simply being outdoors in places where, as Colin Fletcher wrote of the Grand Canyon, people can move "closer to rock and sky, to light and shadow, to space and silence." Thanks to far-sighted citizens and politicians, Arizona has more than 5 million acres (2 million hectares) of legally protected wilderness.

What that means in practical terms is that, no matter how far you hike, there will always be another canyon to explore, another hill to climb, another trail to follow. As a river guide said of her many journeys through the Grand Canyon, "the place is so huge, every trip feels like the first time." ❑

EXPLORING ANCIENT ARIZONA

You can tour prehistoric sites, visit some of the West's
finest collections of artifacts, or join an actual dig
supervised by a professional archaeologist

Land and people are deeply entwined in Arizona. Hike desert trails throughout the state and you'll soon come upon crumbling adobe dwellings, painted and pecked rock art, arrowheads, potsherds, and other reminders that people have been living here for thousands of years. Drive the highways and you'll pass ancient stone cities built into hills and cliffs. Float the Colorado River through the Grand Canyon and almost every side canyon will reveal sealed granaries and mud-walled dwellings that seem to have been abandoned only yesterday.

Arizona's wealth of prehistoric sites is one of its main attractions, and for many travelers the high light of visiting the state is not only touring its many archaeological parks but getting involved in an actual dig. Not sure where to start? Four superb museums offer an overview of Arizona's ancient cultures and an easy way to get up to speed on the state's prehistory before hitting the road and visiting individual sites.

Getting started

Arizona State Museum, founded in 1915 at the University of Arizona in Tucson, is the oldest anthropological institution in the Southwest. An entire gallery interprets the prehistoric Hohokam

and Mogollon cultures, first defined by famed university archaeologist Emil Haury in the 1930s. The museum also houses an important collection of prehistoric Southwest pottery.

The Heard Museum is, quite simply, one of the finest cultural institutions in Phoenix. It was founded in 1929 to display Dwight B. and Maie Bartlett Heard's large collection of Southwest artifacts and does an excellent job of tracing the prehistoric roots of present-day tribes. One of its most impressive exhibits is the Barry Goldwater Kachina Doll Collection, which displays the country's most extensive collection of painted Hopi and Navajo religious carvings. Kachina dolls are traditionally fashioned into the likeness of individual helper spirits and given to Hopi girls dur-

> It's illegal to remove or disturb archaeological remains on public land. If you stumble across rock art, potsherds, or other artifacts, note the location and report them to the managing agency.

LEFT: Betatakin, occupied by Ancestral Puebloans in the 13th century, is set in the safety of Tsegi Canyon.
RIGHT: the exact meaning of some rock art is a mystery.

ing seasonal dances. Other exhibits chronicle the development of pottery, basketry, weaving, jewelry-making, and other arts from prehistoric times to the present.

The Museum of Northern Arizona in Flagstaff focuses on the Indian cultures of the Colorado Plateau. It was founded in 1928 by a Pennsylvania couple, archaeologist Harold Colton and his wife Mary Russell Ferrell Colton, who fell in love with the area and began excavating nearby Wupatki Pueblo. The museum houses artifacts from excavations throughout the Four Corners region and is an active research center.

Research is also the focus of the Amerind Foundation in Dragoon, southeast of Tucson, founded by archaeology enthusiast William S. Fulton in 1937. A large archive of ethnographic materials is available for scholars; casual visitors will be fascinated by the foundation's huge museum, which offers an excellent introduction to the cultures of the Southwest and northern Mexico, with an extensive collection of artifacts from the America-sponsored excavation of Casas Grandes, Mexico.

Can you dig it?

Ever wanted to don an archaeologist's battered hat and help dig up an important piece of the past?

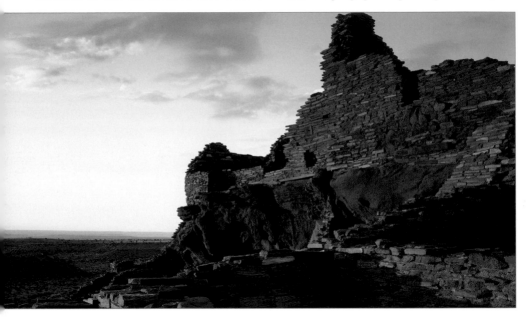

FOOD FOR THOUGHT

The Southwest's most controversial archaeological debate rages around that most taboo of subjects – cannibalism. At the center of the debate is Christy Turner, who, with his late wife Jacqueline, spent 30 years researching cannibalism at Ancestral Pueblo sites after finding signs of butchering and cooking in human bones excavated in northern Arizona. In 1999, the Turners published their findings in *Man Corn*, an allusion to an Aztec word for a ritual meal of human flesh.

Though praised for its scholarship, the book's conclusions have been criticized even by supporters of the authors' work. The Turners suggest that an Aztec warrior cult from Mexico infiltrated Chaco Canyon in New Mexico about AD 900 and used ritual sacrifice to terrorize the local population into submission. The discovery of fossilized excrement containing human remains has prompted even more furor.

Violence is an understandably sensitive issue for the Hopi and other descendants of the Ancestral Puebloans, and two new studies are only adding fuel to the fire. A survey of Pueblo excavations conducted by archaeologist Stephen Le Blanc catalogs numerous examples of violence. Similarly, Polly Schaafsma recently published the results of her study of rock art depicting warfare, which makes clear that conflict was escalating in late Pueblo times.

The romance of archaeology seems to infect everyone. Unfortunately, far more people want to take part in a professionally supervised archaeological dig than there are opportunities for them to do so. But a number of programs are available, with a limited number of slots open to volunteers.

The US Forest Service operates two programs aimed at archaeology enthusiasts. Heritage Expeditions are tours of archaeological sites in national forests. The popular Passport in Time program (PIT) gives you the chance to participate in an actual archaeological excavation in one of the national forests. In recent years, PIT programs have included digs at Mogollon pueblos in

between April and September each year at Elden Pueblo, a 60-to-80-room Sinagua ruin within Flagstaff city limits. The site is open for public participation during the Festival of Science in September and Public Field Days in summer, when visitors get a chance to take part in a supervised dig.

Not far from Flagstaff, the White Mountains are another good bet for anyone interested in archaeology. The White Mountain Archaeological Center, located on a working ranch near St. Johns, offers tours of rock art sites, the chance to assist on a dig at the large Mogollon Raven Site Ruin, moonlit hikes in the surrounding area, and overnight ranch accommodations. Just east of

Apache-Sitgreaves National Forest and fieldwork in Tonto National Forest to map an Apache settlement from the historic period.

The Deer Valley Rock Art Center, run by Arizona State University, offers programs throughout the year that focus on rock art created by the Hohokam. Northern Arizona University, together with Coconino National Forest and other organizations, sponsors the Elden Pueblo Archaeological Project, one of the best participatory experiences in Arizona. Educational programs include site tours, lab work, and excavation techniques and are offered to school groups and institutions

Greer, the X Diamond Ranch also offers the chance to take part in a supervised excavation of a Mogollon ruin with a large kiva. Since 1983, Dr. E. Charles Adams of the Arizona State Museum has operated a summer excavation program at Homolovi State Park near Winslow. The program relies heavily on college students, though volunteers 16 years or older are welcome. If you're interested, contact Earthwatch, a global environmental program. The Smithsonian Institution and National Geographic Society in Washington, D.C., also offer tours of Southwest archaeological sites and are worth contacting.

For a somewhat more formal experience, the Arizona Archaeological Society offers Professional Crew Member certification during summer

LEFT: Wupatki National Monument.
ABOVE: uncovering an ax head at Raven Site Ruin.

programs at Elden Pueblo and Q Ranch, a large Mogollon ruin on a private cattle ranch in the White Mountains. Slots are few, there is a modest fee for the weeklong digs, and you must be a society member.

Arizona State Parks organizes Archaeology Awareness Month, a program of events and activities involving more than 60 different government and private organizations, which takes place in March of each year. More than 100 events include prehistoric site tours, exhibits, open houses, lectures, demonstrations, and other activities throughout Arizona. This is your chance to learn to use an atlatl, or spear thrower; weave a pine-needle basket; attend a

lecture on the latest theories in southwestern archaeology; examine pottery rarely on public display; or take a ranger-led tour into backcountry areas that are usually off-limits.

In addition, the Museum of Northern Arizona, Heard Museum, and Arizona State Museum all sponsor lecture series, special events, cultural programs, and demonstrations as well as occasional field trips to archaeological sites accompanied by experts and working archaeologists.

Several Indian tribes now have their own archaeological resource departments and encourage culture tours led by tribal members. Entrepreneurs on the Navajo Reservation, for example, offer bed and breakfast in traditional Navajo hogans and horseback and jeep tours of nearby prehistoric sites at Canyon de Chelly and Monument Valley. Or you might stop at the Kaibab Paiute Tribal Headquarters next to Pipe Spring National Monument in the Arizona Strip and take a guided tour of rock art sites left behind by Virgin Anasazi and early Paiutes.

Serve and protect

A number of national parks now have Friends groups that raise funds and lobby for increased protection of their prehistoric sites. Site stewardship programs are also catching on fast with local archaeology enthusiasts. Arizona State Parks' highly successful Site Stewardship program trains volunteers to monitor archaeological sites for vandalism, conduct educational presentations about site preservation, and function as a trusted link between nearby communities and the State Historic Preservation Office. Arizona State Museum manages the training for the state parks, working with volunteers to monitor rock art sites east of Tucson.

Of particular interest is the Archaeological Conservancy, a nonprofit organization that purchases threatened archaeological sites across the country. The Conservancy is very active in Arizona, where, in 2000, it negotiated the donation of the Grewe Site, an early Hohokam community on land owned by Wal-Mart Corporation. Fragile archaeological sites are only opened periodically for member tours and volunteer days, but it's exciting to know that your membership dollars are making such a big difference in saving America's cultural heritage. ❏

ROCK ART

Rock art is found throughout Arizona, some dating back to Archaic times more than 2,000 years ago. Images may be pecked (petroglyphs) or painted with ground minerals like red hematite (pictographs) and depict hunting scenes, geometric patterns, and fertility symbols that still have meaning to modern Pueblos. Some rock art had an astronomical purpose; it was used to mark the summer and winter solstices or equinox, indicating the best times to plant or have ceremonies. The most puzzling type may be the huge intaglios or "geoglyphs" that were made on the desert floor near the Gila and lower Colorado Rivers and are best viewed from above.

LEFT: a Sinagua pueblo is tucked under a canyon ledge above Montezuma Well, a natural sinkhole.
RIGHT: White House Ruin, Canyon de Chelly.

GHOST TOWNS

Abandoned mining camps and forgotten outposts are frozen in time, offering insights into the lives of their long-gone inhabitants

Scores of abandoned mining camps that once housed several thousand people can be found throughout Arizona. Some are true ghost towns – mysterious names on a topographical map, completely unpopulated, with dilapidated buildings, empty schools, churches, and collapsed mine works. Most, though, have a few residents who look after the buildings, conduct tours, and keep alive these forgotten places.

A few mining towns never really died. Bisbee, Clifton, Tombstone, Prescott, and Jerome yielded billions of tons of copper, silver, gold, lead, and other precious metals. They grew into the largest and wealthiest towns in the state and became politically important as seats of local and state government. Today, they are undergoing a metamorphosis.

Restless spirits

Whole districts of Victorian mansions, company buildings, hotels, bars, and bordellos are now on the National Register of Historic Places. Many have been restored by artists, retirees, and local historical associations and turned into quirky homegrown museums, art galleries, bed-and-breakfasts, bars,

> *Vulture has only one tree – a hanging tree. The mine supplied the Union with bullion during the Civil War, but miners "high-graded" (stole) as much as 40 percent. Eighteen were hanged for it.*

and restaurants filled with mine memorabilia and, as is the case at the Copper Queen Hotel in Bisbee, haunted by the restless spirits of working girls, former managers, and other ghosts of the past.

LEFT AND RIGHT: rusty vehicles and ramshackle buildings at Gold King Mine near Jerome.

Some ghost towns grew up to serve mining communities. Benson was the railhead for Bisbee and other nearby towns. The Verde Valley Railroad once carried mineral ore and passengers between Clarkdale and Perkinsville, serving mines at the hillside town of Jerome. These historic railroads are now the center of reborn communities, carrying thousands of tourists through the scenic backcountry.

Original buildings, colorful characters, and bloody histories have attracted makers of movie westerns to ghost towns for decades. Many production companies took up permanent residence. Newly constructed "aged" buildings sit alongside original structures in an authentic boardwalk town at Old Tucson Studios, now one of the state's top tourist attractions, with staged gunfights and set tours. A movie set at Pahreah, an 1873 Mormon ghost town just over the Utah line, north of Lake Powell, was constructed for John Sturges's 1962 Western comedy *Sergeants Three* and is now encompassed by Grand Staircase-Escalante National Monument.

The Lord giveth

Residents of the Copper State are proud of their mining heritage. Arizona's motto is "God Enriches." The state seal depicts a miner with a pick and shovel, the likeness of George Warren, the first prospector to hit it big in the Bisbee mines

staked claims, and hoped for a lucky strike. If successful, they usually sold their claims and moved on, leaving the actual hard-rock mining to companies that could afford to invest in the necessary machinery, labor, and infrastructure. The bonanzas that fueled these boomtowns were dramatic, the decline often catastrophic. As mineral deposits played out and miners moved on, fortunes won turned quickly to fortunes lost, and boomtown became ghost town.

Cocktails at 30 paces

Mowry, between Patagonia and the US–Mexico border, is one of the oldest mining camps in Ari-

in the 1860s. Even the state's name is said to be derived from the abandoned silver mining town of Arizonac, just south of the Mexican border. Indian tribes were the first to mine turquoise, malachite, and azurite deposits from marine-formed limestones. Later Spanish and Mexican miners found gold and silver near these beautiful blue minerals. In the mid-1800s, when Anglo miners reopened the Spanish diggings, they located copper seams – the mineral that put Arizona on the map.

It's hard to believe that these dusty ghost towns were once the sites of gold and silver bonanzas that attracted swarms of fortune-seekers – miners and merchants, clergymen and saloonkeepers, lawmakers and lawbreakers, of every nationality. Prospectors followed reports of gold and silver,

zona. The Patagonia Mine was worked by Mexicans in 1857 and perhaps even earlier by Spanish Jesuits. It was renamed when mine executive Sylvester Mowry bought it in 1859. Twelve furnaces reduced the rich ore to 70-pound (32-kg) bars and a reported $1.5 million was shipped. Mowry is now on private land, but FR 214 bisects the townsite and two small adobe ruins can be seen. Nearby are the walls of the mine and smelter site, with a collapsed shaft, powder house, and large slag pile.

Sylvester Mowry was arrested for selling lead for bullets to the Confederates during the Civil War and lost his mine. He is also associated with the former ghost town of Tubac, the oldest European settlement in Arizona. When Edward Cross, editor of the state's oldest newspaper, the *Weekly Arizonan*, criticized Mowry for his support of splitting off Arizona territory from New Mexico, Mowry challenged Cross to a duel with rifles. When each missed his mark, they ended up toasting each other's health.

Situated in the Santa Cruz River valley, Tubac was founded as a *presidio*, or garrison, by the Spanish in 1752, then abandoned by the Mexicans after repeated Apache raiding in 1848. It was re-established in 1855 by American Charles Poston, a politician, entrepreneur, and visionary often called the "Father of Arizona." Today, Tubac is no longer a ghost town. A state historic park pre-

Bloody murder

Another ghost town with a violent history is Ruby, 30 miles (48km) northwest of Nogales. A lead, zinc, and silver mining town that died in 1941, Ruby has more than two dozen roofed buildings, including a jail, a school (with its basketball backboards still in place), mine offices, mill foundations, mine officials' residences, and a miners' dormitory. Bandits from across the Mexican border killed four people during robberies in 1920 and 1921 in the now crumbling adobe store. Only one of the killers was captured, and it's conceivable that one or more are alive today.

The most famous murders of all were those that

serves the remains of the *presidio*, and the town has taken on new life as an art colony.

Tubac was the headquarters for Poston's Sonora Exploring and Mining Company, which reopened Spanish and Mexican silver diggings at Cerro Colorado ("red hill"), west of present-day Interstate 19, in the 1850s. The silver mine established there and named after company president Samuel P. Heitzelman was the outfit's most successful producer. Eventually, though, Apache raids, worker unrest, and the murder of Poston's brother John closed the mine. Poston's grave is all that remains.

FAR LEFT: Washington Camp, south of Patagonia.
NEAR LEFT: the ruins of Jerome's jailhouse.
ABOVE: interior of the assay office at the Vulture Mine.

took place in the 30-second gunfight at the OK Corral in Tombstone in October 1881, killing Tom and Frank McLaury and Billy Clanton, known cattle rustlers, and wounding Virgil and Morgan Earp, brothers of U.S. Marshal Wyatt Earp. Clanton and the McLaurys now lie beneath gravestones in the Boothill Cemetery and the infamous contretemps is commemorated daily in staged gunfights and exhibits at the red-brick 1882 Tombstone Courthouse State Historic Park.

Buildings like the courthouse are evidence that Tombstone's history is not all blood and guts, despite the obvious truth of its claim to being "the town too tough to die." It grew from the Tombstone and Graveyard mining claims filed by prospector Ed Schieffelin in 1877 into one of the largest and wealthiest towns in the West. Schieffelin is buried in a little-known grave west of town under a pyramid-like stone cairn that marks the spot where he spent two nights hiding from the Apache before making his famous strike.

The ghost town trail

East of Tombstone is one of the best concentrations of ghost towns in Arizona. The old copper mining town of Gleeson has the ruins of a jail, school, and hospital. Farther up the road, in the Dragoon Mountains (the stronghold of Apache warrior Cochise), all that remains of Courtland is

its jail, but before World War I the town had its own auto dealership and a population of 2,000. Neighboring Pearce, the site of an 1894 gold rush in the flat Sulphur Springs Valley, has several ruins from its heyday, including the 1884 post office, a school, a jail, a few ruins and foundations, and the Old Store, a large adobe mercantile building with a high false front and an elaborate tin façade. Just to the north, the almost deserted community of Cochise was founded in the early 1880s as a water and fuel stop along the Southern Pacific Railroad. Today, all that's left is the Cochise Country Store, a school, a boarded-up church, and the 1882 Cochise Hotel, which is, remarkably, still open for meals and lodging (both by reservation only).

Mining in the Verde and Prescott Valleys brought fortune hunters to central Arizona in the late 1800s, leading to the choice of Prescott as the first territorial capital in 1912. Gold deposits in the Bradshaw Mountains, southeast of Prescott, yielded $390,000 annually. By 1904, the Crown King mine had enriched its investors with $1.5 million in gold. Problems in reaching the smelter in Humboldt inspired entrepreneur George Murphy to construct what was dubbed "Murphy's Impossible Railroad," linking mining towns in the Bradshaw Mountains over impossibly steep terrain. Trestles, switchbacks, and a tunnel were required in order to lay the tracks for the 51-mile (82-km) standard-gauge railroad. During its 23 years of operation, the railroad transported $1.1 million in gold and silver.

The former tracks now allow visitors to visit Humboldt, Mayer, Cordes, Bumble Bee, Cleator, and Crown King, an easy loop west of Interstate

---

THINGS THAT GO BUMP IN THE NIGHT

Arizona's colorful history has sparked its share of ghost stories. The specters of Bisbee's Copper Queen Hotel are well known. A manager from the early 1900s still strolls the lobby and accompanies visitors in the old elevator. The ghost of Julia, one of many prostitutes who entertained men in the tiny "cribs" in neighboring Brewery Gulch, makes amorous advances toward male guests in a third-floor room that's come to be known as the Ghost Room.

"Soiled doves" and their clients also still seem to be having fun at Tombstone's Bird Cage Theatre. The theater sometimes smells of cigar smoke, and piano music is heard. When it opened as a tourist

attraction, a mannequin of Wyatt Earp was mistakenly placed in the Clanton family's favorite crib. Day after day, Earp's hat sailed mysteriously to the floor, knocked off by some unseen force, until he was moved to a crib of his own.

Guests at the 1917 Vendome Hotel in Prescott report sudden temperature drops, whispered conversations, moving objects, and the appearance of Abby Byr, an owner who died in Room 16. The old hospital in nearby Jerome, now a hotel, also has a female ghost, perhaps a former nurse. "We hear voices," says the night clerk. "Feelings of cold air. Sometimes people have heard a name spoken, have turned around, and nobody's there."

17. The latter is a popular getaway for Phoenicians, with cabins, camping areas, the century-old Crown King General Store, and a saloon-restaurant that was packed in piece by piece from the mining camp of Oro Belle, 5 miles (8km) to the southwest, in 1910.

Colorado River ghosts

Among the earliest Anglo settlements along the Colorado River were Forts Yuma and Mohave, which were built to safeguard gold seekers traveling to mining camps on steamboats that plied the river from 1852 to 1907.

The best-preserved ghost town along the Col-

recreation area, with a relocated historic graveyard and a 2-mile (3-km) hiking tour that takes in the Picacho cave jail and remnants of two mills.

Away from the river, other Mohave Desert ghosts still cling to life. The gold-mining town of Oatman, just south of Kingman, boomed to 10,000 people in 1913. The United Eastern Mine was one of the major producers in the area; the others, Goldroad and Tom Reed, sparked short-lived communities and no longer exist. Today, Oatman has less than 100 residents and is a popular stop for tourists traveling historic Route 66. Several original buildings still stand, including the renovated Oatman Hotel, Mohave County's

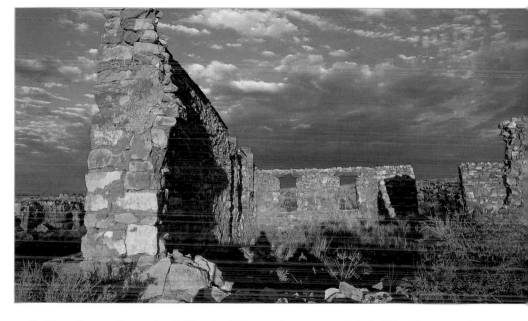

orado River is actually on the California side. Picacho Mine has been worked intermittently since placer deposits were discovered in 1862 beneath 1,300-ft (400-meter) Picacho Peak. By 1907, the site was an "oasis of bustle," according to the *Los Angeles Times*, with a peak population of about 2,500. River damming in 1909 ended cheap transportation of ore and put paid to many mining towns, including Ehrenberg, La Paz, Castle Dome Landing, Hardyville, Aubrey Landing, and Polhamus Landing. Much of Picacho was submerged behind Laguna Dam. Today, it is a state

only two-story adobe building, famous as the spot where Clark Gable and Carole Lombard spent their honeymoon.

Three other ghosts can be found nearby, in the rugged Cerbat Mountains northwest of Kingman. Chloride, named for the silver chloride ore found there in the Silver Hill strike of the 1860s, is one of the earliest Arizona Territory mining camps. The town features a post office and false-front general store, built in 1928. Mineral Park was the seat of Mohave County in the mid-1870s but lost out to Kingman when the railroad arrived in 1887. Nearby Cerbat was settled in the early 1860s, not long after Chloride. Of its three mines – Golden Gem, Esmeralda, and Vanderbilt – only the Golden Gem mill and headframe still stand. ❏

FAR LEFT: the Douglas Mansion at Jerome State Historic Park. **ABOVE:** sunset reddens the walls of Two Guns on old Route 66 east of Flagstaff.

THE ARIZONA COWBOY

His mystique lives on at rodeos
and dude ranches and in the
lives of working buckaroos

O n a crystal-clear spring morning, the Sonoran Desert outside Scottsdale is carpeted
with drifts of Mexican gold poppies,
lupines, owl's clover, and other wildflowers. In
the distance, the 7,000-ft (2,000-meter) peaks of
the Mazatzal Mountains are dusted with snow.

But three men and three women at the Arizona
Cowboy College are oblivious to the scenery.
They're hunched around the hind leg of a patient
gray quarter horse as Rusty, a farrier, gives them a
detailed, three-hour, hands-on lesson on the art and
science of horse shoes. The group is transfixed.

The six students have already spent a day
learning horse basics, including saddling, riding,
and grooming; they've also learned the fundamentals of roping. Tomorrow, under the super-
vision of the cowboy college's instructor, they'll
pack up gear, supplies, and horses and head to a
central Arizona ranch, where, for four days,
they'll be at the beck and call of the rancher,
doing everything from rounding up and brand-
ing cattle to mending fences, sweeping barns,
and shoveling manure.

> *An old cowboy song sums up the difficulties of
> adjusting to life on a dude ranch: "I'm a tough, hard-
> boiled cowhand with a weather-beaten hide, but
> herdin' cows is nuthin' to teachin' dudes to ride."*

Live the legend

For a few days at least, these people will be real,
working cowboys. And like real cowboys, their
working conditions are pretty rough. At the col-

LEFT AND RIGHT: "Cowboys," wrote Walt Whitman,
"are a strangely interesting class ... with their
swarthy complexions and broad-brimmed hats."

lege, they sleep together in an open, concrete-
floored bunkhouse and share one bathroom; on
the range, they sleep on the ground, eschew
showers, and answer nature's call in the brush.
And while real cowboys get paid for their efforts
(though not much), this group of people – and
many like them – pays good money for the experience. After a week of training, "graduates"
could, ostensibly, work on a cattle ranch. Few
do. Most come merely to fulfill a lifelong dream
of cowboying.

Modern-day economics may not support many
authentic ranches or cowboys, but in Arizona, at
least, the cowboy dream lives on. It's a rare visitor to this state who doesn't want to experience
some form of cowboy culture, be it folk art or

fashion, trail rides or steak fries, dude ranches, rodeos, or even something as advanced as the no-holds-barred program at the Cowboy College.

The Spanish connection

Cowboy heritage – both real and legendary – runs deep in Arizona. The state's first cowboy was, arguably, Jesuit missionary Eusebio Francisco Kino, the "Padre on Horseback" who, in the late 17th century, planted the seeds of Spanish cattle ranching and farming throughout southern Arizona.

Cattle ranching during the Spanish colonial period was sporadic. Spain considered the region

and the resident cattle were abandoned, while owners and workers moved into town.

Ranching takes root

After the Gadsden Purchase of 1853, Americans began to trickle into Arizona. Large herds of Texas cattle were driven across the state to supply military and mining concerns in California. After the drives, Texas cowboys brought back tales of southern Arizona's mild winter climate and stirrup-high grasslands.

In 1857, Bill Kirkland became the first American rancher in the state, bringing some 200 head of cattle to what was once a Mexican ranch south

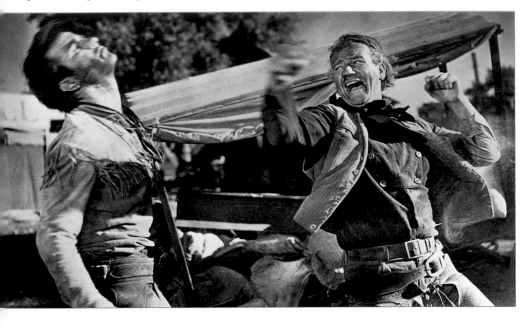

remote at best, and the missions were beset by disease, drought, and Apache raids. After Mexico's independence in 1821, southern Arizona was home to numerous Mexican families who ranched on large land grants, with herds of cattle, horses, and mules that numbered in the thousands.

The influence of early Mexican *vaqueros* on American cowboys is still felt today in ranching techniques, lingo and equipment. Arizona historian Marshall Trimble notes that a vaquero could "ride a horse through steep terrain, rope a cow, roll a smoke, sing a song and do it all with a smile on his lips."

By the 1830s, however, the Apaches had made it impossible for Mexican ranchers and their *vaqueros* to pursue a living; *los ranchos grandes*

of Tucson. But between the outbreak of the Civil War and the continued hostilities of the Apaches, ranching remained in its infancy until Geronimo's surrender in 1886.

With the suppression of the Apaches, ranching flourished in both southern and northern Arizona, spurred on by the arrival of the transcontinental railroad in 1883. It wasn't unusual for large spreads to stretch for miles and support up to 60,000 head of cattle and hundreds of hired hands. Many early ranchers were from Texas and imported their own US-born cowboys. Most of these "buckaroos" (a term derived from the Spanish *vaquero*) fit the same profile: they were young, unmarried, and without family or educational prospects. They worked from dawn to well after dusk in a dangerous profession, all for little more compensation than room and board.

Technically, early Arizona ranches didn't have cowboys at all. The term "cowboy" was a derogatory phrase reserved for cattle rustlers and outlaws. The early ranch hands who tended cattle were referred to as "herdsmen" or "cowpunchers," because they poked at cattle with prods to move them into corrals or railcars. The cowboy moniker didn't take on its present connotation until the turn of the 20th century.

Cowboys were hired hands and tended to move from one job to another as demand or whimsy moved them. Ranchers, on the other hand, often kept their business in the family for generations. Even today, old-time Arizona ranch families are regarded as a sort of royalty, whether or not they're still in the cattle business. Despite economic ups and downs and recurrent droughts, the industry became one of the "four Cs" at the cornerstone of Arizona's economy – cattle, cotton, copper, and citrus.

Cowboys and Indians

It was about this time that rodeos became more prevalent statewide. What started out as a friendly test of cowboy skill became an organized event, complete with prize money. Both Prescott and Payson began having summer rodeos that continue today; Scottsdale's Parada del Sol Rodeo and Tucson's Fiesta de los Vaqueros are large winter events. Major rodeos also developed on Arizona's Indian reservations, particularly in the latter half of the 20th century. In an ironic twist, some of the state's best cowboys are Indians, particularly members of the Navajo and Apache Nations.

By the 1920s, though, cattle ranching changed forever. The state's once-abundant southern grasslands had been overgrazed, droughts had taken a heavy toll, prices dropped, and feedlots began to replace the open range. Where once fortunes could be made by ranchers, and a hard-working cowboy could always find work, there was now only hardship and broken dreams. Today, traditional ranches are few and far between, save for the most remote parts of the state and on some Indian reservations.

Fortunately, conservationists are now stepping in to rescue a few of the most vulnerable old spreads. The historic Slaughter Ranch, adjoining

the Mexican border, for example, was saved from oblivion by preserving the 1890s ranch buildings as a museum. The San Rafael Ranch, also near the border, recently became a state park.

Birth of an icon

But despite the ranching industry's precipitous slide after World War I, the cowboy mystique never lost its appeal. The image was polished early on by popular entertainers like Buffalo Bill, who romanticized the western lifestyle and took it on the road. Countless dime novels fired up the imaginations of city slickers, as did the western novels of Zane Grey (1872–1939), who lived in

Arizona and set many of his stories here.

It wasn't long before Arizona attracted the attention of Hollywood producers. Westerns were big business between the 1920s and 1950s, and a great many of them were filmed in the state. Tom Mix, star of many a silent cowboy epic, made several movies in Arizona. He died when his car flipped on State Highway 79, south of Florence. There's a roadside memorial at the crash site – a metal statue of a riderless horse, which was one of the most-stolen "souvenirs" on Arizona's highways until it was permanently installed.

John Ford came to Arizona in 1938 to film the John Wayne classic, *Stagecoach*, in Monument Valley and returned for more than half a dozen other films, including *Fort Apache* and *She Wore*

LEFT: John Wayne takes a swing at Montgomery Clift in 1948's *Red River*, shot on location in Arizona.
RIGHT: a Navajo cowboy at the O'odham Tash rodeo.

a Yellow Ribbon, making both Wayne and Monument Valley icons of the Western genre. Old Tucson, a "frontier town," was built in 1939 as the set for the epic *Arizona*, starring William Holden and Jean Arthur. The set remained as a desert film location, which, later, counted John Wayne as one of its business partners. Countless movies such as *Rio Bravo* and *The Outlaw Josey Wales* and television series such as *High Chaparral* and *Gunsmoke* were filmed there. The facility, still used as a movie location, is now a popular theme park.

Rex Allen, one of the last of the singing cowboys, was an Arizona native. Allen, whose career spanned radio, film, and television, is honored in his hometown of Willcox in southern Arizona with an annual festival. Memorabilia from his performing career is exhibited at the Rex Allen Arizona Cowboy Museum.

Cash cows

Just as Hollywood was discovering the merits of Arizona as a movie set, tourism began to boom. The industry was boosted in its early days by the marketing efforts of Fred Harvey, who operated hotels and tourist programs throughout northern Arizona and New Mexico on behalf of the Santa Fe Railroad.

Before long, ranchers discovered that accom-

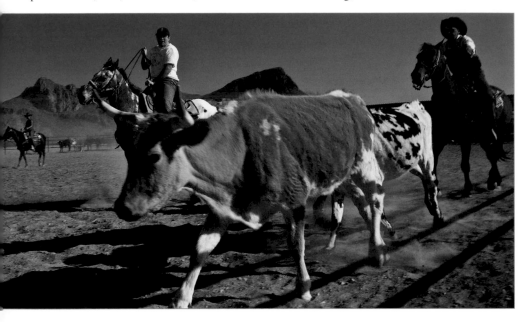

HOW TO CHOOSE A DUDE RANCH

Arizona has scores of dude ranches, ranging from spartan, working cattle ranches to elaborate "resorts with horses." Picking one that suits your needs, interests, and budget can save your dude ranch vacation from turning into one giant dud.

A personal recommendation is the best way to make a selection, but in the absence of firsthand information try searching the Web or calling the ranches directly *(see Travel Tips section for information)*. Be sure to ask about accommodations. Does the ranch have cabins, a bunkhouse, a lodge? Are meals included? How about the riding program? Do guests need to know how to ride or are lessons available? Does the ranch have a children's program? Is accessibility an issue? Also, check the ranch's location. Tucson and Wickenburg, both in the Sonoran Desert, are dude ranch hot spots, but if you like mountains and pine trees you won't be happy there. Consider destinations in the White Mountains or in the mountains around Flagstaff.

A few websites are useful. The Arizona Dude Ranch Association (www.azdra.com) lists comparisons of amenities and programs at their member ranches; Guest Ranches of North America (www.guestranches.com) offers profiles of more than 20 Arizona ranches; and DudeRanches.com (www.duderanches.com) lets you match activities to more than a dozen Arizona ranches. Happy trails.

modating guests could be as profitable as raising cattle, and the Arizona dude ranch was born. At first, they were primarily working ranches that took in guests as a way to supplement their income and offset market fluctuations, but by the 1920s facilities that catered strictly to tourists sprang up in and around Tucson, Wickenburg, and, to a lesser degree, Phoenix. These guest ranches always kept a herd of quiet horses and plenty of steak and beans.

As they grew more competitive, many offered Western-style entertainment, held "dudeos" (rodeos in which guests and staff compete against other guest ranches) and hay rides, and even added swimming pools and golf courses. Many of the old-time dude ranches are still open for the fall-to-spring season. In southern Arizona, these include the Tanque Verde Guest Ranch in Tucson and Rancho de la Osa in Sasabe, while in Wickenburg, it's the Flying E Ranch, Kay El Bar Guest Ranch, and the swanky Rancho de los Caballeros.

Developing at the same time were boarding schools that sprang up in central and southern Arizona, where the scions of New York and Philadelphia society were shipped West to learn the three Rs: reading, riding, and 'rithmatic. In addition to teachers who specialized in the usual subjects, the schools recruited local wranglers to instruct the young whippersnappers on cowboy basics. A few schools still exist – though, sadly, the Judson School, opened in Paradise Valley in the 1920s, was razed to make way for an upscale subdivision.

Lore and literature

But those in search of a bit of the Arizona cowboy mystique don't have to stay at guest ranches, enroll in a boarding school, follow the rodeo circuit or, for that matter, endure the rigors of the Arizona Cowboy College. There are other, less time-consuming ways to soak up snippets of cowboy lore.

The Arizona Historical Society Museum on the grounds of the University of Arizona in Tucson has numerous exhibits that chronicle the state's ranching past. For art, the Desert Caballeros Western Museum in Wickenburg exhibits work by such celebrated cowboy artists as Frederic Remington and Charles Russell, as well as period rooms with

furnishings that reflect the style of the desert frontier. Every October, the Cowboy Artists of America, an organization of noted Western artists formed in Sedona in the 1960s, has a major exhibition of paintings and sculptures at the Phoenix Art Museum. In Prescott, the Phippen Museum specializes in the art of the American West.

For the literary-minded, cowboy poetry festivals abound throughout the state. Prescott hosts a major cowboy poetry gathering at the Sharlot Hall Museum in summer. The event includes music, too.

For cowboy duds you need only visit Stockman's Western Wear in Phoenix or Saba's, with several locations in the Phoenix and Scottsdale

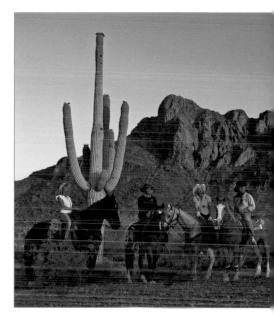

areas, both of which offer jeans, shirts, hats, and cowboy boots. For something ultra luxurious, a pair of custom-made boots may be in order, although a real cowboy wouldn't be caught dead in them. Paul Bond's boot company in Nogales has been making boots for decades, ranging from the utilitarian to the flashy. Customers include dudes, ranchers, and movie stars (ask to see the company's attic, where wooden lasts are kept for the shop's celebrity clients). Stewart's Boots in Tucson also offers a wide range of custom footwear.

The romance lives on at dude ranches, at poetry gatherings, on trail rides, and at every bar in which a cowboy yodels a plaintive lament. The real cowboy may be scarce in Arizona, but cowboy culture lives on. ❏

LEFT: guests at the White Stallion Dude Ranch near Tucson try their hands at a cattle drive.
RIGHT: Sonoran Desert trail ride.

PLACES

A detailed guide to the entire state, with principal
sites clearly cross-referenced by number to the maps

They came, they saw ... they went home. That pretty well sums up the experience of the first Europeans to see the Grand Canyon, a contingent of soldiers dispatched by Francisco Vásquez de Coronado in 1540 to search for the fabled Seven Cities of Gold. Failing after several days to reach the Colorado River, they abandoned the effort and turned back, observing rather matter-of-factly that the canyon was not only big but difficult to cross.

The outcome was only slightly better three centuries later when Lieutenant Joseph C. Ives, leader of the first American expedition into the canyon, was shipwrecked on the Colorado River. Though Ives was awestruck by the "profound grandeur" of the great abyss, he couldn't imagine why anyone would willingly venture into such godforsaken country. "Ours has been the first and will doubtless be the last party of whites to visit this profitless locality," he reported in 1857.

More than 4 million tourists visit the Grand Canyon every year, the vast majority congregating on the South Rim, creating one of the great ironies of the National Park System and one of its biggest headaches – traffic jams in the wilderness. You can now ride a free shuttle bus from Tusayan to Canyon View Plaza and pick up regular shuttles to other areas of the South Rim.

Despite the crowds, the Grand Canyon lives up to its billing. You won't believe your eyes – nor should you – because the vision that sprawls before you is simply too vast to comprehend. It's a common problem in Arizona, where stunning landscapes crop up around every bend.

But there's more to do here than merely enjoy the scenery. Explore the dusty lanes of a ghost town, the graceful interior of a Spanish mission, the dramatic ruins of an ancient Indian village. Pamper yourself at a posh resort. Ride horseback in a sun-drenched desert, cast a line into a cool mountain stream, go bird-watching in a secluded canyon. And get to know the people whose unique combination of Indian, Hispanic, and Anglo cultures, as well as the cultures of recent immigrants, are as complex and colorful as a Navajo rug. ❏

PRECEDING PAGES: exploring Emerald Cave in the Black Canyon of the Colorado
River; Phoenix at twilight; Nankoweap Canyon, Grand Canyon National Park.
LEFT: Monument Valley. **TOP:** Arizona cowgirl. **ABOVE RIGHT:** Route 66 near Oatman.

Northern Arizona

NORTHERN ARIZONA

Monumental landscapes, Indian cultures, and
a scrappy frontier spirit lure travelers
to the canyon country of the north

The Colorado Plateau – a spectacular hunk of continental crust
that sprawls across 130,000 sq miles (337,000 sq km) of the
Four Corners region – dominates northern Arizona. Its sandstone whorls and sinuous canyons give the landscape an animate
quality not found elsewhere in the state. Warmed by the sun, rocks
radiate heat long into the night. Water pulses through arroyos after
heavy summer rains and weeps through fissures in canyon walls.

According to Navajo mythology, the land is indeed a living
thing – *shimah*, mother – and the gargantuan stone formations
that stand upon it are the petrified corpses of gods and monsters who inhabited
the Earth before the coming of humans. To the Hopi, descendants of the
Ancestral Puebloans whose abandoned villages are scattered throughout the
plateau, every aspect of the natural world is infused with spiritual life. They
regard the Grand Canyon as a place of emergence – *sipapu* – where their
ancestors entered the present world before migrating to their mesa-top homes.

Though most visitors don't regard the region as a Holy Land in the same way
that native people do, it's difficult not to be moved by its beauty and scale. The
Grand Canyon is the most popular destination. About 4 million tourists make
a pilgrimage to the park every year, though relatively few venture far from the
main overlooks. Pity. Below the rim, the canyon unfolds like an inverted mountain, passing through a series of ecosystems as you descend
into ever more ancient rock, transected by side canyons that
lead into hidden worlds of waterfalls, hanging gardens, and
narrow corridors of sculpted rock. Only the backpacker and
river runner see this intimate side of the Grand Canyon or get
a close-up view of the mighty waterway that created it.

Beyond the canyon, you'll find no lack of wondrous places.
Pedal a mountain bike through the aspen groves of the San Francisco Peaks
north of Flagstaff. Paddle a kayak into the tortuous canyons that feed into Lake
Powell. Hike around the base of a 1,000-ft-high (305-meter) cinder cone in the
country's largest volcanic field. Explore the ruins of stone pueblos built in protected alcoves beneath soaring cliffs. Shop for silver and turquoise jewelry at an
Indian trading post. Ride horseback with a Navajo guide between the mineral-
streaked walls of Canyon de Chelly. Or drive the back roads of the Arizona
Strip, the "high, wide, lonesome country" north of the Grand Canyon. ❏

TOP: Sedona's red rocks. **ABOVE LEFT:** kayaking Watson Lake, near Prescott.

Map on page 128

Recommended Restaurants on page 145

GRAND CANYON NATIONAL PARK

Humbling, exalting, beautiful beyond words – the canyon is undeniably one of the world's great sights and grows only more fascinating when you venture below the rim

T he ancients spoke of the four basic elements of earth, water, wind, and fire. But at the **Grand Canyon ❶**, another element must be added – light. It is light that brings the canyon to life, bathing the buttes and highlighting the spires, infusing color and adding dimension, creating beauty that takes your breath away. Where else are sunrise and sunset the two biggest events of any day? In early morning and late afternoon, the oblique rays of sunlight, sometimes filtered through clouds, set red rock cliffs on fire and cast abysses into purple shadow.

The Grand Canyon, in northern Arizona, is rightfully one of the seven wonders of the world. Nearly 5 million people a year arrive at its edge and gaze down into this yawning gash in the earth. But the approach to the canyon gives no hint of what awaits. The highway passes a sweeping land of sagebrush and grass, through dwarf pinyon and juniper woodland, and into a forest of tall ponderosa pines. Then, suddenly, the earth falls away at your feet. Before you stretches an immensity that is almost incomprehensible.

The canyon is negative space – it's composed as much by what's not there as what is. After taking time to soak in the scene, one's eyes rove down to the bottom, where there appears to be a tiny stream. Though it looks small from this distance, 7,000ft (2,100 meters) above sea level, it is in fact the **Colorado River**, one of the great rivers of the West. And unbelievable though it may seem, the river is the chisel that has carved the Grand

Canyon. The Colorado rushes through the canyon for 277 miles (446km), wild and undammed. Over several million years, it's been doing what rivers do – slowly but surely eroding the canyon to the present depth of one mile (1.6km).

An awful canyon

To the east, the scalloped skyline of the **Palisades of the Desert** defines the canyon rim. To the north, about 10 miles (16km) as the hawk flies, is the flat-lying forested **North Rim**. To the west, the canyon's cliffs and ledges, cusps and

Main attractions

CANYON VIEW INFORMATION
  PLAZA
HERMITS ROAD
BRIGHT ANGEL TRAIL
HERMIT TRAIL
SOUTH KAIBAB TRAIL
DESERT VIEW DRIVE
THE NORTH RIM
THE INNER CANYON
HAVASU CANYON
GRAND CANYON RAILWAY

LEFT: Toroweap Overlook.
BELOW: mule train on the South Kaibab Trail.

Grand Canyon National Park

Lees Ferry **1**

Marble Canyon **1**

Navajo Indian Reservation

Jacob Lake

Cameron, Flagstaff

Palisades of the Desert

East Entrance

Desert View Watchtower **X**

Desert View **D**

Tusayan Ruin & Museum

Lipan Point **K**

Moran Point

Vishnu Temple 7529

Cape Final 7916

Siegfried Pyre 7913

Nankoweap Mesa 6242

Kwagunt Butte 6377

Colorado

Little Colorado

Point Imperial **F**

Vista Encantada

Walhalla Overlook **G**

Cape Royal

Wotans Throne 7633

Granite Gorge Rapid

Hance Rapid

Horseshoe Mesa 5238

Grandview Point

Desert View Drive

Yaki Point

Yavapai Point

Grand Canyon Village

Grand Canyon Information Plaza

Canyon View **A**

Tusayan

Ten-X

Grand Canyon

Apex

Flagstaff

Bright Angel Pt. 8145

Grand Canyon Lodge **E**

Bright Angel Point

Bright Angel

Phantom Ranch **B**

Tower of Ra

Granite Rapid **L**

Crystal Rapid **M**

Hopi Point

Pima Point

Hermits Rest **C**

Grand Canyon Village

South Rim

North Rim Entrance Station

Kaibab Lodge

De Motte

Kaibab Plateau

Bright Angel Canyon

Crystal Creek

Shinumo Creek

Point Sublime 7458

Havasupai Point 6637

Aztec Amphitheater

Granite Gorge

Kaibab National Forest

Powell Plateau

Colorado

National

Park

Deubendorff Rapid **O**

Steamboat Mtn 7422

Great Thumb Point 8028

Granite Narrows

Chikapanagi Point 5889

Kanab Creek

Kanab Plateau

Grand Canyon

Havasupai Indian Reservation

Havasu Cr.

Havasu **H**

Mooney Falls

Navajo Falls

Supai Falls

Havasu Falls

Supai

Canyon

Hualapai Hilltop

Redlands Camp

Coconino Plateau

The Dome 5487

Colorado

Toroweap Ranger Station

Toroweap Overlook

Lava Falls

Vulcans Throne 5102

Mt Trumbull 8028

Mt Emma 7702

Cliffs

P

Hualapai Indian Reservation

Aubrey

Fraziers Well

Kaibab National Forest

0   10 miles

0   10 km

N

Recommended Restaurants on page 145

curves extend as far as the eye can see, with only distant indigo mountains breaking the horizon. **Grand Canyon National Park** (open daily; tel: 928-638-7888; www.nps.gov/gcra) is more than a million acres (400,000 hectares) of land, and this view encompasses only about a fourth of the entire canyon.

People's reactions to their first sight of the Grand Canyon vary. Some are speechless. Some are brought to tears. Still others, such as early visitor Gertrude B. Stevens, have been overcome in other ways: "I fainted when I saw this awful looking cañon," she declared. "I never wanted a drink so bad in my life."

But with more than the average four-hour stay, a person can begin to explore this miraculous place, savoring different moods throughout the hours of the day, as the light constantly changes the face of the canyon.

The South Rim

Most visitors first see the Grand Canyon from the South Rim, the area that is open year-round and offers the most ample accommodations. The best place to start is at the **Canyon View Information**

Plaza **A**, accessible by free shuttle bus (open 8am–5pm daily; plaza exhibits open 24 hours). This spacious center has wall-size maps, exhibits and books that set the canyon in a larger context and help orient visitors. Park rangers there can answer specific questions. From the plaza, it's a short stroll out to **Mather Point**, for that virgin glimpse of the canyon.

Back at the plaza, buses run at frequent intervals all day to many overlooks along the rim. Other buses go to trailheads to drop off day hikers and backpackers. By extending the public transportation system, the Park Service is aiming to get people out of their cars, and get cars and development away from the rim, seeking to restore that invigorating sense of discovery. Now, the ravens (and a good number of reintroduced condors, which congregate at Lookout Studio) are taking back their rightful place, soaring over the dizzying abyss and croaking their calls of greeting.

Hermit's Road

The historic buildings on the rim, most of them of native stone and timber, will stay, however. One is the **Yavapai Point**

TIP

Cars at the South Entrance Gate often back up during peak summer hours. Traffic tends to be lighter at the East Entrance Gate.

BELOW: sunrise illuminates the canyon rim.

Visitors enjoy the view from Grand Canyon Lodge.

Observation Station (open 8am–6pm daily in summer), on the next point west of Mather. One entire wall of this small museum and bookstore is glass, affording a stupendous view into the heart of the canyon – slices of the Colorado River, a 1928 suspension bridge, and **Bright Angel Campground** and **Phantom Ranch B** tucked at the very bottom.

From here, a paved path along the rim leads to the village area, where shuttle buses head out along 8-mile (13-km) **Hermits Road** (also called **West Rim Drive**). Constructed in 1912 as a scenic drive, it offers several overlooks along the way. At **Trailview Point**, you can look back at the village and the **Bright Angel Trail** switchbacking down to the river. **Indian Garden**, a hikers' campground shaded by cottonwoods, is visible 4½ miles (7km) down the trail. The Bright Angel Fault has severed the otherwise continuous cliff layers that block travel in the rest of the canyon, providing a natural route for hikers.

In the morning, mule trains plod into the canyon, bearing excited greenhorns who may wish they'd gone on foot when the day is done. The trail is also the route of a pipeline that pumps water from springs on the north side up to the South Rim. The benefit of that reliable water supply makes the Bright Angel Trail favored among canyon hikers, especially in the heat of summer. Big flashfloods have washed out parts of the trail and the pipeline, hampering delivery of that most precious commodity in this semiarid land.

Buttes and temples

Other recommended points along Hermits Road are **Hopi**, **Mohave** and **Pima**. From each vista different isolated buttes and "temples" present themselves. There is the massive formation called the **Battleship**, best seen from **Maricopa Point**. There's **Isis** and **Osiris**, **Shiva** and **Brahma**. These overblown names were bestowed by Clarence Dutton, an erudite geologist with the early US Geological Survey and protégé of Major John Wesley Powell. Dutton's classical education inspired names with this Far East flavor. He wrote that all the canyon's attributes, "the nobility of its architecture, its colossal buttes, its wealth of ornamentation, the splendor of its colors, and its wonderful atmosphere… combine with infinite complexity to produce a whole which at first bewilders and at length overpowers."

At **Mohave Point** on a still day, you can hear the muffled roar of crashing waves in **Granite** and **Hermit Rapids** on the Colorado. With binoculars, it may be possible to spy boaters bobbing downriver in rubber rafts. The road ends at **Hermits Rest ⊙**, with a gift shop, a concession stand and restrooms. This is also where hikers head down the **Hermit Trail**, one of the more accessible backcountry trails beyond the main corridors of Bright Angel and South Kaibab. It's about 8 miles (13km) down **Hermit Canyon** to a lovely streamside camp for overnight hikers.

The Santa Fe Railway built the camp as a destination for tourists who arrived on mules, while supplies were shuttled 3,000ft (900 meters) down a cable from the rim. In those days, according to author George Wharton James, the camp furnished accommodations "to meet the

most fastidious demands." The "hermit" was a Canadian prospector named Louis D. Boucher, who settled at an idyllic spot called Dripping Springs, off the Hermit Trail. Known for his flowing white beard and a white mule named Calamity Jane, Louis kept mostly to himself. He prospected a few mining claims, escorted tourists now and then, and by all accounts grew amazing fruits and vegetables down in the canyon.

On a clear day, visibility at the Grand Canyon can exceed 150 miles (240km).

Desert View Drive

Returning to the village, another road, **Desert View Drive**, follows the canyon rim for 25 miles (40km) to the east. Overlooks along the way display still more spectacular canyon scenery. From **Yaki Point**, the panorama includes the massive beveled surface of **Wotans Throne**, and beside it graceful, pointed **Vishnu Temple**. The other main hiking route, the 7-mile (11-km) **South Kaibab Trail**, departs from near Yaki Point, snaking down the side of **O'Neill Butte**

BELOW: tourists take in panoramic views from Mather Point on the South Rim.

Return of the Railroad

Locomotives began beating a path to the Grand Canyon early in the 20th century. It was the end of the trail for the old stagecoach.

In 1883, cowman William Wallace Bass was out chasing doggies south of the Grand Canyon, when he found himself on the brink of the chasm "scared to death." Two years later, he set up cabins on the rim at Havasupai Point, where tourists came to see the great sight. From the small town of Williams, they boarded stagecoaches and bounced along the 72 miles (116km) to the camp, where Bass escorted them into his "dear old Canyon home."

His competition in those days was Pete Berry's Grandview Hotel out at Grandview Point. There, tourists arrived after an 11-hour trip from Flagstaff aboard the Grand Canyon Stage and stayed at Berry's hotel or at John Hance's cabins nearby.

But things changed. On September 18, 1901, the Grand Canyon Railway's Locomotive 282 pulled up to the budding Grand Canyon Village on the South Rim. Passengers found the three-hour train ride from Williams far preferable to the dusty daylong stage trips.

The arrival of the railway spelled the end of Bass's and Berry's tourist headquarters. With construction of the Bright Angel Lodge and Fred Harvey's five-star El Tovar Hotel, Grand Canyon Village became (and has remained) the center for visitors to the South Rim.

El Tovar's patrons were treated to fresh meals, prepared and served by Harvey girls dressed in white starched aprons. Accommodations were luxurious, and rocking chairs on the spacious porch permitted a classic canyon view with little exertion.

Despite the Harvey Company's dominance on the rim, other entrepreneurs came on the scene. Ralph and Niles Cameron staked mining claims and ran the Bright Angel Trail as a toll route for a time. In 1904, brothers Emory and Ellsworth Kolb built their photographic studio at the trailhead. They took pictures of people departing on mule trips in the morning, ran 4 miles (6km) down to a water source at Indian Garden to develop the film, and were ready with prints when the tourists returned. In 1911, the Kolb brothers made a film of their wild trip down the Colorado River, which visitors watched in their studio for 65 years.

Again things changed as Americans embraced the automobile, ending the era of rail service to the Grand Canyon in 1968. But another entrepreneur stepped in, restored the tracks, cars and locomotives, and relaunched the Grand Canyon Railway in 1989. Once again, locomotives chug out of the Williams station each morning, making the 135-minute, 65-mile (105-km) run to the canyon. Passengers have a choice of restored coaches or the more opulent club or parlor cars. The three-hour canyon layover allows plenty of time for lunch, a bus tour or a stroll along the rim.

A night at the canyon is also an option. It's a relaxing ride back, complete with crooning cowboy troubadours and mean hombres who stage a hilarious mock holdup. ❑

● Contact the Grand Canyon Railway at 800-843-8724 or www.grandcanyonrailway.com.

LEFT: the first passenger train to the Grand Canyon prepares for departure, September 1901.
ABOVE: "cowboys" entertain crowds waiting for the train.

through a break in the Redwall Limestone, down to Bright Angel Campground and Phantom Ranch.

Tall tales

Farther east, **Grandview Point** looks down on **Horseshoe Mesa**, site of early copper mines. The **Grandview Trail** starts here, built by miners to reach the ore. But even a short walk will reveal that no matter how pure the ore, hauling it out was not a profitable enterprise.

Grandview was among the first destinations for early tourists to the canyon, who stayed at Pete Berry's Grandview Hotel. One of the regulars there was old John Hance. He arrived at the canyon in the 1880s and built a cabin near Grandview. For a time, John worked an asbestos mine on the north side of the river but quickly realized that working the pockets of "dude" visitors was more lucrative. "Captain" Hance regaled rapt listeners with tales of how he dug the Grand Canyon, how he snowshoed across to the North Rim on the clouds, and other fanciful yarns.

His stamp remains on the canyon – there is a Hance Creek and Hance Rapid,

and the Old and New Hance Trails, rugged routes that drop down into the canyon from Desert View Drive.

In addition to great views and good stories, the drive in this area also gives a look at stands of splendid old ponderosa pines. These cinnamon-barked giants grow back from the rim, here benefiting from slightly higher elevation and increased moisture. Their long silky needles glisten in the sunlight, and a picnic beneath their boughs is a delight. Grazing mule deer and boisterous Steller's jays may be your companions, along with busy rock squirrels looking for handouts. (Resist the temptation; feeding wildlife is strictly prohibited.) The trees growing on the very brink of the rim are Utah junipers and pinyon pines. Sculpted by the wind, they cling to the shallow, rocky soil, never attaining great heights though they can be very old. The warm, dry air rising up from the canyon explains their presence.

In certain good years, pinyon pines produce delicious, edible brown seeds. People gather them, but so do many small mammals and birds. One bird – the dusky-blue pinyon jay – shares an inti-

Mule rides have been a tradition at the canyon for more than 90 years but are not for the faint of heart. Reservations should be made several months in advance; call 888-297-2757.

BELOW: first-time visitors often find the scale of the canyon exalting.

mate relationship with the tree. The jays glean nuts from the sticky cones, eating some and caching others. Inevitably, some of the nuts are forgotten and grow into young pinyon pines.

The eastern tip

Just to the east of Grandview is the entrance to the **Tusayan Ruin and Museum** (open 9am–5pm daily), which preserves the remains of masonry structures constructed some 800 years ago by Ancestral Puebloans. These early farmers were by no means the first humans to inhabit the canyon. Archaeologists have found a tantalizing stone point nearly 13,000 years old left by big-game hunters in the waning days of the Ice Age. For another several thousand years, hunter-gatherers made a living on canyon resources. About 4,000 years ago, they split willow twigs and wound them into small animal figures. They left the figures in caves in the canyon, where modern-day archaeologists have discovered them.

Lipan Point, farther east, provides one of the most expansive views of the canyon and Colorado River from any-

where along the rim. The river makes a big S-turn, with **Unkar Rapid** visible below. A little farther downstream is Hance Rapid, punctuating the entry of the Colorado River into the Inner Gorge.

In autumn, hundreds of hawks – Cooper's, sharpshins, redtails and others – migrate over Lipan Point on their way south. Nearby, in 1540, a detachment of Francisco Vásquez de Coronado's Spanish entrada tried but failed to reach the river. They are believed to be the first Europeans to enter the canyon proper, though Native Americans had long preceded them.

The final destination on this drive is **Desert View ❿** itself. Here the canyon opens out into the wide Marble Platform and east to the huge Navajo Reservation. The **Little Colorado** meets the main Colorado a few miles upstream. And an interesting circular tower stands out on the edge. Mary Jane Colter, architect for the Fred Harvey Company and Santa Fe Railway, designed it. (She also designed Bright Angel Lodge, Hopi House, Lookout Studio, Hermits Rest and Phantom Ranch.) Colter was heavily influenced by Puebloan architecture, and the **Desert**

The Canyon in Winter

Winter weaves a magic spell over the Grand Canyon. In this season the rim is softened by a mantle of ermine snow, and the chilled air bristles with crystals. Pine needles are glazed with frost, and gossamer clouds snag on the tops of pointed buttes. Sounds are muffled, and hectic summer days are a memory.

During the holidays, the fireplace in the lobby of El Tovar Hotel is surrounded with poinsettias. It's tempting to spend the day indoors by the fire, sipping hot chocolate. That's certainly an option, especially if the winds are buffeting the rim. But the outdoors beckons, and with proper clothing and footwear you can walk along the rim path and find yourself nearly alone with the canyon.

Juncos, nuthatches and finches flit in the tree branches. Ravens two-step out on improbable promontories, oblivious to the gaping abyss below. Tracks in the snow hint at dramatic encounters between hawk and rabbit.

Diligence is needed near the rim, though, for snow can hide a slippery drop off and trails may be icy. A ski pole or boots with instep crampons can be helpful. Beware of hypothermia, too. It can strike suddenly in wet, cold, windy weather when you're tired from exertion. Dress in layers, keep a supply of dry clothes, and drink plenty of water.

Recommended Restaurants on page 145

View Watchtower is modeled after structures she'd seen in the Four Corners area. It was built in 1932 of native stone, and on the interior walls are murals painted by Hopi artist Fred Kabotie.

The North Rim

At times, especially during the summer, the concentration of people on the South Rim can get to feel a little crowded. The place to turn is the **North Rim**, the peaceful side of the Grand Canyon.

From the South Rim, it doesn't look terribly far, but the North Rim is 220 miles (346km) away by road. Leaving Desert View, join Highway 89 and head north across the **Navajo Reservation** and part of the **Painted Desert**. Take Highway 89A, cross the bridge over the Colorado River at **Marble Canyon**, and allow time for the 5-mile (8-km) detour to **Lees Ferry**, put-in for Grand Canyon river trips and a vortex of Southwest history. This is the only place for nearly 300 miles (480km) where you can get down to the river, sit on the shore, and marvel that this is the same insignificant-looking stream you saw from the rim.

Back on Highway 89A, drive west across the wide-open, lonesome stretch of **House Rock Valley**, where keen-eyed travelers may glimpse a giant California condor soaring over the **Vermilion Cliffs**. The road then climbs up the east flank of the **Kaibab Plateau**, reentering pinyon-juniper forest and ponderosa pine. At **Jacob Lake**, Highway 67 winds 45 miles (72km) through the forest to the rim.

To the Paiute Indians, who lived on this side of the canyon, Kaibab means "mountain lying down." The North

Murals by Hopi artist Fred Kabotie adorn the interior of the Desert View Watchtower.

BELOW:
Hopi House.

The lookout plaza at Desert View.

Rim's elevation does qualify as a mountain. It averages 8,000ft (2,400 meters), 1,000ft (300 meters) higher than the South Rim, making for a very different forest environment. Here grow dense stands of spiky dark spruce and fir, along with quaking aspen and big grass-filled "parks," or meadows, where coyotes spend their days "mousing." The limestone caprock also holds a few small sinkhole lakes. This forest supports a different variety of wildlife too – the handsome Kaibab squirrel, a tassel-eared tree squirrel of the ponderosa pines, is found only here; there's also blue grouse; a larger population of mule deer; and a consequently larger number of mountain lions, the main predators of the deer. The North Rim is buried in snow in winter, and the entrance road is closed from the end of October through mid-May.

Because of the short season and isolation, the North Rim has never been as fully developed as the South Rim. There is a campground, small cabins, a visitor center, cafeteria, and the **Grand Canyon Lodge E**, which perches on the canyon's edge. One of the prime activities is to nab a rocking chair on the veranda of the lodge and engage in serious canyon watching.

The road to transcendence

From the lodge, a short trail goes to **Bright Angel Point**. Though you're still looking at the same canyon, the north side's greater depth and intricacy are immediately apparent. This is due partly to the Grand Canyon's asymmetry: the Colorado River did not cut directly through the middle of the Kaibab Plateau but slightly off-center to the south. Also because of its greater height and southward tilt, more water flows *into* the canyon here than *away* from it as on the South Rim. Thus the northern side canyons are longer and more highly eroded. The **North Kaibab Trail** along **Bright Angel Creek**, for example, is 14 miles (23km) long, twice the distance of the corresponding trail on the south side. While many people take the North Kaibab all the way down to the river for overnight stays, this trail also lends itself

Recommended Restaurants on page 145

to wonderful day hikes. Other shorter walks on the rim include the **Transept**, **Widforss** and **Ken Patrick Trails**.

A drive out to **Point Imperial Ⓕ** and **Cape Royal Ⓖ**, on the only other paved road, is well worth the time. At 8,800ft (2,700 meters), Point Imperial is the highest prominence on either rim of the canyon. Its eastward-facing view showcases **Mount Hayden**, **Kwagunt Butte** and **Nankoweap Mesa** in the Marble Canyon portion of Grand Canyon.

From there, the road goes out to Cape Royal, where it ends. Clarence Dutton also named this promontory; his description of sunset there strains even his exuberant prose: "What was grand before has become majestic, the majestic becomes sublime, and ever expanding and developing, the sublime passes beyond the reach of our faculties and becomes transcendent."

Go vertical

With the first step down into the Grand Canyon, the horizontal world of the rims turns decidedly vertical. A walk down a trail, even for a short distance, is the only way to begin to appreciate the canyon's great antiquity and sheer magnitude.

A word to the wise, though. Adequate preparation for this backcountry experience is essential. A Grand Canyon trek is the reverse of hiking in mountains: the descent comes first, followed by the ascent, when muscles are tired and blisters are starting to burn. And no matter what trail you follow, the climb out is always a long haul against gravity – putting one foot in front of the other and setting mind against matter. For first-time hikers, the maintained corridor trails are recommended: the Bright Angel, or the South or North Kaibab. Also note that all overnight hikes require permits, available from the **Backcountry Information Center** (tel: 928-638-7875) in Grand Canyon Village; day hikes do not.

There are two other critical considerations – heat and water. As you descend into the canyon, you pass from a high-elevation, forested environment into desert. Temperatures in the inner canyon are routinely 20 degrees warmer than the rim – from June to September that means upwards of 110°F to 120°F (43–49°C) down below. That kind of unrelenting, energy-sapping heat, coupled with a

TIP

Want to learn more? The Grand Canyon Field Institute (tel: 928-638-2485) offers 1- to 10-day trips covering a wide range of topics, including geology, ecology, photography, and cultural history.

BELOW:
Point Sublime, North Rim.

Hikers on the South Kaibab Trail.

BELOW: North Rim panorama.

The Inner Canyon

Dropping below the rims into the canyon's profound silence, you enter the world of geologic time. Recorded in the colorful rock layers is a succession of oceans, deserts, rivers, and mountains, along with hordes of ancient life forms that have come and gone. The caprock of the rims, the Kaibab Limestone, is 250 million years old. It is the youngest layer of rock in the Grand Canyon; every layer beneath it is progressively older, down to the deepest, darkest inner sanctum of black schist that rings in at close to 2 billion years.

As you put your nose up against the outcrop, you'll notice that this creamy-white limestone is chockablock with sponges, shells and other marine fossils that reveal its origin in a warm, shallow sea. The next obvious thick layer is the Coconino Sandstone. Its sweeping cross-beds document the direction of the wind across what were once dunes as extensive as those in today's Sahara Desert. It isn't hard to imagine, because already, even in this first mile of the trail, the canyon begins to look and smell like the

shortage of water, can spell disaster for the unprepared. In summer, each person should carry – and drink – a minimum of a gallon (4 liters) of water apiece. Along with water, a hiker should eat plenty of high-energy foods and take frequent rest stops. A hat, sunscreen, and sunglasses are necessary items. To avoid the extreme heat, hike in early morning and early evening. Or avoid summer altogether and go in spring or fall, which are the best times for an extended canyon hike.

desert – dusty and sun-drenched. Beneath the Coconino is the Hermit Shale, soft, red mudstone that formed in a lagoon environment. Underlying the Hermit is the massive Supai Formation, 600ft (180 meters) thick in places, the compressed remains of mucky swamp bottom 300 million years past. The Redwall Limestone is always a milestone on a Grand Canyon hike, passable only where a break has eroded in the 500-ft-high (150-meter) cliffs. Beneath the Redwall are the Muav Limestone, Bright Angel Shale, and Tapeats Sandstone – a suite of strata that indicate the presence of, respectively, yet another ocean, its nearshore, and its beach. Throughout most of the canyon, the tan Tapeats reclines atop the shining iron-black Vishnu Schist, the basement of the Grand Canyon and arguably its most provocative rock.

At the bottom, embraced in the walls of schist, are the tumbling, swirling waters of the Colorado River, the maker of this, its greatest canyon. The river, aided by slurries of rock and water sluicing down tributary canyons, has taken only a few million years to gnaw down

into the plateau to expose almost 2 billion years of earth history.

Soak hot feet in the cool water. Listen to boulders grinding into gravel on their way to the sea. Consider these old rocks in this young canyon. Ponder our ephemeral existence in the face of deep time.

The Colorado River flows between the sheer limestone walls of the Inner Canyon.

Havasu Canyon

Havasu ⊕, a side canyon in the western Grand Canyon, has been called a "gorge within a gorge." Within it flow the waters of **Havasu Creek**, lined with emerald

BELOW: Havasu Falls spills into a turquoise pool. The water takes its color from calcium carbonate.

Havasu Indian boys play in Havasu Creek.

BELOW: travertine, a sedimentary rock, forms pools of cool water at the base of the falls.

cottonwood trees and grapevines and punctuated by travertine falls and deep turquoise pools, paradise in the midst of the sere desert of the Grand Canyon. A visit is an unforgettable experience, a gentle introduction to the Grand Canyon and to the Havasupai Indians, the "people of the blue-green water," who have made their home here for at least seven centuries.

Getting there is no easy matter. The journey requires a 62-mile (100-km) drive north of Route 66 (about 190 miles/300km from the South Rim) to a remote trailhead, then an 8-mile (13-km) hike or horseback ride to the small village of **Supai** on the canyon bottom.

The pace at Supai is slow and easy. Development is limited to a small café, general store, post office, school, tourist lodge and tribal museum. Mail and supplies arrive by mule or horse (and these days by helicopter and Internet). In past times, the Havasupai partook of what the land offered. Evidence is seen along the trail in large rock piles, the pits used year after year for roasting the sweet stalks of agave. In their rocky homeland are distinctive natural features that hold great significance to the Havasupai. Rising high above the village is a pair of sandstone pillars known as Wigleeva. To the Havasupai, these are their guardian spirits; as long as they are standing, the people are safe.

Waterfalls

About 1½ miles (2½km) beyond the village is the first of the famous waterfalls – **Navajo Falls**. A short distance beyond is 100-ft-high (30-meter) **Havasu Falls** and the campground. The trail continues on to **Mooney Falls**, known as the Mother of the Waters to the Havasupai. To go farther down canyon requires a steep descent next to the falls on a water-slickened cliff face, with the aid of a chain railing. It's another 3 miles (5km) to **Beaver Falls**, a popular day hike for boaters coming up from the river to frolic in the beautiful pools. Those who make the journey know why Havasu is often called the Shangri-la of the Grand Canyon.   ❑

RESTAURANTS

Prices for a three-course dinner per person, excluding tax, tip, and beverages:
$ = under $20
$$ = $20–45
$$$ = $45–60
$$$$ = over $60

Arizona Room
Bright Angel Lodge
Tel: (928) 638-2631
Open: L, D daily $–$$
A logical second choice if El Tovar is full, this steakhouse has wonderful sunset views of the canyon. Steaks, barbecue, and wild salmon are popular. Fast for lunch but very slow at dinner, as there are no reservations.

Bright Angel Coffee
Bright Angel Lodge
Tel: (928) 638-2631
Open: B, L daily $
Located inside the lounge of the lodge, this is a good place for morning java and pastries.

Bright Angel Restaurant
Bright Angel Lodge
Tel: (928) 638-2631
Open: B, L, D daily $
A coffee shop serving diner-style food that should fuel you up for a day of hiking. Lots of kids' choices, including breakfast eggs, burgers, steaks, patty melts, spaghetti, and chili.

Canyon Star Restaurant
The Grand Hotel, Tusayan
Tel: (928) 638-3333
Open: B, L, D daily $–$$
The cavernous cowboy-themed dining room in this rustic hotel offers twice-nightly dinner shows with Indian dancing. The waitstaff is indifferent, but a few dishes show surprising flair. The seared elk tenderloin with berry reduction puts you in the mood for the Native American entertainment. There's a buffet breakfast and lunch and a bar with cowboy saddle seats.

Coronado Room
Best Western Grand Canyon Squire Inn, Tusayan
Tel: (928) 638-2681
Open: B, L, D daily $$
This is an excellent alternative if all the South Rim restaurants have long lines. American and Continental fare is done well and includes filet mignon, salmon, and spare ribs.

Delicatessen at the Marketplace
Market Plaza
Open: B, L, early D $
This deli in the South Rim's main grocery store serves surprisingly decent food and is a good choice for a quick bite. Try meat chili served in a sourdough bread bowl, roasted chicken and turkey sandwiches, salads, fruit, yogurt, and other healthy choices. The coffee here is superior.

El Tovar Restaurant
El Tovar Lodge
Tel: (928) 638-2631
Open: B, L, D daily $$–$$$
The views are spectacular at the tables near the windows in this rustic dining room, which has dark-paneled walls and Indian murals, crisp white linen, silver on the tables, and an attentive staff. The cuisine is Continental with Southwest flourishes and leans heavily toward steak, seafood, and pasta. It's by far the best on the South Rim, but you shouldn't expect miracles: it's nearly impossible to produce gourmet fare in such a busy dining room. Make dinner reservations weeks ahead, or plan on eating very late. Ask for a table near the huge picture window at sunset.

Grand Canyon Lodge Dining Room
Grand Canyon Lodge
Bright Angel Point
Tel: (928) 638-2611
Open: B, L, D daily $$
The only full-fledged restaurant on the North Rim is set in a grand window-wrapped room on the edge of the canyon. The menu is dominated by American and Continental dishes – prime rib, rosemary chicken, pasta with pesto sauce and asparagus. The food is mediocre, and the service is inconsistent, but the setting – the reason people come – is magnificent. If possible, make dinner reservations weeks in advance.

Grand Canyon Quality Inn & Suites
Tusayan
Tel: (928) 638-2673
Open: B, L, D daily $$
This light, bright, modern dining room in the Quality Inn at the far end of Tusayan is a popular choice with locals, who enjoy the large buffet at breakfast, lunch, and dinner. There is also an a la carte menu. Entrees are the typical steak and seafood at lunch and dinner with some interesting additions, such as *wienerschnitzel* and Navajo tacos. Vegetarians will find plenty of salads and fruit.

Jennifer's Bakery & Internet Cafe
Highway 64, Tusayan
Tel: (928) 638-3433
Open: B, L $
This tiny bakery is a find. It has good coffee, homemade pastries, egg dishes, sandwiches, and a close approximation of a hip atmosphere in bland Tusayan. Closes at 5pm.

Maswik and Yavapai cafeterias
Maswik and Yavapai lodges
Tel: (928) 638-2632
Open: B, L, D daily $
You'll find no frills here, just cheap, fast, filling food. If you're famished after a day of hiking and the Delicatessen at Marketplace is closed, this is a good choice.

Pine Country Restaurant
107 N. Grand Canyon Blvd, Williams, AZ
Tel: (928) 635-9718
Open: B, L, D daily $
This homestyle restaurant offers inexpensive family fare and is a good choice if you're in Williams to take the Grand Canyon Railway. The pie's the thing. Selections include double chocolate, coconut, chocolate peanut butter, and cherry, among others.

A MOUNTAIN IN REVERSE

The ecology of the Grand Canyon is determined largely by elevation, ranging from sere desert along the Colorado River to forested plateaus at the canyon's rims

Hiking into the Grand Canyon offers intimate views of the plants and animals that live at different elevations. Dwarf piñon-juniper thickets grow below the rim, and airy forests of virgin ponderosa pine and gambel oak dotted with natural clearings called "parks" dominate the 7,000-ft (2,000-meter) South Rim, alongside native grasses, cliffrose, sagebrush, pricklypear cactus, scarlet Indian paintbrush, and purple lupine. The higher, moister 8,200-ft (2,500-meter) North Rim supports fir and aspen, biological pioneers that grow up in the sunlight at the margins of meadows. Alpine fir-spruce forests are found at the North Rim's highest elevations.

Rim residents include Steller's jays, woodpeckers, great horned owls, huge desert ravens, and restored populations of California condors. Cottontails, gophers, and other rodents form the diet of nocturnal coyotes and bobcats. Long-eared mule deer emerge at dusk to feed. They are the principal prey of cougars, one of the West's most timid creatures. Look for two distinct species of squirrel, which evolved as the canyon widened: the Abert's on the South Rim and the Kaibab on the North Rim.

In the canyon bottom, adjoining desert and riparian habitats create a striking contrast. Shy bighorn sheep are sometimes seen among rocks, picking among cacti and yucca, startling chuckwallas, collared lizards, and the occasional rattlesnake. Mingling with the sound of trickling water is the sweet, descant song of the canyon wren, which hops among rocks, native willows, and exotic tamarisk. Birds rely on the Colorado River for survival and include ducks, sandpipers, endangered Southwest willow flycatchers, great blue herons, and bald eagles attracted by coldwater fish like rainbow trout and carp. Where water seeps through sandstone, look for lovely "hanging gardens" of maidenhair fern, monkeyflower, and columbine.

LEFT: the endangered California condor is the largest flying bird in North America. The Arizona population was 63 birds in 2008. A second population has been established on the California coast.

ABOVE: hikers pass through a ponderosa pine forest on Widforss Trail on the North Rim of the Grand Canyon; ponderosa pines grow at elevations between 6,500ft and 8,200ft (2,000–2,500 meters).

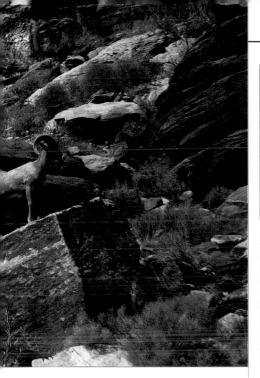

ABOVE: bighorn sheep thrive in the vertical terrain of the canyon. Sharp, cloven hooves allow them to stand on ledges only inches wide, and powerful legs propel them away from predators at speeds up to 30mph (48kmh). **BELOW:** rattlesnakes use their formidable fangs for both hunting and defense. Their venom prevents blood from clotting; a bite should be treated immediately.

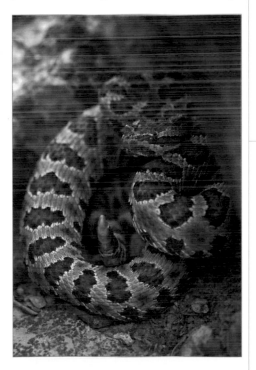

MERRIAM'S LIFE ZONES

In 1889, naturalist Clinton Hart Merriam hiked down the Old Hance Trail to the bottom of the Grand Canyon, climbed the surrounding San Francisco Peaks, and explored the badlands of the Painted Desert. Merriam concluded that plants and animals in the Southwest live in habitats that can broadly be arranged in horizontal bands, or life zones, according to elevation and temperature, that normally would only be found by crossing the United States from northwest Mexico (lowest) to Canada's Arctic Circle (highest).

The 7,000-ft (2,000-meter) elevation difference at the Grand Canyon accounts for five of the seven life zones and includes the **Lower Sonoran** (up to 4,000ft/1,200 meters), **Upper Sonoran** (4,000–6,800ft/1,200–2,100 meters), **Transition** (6,800–8,000ft/2,100–2,400 meters), **Canadian** (8,000–9,500ft/2,400–2,900 meters), and **Hudsonian** (9,500–11,000ft/2,900–3,350 meters). Typically today, biologists refer to life zones in terms of the specific plant associations within each zone: cacti in the Lower Sonoran, piñon and juniper in the Upper Sonoran, ponderosa pine in the Transition, aspen and fir in the Canadian, and alpine fir-spruce in the Hudsonian.

These broad-brush categories don't account for the numerous ecotones found throughout the park, where a change in soil type, exposure, or moisture allow small islands of wildlife to get a foothold. More than 1,500 plant, 355 bird, 89 mammalian, 47 reptile, 9 amphibian, and 17 fish species are found in the park.

TOP: snow blankets the South Rim. **BELOW:** bald eagles returned to the Grand Canyon in the mid-1980s, possibly attracted to the presence of trout in the Colorado River and an increase of migratory waterfowl.

COLORADO RIVER RAFTING

The West's mightiest waterway transports boaters on a breathtaking journey through the heart of the Grand Canyon

On a hot July day, a flotilla of rubber rafts floats down a serene stretch of the **Colorado River** in the **Grand Canyon**. A high-pitched buzz echoes off the sun-drenched cliffs. It's a peregrine falcon sounding an intruder alarm as it swoops down to the water, then soars up into the blue sky.

For boaters, the sight of this majestic raptor is an awesome spectacle, and one of the many reasons that a journey through the canyon is such a singular adventure. Here boaters enter the heart of the Southwest's remaining great wilderness and one of the planet's deepest gorges. They encounter wild creatures, pass in wonder through stunning desert canyons, and ride some of the biggest whitewater in the West.

The Rio Colorado courses wild and free through the million acres (405,000 hectares) of **Grand Canyon National Park** (tel: 928-638-7888) in northern Arizona. From the launch point at **Lees Ferry ❶**, the only way out in the next 227 miles (365km) is by foot on long, steep trails up to the canyon's rims.

Summer is prime season for running the "Grand," and while private individuals with the proper gear and experience are allowed to make the trip, a Park Service permit can take years to obtain. That's why most of the 22,000 people who boat the canyon each year go as paying passengers with outfitters licensed by the Park Service. On these trips, experienced guides row the boats, and the company furnishes all the food and gear. The guides know the river, the best places to hike and camp, and the canyon's stories. It's a tough job – part navigator, part tour guide, part entertainment director. They're up before dawn to make the coffee, they rig and row the boats, they lead hikes and side trips, and they strum their guitars under the stars.

Rules and risks

Even with seasoned guides, passengers need to know a few rules and risks. The rules: wear shoes on shore, don't

Main attractions
MARBLE CANYON
PHANTOM RANCH
HANCE RAPID
GRANITE RAPID
REDWALL CAVERN
CRYSTAL RAPID
THE JEWELS
LAVA FALLS

PRECEDING PAGES: a dory drifts through a stretch of calm water. **LEFT:** rafters stop at Vasey's Paradise. **BELOW:** river guide.

ABOVE AND BELOW: rafters punch through a series of rapids churned into a silty froth.

stream. The reason is twofold: first, to ward off rocks with your feet rather than your head and, second, to prevent your feet from getting trapped on the bottom, which can cause you to be dragged under by the current. Get back into the boat if possible; if not, swim to shore and wait for your party to pick you up. The water temperature hovers around 50°F (10°C), and even a short dip can be a numbing experience.

The Grand Canyon is a remote and wild place; emergency help is more than a phone call or a short drive away. But if you're armed with proper information and take sensible precautions, the journey can be safe and pleasurable for everyone.

Choosing a vessel

Many companies run both oar-powered and motorized boats. Oar boats are smaller, holding four or five people, and trips usually last two weeks (though partial trips are an option). Motor trips last a week or less, and each boat carries many more passengers. Purists eschew the motors because they disturb the canyon's sub-

use soap in the water, drink plenty of fluids, never litter, and most important, wear life jackets at all times on the river. Helping in camp and kitchen is welcome but certainly not mandatory.

The chief risks: boats can flip, and they do once in a great while. Should this happen, the best advice is to keep your feet up and point them down-lime silence. Others who go by motor swear their journey could not have been more profound. As one riverman put it, you could go down the Colorado in a bathtub and still have a peak experience.

Yet another option is a dory – an elegant, wooden, oar-powered boat that is reminiscent of (though much more river worthy than) the vessels used by such early explorers as Major John Wesley Powell, who first ran the Colorado River in 1869.

No matter what kind of boat you choose, you're guaranteed a white-knuckle ride unlike any river you may have paddled elsewhere in the West. Though most of the Colorado's rapids aren't technical in the sense that they require a rapid-fire succession of precise maneuvers, the sheer size of the waves packs a mighty wallop and should never be underestimated. Unlike other rivers, which are rated on the familiar International Scale of Whitewater Difficulty, the Colorado has its own rating system, 1 being the most tranquil, 10 the most challenging.

Canyon time

Canyon trips start at Lees Ferry, a desert outpost where a road goes down to the river's edge. It's a busy place on summer days, with several parties rigging at the same time. Tanned, muscled guides lash bags, coolers and metal ammo cans onto boat frames and laugh and joke with their pals. Then, a big bus or van pulls up, disgorging passengers, many of whom have never met before but who will be sharing perhaps the most intense two weeks of their lives together. It's hard to imagine, standing by the gentle, gurgling water, just what the Colorado has in store for them.

With everything neatly stowed and ready, the passengers buckle on life jackets and climb aboard. The boats push off from shore and bounce through the Paria riffle. Everyone stares up at **Navajo Bridge**, 300ft (90 meters) overhead, the last bit of civilization they'll see for many, many miles.

Around lunchtime, **Badger Rapid** bellows its presence. Boats slide easily down the shining tongue at the top, and passengers squeal with shock and

TIP

It can take 10 years to get a private permit, but you can bypass the process by signing on with one of the commercial outfitters who support kayakers wishing to pilot their own boats.

BELOW: dories give a "dry ride" even through big water and can be steered with amazing precision.

BELOW: a lone
dory drifts through
the canyon.

delight at their baptism in the river's chilly water. The trip continues down through **Marble Canyon** ❶, past canyon walls rising ever higher.

The river routine sets in – eat breakfast, pack boats, travel downriver for a few miles, walk up to an ancient Pueblo granary or stop to view a historic inscription on a boulder, lunch under a shady tamarisk, boat a few more miles, then pull up onto a sandy beach for the night. Change into dry clothes, enjoy social hour and dinner, then hit the sleeping bag under a starry sky.

By the third or fourth day of a trip, the sense of being in and of the earth is palpable. Skin toughens to the sun and dry air, people start to talk more about what they're seeing around them than what the stock market is doing back home. Wristwatches and worries are shed as canyon time takes over.

Past the scalloped cliffs of the **Desert Palisades**, the stone tower at **Desert View** punctuates the rim skyline. Soon, the aquamarine waters of the **Little Colorado River** interweave with the main Colorado. Guides often pause here to let their passengers enjoy

a swim in the Little Colorado's relatively warm, turquoise waters, slather themselves with mineral-rich mud, or hike to the remains of a hermit's cabin.

A little farther on, at Mile 77, the canyon walls change from colorful sandstones and limestones to the ominous dark black schist of the **Inner Gorge**. Here is **Hance Rapid** ❿, the first big drop on the river. Its predecessors were only teasers. Hance is a long jumble of rocks and waves, featuring a nasty hole midway through called the **Mixmaster**. At low water it earns a rating of 10.

As the canyon closes in, boaters gear up for another series of rambunctious rapids including **Sockdolager**, translated as "the knock-out punch." A taste of rustic civilization rears its head briefly at **Phantom Ranch**, where people can sip an ice-cold lemonade, watch backpackers toiling into camp, and send home a postcard that will be carried out of the canyon on the back of a mule.

This is the point at which an interchange of passengers may occur. Some hike out of the canyon, while others join the trip. They have no idea what's in store for them below Phantom Ranch, because rapids that heretofore inspired awe and fear will soon pale in comparison to those ahead.

Whitewater quartet

At lunch, the usually garrulous guides get a little serious. Furrowed brows, furtive conversations, gear tied down a little tighter. Then it's **Horn Creek**, a short, sweet jolt. At lower water levels, when the vicious rocks, or "horns," are showing, this rapid requires a precise entry and one or two strategic oar strokes.

A few miles downstream, the roar of **Granite Rapid** drowns out jokes and laughter. Formed by boulders washed in from **Monument Creek**, Granite is a chaotic flume of monstrous waves issuing off the right wall, along with a few crushers coming in from the left, not to mention dreaded **King Edward**, a major eddy at the bottom. A left entry into Granite is desirable, but the river often has other ideas, as all the current piles into the right. Granite's been known to flip a few boats, so everybody's happy to be right side up at the bottom and beyond the clutches of King Edward.

Hermit Rapid awaits – a series of five beautiful, standing waves – approached head on, right down the middle. The fifth wave, the granddaddy of them all, can grab a raft and hold it in a watery grip for a few seconds – though it feels like an eternity – as it decides whether to permit passage or to capsize the prisoner.

With adrenaline nearly exhausted, some guides elect to stop for the night on a pleasant little beach before attempting the last of the quartet – infamous **Crystal Rapid**. Crystal – the name is pronounced with reverential dread – deserves its 10-plus rating and is generally regarded as one of the most dangerous rapids on the Colorado. Before 1966, Crystal was a mere riffle. But during a storm that winter, a flash flood deposited a mass of boulders in the riverbed, transforming Crystal into

ABOVE: the rigid frame and long oars of an oar raft give pilots power and maneuverability.
BELOW: Nankoweap Canyon.

A motorized raft powers through whitewater.

BELOW AND BOTTOM RIGHT: Redwall Cavern, created by river erosion in a layer of limestone, is a favorite place to stop and rest.

one of the two toughest runs on the river.

A far-right entry in this rapid is almost mandatory. A faulty start can send a boat into the frightening maw at center-left, which may result in a trip through the strainer known as the **Rock Garden** down below.

Heart of the earth

Once all the excitement is over, passengers can enjoy the beauty of the Inner Gorge, surrounded by walls of fluted, blue-black Vishnu schist gleam-

ing like forged iron. The Vishnu, nearly 2 billion years old, is the oldest rock in the canyon. All the rock on top, and all the rock since leaving Lees Ferry, is younger. The Grand Canyon lays out in textbook fashion a neat chronology of the Earth's history, one of the most complete records anywhere, from 2 billion through about 250 million years ago, with only a few gaps.

The rock is old, but the canyon is young. It took the Colorado River less than 6 million years, and maybe as few as 1–2 million, to carve the mile-deep Grand Canyon. It wasn't merely flowing water that did the work, however. The Colorado once carried millions of tons of sediments in its waters. That heavy load of sand, gravel, and boulders acted like a giant rasp, grinding against the streambed, abrading the rock, and carrying it bit by bit to the delta at the Gulf of California. The river is still trying to cut deeper, but the old, hard, crystalline schist is resisting mightily.

Altered environment

Another major impediment has slowed the work of the river. **Glen Canyon**

Dam, 15 miles (24km) above Lees Ferry, was completed in 1963. This 710-ft-high (216-meter), 10-million-ton concrete plug now holds back the waters of the Colorado in **Lake Powell**. The hydroelectric power generated at the dam electrifies cities all over the West. The water that goes through the turbines is pulled out of the lake about 200ft (60 meters) below the surface. For boaters downstream, that means cold, clear, green water. In the old days, the Rio Colorado was choked thick with mud and silt, but no more. Also, electricity demand now determines water levels on the Colorado, which has caused more stable and predictable levels over the course of the year, though daily fluctuations can be dramatic. In some cases boats are left high and dry on beaches in the morning when the water level drops precipitously during the night.

Glen Canyon Dam has also been the single most important influence on the river ecosystem in modern times. Native fish and plants, like humpback chuba and willow trees, have given way to introduced trout and tamarisk.

Altered though it may be, the river corridor still harbors a wealth of wildlife – bighorn sheep perched on impossibly sheer cliffs, coyotes coming down to the river to drink, great blue herons standing stock-still on a mudflat, Bell's vireos calling from the thickets, bats fluttering overhead at dusk, collared lizards scampering from boulder to boulder in search of shade, canyon wrens warbling their distinctive liquid trill.

While the river remains the focus, each day brings new places and new discoveries. Boaters frequently stop and walk up side canyons, paradises in the desert with year-round flowing streams, pools reflecting canyon colors, waterfalls where hummingbirds hide, and freshwater springs lush with maidenhair ferns and crimson monkeyflowers. The names of these places are legendary among river

A dory pilot punches through Sockdolager Rapid.

A boater crashes through Lava Falls.

BELOW: Umbrellas provide welcome shade. Summer temperatures on the river can reach 115°F (46°C).

rats. **Redwall Cavern**, where a sandy beach is sheltered by an enormous rock alcove, frames glorious views of the canyon; spring water pours hundreds of feet down the mineral-stained walls of **Vasey's Paradise**; **Nankoweap** is known for ancient Pueblo granaries tucked into the canyon 600ft (180 meters) above the river; **Shinumo Creek** is favored for its inviting swimming hole and the ruins of an old mining camp; **Elves Chasm** and **Matkatamiba Canyon** have trickling streams, beautifully eroded rock formations, and lush hanging gardens of water-loving plants.

Lava and beyond

Moving ever downstream, boaters soon come to a stretch of the river below Crystal Rapid known as the

Jewels N: Agate, Sapphire, Turquoise, Ruby, Serpentine, Garnet. Boats swirl peacefully past the colonnade of **Conquistadore Aisle**, down to Mile 130 and **Bedrock Rapid**, and below it to **Deubendorff O**, a long rapid to be run before camping for the night. **Tapeats** and **Deer Creeks** are fine places to linger before facing **Upset Rapid** with its sharp surprises.

On to Mile 157 and **Havasu Canyon**, "place of the blue-green waters," home of the Havasupai Indians, where river trips often spend the better part of a day exploring the canyon's travertine ledges and splashing in the plunge pool at the base of **Beaver Falls**.

Farther on, the rocks assume a new form. Black volcanic rocks fill side canyons and form etched pillars. **Vulcan's Anvil**, a remnant of basalt standing in the middle of the river, is an ominous marker of what lies just ahead.

Lava Falls P is yet another Grand Canyon legend, the one the guides have been talking about ever since the trip began. It's a frightful maelstrom of foaming, seething turbulence stretching the width of the river, and it's rated a 10 at all water levels.

After a scouting session that seems to last forever, everyone walks back down the hot, dusty trail to the boats, hushed and sobered. Life jackets are buckled tight, the guides check every loose line, cameras and binoculars are securely stowed. This one's for real, and everyone seems to know it.

Untied, the boats swing into the current. The guide stands up for a better view, searches for the proverbial "bubble line" that marks the entry. "Hang on," he says, and the passengers clutch whatever handhold they can find. The boat slips down the tongue. Slam. A wave hits the bow like a two-ton truck. Then the boat drops down into a trough of air and climbs up the front of another wave. In a brief second, people stare over into the gargantuan hole formed by Lava's famous V-wave. The boat just kisses it, and the guide shouts, "Get ready!" Another slam of water engulfs boat and passengers. Seconds later, the boatman whoops and orders: "Bail! Bail!" The passengers oblige, tossing bucket after bucket of water back into the Colorado.

Relief. Exultation. Joy. Camp below Lava is always a big celebration. Of course, the trip isn't over. This is only Mile 179.6. There are still another 50 miles (80km) to go. The terrain changes again as the canyon widens and the river drops into even more austere desert. Finally, **Diamond Peak** spears the horizon. The trucks wait at the **Diamond Creek** take-out. Boats are unpacked one last time, the fine canyon sand sloshed away. It will be a while, though, before all the sand and all the memories are washed clean. Dreams of diving falcons and the sweet songs of canyon wrens will fill many nights to come. Dreams of the canyon and river may last forever. ❑

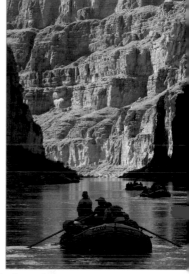

Muav Gorge.

BELOW: a rafter on a hiking expedition fills her water bottle at Dutton Spring in Deer Canyon.

PAGE AND THE ARIZONA STRIP

A modern town built to harness the power of the Colorado River is a gateway to the lean and lonesome country north of the Grand Canyon

"High, wide, lonesome country" is what cowboys called the **Arizona Strip**. Even many Arizonans have never heard of this quiet stretch of high desert on the Arizona–Utah border, sandwiched between the **North Rim of the Grand Canyon** and the **Vermilion Cliffs**. For most visitors, it's the Highway 89A Grand Canyon corridor, connecting the communities of northern Arizona with those of southern Utah via the only road bridge over the **Colorado River** in 600 miles (970km).

To the Kaibab Paiute Tribe, whose small reservation surrounds Pipe Spring National Monument, the Strip was once a bountiful homeland of tallgrass prairie, sunflowers and hundreds of other food plants. Some 5,000 of their ancestors roamed long distances seasonally, living in wickiup brush shelters and weaving beautiful baskets to gather pinyon nuts, seeds and other foods.

In summer, they hunted deer and elk on the Kaibab Plateau, then returned to stone houses beside springs to harvest corn and squash like their predecessors, the Virgin River Anasazi. Springs "belonged" to individual families, who acted as caretakers on behalf of the natural world, learning the songs of each rock and tree, much as Australian aborigines follow "songlines" across the Outback. "They cannot describe a country to you," wrote explorer John Wesley Powell, who mapped this area with Paiute guides in 1871, using Pipe Spring as his base. "But they can tell you all the details of a route."

The road to recovery

The Kaibab Paiute were almost wiped out by 18th-century Spanish diseases and 19th-century Navajo and Ute slave trading. Then, in the 1860s, Mormon colonists took over water sources and traditional hunting and gathering lands for farms, ranches, and settlements, and the Kaibab Paiutes quickly lost their self-sufficiency and became poverty-stricken. The situation has changed, due largely to education, legal challenges over self-determination and access to water, and modest commercial development on the reservation.

Main attractions
LAKE POWELL
GLEN CANYON DAM
GLEN CANYON NATIONAL
  RECREATION AREA
RAINBOW BRIDGE
HORSESHOE BEND
VERMILION CLIFFS
PARIA CANYON
PIPE SPRINGS

PRECEDING PAGES:
Rainbow Bridge.
LEFT: Paria Canyon.
BELOW: bighorn sheep inhabit the Vermilion Cliffs.

The Canyon King *offers sunset, dinner and short scenic cruises on Lake Powell.*

BELOW: the Glen Canyon Dam impounds the waters of Lake Powell.

Things look less rosy for the land itself. The huge cattle drives of the 1870s and 1880s badly overgrazed the Strip. Lush grasslands have been replaced by sagebrush and erosion of deep arroyos, and despite better stewardship of the land under the watchful gaze of the Bureau of Land Management (BLM), it struggles to recover. Although ranching, logging, and mining are still in evidence, tourism and outdoor recreation are becoming more important economically. Four-wheel-drivers, river runners, hikers and other outdoor-lovers can explore some of the most beautiful and little-traveled backcountry in the state in **Grand Canyon National Park**, four national monuments, and eight wilderness areas.

Unnatural beauty

Given this abundant natural beauty, it's ironic that the area's most popular attraction is unnatural. Some 130 miles (210km) north of Flagstaff, on Highway 89, is 180-mile-long (290-km) **Lake Powell ❷**, the second largest man-made lake in the Western Hemisphere. The lake is formed by 710-ft-high (220-meter) **Glen Canyon Dam**, downstream at **Page ❸**, which generates 1,200 megawatts of hydroelectricity for the megalopolises of Phoenix and environs – and ample controversy.

When it was begun in 1956, the dam had the blessing of almost everyone concerned. By the time it was finished in 1963, conservationists like the Sierra Club's David Brower and writer Wallace Stegner had belatedly recognized that Glen Canyon was comparable in grandeur to anything – including the nearby Grand Canyon – on the Colorado Plateau.

Since 2000, drought has pushed lake levels 118 ft (36 meters) below capacity. As the lake drops, hiking and primitive camping on new beaches and side canyons are once again becoming popular in the northern reaches of the lake, where archaeological remains are reappearing like the mythical lost city of Atlantis. Once mourned as "The Place No One Knew," Glen Canyon is beginning to reemerge of its own volition, even as the dam faces an uncertain future.

That said, Lake Powell, administered

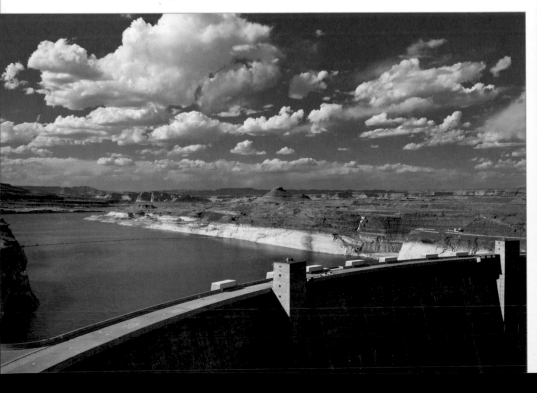

Recommended Restaurants on pages 172–3

by the National Park Service as part of 1.2-million-acre (486,000-hectare) **Glen Canyon National Recreation Area** (open daily 7am–4pm; tel: 928-608-6200, www.nps.gov/glca), is a stunning place to waterski, fish, and explore the shoreline. Miles of blue water and a 1,961-mile (3,156-km) shoreline of carved sandstone cliffs make the lake a photographer's dream. Houseboats, popular with vacationers, may be rented at **Bullfrog Marina** (tel: 435-684-7400), one of four marinas, along with fishing tackle and powerboats. Sea kayaks, ideal for exploring the dozens of side canyons that spill into the lake, are also available.

Carl Hayden Visitor Center (open daily 8am–6pm in summer, 8am–5pm Dec–Feb, 8am–5pm rest of year; tel: 928-608-6404; admission charge), next to the dam in Page, has exhibits, interpretive presentations and information on hiking side canyons and river trips. It offers frequent self-guided and guided tours of the dam and powerplant, which is operated by the US Bureau of Reclamation. Expect tight security measures at Glen Canyon Dam. No bags, purses, knives, weapons, or food are allowed inside the visitor cen-

ter. You may only bring in wallets, cameras, and water bottles.

The Park Service operates a developed campground at Lees Ferry and five primitive campgrounds at Lone Rock Beach, Stanton Creek, Hite, Dirty Devil, and Farley. A concessionaire operates well-developed campgrounds at Wahweap and Bullfrog inside the park. There are numerous undeveloped sites along the shoreline and camping on the southern shore of Lake Powell with permission from the Navajo Nation.

Also on Navajo land is 290-ft-high (90-meter) **Rainbow Bridge National Monument** (open daily; tel: 928-608-6200), the world's tallest known natural bridge. The bridge may be reached by boat trip and a 1.25-mile (2-km) hike into a side canyon directly from Lake Powell, but the site is sacred to the Navajo who control overland access on two rugged trails. For hiking and camping permission, contact Navajo Parks and Recreation, PO Box 9000, Window Rock, AZ 86515 (tel: 928-871-6647). Hiring a Navajo guide is recommended for trips into **Antelope**

Houseboaters stop for a swim at a sandstone beach.

BELOW: Antelope Canyon is one of the most accessible slot canyons in the Page area.

Canyon, one of the easiest slot canyons in the area to reach and explore.

You'll find equally stunning vistas at the **Horseshoe Bend** viewpoint, which is set on the cliffs over a hairpin loop in the Colorado River. It's roughly a half mile (800 meters) to the overlook from the trailhead, which is about 5 miles (8km) south of the Carl Hayden Visitor Center on Highway 89.

Lake Powell was named for explorer John Wesley Powell, whose 1869 and 1871–72 river-running trips were the first to explore the Green and Colorado River Gorges. **John Wesley Powell Memorial Museum** (open Mon–Fri 9am–5pm; tel: 928-645-9496; admission charge) has old drawings and photos about Powell's life and voyages, geological displays, and Indian artifacts. The museum is located in downtown Page, which has grown from a makeshift shantytown for dam workers into far northern Arizona's largest community, with a variety of mainstream lodgings, restaurants, and gas options.

Into the Strip

To enter the Arizona Strip itself, head back south to the junction of Highway 89 and 89A, at **Bitter Springs**, and drive west on Highway 89A via **Marble Canyon**. When it opened in 1929, the narrow, 467-ft-high (142-meter) **Navajo Bridge** over the Colorado River was the highest steel structure in the world. A wider bridge was opened in 1997, and you can walk across the old structure. The small **Navajo Bridge Visitor Center** (open Apr–Oct, 9am–5pm; tel: 928-355-2319) is an impressive piece of desert architecture, with pueblo-style sandstone walls and a fine little bookstore. This is a popular spot to look for one of the 63 reintroduced California condors now living in and around the Grand Canyon. Birds can be seen circling Marble Canyon looking for food in the cliffs below.

Behind the dramatic Vermilion Cliffs is **Lees Ferry** ❹, once a ferry crossing operated by John D. Lee, a prominent Mormon elder. He was sent here by Mormon leader Brigham Young after the 1857 Mountain Meadow Massacre in Utah of a wagon train bound for California, for which he would be executed. At the mouth of the **Paria River**, Lee's old homestead, **Lonely Dell Ranch**, is a

Buffalo Jones

Jesse "Buffalo" Jones was an aging buffalo hunter who had participated in the mass slaughter of the shaggy beasts on the Great Plains in the 1870s. In 1906, realizing that the buffalo were close to extinction, he drove a herd of survivors to the Arizona Strip, where he set up a buffalo preserve and tried unsuccessfully to breed "cattalo," a cross between buffalo and cattle.

Celebrated western writer Zane Grey was introduced to Jones in 1907, while the colorful frontiersman was on a fund-raising tour of the East Coast. Jones, clad in fringed buckskin, held audiences spellbound with stories of lassoing wild mountain lions in the Grand Canyon and other tales of life on the western frontier. Grey, who had honeymooned in northern Arizona the year before, was intrigued. He traveled to Arizona and witnessed Jones's lion-hunting skills firsthand, which became a key inspiration for *Last of the Plainsmen* and other stories.

Although Grey admired Jones, he was dismayed by Jones's ruthless pursuit of his prey. "He shore can make animals do what he wants," wrote Grey in *Don, the Story of a Lion Dog*. "But I never seen the dog or horse that cared two bits for him." Descendants of Jones's original buffalo herd may still be seen in House Rock Valley today.

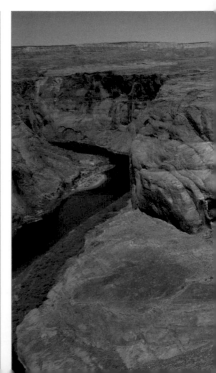

Recommended Restaurants on pages 172–3

pretty spot with a log cabin, a blacksmith shop, ranch house and shady orchards, a good place to stop and watch the river runners putting in on the Colorado River.

Canyons and crossings

The 293,000-acre (119,000-hectare) **Vermilion Cliffs National Monument** ❺ incorporates **Paria Canyon–Vermilion Cliffs Wilderness**, which has no fewer than three spectacular slot canyon hikes. The most popular is the 38-mile (61-km) hike through the narrow, 2,000-ft-deep (600-meter) **Paria River Canyon** to **Paria, Utah**, a trip of four to six days. The southern trailhead is at Lees Ferry. Day users must register before setting out; all overnight trips are by permit only, with daily quotas in force. The best time to do this river hike (which requires wading in places) is mid-March to June. This is not a place you want to be during a flash flood in the summer monsoon season.

Hiking tips, permits, and up-to-date weather information can be obtained from the BLM Arizona Strip Field Office (345 E. Riverside Dr, St George, Utah; tel: 435-688-3200; open Mon–Fri 7.45am–5pm, Sat 10am–3pm).

The first white men to see the mouth of the Paria River were Spanish Padres Dominguez and Escalante whose expedition left Santa Fe, New Mexico, in 1776, hoping to forge an overland route to Monterey, California. They were forced to turn back near St. George, then tried, unsuccessfully, to cross the Colorado River at Lees Ferry. Eventually, they found a good ford, 40 miles (64km) upriver, at a spot known as the Crossing of the Fathers (it has since been flooded by Lake Powell). The **San Bartolome**

The Glen Canyon Bridge spans the chasm just below the dam.

BELOW: Horseshoe Bend is a dramatic U-shaped meander in the Colorado River.

Swirling sandstone and dramatic lighting make Antelope Canyon a favorite of photographers.

BELOW:
the Colorado River at Lee's Ferry.

Historic Site marker on the north side of Highway 89A, marks one of their campsites. You'll find it west of the 1890 **Cliff Dwellers Lodge**, a tiny redstone oasis built beneath a huge boulder, with overnight lodging, a decent restaurant, a gas station, a small store and stunning views.

The Vermilion Cliffs support desert bighorn sheep, pronghorn, mountain lion and, since 1996, California condors, which were reintroduced at **House Rock Valley**, a grassy break in the cliffs. House Rock Valley was home to Mormon pioneer Jim Emett, who operated Lees Ferry in the early 1900s. Emett and his neighbor, frontiersman Jesse "Buffalo" Jones *(see box, page 166),* guided Zane Grey on his first mountain lion hunting trip to Arizona in 1907, when they spent time at both ranchers' homesteads on the Strip and explored **Surprise Valley**, near the Grand Canyon. Grey later wrote that Emett was "the man who influenced [me] most," noting

Emett's love of the West and all living things despite "so few of the joys commonly yearned for by men." The frontier spirit embodied in men like Emett became recurrent themes in such classic Grey novels as *Riders of the Purple Sage* and *Last of the Frontiersmen.*

The Kaibab Plateau

The road winds onto the 8,000-ft (2,400-meter) **Kaibab Plateau** through old-growth ponderosa pine forest. The turnoff for the North Rim of the Grand Canyon is at **Jacob Lake ❻**, named for Mormon missionary Jacob Hamblin, whose exploring party came through in the 1860s. Starting in 1866, Franklin Woolley, followed by his brother Edwin "Dee" Woolley, explored the plateau's potential for lumber, grazing, and Mormon settlements and hatched numerous schemes for development.

Woolley's most extravagant caper came in 1892, when he and Brigham Young's son John, on a mission in England, hired Buffalo Bill, whose famous Wild West Show was currently in London, to escort a party of wealthy English nobles interested in game hunting and

Recommended Restaurants on pages 172–3

ranching in the region. None of the Brits decided to purchase ranches, but they stopped at Jacob Lake, where Buffalo Bill reputedly said grace at one meal, offering thanks for many blessings, specifically "Emma Bentley's custard pie."

Excellent homemade pies and milkshakes are still served at historic **Jacob Lake Inn**, operated by descendants of Edwin Woolley. Tiny **Jacob Lake Visitor Center** has exhibits and information on visiting the rough backcountry of **Kaibab National Forest**. One of the best hikes here is in **Snake Gulch**, where you'll see remarkable Virgin River Anasazi rock art. Camping and horseback rides are also available near the inn.

From Jacob Lake, Highway 89A spirals 3,000ft (900 meters) off the plateau, descending from ponderosa pine into pinyon-juniper dwarf forest. Views of the western Arizona Strip and southwestern Utah's Color Country are breathtaking. It's hard to drive and goggle at the scenery, so pull off at **Le Fevre Overlook**. From here, you can see the geological formation known as the **Grand Staircase**, including the **White Cliffs** of Navajo Sandstone in **Zion National Park**

At the base of the Kaibab Plateau, the small Mormon community of **Fredonia** 7 (a contraction of the English word "Free" and the Spanish word "Doña" to signify a free woman – a reference to the town's polygamous past) is a good place to spend the night, with small motels, Mexican restaurants, gas stations, and convenience stores. If you're heading south, you can also pick up information on Kaibab National Forest at the US Forest Service headquarters.

Mormon outpost

Turn west on Highway 389 and continue to **Pipe Spring National Monument** 8 (open 7am–5pm in summer, 8am–5pm rest of year; tel: 928-643-7105; admission charge), a small 1870 fortified ranch where the Mormon-owned Canaan Cattle Company ran the Church's large tithe cattle herd. The two-story fort was ostensibly built to enclose springs from the nearby Sevier Cliffs and to keep out Navajo raiders; in reality,

Curious rock formations are found throughout Glen Canyon National Recreation Area.

BELOW:
Winsor Castle is the main building at Pipe Springs.

TIP

Contact the Glen Canyon Natural History Association (tel: 877-453-6296; www.glen-canyonnha.org) for help with trip planning in the Arizona Strip and adjoining public lands in Utah.

BELOW: erosion exposes a fin of tilted sedimentary rock deposited during the age of dinosaurs.

there was more to fear from government officials hounding polygamous families (including Dee Woolley and his young wife Flora). The women were kept busy making pies, bread and stews for travelers, explorers, miners and, after the St. George Temple had been completed, Mormon newlyweds who had been "sealed" and were returning home on the Honeymoon Trail. John Wesley Powell used the West Cabin as a headquarters during his 1872 survey, which ascertained that lands originally thought to be in Utah were actually in Arizona, creating the area we know today as the Arizona Strip.

In summer, rangers in period costume offer fascinating living-history demonstrations of pioneer life. Year-round tours leave from the visitor center and pass through the heavy wooden doors of the fort into two buildings joined by a catwalk. Spring water was piped into a ground-floor spring room where milk was kept cool, then processed into butter and cheese. Milk, meat, butter, and cheese were sent by the wagonload to St. George, Utah, every two weeks to feed workers constructing the new St. George

Temple. A second-floor room housed Arizona's first telegraph. A self-guided tour through the orchards has a push-button oral history by Maggie Heaton, a hired hand at Pipe Spring in 1898. The Kaibab Paiute Tribe, whose reservation surrounds the monument, participates in the management of the site and a new on-site museum documenting Kaibab Paiute history at Pipe Spring. The tribe runs a campground, offers guided tours of rock-art sites, hikes, and cultural activities, and holds a powwow every October. Many tribal members work at the tribe's new gas station and convenience store or at tribal headquarters opposite the visitor center, and live in nearby Kaibab and Moccasin.

All in the family

The Arizona Strip tends to attract non-conformists. **Colorado City ❾**, on the Arizona–Utah border, is one such town. Its massive, half-finished houses with more than one door, bonneted wives, and young girls in quaint leggings and floral shifts are just a few outward signs of the polygamous lifestyle still practiced here. Once subject to government raids (the

Recommended Restaurants on pages 172–3

last was in 1957), the residents of Colorado City are tolerated by the authorities and are beginning to interact with tourists needing gas, food, and other services. A small city park has steep trails into the 6,500-acre (2,600-hectare) **Cottonwood Point Wilderness**, which contains 1,000-ft (300-meter) multihued cliffs, pinnacles, and canyons.

Views to the south take in an area of spare beauty that includes the **Shivwits Plateau**, **Mount Trumbull** and **Mount Logan Wildernesses**, **Grand Wash Cliffs Wilderness** and **Paiute Wilderness** in the **Virgin Mountains**. All of these are now part of the newly created 1.1-million-acre (450,000-hectare) **Grand Canyon–Parashant National Monument** ❿ (345 E. Riverside Dr, St George, Utah; tel: 435-688-3200; open Mon–Fri 7.45am–5pm, Sat 10am–3pm). The very remote monument expands the geological story of the Grand Canyon by including volcanic landmarks like 8,028-ft (2,447-meter) **Mount Trumbull** (which provided the wood for the St. George Temple). It is also an ecologically unique area where the Sonoran, Great Basin, and Mohave Deserts

intersect, providing critical habitat for endangered California condors, desert tortoises, Southwest willow flycatchers, desert bighorn sheep, and pronghorn antelope.

Remote outpost

Long, very rough dirt roads are the norm in this undeveloped monument. Avoid them during the summer monsoon season, and don't travel here without several gallons of backup gas and water, food and spare tires. The monument's size and the long distances required to reach its features are intimidating, but adventurous travelers will enjoy the 60-mile (100-km) kidney-bruising drive to 6,393-ft (1,947-meter) **Toroweap Overlook**, where the Grand Canyon drops away 3,000ft (900 meters) right below your feet. **Tuweep Ranger Station**, about 6 miles (10km) before the overlook, is open year-round and has information on hiking, camping and road conditions.

The BLM's excellent Arizona Strip map offers an overview of the region and is essential for navigating the monument's backcountry roads.   ❑

The jackrabbit's powerful legs allow it to escape prey with bursts of speed up to 40 mph (65 kmh).

BELOW: green from a spring algae bloom, the Colorado River flows through Marble Canyon.

RESTAURANTS

Prices for a three-course dinner per person, excluding tax, tip, and beverages:
$ = under $20
$$ = $20–45
$$$ = $45–60
$$$$ = over $60

Bella Napoli
810 N. Navajo Drive, Page
Tel: (928) 645-2706
Open: L, D daily in summer, Mon–Sat rest of year, closed late Dec–mid-Feb **$$**
Upscale Italian dining includes many pasta dishes with assorted sauces.

Bene Pizza
Lake Powell Resort, Page
Open: May–Sept **$**
This casual joint situated on the resort premises has patio dining and is a good place to find a gourmet pizza. Ask for an

outdoor table in fine weather.

Butterfield Steakhouse
704 Rimview Drive, Page
Tel: (928) 645-2467
Open: L, D daily **$–$$**
Set on a bluff overlooking Lake Powell, this family-friendly restaurant serves satisfying portions of straightforward American and Southwestern food. There are no surprises and few disappointments.

Dam Bar and Grille
644 N. Navajo Drive, Page
Tel: (928) 645-2161
Open: L, D daily (no lunch on Sun) **$–$$**
Upscale and hip, this restaurant is a surprise in staid Page. It works the dam theme hard, including a transformer at the entrance that

shoots off neon sparks and a wall of concrete sculpted like the dam, but the food can keep up. Steak and seafood are the main stars, along with pasta, chicken, sandwiches, burgers, and salads.

Fernando's Hideaway
332 N. 300 West Street, Kanab, UT
Tel: (435) 644-3222 **$**
Slightly off the main drag in Kanab, on the Utah side of the Strip, this neighborhood Mexican restaurant serves unexpectedly good food. Dine on the patio or inside, where there is a fresh southwestern ambiance, with tile floors and whitewashed walls adorned with Mexican folk art. The consistently good food, killer margaritas, and inexpensive prices make this a restaurant locals recommend to visitors over and over. Full liquor license.

Fiesta Mexicana Family
125 S. Lake Powell Boulevard, Page
Tel: (928) 645-4082 **$**
Reliably good but pretty mainstream Mexican food in Page. Try the Fiesta Salad.

Jacob Lake Inn
Highway 67 and 89A, Jacob Lake
Tel: (928) 643-7232
Open: B, L, D daily **$**
This inn's chummy cof-

fee shop is a welcome break during a long, lonesome traverse of the Arizona Strip. There's a cozy dining room with regular table service, but the old-fashioned counter is more fun. The menu features Mormon family recipes such as Southwest-baked chicken, *jagerschnitzel,* and baked trout. In the late 1800s, Buffalo Bill was enamored of the pies at this historic place ("I kiss the hand that made the pie," he exclaimed). The famous milkshakes are a meal in themselves. Expect lots of hunters fueling up at breakfast here in the fall. Stop here for a hearty meal before pressing on to the North Rim of the Grand Canyon.

Kaibab Lodge Restaurant
Kaibab Lodge, US 67
Tel: (928) 638-2389
Open: B, D daily **$–$$**
This cabin resort in the woods, near the entrance to Grand Canyon's North Rim, offers reasonably priced breakfasts and dinners. Breakfast might include your choice of omelets and egg dishes, fresh fruit smoothies, French toast, huevos rancheros, and biscuits and gravy. At dinner, there are hot sandwiches and American steaks and seafood options, such as salmon, Kaibab chicken (basted in beer),

LEFT: tacos, burritos, and other Southwestern dishes are usually a good choice for an inexpensive and filling meal. **RIGHT:** a breakfast of bagel and lox at a lakeside restaurant.

mesquite-grilled chicken on salad greens, and St. Louis ribs. Light soup and salad options and kids' menu are available. Dessert is a major draw. Try their homemade cheesecakes, pies, and cobblers, the Mountain Lion triple-chocolate cake, and ice cream. Closed in winter.

Lees Ferry Lodge
US 89A, Marble Canyon
Tel: (928) 355-2231
Open: B, L, D daily $-$$
Simple, hearty American fare served in a rustic, wood-paneled dining room makes this Western lodge popular with rafters who are preparing to take on "the Grand" at nearby Lees Ferry. An extensive selection of beers is available, and the wine list is an unexpected pleasure.

Mandarin Gourmet Restaurant
683 S. Lake Powell Blvd, Page
Tel: (928) 645-5516
Open: L, D daily $
Don't take "gourmet" too literally – the food's nothing to write home about. But the all-you-can-eat buffet is reasonable value if you're hungry.

Parry Lodge
89 E. Center Street, Kanab, UT
Tel: (435) 644-2601
Open: B only daily $
The lodging of choice for Hollywood's stars filming westerns in the area, Parry Lodge is well worth a look if you're passing through Kanab. The walls have many autographed photos of stars. The dining room is open for breakfast between April and October. A very reasonably priced buffet offers many items, from croissants and fruit to

eggs. Hotel guests eat half price.

Rainbow Room
Wahweap Lodge, Page
Tel: (928) 645-2433
Open: B, L, D daily $-$$$
The dining focal point of the large Lake Powell Resort, this two-story window-wrapped dining room dishes up above-average fare in its lovely waterside location. There's a buffet for breakfast, and soups, sandwiches, and salads at lunchtime. At dinner, prime rib, seafood, chicken, salads, and American Indian dishes are well done. Four-course special Chef's Table dinners, served in a section of the adjoining Driftwood Lounge, are offered June through September, highlighting the chef's use of sustainable foods, such as wild salmon, grass-fed beef, organic greens, and wild mushrooms.

Rewind Diner
18 E. Center Street, Kanab, UT
Tel: (435) 644-3200
Open: B, L, D daily $
Don't be fooled by this 1950s diner. It looks like a soda fountain, but the menu is surprisingly sophisticated, with unusual offerings such as faux gyros, falafel, and other vegetarian items alongside classic diner food such as burgers and milkshakes. Locals recommend it highly.

Rocking V Cafe
97 W. Center Street, Kanab, UT
Tel: (435) 644-8001
Open: D daily, Mon–Tue in Mar, Nov, and Dec, closed Jan and Feb $-$$
Kanab's best restaurant is an unexpected Slow

Food haven, where you'll enjoy real food, freshly prepared, cooked to order, and beautifully presented in an artsy atmosphere. The dining room is eye-poppingly colorful and has art on the walls, cool music on the stereo, and a fun, laid-back atmosphere. Choose from a variety of salads made from organic greens, grass-fed beef and bison, locally raised trout, and wild Alaskan salmon, flown in four times weekly in season. There are many vegetarian and vegan items. For dessert, try the house specialty: crème brulée. Dining with pets and smoking allowed on outside patio; full liquor license.

Stromboli's Restaurant and Pizzeria
711 N. Navajo Drive, Page
Tel: (928) 645-2605 $-$$
This sister restaurant to the hugely popular pizza spot in Flagstaff serves

up large thin-crust pizzas and lots of traditional Italian dishes and calzones, and salads. A popular boaters' gathering place. Closed Nov–Feb.

Vermilion Cliffs Bar and Grill
Lees Ferry Lodge, Hwy 89A at Vermilion Cliffs
Tel: (928) 355-2231
Open: B, L, D $$-$$$
Steaks, burgers, and baby back ribs are served in a down-home rustic atmosphere at this remote Arizona Strip eatery frequented by river runners and other adventurers. There are 80 different kinds of beer.

Zapata's
614 N. Navajo Drive, Page
Tel: (928) 645-9006
Open: L, D daily $
Burritos, enchiladas, and other Mexican staples are specialties at this casual eatery. Wash your meal down with a margarita or two.

Desert Blossoms

Engaged in a competition to attract pollinators, wildflowers bring a splash of vibrant color to even the harshest environments

Arizona has two main wildflower seasons – the result of steady winter rains and violent summer "monsoons" that awaken first delicate annuals and later hardy perennials. As a result, flowers are blooming somewhere in Arizona from late January all the way to October, starting with low-elevation deserts and ending with the high country of the White Mountains and San Francisco Peaks near Flagstaff.

But it is the brilliant March displays of brightly colored annuals below an elevation of 6,000ft (1,830 meters) that catch the headlines and send photographers scrambling for their cameras. With the right balance of rain and sunshine between October and January – an event that occurs only every five years or so – expect a wildflower extravaganza the following February to May. Displays of annuals are unpredictable. To find out what is blooming and where, check in with wildflower reports on the Web and at local parks, in newspapers like the *Arizona Daily Star*, and the 602-542-4988 Arizona Wildflower Hotline set up each spring.

In February, Organ Pipe Cactus National Monument and other low-elevation spots in the west deserts are the first to bloom, in delicate waves of desert chicory, bladderpod, desert marigolds, and verbena. They are followed by showy displays of sulfur yellow brittlebush, a shrub that, like creosote, appears to die in summer heat, only to releaf a few days after consistent rains.

In late March and early April, trails along hillsides in Catalina State Park and Picacho Peak, north of Tucson, are carpeted with Mexican and California poppies in shades of gold, yellow, and peach, interwoven with bunches of white-purple Coulter's lupine, blue toadflax, pink owl clover, white desert phlox, and yellow evening primrose.

By May, pricklypear, hedgehog, claret cup, and cholla cactus begin wearing topknots of neon red, purple haze, and acid yellow to attract birds for pollination and to spread their seeds through juicy fruits. Green-barked paloverde trees are decked out in a golden rain of blossoms; long-lived ironwood trees erupt into a riot of lilac blooms. Living fences of ocotillo branches, rooted in the ground, are tipped with red blooms in villages all over Sonora, Mexico.

Just as low-elevation wildflowers start to wilt under triple-digit temperatures in the deserts, the race to reproduce is heating up in the reawakening high country. After wet winters, look for outrageous displays of penstemons atop the rocky limestone and volcanic soils around Flagstaff, including one species that grows only

LEFT: the century plant blooms only once in its lifetime. **ABOVE:** pricklypear cactus blossom. **TOP RIGHT:** fissures in sandstone channel moisture and support a lush growth of vegetation **RIGHT:** ocotillo flowers attract hummingbirds, whose long, thin bills are the right shape to feed on the tubular blossoms.

at Sunset Crater Volcano National Monument.

Monsoons saturate the soil, and by August, wildflowers are drinking up moisture greedily. Flame-colored Indian paintbrush, a parasitic beauty, roots atop other plants. Five-fingered purple lupines "wolf" down nitrogen. Red skyrocket gilia and a variety of salvias, or sages, attract hummingbirds. Along shady streams and washes, bog iris, Rocky Mountain columbines, nodding bluebells, pink shooting stars, and jolly yellow and red monkeyflowers keep their feet wet, while in open sandy areas, like those on the Navajo Reservation, vetches and princes plume occupy sandy ridges rich in selenium.

Yellow sunflowers and purple asters are the summer stars of the high country. They line roadsides and form joyful throngs in meadows, allowing tits and finches to stock their larders with seeds before the first snows of October once more blanket the mountains.

Surrounded by such beauty, it's easy to forget that wildflowers are actually engaged in a competitive struggle to reproduce. Their shape and color are designed to attract the animals they rely on for pollination and seed dispersal. Night-blooming white flowers are a magnet for visiting Mexican long-nosed bats and hawkmoths; pastel purples and pinks attract butterflies; yellow flowers lure carpenter

bees; red trumpet flowers advertise for hummingbirds. It's all part of an evolutionary scheme that links one living thing to another. As is always the case in nature, the survival of any one species depends on the health of the whole ecosystem. ❑

Recommended Restaurants on page 189

NAVAJO AND HOPI RESERVATIONS

At home in remote and sacred valleys and mesas, the Navajo and Hopi tread a path between centuries-old rituals and modern lifestyles

Travel anywhere in Indian Country and you will encounter beauty. It haunts the eerie rock formations, deeply etched canyons, sacred peaks, and serpentine rivers that give form and meaning to the Navajo and Hopi homelands. Life in such huge, empty, dry country seems ephemeral – a question of chance. What is really required is adaptation and a deep understanding of the land, the seasons and the rituals that help humans remember their place in the cosmos.

Both the Hopi and Navajo understand this. The Hopi say that, after being expelled from three lower worlds because they fell out of harmony with the Creator Spirit, the people entered this Fourth World and encountered Masaw, the caretaker of the Earth. Masaw offered them a short ear of blue corn, from which they realized that life would be difficult, and, in order to cultivate the corn, they would have to learn humility, cooperation, respect, and earth stewardship. The Hopi clans migrated for countless generations, traveling in all four directions in search of the Center of the Earth. They finally settled on this arid plateau between the Rio Grande and the Colorado River, a place so barren they would be forced to depend on prayer for rain and food. Never again would they forget to be thankful to the Creator.

Indian country gateway

Begin your tour of the 29,817-sq-mile (77,225-sq-km) **Navajo Nation** ⓫ and much smaller adjoining **Hopi Reserva-** **tion** north of Flagstaff, on Highway 89. In about 30 miles (50km), the elevation drops from 7,000 to 6,000ft (2,100–1,800 meters), with a corresponding change in scenery from ponderosa pine forest to sagebrush rangeland dotted with pinyon and juniper. The road passes through the large volcanic field that gave birth to **Sunset Crater Volcano** and the 12,000-ft (3,600-meter) **San Francisco Peaks**, revered by both the Navajo and Hopi. To the east are the pastel-hued badlands of the **Painted Desert** and the distant **Hopi Mesas**.

Main attractions

CAMERON TRADING POST
NAVAJO NATIONAL MONUMENT
MONUMENT VALLEY
HUBBELL TRADING POST
 NATIONAL HISTORIC SITE
CANYON DE CHELLY
 NATIONAL MONUMENT
HOPI CULTURAL CENTER

LEFT: Navajo dancer, Navajo Nation Fair.
BELOW: sandstone pillars, known as the Elephant Feet, off US 160.

A mechanized coal line runs from mines on Black Mesa.

Trading post and dino tracks

Ahead is the **Little Colorado River**, which rises on Mount Baldy in the White Mountains and flows northwest to its confluence with the Colorado River in the Grand Canyon. A good view of the river can be had from the historic **Cameron Trading Post ⑫** (PO Box 339, Cameron, AZ; tel: 800-338-7385) left of the highway bridge, established by Mabel and Hubert Richardson in 1916. Still in the Richardson family, there's now a 65-room motel, an RV

park, a gas station, a post office, and an art gallery. The original trading post retains its authentic atmosphere, with creaky wood floors and dry and canned goods traded for rugs, jewelry, and the other Indian arts and crafts sold here. Skip the cheap souvenirs in the front rooms and head for the stone gallery, where big-ticket, museum-quality artifacts are sold. The dining room serves a tasty Navajo frybread taco (voted Arizona's state dish in a 1995 *Arizona Republic* poll). It's a good idea to get here early to avoid the tour bus lunch crowd and to obtain a room, if you wish to spend the night.

Drive east on Highway 160 through a spectacular landscape of rocks laid down during the Time of the Dinosaurs, 200 million years ago. Handmade signs lead north of the highway to the famous **Dinosaur Tracks** in the red Kayenta Formation, where, for a few dollars, a young Navajo guide will show you the three-toed tracks of dilophosaurus, a "running dinosaur." This dinosaur weighed 1,000 pounds (450kg), stood 8 to 10ft (2.4–3 meters) tall, and ran on its powerful hind legs. It used short forearms and clawed fingers for grasping and tearing apart its prey. Claw marks can be seen in the tracks.

Mormon way station

To the north is **Hamblin Ridge**, named for Mormon missionary Jacob Hamblin, who was sent by Church President Brigham Young to make contact with the Hopi and Navajo and assess the area's potential for colonization in 1858. Hamblin farmed here for several years, after befriending Hopi Chief Tuuvi, who subsequently converted to Mormonism. **Tuba City ⑬**, founded by Mormons in 1877, honors this chief. The town was used as a way station for Mormons traveling south from Utah to develop communities on the Colorado River and still displays the Lombardy poplars that typically mark such settlements.

Even before the Mormons arrived, Charles Algert had opened the **Tuba Trading Post** in 1870. This unusual octagonal trading post, built in 1906 to resemble a traditional Navajo hogan, is a good place to buy a Storm Pattern rug, the signature design of the Western Navajo Reservation, with symbols that vividly recall the landmarks and colors of this dramatic area.

The Mormons never obtained clear title to the land on which Tuba City was built, and in 1903 it was withdrawn by the US government and added to the Navajo reservation. In 1905, the Bureau of Indian Affairs built the large two-story sandstone complex of Tuba City Boarding School. Schools like this one aimed to assimilate Indian children by taking them from their families, cutting their hair, forbidding them to speak their language, and enforcing military-style discipline.

Today, despite 50 years of educational reform and a renaissance in Indian culture, only half of the 300,000 tribal members speak Navajo, although reservation schools have been required to teach the language since 1984. Sixty percent of the Navajo Nation is now between the ages of 19 and 38 and exposed every day to the more materialistic Anglo culture. Many, though by no means all, see little value in the old land-based traditions.

South of the highway, between Red Lake Trading Post and Kayenta is 8,210-ft (2,500 meter) **Black Mesa**, the largest

> *Happily may I walk.*
> *May it be beautiful*
> *before me.*
> *May it be beautiful*
> *behind me.*
> *May it be beautiful*
> *below me.*
> *May it be beautiful*
> *above me.*
> *May it be beautiful*
> *all around me.*
> *In beauty it is finished.*
>
> —Navajo Night Chant

BELOW: the hands of a Navajo weaver and sheepherder reflect years of hard work.

A Navajo rug weaver at a reservation trading post.

single landform in northern Arizona. Peabody Western Coal Company operates two of the largest open pit strip mines in the country here and pays royalties to both the Navajo and Hopi tribes. Coal from the Black Mesa Mine goes to the Mohave Generating Station on the Nevada–Arizona border through the Black Mesa Pipeline, which uses a billion gallons of pristine aquifer water a year to slurry the coal more than 273 miles (440km) around the Grand Canyon. This has prompted a great deal of concern by residents about spring depletion, and alternatives are now being explored.

The ancient ones

North of Black Mesa, a 10-mile (16-km) drive on Highway 564 leads through swirling pink slickrock country to **Navajo National Monument ⓮** (open daily, May–Sept 8am–7pm, closes 5pm rest of year; tel: 928-672-2700; free), which protects some of the largest and best preserved prehistoric cliff dwellings in the nation. Snugged into a 450-ft-high (140-meter) alcove above **Tsegi Canyon**, the 135-room pueblo of

BELOW RIGHT:
Navajo National Monument.

Betatakin ("Ledge House") was built in AD 1250 and housed about 135 people for 50 years. It harmonizes so perfectly with its surroundings, visitors standing at the overlook at the end of the short Sandal Trail usually don't see it at first. Free 5-mile (8-km) hikes to Betatakin are led by rangers each morning in summer (on weekends in winter) and are limited to 25 hikers. To avoid disappointment, stay in the monument's delightful 47-site campground and high-tail it to the visitor center first thing in the morning to pick up a ticket.

A second, larger pueblo, **Keet Seel**, lies 8 miles (13km) in the backcountry and requires a permit and challenging overnight hike to view. A limit of 20 visitors per day is strictly enforced; make reservations before your trip and be sure you're up to it. Elevation loss and regain is 1,000 ft (300 meters) and the hike is very hot, dry, and exposed the whole way. Temperatures reach 100°F (38°C) in summer. Wear a hat, sunscreen, sunglasses, and sturdy boots, and carry high-energy food and at least a gallon (4 liters) of water. A ranger guides hikers through the ruins.

Navajo–Hopi Land Dispute

The Navajo and Hopi tribes have had their differences over the years, especially regarding the disposition of tribal lands and resources. The Hopi, whose mesa-top homes are completely surrounded by the larger Navajo Nation, have long claimed that the expansion of the Navajo reservation in several stages during the 19th and 20th centuries was made at the expense of Hopi land.

Tensions seriously escalated in 1974, when the US Congress passed the Navajo–Hopi Relocation Act. The law, which divided nearly 2 million acres (800,000 hectares) between the tribes, was supposed to compel 11,000 Navajo and about 100 Hopi to leave homes they had known for generations. Many of the Navajo moved to new government housing; others still resist relocation.

In recent years, public attention has been focused on a resolution of the so-called Bennet Freeze, a decree handed down by the US Department of Interior in 1966 that prevents Navajo living on contested land from building new homes or making substantial repairs to old ones. The ruling affects as many as 7,000 Navajo living on a 1½-million-acre (607,00-hectare) disputed area, only 10 percent of whom have running water and 3 percent have electricity, according to a Navajo survey.

Recommended Restaurants on page 189

Monument Valley

Kayenta ⑮ is a large prosperous town with good food and lodging. It has benefited from its proximity to the Black Mesa Mine and **Monument Valley** ⑯ (open daily 6am–8pm summer, 7am–7pm rest of the year; tel: 435-727-5870, www.navajonationparks.org;   admission charge), the crown jewel of the Navajo tribal park system. Begin your tour at the visitor center, 20 miles (32km) north of Kayenta on Highway 163, which has exhibits about the Navajo, or Diné, way of life, a gift shop, restrooms, and water.

This is the place to watch the world's most awe-inspiring sunrise illuminate the Owl, Mittens, Totem Pole, and other fiery sandstone landmarks familiar from such John Ford Westerns as *Stagecoach*, *She Wore a Yellow Ribbon* and *Cheyenne*. Local Navajo pose for photos in traditional dress, but always ask first and offer payment. Families rely on tourism income.

A tour booklet has information on 11 scenic overlooks along the 17-mile (27-km) unpaved scenic drive, including John Ford Point, the most famous view in the valley. You'll need to hire a

Navajo guide to go into the backcountry. Horseback, van, and open Jeep tours usually include a visit to the hogan of famed Navajo weaver Susie Yazzie and her family, and the chance to view some of the more than 200 Ancestral Pueblo ruins and petroglyphs in the valley. Bring your own food and water and cash to pay tour guides and tips for Navajos who pose for pictures.

Make arrangements at the visitor center or at the 62-room Gouldings Lodge (tel: 435-727-3231). The old 1930s trad-

The Sandal Trail at Navajo National Monument leads to a dramatic view of the Betatakin cliff dwelling.

BELOW: West Mitten Butte, Monument Valley.

TIP

The Navajo Nation Fair,
held in Window Rock in
September, features
traditional dances, a
rodeo, a parade, carni-
val rides, and plenty of
arts and crafts exhibits.

ing post started by Harry Goulding and his wife Mike is now a museum filled with memorabilia from Harry's friendships with John Ford, John Wayne, and other Hollywood celebrities. The lodge offers the only accommodations in Monument Valley. The restaurant serves Navajo and American fare, but it's the view, not the food, that leaves the biggest impression.

The Navajo-owned **View Hotel and Restaurant** (435-727-3470; www.monumentvalleyview.com), adjoining Monument Valley tribal visitor center, opened in 2008. The first lodging to be built inside the tribal park, the hotel will feature incredible view rooms, Indian arts and crafts, and native foods.

Monument Valley isn't a valley at all but the Monument Upwarp, a geological uplift, or monocline, riddled with faults. It stretches from Comb Ridge and the San Juan River on the Arizona–Utah border to the north and Black Mesa to the south. Restless earth movements have created all kinds of strangely tilted cliffs (long mined for valuable minerals) and major landmarks. Looming on the northern horizon is 10,416-ft (3,175-meter)

BELOW: an elder
demonstrates
traditional Navajo
weaving outside a
hogan in
Monument Valley.

Navajo Mountain, sacred to the Navajo and Hopi, and the twin buttes called the **Bear's Ears**. At the valley's southern perimeter is craggy **Agathla Peak**, a dark basaltic volcanic neck bared by erosion that once marked the southern boundary of Ute territory. The only camping in the park is in Mitten View Campground, which has 100 sites. Gouldings Lodge runs a developed campground next to Oljato Mesa on the opposite side of the valley.

Four Corners

Highway 160 continues east from Kayenta on the south side of **Comb Ridge** (try to do this drive at dusk when the oblique rays of the sun turn the sandstone blood red). In 64 miles (103km), you'll reach historic **Teec Nos Pos Trading Post** ⓗ (tel: 928-656-3224), a good place to get gas, have a quick bite to eat, and view superb examples of large, intricately patterned Teec Nos Pos rugs. Many say the design is reminiscent of Persian rugs – with a price tag to match. A brief detour north takes you to **Four Corners Monument Navajo Tribal Park** (open daily

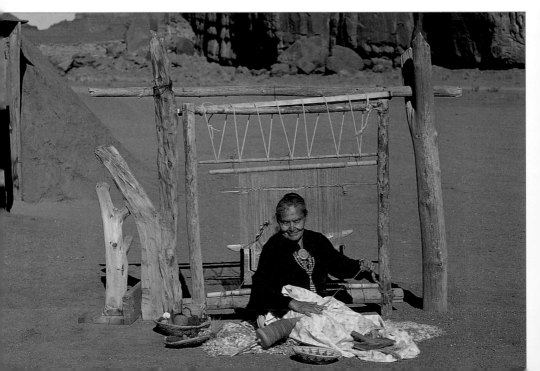

Recommended Restaurants on page 189

7am–8pm in summer, 8am–5pm rest of year; admission charge), the only place in the United States where you can stand simultaneously in four states – Utah, Arizona, New Mexico, and Colorado. There is a modest vistors center but no water.

Highway 191 heads south on the west side of the **Carrizo**, **Lukachukai**, and **Chuska Mountains**. So many of the reservation's overscaled, fantastically shaped rocks seem alive. Indeed, Navajo legends state that many of these formations were once fearsome, human devouring monsters, slain by the mythic Hero Twins – Monster Slayer and Born for Water – thereby freeing the Navajo to pursue *hozho*, the Beauty Path in the Fourth World. The Chuskas, Lukachukais, and Carrizos are said to be the head, torso, and feet of the male god Yootzill.

Navajo capital

Northwest of **Window Rock ⑱** is **Fort Defiance**, the site of an 1851 fort built by the US Government to calm tensions between Navajo and newly arrived Anglo residents. By 1863, things had

deteriorated to the degree that US Army Captain Kit Carson, under the orders of General James Carleton to "solve the problem," instigated a five-year scorched-earth campaign to drive out the Navajo. Homes and possessions were burned, fruit trees cut down, and livestock slaughtered. As many as 8,000 Navajo were sent on a 300-mile (480-km) forced march to Bosque Redondo (Fort Sumner) on the Pecos River in New Mexico, while several thousand others hid in remote Canyon de Chelly, the Grand Canyon, and Monument Valley.

Although many Diné starved or died of disease in confinement, survivors of the Long Walk were eventually allowed to return to a fraction of their original homeland in 1868. They quickly rebounded in numbers and livestock holdings and began to thrive. The federal government built a Bureau of Indian

A butte in the northern Navajo Reservation rises above bands of sedimentary rock.

BELOW: Navajo sheep herders in Monument Valley.

Navajo rugs, some costing thousands of dollars, are displayed at Hubbell Trading Post.

BELOW: Spider Rock rises about 800ft (245 meters) from the floor of Canyon de Chelly.

Affairs agency at Fort Defiance in 1868, followed by the first reservation boarding school.

A few miles to the south is Window Rock, the capital of the Navajo Nation. In 1923, after vast oil reserves were found underneath the Navajo Reservation, the federal government created the Navajo Tribal Council to facilitate negotiations of lease agreements with oil companies. Later discoveries of oil, gas, and uranium further concentrated the power of the tribal council, and eventually widespread corruption necessitated a complete reorganization in 1991. It now has 88 delegates from 110 chapter houses, or local councils, across the reservation, which meet four times a year (and on many special sessions) in the beautiful Navajo Nation Council Chambers. Delegates speak in Navajo while the council is in session, and visitors are welcome to observe the proceedings.

Navajos fought bravely in World War II, Korea, Vietnam, and other recent conflicts. Their finest hour may have been when Navajo Code Talkers foiled Japanese codebreakers by transmitting important communications among allies in Navajo. Commemorating the tribe's distinguished military service is the **Navajo Nation Veterans Memorial Park** in **Window Rock Tribal Park**, a pleasant spot for a picnic and a closer look at Window Rock itself, a geological opening in the Cow Springs Sandstone.

Stop at the Navajo Nation Parks and Recreation Department (open daily; tel: 928-871-6647, www.navajonationparks.org) off Highway 264 to pick up information on Navajo tribal parks and visitor permits for hiking, camping, and fishing. Next door is the delightful **Navajo Nation Zoo and Botanical Garden** (open Mon–Sat 10am–5pm; tel: 928-871-6574; www.navajofishandwildlife.org/nnzoo; free), which exhibits mountain lions, coyotes, Mexican wolves, churro sheep, and other native animals, interpreting them from the Navajo point of view. Well worth a look, too, is the adjoining **Navajo Nation Museum** (open Tues–Fri 8am–8pm, Mon

Recommended Restaurants on page 189

8am–5pm, Sat 9am–5pm; tel: 928-871-7941; free) an oversize, hogan-style building with permanent and revolving exhibits.

Historic trading post

Highway 264 leads west to **Ganado**, named for Navajo leader Ganado Mucho, a friend of trader Lorenzo Hubbell, who, in 1876, opened a trading post here. The still operational **Hubbell Trading Post National Historic Site ⑲** (open daily 8am–6pm in summer, 8am–5pm rest of year; tel: 928-755-3475; admission charge) is a fine place to learn about the important role of trading posts in the late 1800s.

Hubbell became a powerful political figure in Arizona, hosting Theodore Roosevelt and other dignitaries. He is best remembered, though, as a loyal friend and mentor to the Navajo, whom he encouraged to make heavier, better designed rugs and to eschew new artificial dyes from back east in favor of natural dyes. The trading post is known for the Ganado Red blanket, a bright-red design with a diamond or cross in the center. Pottery, baskets, and renderings of rug designs by famous artists hang in the Hubbell Home next door. Daily tours are limited to 15 people. Navajo rug weavers and silversmiths demonstrate in the visitor center. There is an excellent gift shop. Arts and crafts auctions, held in May and October at the trading post, should not be missed if you are in the area. Rugs, katsinas, and other items can be purchased at reasonable prices.

Sacred canyons

About 30 miles (50km) north of Ganado, off Highway 191, is **Chinle**, headquarters of 130-sq-mile (340-sq-km) **Canyon de Chelly National Monument ⑳** (open daily 8am–5pm; tel: 928-674-5500; free), where the Rio de Chelly has carved 1,000-ft-deep (300-meter) **Canyon de Chelly** and **Canyon del Muerto** into the Defiance Plateau. Two 35-mile-long (56-km) scenic drives along the North and South Rims offer heart-stirring views

Navajo girl, about 1910, in traditional skirt and velveteen blouse.

BELOW: a Navajo girl plays at the family sheep camp.

White House Ruin, at the bottom of Canyon de Chelly, can be reached via a steep trail from the rim.

BELOW: Hopi women grinding corn, *c.*1906.

into inner canyons and historic overlooks, such as the one above **Massacre Cave**, where 90 men and 25 women and children were massacred by Spanish Lieutenant Antonio de Narbona in 1805. The 2½-mile (4-km) **White House Trail** down Chinle Wash is the only route accessible without a Navajo guide. It leads to the multilevel pueblo cliff dwelling called **White House**. These canyons were home to Ancestral Pueblo farmers for centuries before the arrival of the Navajo. The trail is a wonderful introduction to this most beautiful of Southwest canyons. Swallows swoop down to the wash from the clifftops. Raven caws rend the silence. And in summer, you'll encounter Navajo residents tending corn near hogans on the canyon floor.

If you have a four-wheel-drive vehicle, consider hiring a Navajo guide who can accompany you deeper into the canyons to see cliff dwellings like **Antelope Ruin**, **First Ruin** and **Junction Ruin**, remarkable rock art on canyon walls from the Ancestral Pueblo, Spanish, and Navajo eras, and stunning formations like **Spider Rock**, a sandstone spire that rises 800ft (240 meters) from the canyon floor. Guides are available at the 1902 Thunderbird Lodge, a beautiful historic building with lodgings, reasonably priced rugs and other artworks, and a popular cafeteria. Half- and whole-day tours in large, jostling open-air vehicles (jokingly referred to as "shake-and-bakes") also depart from here.

Hopi homeland

Highway 264 continues west to the **Hopi Reservation ㉑**, which is made up of a series of 12 compact, autonomous stone villages atop windswept **First**, **Second**, and **Third Mesas,** and **Moenkopi**, several miles to the west, near Tuba City. The Hopitu, the "peaceful people," are the descendants of the Ancestral Puebloan culture, which they call Hisatsinom. A proud, private people, the Hopi live a very different kind of life

Recommended Restaurants on page 189

than their Navajo neighbors, whose much larger reservation completely surrounds theirs. Their east-facing villages have changed little since late Pueblo times. Hopi men dry-farm untilled plots of corn, melons, squash and other crops at the base of the cliffs and in terraces that catch the scant 10 inches (25cm) of rain that falls here each year. Women make pottery and baskets. Children play in dusty streets. Visiting the villages is about as close to stopping time as you may ever experience – which is, of course, its greatest attraction to travelers and, ironically, one of the biggest threats to the Hopi way of life.

It is believed that the Bear Clan was the first to arrive on the mesas. In time, other clans arrived from their migrations, and each was asked to contribute a different skill or ceremony to ensure the well-being of people on earth. From this, a complex seasonal ceremonial calendar was devised, with sun priests in each village determining the timing of ceremonies based on the positions of the sun, moon, and planets.

The most important ceremony of the year is the Niman, or Home Dance, in July, when the *kachinas*, serving as supernatural intermediaries between the Creator Spirit and the people of Earth, return to their winter home in the San Francisco Peaks after blessing the crops and bringing rain. The hypnotic singing and dancing of the *kachinas* symbolize the harmony of good thought and deed necessary for a balanced life and to bring the blessing of rain.

Sacred dances

Though the crowd may seem nonchalant, Hopi dances are deeply spiritual and should be accorded the same respect as any other religious event. Dancers are required to undergo extensive preparations for their roles. Spectators have a role, too: they contribute their prayers to the successful completion of the dance's mission. Disrespect by outsiders means that some dances have been closed to non-Hopis. If you are lucky enough to attend a dance, both men and women should

Navajo riders gallop through Canyon de Chelly.

BELOW: the Hopi are known for crafting exquisite handmade pottery.

SHOP

Shopping for Hopi crafts? Try McGee's Indian Art Gallery (Hwy 264; tel: 928-738-2295; www.hopiart.com) in Keams Canyon or Monongya Gallery (Hwy 264; tel: 928-734-2344) near Oraibi.

BELOW: Hopi cornfields sprawl around the village of Moenkopi.

dress modestly; refrain from talking, asking questions, or following the *kachinas*; and never photograph, sketch, videotape or record the dances in any other way. Information on current dances is available at the **Hopi Cultural Center** (open Mon–Fri 8am–5pm, Sat–Sun 9am–3pm; closed weekends in winter; tel: 928-734-2401; admission charge to museum, *for information, see below*) on Second Mesa, the best place to orient yourself to the reservation.

Artistic specialties

Inside the cultural center is the **Hopi Museum**, which has modest but effective displays on Hopi art and culture. Each mesa specializes in a particular craft. First Mesa is known for its pottery, which women coil by hand, smooth with a polishing stone, and fire outdoors, usually with dung. The pots are then hand-painted with intricate designs using fine yucca-fiber brushes and natural paints. Second and Third Mesas are renowned for basketry, one variety made of woven wicker, the other of coiled yucca. Kachina dolls, perhaps the best known of the Hopi crafts, are made by

craftsmen on all the mesas and carved from cottonwood roots. Hopi silversmiths specialize in the distinctive overlay style, although a number of talented jewelers are now branching off into inlay and channel work with turquoise, jet, coral, shell, and other semiprecious stones, and a few jewelers work with gold settings. Many craftspeople work out of their homes and sell directly to the public.

The cultural center offers tours that include workshops, craft stores, villages, and other places of interest. The villages of **Shungopavi** (home of artist Fred Kabotie, who painted the mural inside the Grand Canyon's Desert View Tower), **Shipaulovi** and **Mishongnovi** all feature dances.

The 33-room motel next to the Hopi Cultural Center (tel: 928-734-2401) fills up quickly in summer. A restaurant serves all-American fare as well as Hopi specialties, such as paper-thin blue-corn *piki* bread and traditional stews, though these will seem bland to most palates. The blue-corn pancakes are the best bet. You can also stay at **Keams Canyon**, an administrative town east of the Hopi Mesas. Before 1860, it was known to the Hopi as Peach Orchard Springs. It was renamed in honor of English trader Thomas Keam, who established a trading post there in 1875 and defended the Hopi from repressive government practices.

Ancient villages

Behind Keams Canyon is the abandoned 12th-century village of **Awatovi** on Antelope Mesa. Awatovi was the only Hopi village to be converted by Spanish missionaries, who built a church here in 1629. In 1680, the Hopi joined their New Mexican Pueblo neighbors and killed or exiled the Spanish. When the mission was reestablished in 1700, the Hopi grew so angry over the continued Christian influence, they destroyed Awatovi, massacred all the men of the village, and removed the women and children to other villages. You'll need a permit and a Hopi guide to visit.

See below for Recommended Restaurants

Of all the Hopi villages, be sure not to miss **Walpi**, atop First Mesa. A traditional village, with no running water or electricity, residents live much as they have since prehistoric times. The village may be entered only with a Hopi guide on free 40-minute walking tours that leave from Ponsi Hall in **Sichomovi** or from the tourist booth at the Walpi parking lot. Interestingly, **Hano**, the first village you reach, is not Hopi; it's a Tewa village built by people from the Rio Grande region of New Mexico, who sought refuge here during an unsuccessful revolt against the Spanish in 1696. The village at the base of the mesa is **Polacca** – also a latecomer – made up of residents of the three villages on First Mesa.

Old Oraibi, on Third Mesa, constructed in AD 1125, is often dubbed the oldest continuously inhabited community in the United States. The ruins of a Spanish mission built in 1629 are visible north of the village. In 1900, Old Oraibi had one of the reservation's largest populations (800), but disputes between chiefs caused many to leave. In the first major dispute, in 1906, two leaders

staged a "push-of-war" contest, where two groups pushed against each other until one side crossed a line marked in the dust.

The loser, You-ke-oma, left with his followers and established **Hotevilla**, 4 miles (6.5km) away. Eventually, some tried to return to Old Oraibi, but were ousted again in 1909. They settled at a new site called **Bacavi**, opposite Hotevilla. Other residents moved to join New Oraibi, at the foot of the mesa, otherwise known as **Kykotsmovi**.

Today, Kykotsmovi is the location of the modern Hopi tribal government, which has itself been the source of a continuing conflict among the traditionally self-determined villages ever since it was created by the federal government in the 1930s. "One is not born Hopi," explains one tribal member, when asked what it means to be Hopi. "One becomes Hopi." ❑

Blue corn is a staple of traditional Hopi cooking.

RESTAURANTS

Blue Coffee Pot
US 160/US 163, Kayenta
Tel: (928) 697-3396
Open: B, L, D daily **$**
The food is nothing special at this diner, although you'll find Navajo tacos and mutton stew. The building has more character than most establishments in town.

Garcia's Restaurant
Holiday Inn – Canyon de Chelly, Indian Route 7, Chinle
Tel: (928) 674-5000
Open: B, L, D **$**
There's predictable southwestern and American food and a few Navajo specialties at this well-maintained restaurant near the entrance to Canyon de Chelly National Monument.

Hopi Cultural Center Restaurant
Second Mesa
Tel: (928) 734-2401
Open: B, L, D **$**
The most interesting items here are Hopi *piki* bread, paper thin and cooked on a griddle, lamb stew, and blue-corn pancakes.

Quality Inn Navajo Nation Capital
48 Highway 264,
Window Rock
Tel: (928) 871-4108
Open: B, L, D **$**
A favorite meeting place for locals and people visiting on business. Navajo tacos and a few local specialties and standard American diner food.

Stagecoach Dining Room
Goulding's Lodge,
Monument Valley, UT
Tel: (435) 727-3231
Open: B, L, D **$**
The lodge's dining room has gorgeous views of Monument Valley and a collection of movie memorabilia. Solid American fare and Navajo tacos.

Thunderbird Lodge
Chinle
Tel: (928) 674-5841
Open: B, L, D **$**
At the mouth of Canyon de Chelly, this old stone trading post now serves as a cafeteria. The food is cheap and tends toward greasy fast-food-type items. The walls are hung with

beautiful Navajo rugs.

Wagonwheel Restaurant
Holiday Inn – Kayenta, Kayenta
Tel: (928) 697-3221
Open: B, L, D **$**
Standard motel restaurant with parts of the decor modeled on an Ancestral Pueblo ruin. The menu offers good American food with a few local specialties like Navajo tacos. Bus tours often stop here, so don't be surprised to find a crowd.

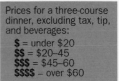

Prices for a three-course dinner, excluding tax, tip, and beverages:
$ = under $20
$$ = $20–45
$$$ = $45–60
$$$$ – over $60

American Indian Art: A Buyer's Guide

Jewelry, pottery, and other art-works made by Arizona's native people are things of beauty, and, in some cases, good investments

The quality of Indian craftsmanship varies from artist to artist and from piece to piece. Obviously, the finer the workmanship, design, and materials, the more a piece is worth. And, while it's true that beauty is in the eye of the beholder – and that it is sometimes the imperfections of a work that make it most endearing – there are a few essential points you may wish to keep in mind when judging arts and crafts.

Jewelry

Most Navajo and Hopi jewelry is made with silver and semiprecious stones. The Hopi are known for the "overlay" style in which a design is cut out of a sheet of silver and welded onto a blackened layer below. The Navajo are best known for their work with silver and turquoise and such distinctive forms as "squash blossom" necklaces and concha belts. Be

sure to ask what kind of silver you are buying. If it is sterling, there should be a stamp on the back. Nickel silver, a lower grade alloy, is also sometimes used.

You should also ask the seller to identify the types of stones that are used. Be especially careful of turquoise; various forms of mock turquoise can fool an inexperienced eye. Jewelry should look clean and finished. Check the piece for file marks, sloppy soldering, and other irregularities. Check the stones for cracks, pits or discoloration, and make sure the settings are adequate to hold the stones.

Pottery

Traditional Indian pottery is made by hand without a potter's wheel, painted with natural dyes, and fired over an open flame. The first thing you should ask about pottery is whether it is handmade or manufactured. Because the price of handmade pottery is so high, manufactured (or "ceramic") pots have become quite common. They are often hand-painted in the traditional way and – so long as you know what you're buying – can be quite beautiful. Most Indian vendors make a point of distinguishing between handmade and manufactured pottery. Gift shops may not always be so scrupulous. Manufactured pots tend to be lighter in color and weight and uniform in size and shape.

If you're shopping for handmade pottery, look for a graceful, symmetrical form, fairly thin walls, and precise, neatly applied decoration. As always, watch out for irregularities: cracks, discoloration, bumps, or pits in the clay, lopsidedness, slanted or uneven decorations. Keep in mind that firing clouds, which usually appear as dark smudges, are sometimes quite desirable, even though many potters consider them a problem.

Basketry

Fine, handmade baskets are quite rare these days, but there are still a few Indian people who are pro-

LEFT: Navajo sandpainting **TOP:** bracelet by Hopi artist Charles Loloma. **ABOVE RIGHT:** the Heard Museum in Phoenix has one of the country's best collections of Native American art. **RIGHT:** pictorial-style Navajo rug.

ducing exquisite traditional work. First of all, make sure you are buying an American Indian basket. Imports have found their way into the Southwest and occasionally crop up next to genuine American Indian work without any explanation.

There are basically two types of basketry: coiled and woven. In both cases, look for tight, even, and sturdy construction, a pleasing shape, and clear and even designs. To test the tightness of the weave, hold the basket up to the light. You should also check how the basket was started; the first coil should not stick out or be loose.

Weaving

Again, be absolutely sure you are buying Indian work. The popularity of Navajo rugs has created an entire industry of imitations. A few Navajo weavers still do their own washing, carding, dyeing, and spinning, but most buy prepared wool. Some use a mixture of commercial products and traditional techniques. In any case, the finished product should be tightly woven, with a "balanced tension" of design and color.

The rug or blanket should have a smooth texture and the corners should not curl. It should also have fairly even edges (all four corners should meet when folded). Ask if the rug is 100 percent wool. Some weavers will use cotton or synthetic fibers in the warp. You should also know if the dyes are veg

etal, commercial, or both. Commercial dyes tend to give brighter, more saturated colors. Vegetal dyes are subtler and made by hand.

Kachina carving

Although most often associated with the Hopi, kachina dolls are also made by other Pueblo people as well as by the Navajo. The most valuable kachina dolls are carved from a single piece of cottonwood root. Less expensive pieces may have separate arms or legs and possibly leather, feather, or other adornments attached to the figure. Most reputable dealers will tell you if the figure is Hopi-made. Many people feel that Navajo kachinas are less authentic, but considering the high price of Hopi work, Navajo work may be a reasonable option. As with any purchase, let your eyes, conscience, and wallet be your guide. ❑

Recommended Restaurants on pages 204–5

FLAGSTAFF AND ENVIRONS

Ancient Indian ruins, a historic observatory, and one of the state's most beautiful mountain ranges are just a few of the attractions in and around this former frontier outpost

O n the road up **Mars Hill**, there's a pull-off where you can look out over **Flagstaff ㉒**. The railroad tracks weave a steel ribbon through the middle of town. Famed **Route 66** parallels the tracks, and sturdy brick and stone buildings line the road. From this vantage point, Flagstaff looks for all the world like a toy railroad town, just like those miniature cardboard villages that came with your model train set.

And so it should, for the railroad made Flagstaff and has been its beating heart for more than a century. Freight trains rumble through like clockwork all day long, their whistles echoing through town, and Amtrak's passenger train, the *Southwest Chief,* stops twice a day, eastbound in the morning, westbound at night.

In the 1850s, government surveyors plotted a railroad route along the 35th Parallel. By the early 1880s, loggers rolled their big wheels into the ponderosa pine forests of northern Arizona, felled the tall trees, then sawed and stockpiled nearly a half million ties for the rails, as they blazed west. A spring at the base of Mars Hill furnished precious water for advance crews, and in 1882 the Santa Fe Railway arrived there at the first depot, a boxcar. The steep uphill grade soon mandated a move back to flatter terrain a half mile east, from Old Town to what soon became known as New Town. Across the street, a thirsty man could find not only a cup of water but stronger brew as well in this wild and woolly newborn burg.

Crossroad town

A few Anglo-Americans had preceded the railroad. The Boston Party, a group of colonists who undertook an arduous westward journey in response to claims of good, cheap farmland, celebrated the nation's centennial in 1876 by hoisting the flag up a pine tree on the Fourth of July. Though their patriotic act gave Flagstaff its name, few of the immigrants stayed. Disillusioned, they discovered that the glowing promises of agricultural possibilities were so much promotional puffery.

Main attractions

LOWELL OBSERVATORY
MUSEUM OF NORTHERN ARIZONA
SAN FRANCISCO PEAKS
ARIZONA SNOWBOWL
SUNSET CRATER VOLCANO NATIONAL MONUMENT
WUPATKI NATIONAL MONUMENT
WALNUT CANYON NATIONAL MONUMENT
METEOR CRATER

LEFT: Lowell Observatory.
BELOW: Flagstaff mural.

The Babbitt Building, downtown Flagstaff.

BELOW: the Coconino County Courthouse in Flagstaff was built in 1894.

Stockmen found the grasslands fine, though. A handful of them, such as Thomas McMillan and John Clark, settled in. Another pioneer, merchant P.J. Brannen, had faith in the railroad. He erected his store across from the New Town depot. Soon thereafter came five brothers from Cincinnati, Ohio, by the name of Babbitt. Through their efforts, and others, Flagstaff was on its way to becoming an established town.

Now a small and growing city of 60,000, Flagstaff hosts a lively, eclectic mix of small business owners, students, writers and artists, travelers, cowboys and Indians, river runners and Rastafarians, old-timers and newcomers. It's been characterized as a crossroads and a destination. Millions from all over the world pass through on their way to the Grand Canyon each summer. Big-city folks wander up on weekends, sampling the small-town feeling. Students stay for a few years to obtain an education at **Northern Arizona University Ⓐ**. The rest – hearts captured by the town's friendliness and the surrounding beauty of forests, mountains, and canyons – find themselves permanent Flagstaffians.

Art and history

Downtown Flagstaff is a good place to start a visit. At its center is **Heritage Square Ⓑ**. This outdoor plaza features a small amphitheater where concerts are presented nearly every weekend through summer and fall. Diagonal to the square is the landmark **Weatherford Hotel**. Judge John Weatherford opened this elegant establishment on New Year's Day in 1900. Like many downtown structures, the hotel is built of locally quarried sandstone called Arizona Red. The present owners have faithfully restored the hotel's original face, including a restored balcony that wraps around the second story; it's a perfect place to sip a cold drink and view the parade of humanity on the sidewalk below.

For a more in-depth look at downtown's many other turn-of-the-century stone buildings, two publications will help: *Flagstaff Historic Walk* and *Stone Landmarks*, both available at the **Visitor Center Ⓒ** (open Mon–Sat 7am–6pm, Sun 7am–5pm; tel: 800-842-7293 or 928-774-9541) in the train station a block from the Weatherford Hotel or at local bookstores.

Flagstaff is no Santa Fe, but in recent years a slew of galleries has opened downtown. On the first Friday of each month, several stay open between 6pm and 8pm for the **First Friday Art Walk**. Visitors have a chance to meet the artists, many of them local, who produce fine art and crafts in glass, wood, cloth, and other media.

Lowell's legacy

A trip up to **Lowell Observatory** Ⓓ (open daily 9am–5pm in summer, noon–5pm rest of year, evenings June–Aug Mon–Sat from 8pm, rest of year Wed, Fri and Sat from 7.30pm) just west of downtown affords that toy-town view of Flagstaff from Mars Hill. Wealthy Bostonian Percival Lowell chose the hill as the site for his observatory, where he ordered a telescope erected to view the planet Mars. Lowell arrived in 1894 in time to make those observations and lived part-time there for the rest of his life. The planet Pluto was discovered at the observatory in 1930, and astronomers continue to make significant contributions in their various specialties. The **Steele Visitor Center** and the **Slipher Building** contain

fascinating interactive exhibits on the work of astronomers and the history of the observatory. With the clear, dark sky bursting with stars, it is a distinct treat to attend a nighttime viewing through Percival's original Clark telescope.

Flagstaff is also a center of other scientific pursuits. A branch office of the US Geological Survey is located in town and is the place where the late Eugene Shoemaker founded the discipline of astrogeology. A 10-day **Festival of**

Weatherford Hotel.

BELOW LEFT:
Percival Lowell, founder of Lowell Observatory, believed that "canals" on Mars were built by intelligent life.

Lowell and the Red Planet

Percival Lowell may have seen little green men on Mars, but he never said so. What he did say was that life probably existed on the red planet. His belief in Martian life was based on observations of lines radiating from various points on the planet's surface, which he thought were a network of canals.

The canal idea had been posed some years earlier. Italian astronomer Giovanni Schiaparelli claimed to have seen such lines, which he called *canali*, or channels. Lowell expanded on this, writing that "A mind of no mean order would seem to have presided over the system [of canals] we see." Because Mars was presumably an arid place, an irrigation system would have been necessary to gather water from melting polar ice caps and dew or frost. Lowell also suggested that Mars had an atmosphere, thin and cloudless but adequate to support life.

Percival Lowell wasn't shy about publicizing his findings. The press picked up the stories, sometimes poking fun at them. Support from astronomers was mixed at first but later soured into scathing criticism. If Lowell were alive today, he might find some vindication in recent photographs of Mars that show signs of water in old riverbeds and possible evidence of organic material in rocks.

One of several telescope domes at Lowell Observatory.

BELOW: Museum of Northern Arizona.

way 180 (Fort Valley Road) north until you reach a white stone building, originally the county hospital, that locals once called "the poor farm." Along with housing the small staff, the hospital had room for about a dozen patients. In 1908, the local newspaper described the new building as "a substantial one of stone, fitted up with hot and cold water in each of the airy rooms, situated among the pines on a small hill overlooking the rich little valley to the south."

Outside the museum stands old **Number 12**, a shiny black steam locomotive put into service in the Northwest woods in 1929 and used in the Flagstaff area in the 1950s. Inside, individual rooms contain artifacts of early medicine, logging and transportation in northern Arizona. A display of old dolls, games, children's books, tea sets, quilts and more – called Playthings of the Past – is held each holiday season. The museum's two big events each year are the **Wool Festival** on the first weekend in June, and the **Independence Day Festival** marking the Fourth of July, with live demonstrations at each.

Science is held each fall, with a constant round of public events. Recognizing the area's botanical diversity, the **Arboretum at Flagstaff** ⓔ (open Apr–Oct daily 9am–5pm) features native plant gardens, nature walks, and other activities on the grounds on Woody Mountain Road, 4 miles (6.4km) from town.

The Arizona Historical Society's **Pioneer Museum** ⓕ (open Mon–Sat 9am–5pm) displays interesting artifacts from Flagstaff's past. To visit, follow High-

Immediately behind the Pioneer Museum is the **Coconino Center for the**

Recommended Restaurants on pages 204–5

Arts **G** (open Tue–Sat 11am–5pm; tel: 928-779-2300), exhibiting the work of local artists and providing a venue for live music and other programs. Next door is the **Art Barn**, location for classes and opportunities for resident artists.

Family treasures

A mile farther out Highway 180 resides the **Museum of Northern Arizona ❶** (open daily 9am–5pm; tel: 928-774-5213). Dr. Harold Colton, his wife Mary-Russell Ferrell Colton, and other community members founded this institution in 1928. This gem of a museum, standing amid ponderosa pines beside the Rio de Flag, shares the wealth of geology, biology, and culture of the Colorado Plateau, the geologic province in which Flagstaff is located. Rotating exhibits showcase some of the museum's extensive collections of basketry, pottery, paintings, and kachina carvings. Mrs. Colton, an accomplished artist in her own right, encouraged Native American artists. Her legacy continues at the museum to this day, with a series of shows and marketplaces in summer and early fall featuring some of the best arts and crafts produced in the region.

The old administration building at the University of Northern Arizona.

Back in town near Northern Arizona University, another piece of Flagstaff's history has been preserved in a state park. **Riordan Mansion ❶** (open May–Oct daily 8.30am–5pm, Nov–Apr daily 10.30am–5pm, hourly tours start at 11am, reservations recommended; tel: 928-779-4395) was the home of businessmen and brothers Michael and Timothy Riordan. The 40-room, 13,000-sq-ft (1,200-sq-meter) house, designed by Charles Whittlesey, architect of the Grand Canyon's

BELOW: Old Number 12 sits idle outside the Arizona Historical Society's Pioneer Museum.

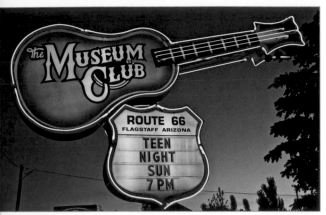

Hankering for live country music? Check out the Museum Club (928-526-9434) on old Route 66, a classic log roadhouse known as the Zoo for the trophy heads that adorn the walls.

BELOW: a shop in downtown Flagstaff.

the Riordans weren't immune to grief. In daughter Anna's bedroom is her hoop dress, which she wore as a young woman. On the night of her engagement party in 1927, she was stricken with polio and her life was cut short.

Sacred peaks

The **San Francisco Peaks** ㉓ sweep up behind Flagstaff, a small range as far as mountains go but an extremely captivating one. The Peaks are sacred mountains to nearly everyone who has felt their attraction – considered so by the Hopi, Navajo, and many other Native Americans and non-Indians as well.

The Peaks rank as the highest mountains in Arizona – 12,643ft (3,854 meters) at the windswept tundra atop **Humphreys Peak**. A trio of separate summits complete their impressive profile: **Agassiz**, **Doyle**, and **Fremont**.

Franciscan friars who saw the mountains from the Hopi Mesas in 1629 named them in honor of their founder, St. Francis. Early travelers headed for the springs that issue from them, and a fledgling Flagstaff relied on those water sources for the town's sustenance. Now

El Tovar Hotel, was built in 1904. Stone, plank, and shake construction was used; some of the wood was scrap ponderosa pine from the nearby Arizona Lumber and Timber Company mill, which the Riordans owned. The two brothers married the Metz sisters, and each family had separate living areas in the mansion, connected by a common space called the "cabin room." The Steinway piano, Tiffany stained-glass windows, velvet upholstered seats, and six-car garage show what life was like for the "upper crust" in Flagstaff in the early years. But people flock to the mountains for recreation and inspiration. They hike the trails in summer, gawk at golden aspens in the fall, sled and ski in winter, and watch for the first candytuft to bloom in spring. Botanists search the alpine tundra for rare plants, hunters scan the ridges for elk, and woodcutters load up logs for their stoves.

Geologists classify the Peaks as a "stratovolcano." Numerous explosions piled layer upon layer of lava, cinders, and ash to an elevation of nearly 16,000ft (4,800 meters) about 400,000 years ago; on the north side, the mountain collapsed into a huge bowl called the Inner Basin.

1951) 17 miles (27km) from town, off Highway 180. The **Humphreys Trail** ascends steeply through dense evergreen forest to the rocky tundra of the highest summit. The **Kachina Trail** is a gentler path that follows the lower slope. Northward stretches the grassy expanse of **Hart Prairie**, home to a Nature Conservancy preserve with rental cabins. Forest Road 151, accessible from Highway 180, is a scenic unpaved drive that gives unending views of the Peaks.

Wildflowers carpet a meadow in the San Francisco Peaks.

Mountain wilderness

The uppermost reaches of the San Francisco Peaks are protected as the **Kachina Peaks Wilderness Area**. While no motorized or wheeled vehicles are allowed, hikers walking the wilderness may be rewarded with the sights and sounds of gray fox, Mexican owls, and bugling elk. Two popular trails, the Humphreys and Kachina, can be reached by driving to the **Arizona Snowbowl** (open daily 9am–4pm; tel: 928-779-

Ski country

With the first dusting of snow on the Peaks in early winter, Flagstaffians rejoice at the prospect of downhill skiing. The sport arrived here in 1915. That winter, with 6ft (2 meters) of snow on the ground, Ole and Pete Solberg strapped on homemade wooden skis and swooshed down Mars Hill. Townsfolk gathered to watch, and the local paper exclaimed, "They call it 'skiing'!" In the 1930s a local ski club was formed

BELOW: a fanciful mural adorns a building in downtown Flagstaff.

TIP

Amateur archaeologists can help excavate Elden Pueblo, a Sinagua ruin in Flagstaff. Educational programs include site tours, lab work, and excavation techniques. Call 928-527-3452 for information.

BELOW: a ponderosa pine at Sunset Crater National Monument.

to foster the sport, and the first lodge was built at what is now the Arizona Snowbowl. It's music to skiers' ears when the snow report reads "67 inches of packed powder at Midway, all runs open." The Snowbowl's four lifts serve beginner to advanced skiers. (In summer, one lift operates as a scenic skyride, taking riders to an elevation of 11,500ft/3,500 meters.)

Without snow-making equipment, the Snowbowl depends on mother nature. In dry years the season can be short; but in average years, with 260 inches (660cm) of snow possible, the slopes are open from mid-December through March.

For a lower-tech experience, the **Flagstaff Nordic Center** (open daily 9am–4pm; tel: 928-220-0550) is the place to go. On Highway 180, 8 miles (13km) past Snowbowl Road, the center offers a variety of groomed cross-country and snowshoe trails through the forest and meadows. Cross-country skiers will also find a nearly endless supply of back-roads, most of them closed in winter, in **Coconino** and **Kaibab National Forests** that provide a wealth of possibilities for winter trekking.

During the entire month of February, a kind of cold-weather mania grips Flagstaff during **Winterfest**. All manner of snow-related activities are scheduled, including skiing, dogsledding, snowshoeing, ice skating, and skijoring (a cross between cross-country skiing and dogsledding), not to mention the Snowball Slide and Icicle Walk and Gawk. An array of music, food, and dance events complements the more vigorous endeavors.

Volcanic origins

Like the San Francisco Peaks, the landscape around Flagstaff owes its character to a long period of volcanism. Hundreds of cinder cones are scattered throughout the grassy plains surrounding town. And though some of the cones date back several million years, the most recent is less than 1,000 years old. That one is **Sunset Crater Volcano National Monument** ❷❹ (open daily 8am–5pm, from 9am in the winter; tel: 928-526-0502). This black 1,000-ft-high (300-meter) cone was formed when hot ash and lava exploded from a vent around AD 1064–65. It continued erupting for 150 years or so, pouring out fiery lava and other

Southside

South of the tracks, along South San Francisco and South Beaver Streets in Flagstaff, is what's known as Southside – a funky neighborhood of ethnic restaurants, coffee shops, dance studios, sport shops, youth hostels, historic churches and modest homes.

Southside has always been the working-class side of town. Its residents claim a mixture of Mexican, Basque and African-American heritage. They moved here between the 1870s and 1930s to escape revolution in Mexico and to find jobs, mostly as sheepherders and mill workers.

They built modest stone cottages and frame bungalows and gathered at Zaragosa Hall on South San Francisco for dances and boxing matches. Billiards and handball played at a traditional Basque *pelota* court (which still stands on South San Francisco Street) provided other pastimes.

Today, the grandchildren of those early pioneers still live in the same houses and run family businesses. The streets are filled with the scent of fresh tortillas and roasted coffee. Diners can enjoy every kind of cuisine from Chicago-style hot dogs to hemp burgers. On most days, some of the 15,000 students at Northern Arizona University pedal and skateboard through this down-home neighborhood that relishes its individuality and history.

volcanic debris that has frozen into a black, jagged moonscape.

To see Sunset Crater up close, travel 12 miles (19km) north of Flagstaff on Highway 89 and turn at the national monument sign. After a stop at the visitor center, continue on the loop road at the base of Sunset Crater. Though the crater itself is now off-limits to hikers due to erosion, you can walk around it on the mile-long **Lava Flow Trail**. Along the way you'll see the many byproducts of the eruption – football-shaped volcanic bombs, upturned slabs of lava descriptively called squeeze-ups, and the entrance to an ice-filled lava tube.

After the eruption

When the volcano first erupted, the people living in the vicinity must have thought the world was coming to an end. But the fine cinder mulch the volcano deposited, along with a favorable period of precipitation after the eruption, lured them back. Harold Colton, founder of the Museum of Northern Arizona, named these people the Sinagua, which means "without water," for their arid homeland. He and other archaeologists believed the

"new" volcanic farmland lured thousands of settlers into northern Arizona.

Ancestral Puebloans were probably among them. Their stunning architectural stonework is on display at **Wupatki National Monument** ㉕ (open daily sunrise to sunset; tel: 928-679-2365), 22 miles (35km) beyond Sunset Crater on the loop road. Several beautiful pueblos have been excavated and are open to visitors. The largest is namesake **Wupatki Pueblo**. From the visitor center, a half-mile self-guiding path leads through this

A lava flow at Sunset Crater is gradually being reclaimed by vegetation.

BELOW: Kachina Peaks Wilderness, Coconino National Forest.

WUPATKI
PUEBLO
OPEN. TILL SUNSET

Wupatki National Monument encompasses the ruins of several Sinagua pueblos: Wupatki, Lomaki, Wukoki, Citadel, and Nalakihu.

BELOW:
snowshoeing at the base of the San Francisco Peaks.

four-story dwelling built of sandstone slabs set in mud mortar. Some of the masonry resembles that of Chaco Canyon in New Mexico. Wupatki Pueblo's more than 100 rooms ramble without any apparent plan, and recent work suggests it was built in several phases from the mid- to late 1130s through the early 1200s. Cached in several rooms were remains of such tropical birds as scarlet macaws and thick-billed parrots. These and other finds have led archaeologists to suggest that Wupatki was a site of high political or spiritual significance. Other intriguing sites in the park – **Wukoki**, the **Citadel**, and **Lomaki** – certainly support this thought.

Wupatki is located in the high-desert valley of the **Little Colorado River**. For a real backroad trip, take a ride to the **Grand Falls** ㉖ of the Little Colorado. The river's muddy brown waters tumble over a 185-ft (56-meter) ledge, a virtual Niagara in the desert. Keep in mind, however, that Grand Falls flows only seasonally, when the river is running with springtime snowmelt or summer storm water, and requires quite an undertaking to reach.

Take Highway 89 just north of Flagstaff, turn right onto the Townsend–Winona Road, go 8 miles (13km) to Leupp Road, turn left and go another 15 miles (24km) to the boundary of the Navajo Nation. Turn left (north) onto Navajo Route 70, a good gravel road when dry, but impassable when wet. In another 9 miles (15km), you'll spot picnic ramadas and find yourself at Grand Falls.

Relics of the past

Returning to Flagstaff, head east on Interstate 40 for 10 miles (16km) to the area's third national monument – **Walnut Canyon** ㉗ (open daily 8am–5pm in summer, 9am–5pm rest of year; tel: 928-526-3367). The Sinagua lived here too, though in a totally different setting than Wupatki. They tucked their living quarters beneath limestone ledges in a deep canyon. Descend the **Island Trail** to the small rooms and smoke-blackened walls of their abodes. A host of plants along the streamcourse, on the drier hillsides, and on the forested rim sustained them with wild foods and material for clothing and other utilitarian items. By building small rock dams across gullies, the

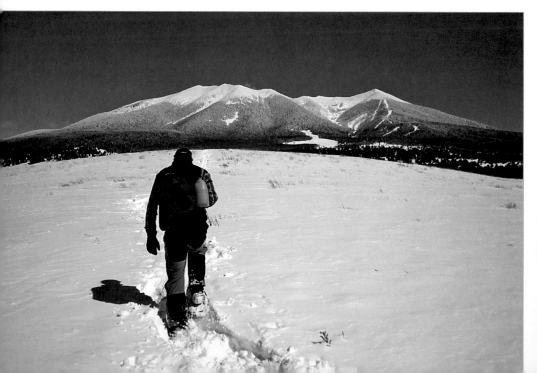

Recommended Restaurants on pages 204–5

Sinagua gathered pockets of soil where they grew corn, beans and squash. Some of these are visible along the **Rim Walk**, a fine place to gaze into Walnut Canyon or up into the sky for soaring hawks and eagles.

Continuing on Interstate 40 another 25 miles (40km), there's a big hole in the ground about 6 miles (10km) south of the highway that interests many people. And well it should. About 50,000 years ago, a chunk of iron traveling at about 40,000 mph (65,000 kph) hit the Earth. With the force of about 20 million tons of TNT, it blew out a depression known as **Meteor Crater ㉘** (open daily 7am–7pm in summer, 8am–5pm rest of year; tel: 928-289-2362; admission charge). This natural landmark – 4,000ft (1,200 meters) across and 560ft (170 meters) deep – is open for guided tours, or the crater can be viewed through windows at the fine museum on the rim.

Another 25 miles (40km) beyond Meteor Crater is the railroad town of **Winslow ㉙** Beside the tracks stands **La Posada**, a grand hotel that dates to the heyday of American passenger trains in the 1930s. Private owners have superbly restored the huge mission-style structure, and it is well worth a visit.

A few miles north of town is **Homolovi Ruins State Park ㉚** (8am–5pm daily; tel: 928-289-4106). Situated atop high mounds overlooking the **Painted Desert** are 14th-century pueblos. Certain Hopi clans claim Homolovi as the home of their ancestors, the *hisatsinom*, who made this their last stop before arriving at present homes on the mesas about 60 miles (100km) to the north. Homolovi sites I and II are accessible to visitors. Hiking trails, a campground, picnic areas, and a chance to watch archaeologists at work are features of the park. Check at the visitor center for the latest information. ❑

Meteor Crater was blasted from the Earth's surface about 50,000 years ago.

BELOW: Wupatki Pueblo National Monument.

RESTAURANTS

Prices for a three-course
dinner per person,
excluding tax, tip, and
beverages:
$ = under $20
$$ = $20–45
$$$ = $45–60
$$$$ = over $60

Beaver Street Brewery & Whistle Stop Cafe
11 S. Beaver Street, #1,
Flagstaff
Tel: (928) 779-0079
Open: L, D daily **$**
This popular micro-
brewery, south of the
tracks near the univer-
sity, pairs delicious wood-
fired pizza, hefty salads,
fresh steaks and
seafood, fondue, and an
assortment of bar food
with an interesting selection of suds, from a
robust stout to a light
berry ale. Expect a spir-
ited college crowd.

Black Bean Burrito Bar and Salsa Company
12 E. Route 66, Flagstaff
Tel: (928) 779-9905
Open: L, D daily **$**
A tasty variety of rib-stick-
ing burritos are the spe-
cialty here, served in foil
and plastic and eaten at
the counter. Just the thing
for a cheap filling feast.

Brandy's Bakery & Restaurant
1500 E. Cedar Avenue,
#40, Flagstaff
Tel: (928) 779-2187
Open: B, L, D **$–$$**
This sister restaurant to
downtown's La Bellavia
is hidden in a shopping
center on the east side
of town but is worth
searching out. It's larger
and airier than La
Bellavia but has similar

menu items. They stage
art openings monthly.

Brix Restaurant and Wine Bar
413 N. San Francisco Street,
Flagstaff
Tel: (928) 213-1021
Open: L, D Mon–Sat **$$**
Set in an old carriage
house, Brix's New
American menu focuses
on light Mediterranean
cuisine made with local
and organic foods. An
artisanal cheese plate
paired with poached apri-
cots features creamy
goat cheese from Black
Mesa Ranch in the White
Mountains. Entrees
include pan-seared
seasonal fish served with
polenta and corn soufflé,
an authentic bistro steak-
frites using hormone-free
beef, and pork, lamb, and
chicken dishes from simi-
larly cosseted livestock.
Vegetarians may swoon
over the golden beet ravi-
oli paired with baby
spinach, roasted apples,
spiced walnuts, blue
cheese, and lemon broth.
Soups, salads, sand-
wiches, and burgers
round out the lunch
menu.

Cafe Espress
16 N. San Francisco Street,
Flagstaff
Tel: (928) 774-0541
Open: B, L, D daily **$**
A favorite with the moun-
tain-biking crowd, this
arty, laid-back cafe offers
fresh, healthy food rang-
ing from huevos
rancheros and other fill-
ing Mexican specialties
such as tofu and mushroom
stroganoff and artichoke

scampi. The baked goods
and desserts are yummy.

Charly's Pub and Grille
23 N. Leroux Street, Flagstaff
Tel: (928) 779-1919
Open: B, L, D daily **$$**
Housed on the ground
floor of the historic
Weatherford Hotel,
Charly's has one of the
best locations in town.
Food here is reliably
good southwestern fare,
and the wine list offers
many selections. There
are sidewalk tables to
watch the people go by.

Cottage Place Inn
126 W. Cottage Avenue,
Flagstaff
Tel: (928) 774-8431
Open: D daily **$$**
This unassuming 1909
bungalow, next door to a
New Age bookstore, har-
bors an elegant little din-
ing room where customers
feast on rich Continental
dishes such as
chateaubriand, gor-
gonzola-crusted filet,
Dijon-crusted salmon, veal
chops, and seafood ravi-
oli, presented with silver-
platter fanfare – snooty to
some, a delight to others.

Delhi Palace
2700 S. Woodlands Village
Boulevard, Flagstaff
Tel: (928) 556-0019
Open: L, D daily **$–$$**
This excellent north
Indian restaurant is in
the Woodlands Plaza
shopping center on the
south end of town and
offers authentic Asian
food. You can't go wrong
with the lunch buffet, a
great option if you're on
a budget. White-table-
cloth service from family

members make this a
good dinner option, too.

Downtown Diner
7 E. Aspen Avenue, Flagstaff
Tel: (928) 774-3492
Open: B, L, D daily **$**
A classic greasy spoon
with typical diner fare
and historic photos of
Flagstaff on the walls.

Jackson's Grill at the Springs
Hwy 89A, Flagstaff
Tel: (928) 213-9332
Open: D daily **$$–$$$**
En route to Sedona, at
the edge of a meadow in
the national forest, Jack-
son's is a popular spe-
cial-occasion restaurant.
Continental cuisine is
done well and includes a
large array of steaks,
seafood, wood-fired piz-
zas, and salads. The
wine list is long, and the
views are spectacular.

Josephine's
503 N. Humphreys, Flagstaff
Tel: (928) 779-3400
Open: L, D daily **$$**
Following on from the
long-time success of
Chez Marc in the cozy
1911 Craftsman bunga-
low at this location,
Josephine's serves
appealing New American
bistro food. The menu is
globally inspired and
includes lamb meat loaf,
seared ahi tuna, as well
as steak and seafood
classics. Vegetarian
items are available. The
wine list is extensive.

La Bellavia
18 S. Beaver Street,
Flagstaff
Tel: (928) 774-8301
Open: B, L daily **$**

Bellavia is a great little breakfast spot with good pancakes and egg dishes. The breakfast trout, Swedish oat pancakes, and build-your-own omelettes are Flagstaff classics. There's often a line; get here early.

Late for the Train Coffeehouse
107 N. San Francisco Street, Flagstaff, AZ 86001
Tel: (928) 779-5975
Open: B, L, D daily $
Located downtown, on the ground floor of the historic Babbitt Building, this superb little coffeehouse roasts its own delicious joe and serves cleverly monikered coffee drinks, pastries, and sandwiches.

Macy's European Coffeehouse and Bakery
14 S. Beaver Street, Flagstaff
Tel: (928) 774-2243
Open: B, L, D daily $
When Californian Tim Macy opened his eponymous café south of the tracks in 1980, his was the first coffeehouse in Arizona to roast its own beans. Today, the java is still rich and dark and the fresh pastries healthy yet sinful at this classic college-town hangout. Sandwiches, pasta, and an all-vegetarian menu round out the offerings.

Monsoon on the Rim
6 E. Aspen Avenue, Flagstaff
Tel: (928) 226-8844
Open: L, D daily $
Located in a large, attractive building on Heritage Square, this combo Asian restaurant and sushi bar is in a cavernous space. You can sit in the main dining room, at a sidewalk

table, or in the Martini Bar, a hip spot among Flagstaff's sophisticates.

Mormon Lake Lodge Steak House and Saloon
Mormon Lake Road, Mormon Lake Village
Tel: (928) 354-2227
Open: L, D daily $$–$$$$
In business since 1924, this steak house in the White Mountains, 28 miles (45km) southeast of Flagstaff, is a real ranch country experience. Locally raised mesquite-grilled ribs, chicken, and trout are the centerpieces of the menu. The dining room has Arizona brands seared into the wood paneling. Just the thing after a day on the trail.

Morning Glory Cafe
115 S. San Francisco Street, Flagstaff
Tel: (928) 774-3705
Open: L Tue–Sat, Br Sat $
A staple of the university district for years, Morning Glory is your typical college-town, crunchy-granola café. The tasty food is mostly organic and vegetarian and runs the gamut from blue corn tamales and pancakes to soups and salads.

Mountain Oasis
11 E. Aspen Avenue, Flagstaff
Tel: (928) 214-9270
Open: B, L, D daily $$
Fresh, globally inspired cuisine; a romantic, airy, plant-filled dining room in an historic building; and very reasonable prices are among the selling points of this friendly restaurant. The menu spans the world and includes appetizers like sushi, spring rolls, dolmas, and hummus. The list of entrees is as long as your arm. Try the

salmon or chicken curries, the Thai plate, prime rib, or pasta. There are wonderful salads, including one with organic chicken. A romantic night out that won't break the bank.

Pasto
19 E. Aspen Street, Flagstaff
Tel: (928) 779-1937
Open: L, D daily $
From the original owners of Cafe Espress, another restaurant for the hip and hip-at-heart. This one specializes in creative Italian fare, with a few local twists, such as the Southwestern black-bean ravioli. The atmosphere is casual, the decor imaginative.

Racha Thai
Monte Vista Hotel, 104 N. San Francisco Street, Flagstaff
Tel: (928) 774-3003
Open: L Tue–Sat, D Tue–Sun $
One of two good Thai restaurants in Flagstaff, Racha has many unusual offerings, including a curry pot pie. It occupies an old hotel coffee shop,

so there's lots of retro atmosphere.

Sakura Restaurant
1175 W. Route 66, Flagstaff
Tel: (928) 773-9118
Open: L Mon–Sat, D nightly $–$$
This Japanese restaurant is in the elegant Radisson Woodlands Hotel on the west end of town. Menu highlights are teppanyaki steak, chicken, and seafood, but it's also the best sushi restaurant in town.

Szechuan
1451 S. Milton Road, Flagstaff
Tel: (928) 774-8039
Open: L, D daily $–$$
Spicy Szechuan food is well done at this popular Chinese restaurant. Try General Tso's chicken or crackling san shein, a sauté of beef, chicken, shrimp, and vegetables in a mandarin sauce. A big lunch and dinner buffet allow you to sample numerous dishes.

RIGHT: al fresco dining at Pasto.

Reach for the Stars

Dry air and dark skies produce what astronomers call "good seeing," attracting both professional and amateur skywatchers to Arizona

Three major observatories are located in southern Arizona, each atop a mountain peak far from the glare of city lights and the dust and moisture that tend to settle at lower elevations. A fourth and much older facility, Lowell Observatory, is in Flagstaff and has been engaged in fundamental research for more than a century.

Kitt Peak, the best known of the state's observatories, stands at an elevation of about 6,900ft (2,100 meters) in the Quinlan Mountains 56 miles (90km) southwest of Tucson. The ridge bristles with the largest array of telescopes in the world, including three major nighttime telescopes and the facilities of consortia that operate 19 optical telescopes and two radio dishes on this site. The largest is the 4-meter Mayall reflector, which is housed in an 18-story dome. About half a mile away, the white angular housing of the McMath Solar Telescope rises from the mountain's south

end, looking more like a modern sculpture than an astronomical instrument. At the top of the structure is a 2-meter mirror that collects the sun's rays and reflects the light down a 530-ft-long (162-meter) diagonal shaft into an underground laboratory.

Given that Kitt Peak is one of the country's most sophisticated astronomical facilities, the observatory is remarkably welcoming to visitors. Tour groups set out from the visitor center daily, though most people choose to follow the self-guided tour. Either way, visitors get an uncommonly close-up look at the workings of the observatory. Nightly viewings give amateurs a chance to probe the heavens with a 16-inch reflector under the guidance of a graduate student. An advanced program limited to two participants per night let's you work side-by-side with professionals. Reservations should be made well in advance; call 520-318-8726 for information.

To the east, in the Pinaleño Mountains outside Safford, Mount Graham International Observatory is operated by Steward Observatory, the research arm for the Department of Astronomy at The University of Arizona. Tours depart from Discovery Park (Mon–Sat May–mid-Nov 9.30am–4.30pm by advance reservation; tel: 928-428-6260; tour fee), a visitor center at the base of the mountain, followed by stargazing through the 20-inch telescope in the evening.

Fred Lawrence Whipple Observatory, in the Santa Rita Mountains 35 miles (56km) south of Tucson, offers 6-hour bus tours (mid-Mar–Nov; tel: 520-670-5707). The highlight is a close-up look at the Multiple Mirror Telescope which combines the light from six 1.8-meter mirrors constantly realigned by laser sensors.

LEFT AND RIGHT: Kitt Peak. **TOP:** spiral galaxy photographed from Kitt Peak. **ABOVE RIGHT:** star trails streak the sky in a time-lapse photo of Monument Valley.

Lowell Observatory (Mon–Sat 9am–5pm Mar–Oct, 5.30pm–10pm June–Oct, noon–5pm Nov–Feb, and Mon, Wed, Fri, Sat 5.30pm–9.30pm Sep–May; no reservations required; tel: 928-774-3358) is the most visitor-friendly of the four, with a host of interactive exhibits, informative tours, and an array of viewing programs and special workshops. Although best known for Percival Lowell's obsessive search for Martian life, the observatory is also credited with Clyde Tombaugh's discovery of Pluto and observations that led to the discovery of the expanding universe.

Nowadays, a staff of some two dozen astronomers conducts research on the planets, stars, galaxies, comets, and asteroids, including a project that locates and tracks objects that could collide with Earth, causing the same ecological catastrophe that wiped out the dinosaurs.

Space junkies can continue the star tour at Tucson's Flandrau Science Center and Planetarium (tel: 520-621-STAR), where visitors can see a 200-pound (90-kg) chunk of the Barringer iron that blasted out Meteor Crater, take in a planetarium show, and gaze through a 16-inch telescope in a rooftop observatory. Nearby is the Steward Observatory's Mirror Laboratory, which produces optics for some of the world's biggest telescopes.

Travelers can rub elbows with stargazers at the

annual Grand Canyon Star Party in June, a gathering of amateur astronomers for several days and nights of viewing at the edge of the great abyss. Another option is to check into the Astronomers Inn (tel: 520-586-7906), a bed-and-breakfast near Benson that caters to astronomers, with an indoor and outdoor observatory, high-end telescopes, and all the comforts of a fine inn. ❏

CENTRAL ARIZONA

Phoenix, the state's urban heart, anchors a region of varied charms

Central Arizona

0   20 miles
0   20 km

P hoenix and its suburbs, known collectively as the Valley of the Sun, form the nucleus of central Arizona. Built upon the bones of an ancient Hohokam settlement, the city has grown from a drowsy desert outpost to a booming metropolis of more than 1.4 million souls, with an additional 2.2 million in the greater metropolitan area. It has never been a cultural heavyweight, but that's changing: two new sports venues, two new performing-arts centers, and a cluster of expanding museums, theaters, parks, shops, and gourmet restaurants in the restored downtown area – long derided for its nonexistent nightlife – have given the city a much-needed center of gravity.

Beyond the Valley of the Sun is a region that too many travelers overlook in their dash to the Grand Canyon. In the White Mountains, for example, you may hardly suspect you're in Arizona at all. Ponderosa pine and Douglas fir tower above you, cool breezes tousle your hair, and cold streams feed the headwaters of the Salt River.

To the northwest, in another dramatic change of scenery, are the red-rock formations of Sedona, whose reputation for "spiritual hot spots," known as vortexes, and trendy shopping have made it a popular weekend getaway. It's about 50 miles (80km) and yet another distinct set change to historic Jerome, a former rough-and-tumble mining town.

Far to the west, where the Colorado River has been fashioned into a series of reservoirs, is Arizona's "West Coast," a 350-mile-long (560-km) water world with resort towns, wildlife refuges, and an abundance of boating and fishing. There's also the state's second most popular tourist attraction, the London Bridge, which, as an extravagant marketing gimmick, was shipped to the desert brick by brick and rebuilt on the banks of Lake Havasu.   ❑

PRECEDING PAGES: Old Route 66, near Oatman.

ARIZONA'S WEST COAST

The Colorado River forms a 350-mile coastline on the state's western border, with palm-shaded beaches, excellent boating and fishing, wildlife refuges, and, improbably, the London Bridge

t seems a misnomer at first. After all, Arizona's "west coast" is far from any ocean, in a desert so hot and dry that rain often evaporates before it can reach the ground. In the eyes of newcomers, this harsh landscape may seem completely devoid of life. Yet first impressions can be deceptive. There are, in fact, many life-forms that thrive here, including humans, along the all-important coastline of the **Colorado River**.

"Where you see a barren wasteland, we see a supermarket," a member of one of the area's indigenous groups once told an anthropologist. Indeed, the Hualapai, Yavapai, Mohave, Quechan, Chemehuevi, Cocopa, and Maricopa cultures flourished here for millennia, hunting and gathering wild foods as well as cultivating gardens. Descendants of some of these early residents remain, commingling with Hopi and Navajo who have migrated from northeastern Arizona. The secret of their survival is the Colorado's delivery of the region's most precious commodity – water.

In 1540, Hernando de Alarcón became the first European to sail the Colorado. The Spaniard navigated its broad delta and, near present-day Yuma, met Quechan Indians with facial tattoos "covering their faces almost entirely" and ear piercings "in which they placed beads and shells." Juan de Oñate pushed farther upstream 64 years later, encountering the Mohave and other tribes. In 1699, the peripatetic Father Eusebio Kino crossed the river and paused to name it.

Colorado means *red* in Spanish, a reference to the iron-laden silt the waterway historically carried from the north.

Troubled crossing

Over the next two centuries, the Spanish developed trails that linked their settlements in California and New Mexico. Following their official exit from the area in the early 1800s, western Arizona drew Mexican farmers and American adventurers. In 1849, thousands of fortune-seekers used Yuma Crossing, where the Gila Trail met the Colorado, en route to

Main attractions

LAKE MEAD NATIONAL RECREATION AREA
CHLORIDE
KINGMAN
OATMAN
ROUTE 66
GRAND CANYON SKYWALK
LAKE HAVASU CITY
LONDON BRIDGE
KOFA NATIONAL WILDLIFE REFUGE
YUMA

LEFT: Lake Havasu.
BELOW:
Route 66 gift shop

Arizona's West Coast

California's goldfields. This had a devastating effect on the Quechans, who had historically controlled the ford and gathered food nearby. Americans took over the crossing, established a fort, and allowed their livestock to eat most of the mesquite beans that Quechans depended on for sustenance. Similar incursions to the north routed the Mohave people from their homelands.

Eventually, the mighty Colorado was tamed and the remaining indigenous people were granted reservations along the river: Fort Mohave, Chemehuevi, Colorado River, and Yuma. Now that the Colorado is the most harnessed river in the United States, thousands of acres of farmland have been developed along its course with the use of elaborate irrigation systems.

The lure of water

Today, Arizona's West Coast is an aquatic playground in a land that averages a mere 3 inches (8cm) of rain annually. Snowbirds and retirees are attracted by the year-round sunshine, carefree lifestyle, easy access to casinos and endless outdoor recreation. Thousands of vacationers converge from Las Vegas, Phoenix, and Los Angeles, most heading for the reservoirs formed by a series of dams along what is now a tame stretch of the once-unpredictable Colorado.

Fortunately, at least a small percentage of the river's extraordinary biodiversity is protected at several wildlife preserves, which maintain vital wetland habitats used by migrating birds as well as resident flora and fauna.

Three east-west interstate highways traverse western Arizona and connect it with the Southwest's major cities. Interstate 40 bisects the state via Kingman as it connects central California with Flagstaff and points east; Interstate 10 links Phoenix and Los Angeles through Quartzsite; Interstate 8 flows through Yuma, halfway between San Diego and Phoenix. In the northwest, US Highway 93 links Kingman with Las Vegas, Nevada. State Route 95 follows a north-south axis, roughly parallel to the Colorado, from Davis Dam (straddling the border with Nevada) through Parker and Yuma to Mexico.

Recreational oasis

The tour begins in Arizona's northwest corner along US Highway 93 at **Lake Mead National Recreation Area ❶**, which encompasses the largest reservoir in the United States (twice the size of Rhode Island). Created by the impoundment of the Colorado River at **Hoover Dam**, Lake Mead extends more than 100 miles (160km), nearly into the Grand Canyon. The reservoir, which straddles the Arizona–Nevada line and is stocked with gamefish, has six marinas and more than 500 miles (800km) of shoreline that have made it a sun-drenched mecca for those keen on boating, water-skiing, fishing, sunbathing, picnicking, and RV or tent camping. Boats and sports equipment can be rented in many locations, and you'll also find numerous tackle shops, restaurants, motels, and groceries.

Popular scenic boat tours of Lake Mead and Hoover Dam are offered by park concessionaire Lake Mead Cruises (702-293-6180). Tours leave from **Boul-**

der Beach**, 2 miles (3km) north of Highway 93 on Nevada State Route 166. The three-deck steamboat *Desert Princess* makes a two-hour cruise six times a day from the main **Lake Mead Cruises Landing** on Route 166. From the Arizona side, the reservoir is accessible from Highway 93 at **Temple Bar** (via Temple Bar Road) and **Meadview** (via Dolan Springs-Meadview Road). The **Alan Bible Visitor Center** (open daily 8.30am–4.30pm; tel: 702-293-8907) is located at the junction of Highway 93 and Lakeshore Scenic Drive, 4 miles

Powerboats crowd the beach at a Lake Havasu City hotel.

BELOW: houseboats are a leisurely way to explore Lake Mead National Recreation Area.

Golfers have a choice of several courses around Lake Havasu City.

BELOW: Route 66 memorabilia in Kingman.

(6.5km) west of Boulder City. Free literature is available, along with fascinating, fact-filled videos about desert ecosystems and wildlife and the dam's construction.

Due to an extended drought, water levels in the Colorado River and, by extension, Lake Mead continue to fall, jeopardizing marinas. Lake Mead Marina, the main marina, has now been moved to Hemenway Harbor and has become part of Las Vegas Boat Harbor.

Without Hoover Dam's water and power, not only would Lake Mead not exist but the neon-lit oasis of Las Vegas (30 miles/48km northwest) would have remained a tiny settlement. The structure is the keystone of the Colorado River Reclamation Project, which serves millions of users in Nevada, Arizona, and California. US Highway 93 passes over this edifice, at 726ft (221 meters) the highest concrete arch dam in the West-

ern Hemisphere. Hoover was completed in 1935 (by 5,000 men working in 24-hour shifts) and can retain some 30 million acre-feet of water.

Hoover Dam Visitor Center (open daily: 9 am–6 pm summer, until 5 pm winter; 702-494-2517; admission) has a parking garage ($7 charge, cash), exhibits, and a viewing area. Tours last 30 minutes and are offered several times each day except Thanksgiving and Christmas (tel: 702-294-3523, charge). Motorized raft trips can be taken from a dock below the dam to and from Willow Beach, about 20 miles (32km) downstream. Due to heightened post-9/11 security, visitors must pass through a security checkpoint. Cameras, purses, and small-size backpacks are permitted. ◆

Services are available in nearby **Boulder City**, the Nevada town created by the US Bureau of Reclamation for those who built and continue to manage the dam. (Boulder is the dam's original name, changed in 1947 to honor former President Herbert Hoover.) About 50 miles (80km) below Hoover is **Davis Dam**, one of three smaller dams that control the river's flow along the rest of Arizona's

Recommended Restaurants on page 225

West Coast. Davis creates **Lake Mohave**, a part of Lake Mead National Recreation Area accessible from both banks but relatively undeveloped.

Boom and bust

Below Davis Dam are the twin cities of **Bullhead City ❷**, Arizona, and **Laughlin**, Nevada, about 20 miles (32km) east of US Highway 95. As recently as the 1980s, these communities barely existed. They have since morphed into a bridge-connected metropolis with more than 11,000 hotel rooms, scores of restaurants, and, in Laughlin, nine major casinos, including a few on old-fashioned riverboats. These cities provide gaming and other amenities (notably golf) to those who don't want to drive another 100 miles (160km) to Las Vegas or who simply prefer a less glitzy atmosphere.

Switching from the modern to the historic, the colorful mining legacy of western Arizona is well preserved in **Chloride ❸**, 20 miles (32km) north of Kingman on US Highway 93 and another 4 miles (6½km) east via Chloride Road. Home to 2,000 people during its 1860s boom, Chloride's name derives from the

silver-chloride ore extracted from mines in the nearby **Cerbat Mountains**. Only a few hundred residents remain in the rustic, frontier-style buildings, but at the end of June each year the town comes alive during Old Miners Day. Festivities are marked by burro (donkey) rides, a swap meet, a crafts fair, and a parade. Gunfights are held every Saturday at noon (every other Saturday in summer). For more information, contact the Chloride Chamber of Commerce (tel. 928-565-2204).

Honeymoon suite

The sprawling city of **Kingman ❹** extends from the intersection of Interstate 40 and US Highway 93, 48 miles (77km) east of the California border in the brown plain of the **Hualapai Valley**. Established as a turquoise-mining center and railroad stop, the town now mainly serves highway travelers and retirees. Learn about the region's history at the worthwhile **Mohave Museum of History and Arts** (400 W. Beale St; open Mon–Fri 9am–5pm, Sat–Sun 1–5pm; tel: 928-753-3195; admission charge). See a detailed replica of a Mohave village, an impressive collection of carved

TIP

Look for colorful murals painted by artist Roy Purcell on boulders outside of Chloride. Follow Tennessee Avenue into the hills about a mile from town.

BELOW LEFT: an iconic star for an iconic road; the longest remaining stretch of the legendary Route 66 runs through western Arizona.

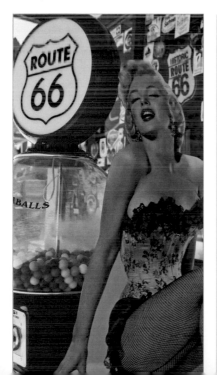

Route 66: The Mother Road

For generations, US Route 66 drew hundreds of thousands of travelers to the Southwest, providing a concrete trail between Los Angeles and Chicago for those in search of a better life. Most of Route 66 was destroyed to create Interstate 40, and many communities along the highway nearly died. But nostalgia and shrewd promotion revived interest in "the Mother Road," now commemorated in places like Kingman and Flagstaff, where Route 66 is still the main thoroughfare.

The longest remaining stretch of the highway is open between Topock (east of the Colorado River) and Ash Fork. Besides spectacular desert scenery, Route 66 provides access to the Hualapai Indian Reservation on the edge of the Grand Canyon. Near Peach Springs is Grand Canyon Caverns, where you can take an elevator 21 stories into the earth for a 45-minute tour (tel: 928-422-3223). A fun stop in Seligman is the Snow Cap Drive-In, a popular hamburger joint for some 40 years.

The Route 66 museum celebrating this stretch of highway is located at the Kingman Visitor Center (tel: 928-753-9889). Nearby is Mr. D's Route 66 Diner (106 Andy Devine), a 1950s-era eatery filled with memorabilia from the road's glory days.

Burros roam freely in Oatman; they are descendants of animals used by gold miners.

BELOW:
reconstruction of London Bridge was completed in 1971; the channel beneath was dredged afterward.

turquoise, and an entire room dedicated to the memory of Kingman's most famous native son: "good guy" actor Andy Devine, who died in 1977. Nearby is the **Powerhouse Visitor Center** (120 W. Andy Devine; open Mon–Fri 9am–6pm in summer, 9am–5pm rest of year; tel: 928-753-6106). The center has information about historic sites in the area and a Route 66 museum. Fourteen miles (23km) southeast is **Hualapai Mountain Park** (open 5am–3pm; tel: 928-757-3859, admission charge), a pine-forested enclave that rises to 8,500ft (2,600 meters) above sea level, with scenic hiking trails, a campground, and picnic areas.

A scenic detour from Kingman takes you to the old mining town of **Oatman** ❺, 25 miles (40km) southwest on Historic Route 66 (Oatman Road). Oatman's single dusty street is lined with tourist-oriented curio shops, saloons, cafés, and hotels. Among the more venerable institutions is the ramshackle **Oatman Hotel** (Route 66, Oatman; 928-768-4408), a virtual museum of century-old memorabilia where Hollywood legends Clark Gable and Carole Lombard spent their wedding night in 1939, after getting hitched in Kingman. Wandering throughout the town are good-natured burros (a prospector's favorite helper), eager for hand-outs of carrots and similar goodies. Fake shoot-outs are staged on the main drag on weekends and holidays.

Skywalk

Kingman is also a good base for visiting **Grand Canyon West** on the Hualapai Indian Reservation. The western end of the Grand Canyon, east of Hoover Dam (just before the Colorado River turns south along the state border to form the West Coast), offers a very different experience from the main Grand Canyon.

Grand Canyon Resort is aimed at tourists arriving from the West who want a quick visit to the Grand Canyon. Las Vegas in Nevada to the northwest, and Kingman and Peach Springs, both in Ari-

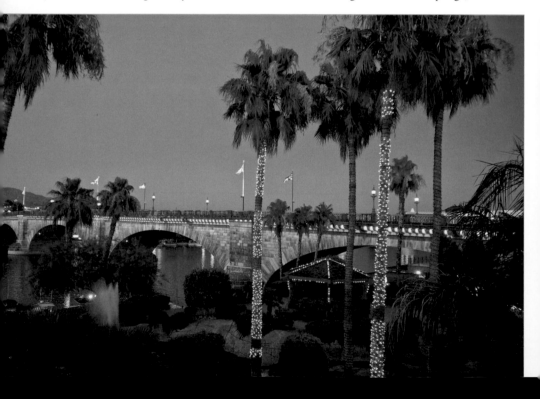

Recommended Restaurants on page 225

zona off old Route 66, are all 2½ hours away. Small commuter airlines offer day trips directly to Grand Canyon West Airport from Flagstaff and Las Vegas.

The Hualapai Tribe have already built a casino, and a large hotel and campgrounds are also planned for Grand Canyon Resort. At present, **Hualapai Lodge** (tel. 888-255-9550), in the small tribal headquarters community of Peach Springs, is the only lodging available. A variety of day tours may be reserved through the concierge desk; 24 hours notice is required.

Scenic helicopter rides are offered daily from the airport. Hualapai Tours offers a popular van tour into the Grand Canyon with guides who share information about their culture with visitors. The tour stops at dramatic overlooks like Eagle Point, 4,300 feet (1,290 m) above the river, and travels Diamond Creek Road, the only route into the Grand Canyon. Smooth-water pontoon boat tours on the Colorado by **The River Runners** (tel. 888 255 9550) allow you to experience all of the above by flying into the canyon by helicopter and boarding an eight-passenger motorized boat on the river (March through October).

Eagle Point is the site of the **Grand Canyon Skywalk ➏**, an observation deck that juts 75ft (23 meters) out over the canyon. The platform is mostly made of 4-inch (10-cm) thick Plexiglass, allowing visitors a clear (and vertiginous) view of the Colorado River 4,000ft (1,200 meters) below. Opened in 2006, the sleek structure has been designed to withstand earthquakes and 100mph (160kph) winds.

London Bridge

Follow Interstate 40 and State Route 95 for about 60 miles (95km) to the south of Kingman to arrive at the improbable "instant city" of **Lake Havasu City ➐**, developed on the Colorado River during the early 1960s by the late tycoon Robert McCullough. McCullough's chain-saw factory moved from here to Tucson years ago but not before his town acquired its greatest single attraction: **London Bridge**. Yes, the same graceful, arched structure of granite – quarried at Dartmoor in southwest England – built in 1824 across the River Thames in London, England. When it was replaced in

TIP

The breathtaking views from the Grand Canyon Skywalk don't come cheap. There's a $20 parking fee, a $29.95 entrance fee, and an additional $29.95 for the Skywalk. Children aged between 3 and 11 get a 25% discount. Cameras are not permitted on the Skywalk.

BELOW: the Grand Canyon Skywalk is owned by the Hualapai Indian Tribe.

Water Issues

The big challenge for the Colorado River in our time is quenching the thirst for power of a burgeoning populace in the desert Southwest

"Too thick to drink, too thin to plow." That's what they used to say about the Colorado River. Not anymore. The 1,450-mile-long (2,330-km) Colorado, rising in the Rocky Mountains and draining an area the size of France, has been tamed – dammed, diverted for irrigation and power, and so heavily used by the states it flows through that it is no longer a river by the time it passes over the Mexican border. The river once known as the Grand is now a managed resource, not the wild, churning, seasonally flooding Great Unknown that so intimidated John Wesley Powell's 1869 and 1871 river expeditions.

Historically, the Colorado was a warm river that swelled into a red, silty, roaring froth when snow in the high country melted. Two-thirds of its volume comes from the Green River, which confluences with the Colorado in what is now Canyonlands National Park in Utah. The Colorado then rages in

a series of whitewater rapids through the narrow confines of Cataract Canyon.

Plants and animals in the Grand Canyon, carved by the Colorado, evolved to deal with seasonal surges in the river. Humpback chub appeared in the warm waters of the Colorado some 3 million to 5 million years ago, when the river first cut through the layer-cake strata of the uplifted Colorado Plateau. Now, warm-water fish like the chub and razorback sucker struggle to survive in the colder waters exiting Glen Canyon Dam, which has created Lake Powell. In the words of environmental analyst Stephen Corothers, the Grand Canyon is now a "naturalized" environment rather than a natural one, meaning that the ecosystem has changed to suit man-made conditions.

The greatest challenge today is to provide for the needs of a burgeoning Southwest population in the nation's fastest-growing region while conserving its natural habitats, such as those of the Grand Canyon and the lower Colorado. Daily surges in demand for power in large metropolitan centers like Phoenix once drove dam releases, creating damaging high and low river levels. This has been improved by the passage of the 1992 Grand Canyon Protection Act, which requires the dam's operators to smooth out flows to ensure that the natural habitat downstream is not subjected to extreme fluctuations.

On the other hand, infrequent great floods were once a feature of the Colorado and may have a place in the downstream environment. In 1996, the floodgates at Glen Canyon were opened to allow the river to run unchecked through the Grand Canyon. Beaches were renewed, old vegetation whisked away, and habitat improved in the weeklong flood.

As former Secretary of the Interior Bruce Babbitt put it: "When the dam was going up in the 1950s, it never occurred to anybody that they needed to think about what would happen a hundred miles downstream because we tended to see the landscape as fragments and each one of them independent. What we've learned ... is that nature doesn't operate that way." ❏

LEFT: kayakers paddle the Colorado River below the Hoover Dam. **ABOVE:** Glen Canyon Dam.

Recommended Restaurants on page 225

1971, it was sold for $2.5 million and shipped in numbered pieces to the Arizona desert, where it was reassembled on a peninsula jutting into the lake.

Despite its unlikely relocation, this is an authentic piece of history: note the strafing scars left on the stones by German bombers during World War II. Next to the 900-ft (275-meter) span is **English Village**, a tourist-oriented promenade of shops and restaurants decked out in an "old London" theme. Lake Havasu City, London Bridge, and these cute Olde England buildings were the brainchild of the retired general manager of Disneyland. Now, unfortunately, the once-bustling shopping center is looking a little worn out. There are still a few gift shops here, including **Village Gifts and Souvenirs** and **London Bridge Candle Factory**, which claims to be the world's largest candle shop.

The city itself has thrived and become home to more than 56,000 year-round residents, including many retirees. A full spectrum of water recreation, golf courses, tennis courts, and related services is available. Although you can hike up nearby **Crossman Peak**, most of the action is on Lake Havasu, a 45-mile-long (72-km) artificial lake. Be advised that, like others on Arizona's West Coast, this reservoir is extremely popular with the spring-break crowd during March and April, when thousands of party-hungry college students arrive.

Those who favor somewhat more sedate pursuits may wish to visit nearby **Buckskin Mountain State Park**, **Bill Williams National Wildlife Refuge** or **Lake Havasu National Wildlife Refuge**, each of which protect scenic

The Dixie Belle waits for passengers at a dock near the London Bridge

BELOW: spring-break revelers work on their tans at Lake Havasu.

Mohave Girl, by Edward Curtis, 1903. The tribe numbered about 6,000 at the arrival of the first Europeans.

BELOW: canoeing on the Lower Colorado River.

areas and key ecosystems along this particular stretch of the river. The parks provide a mix of boat-launch ramps, campgrounds, swimming beaches, picnic areas, and hiking trails.

Parker Dam, which impounds the Colorado about 20 miles (32km) south of Lake Havasu City, is not as stunning as Hoover, although workers were required to dig an amazing 230ft (70 meters) into bedrock below the river in order to make the structure secure. Self-guided tours are no longer available at Parker Dam. However, visitors are welcome to park in the turnout on the California side of the dam and view the features and interpretive panels around the site. For more information, call 760-663-3712.

Another 15 miles (24km) downstream is the small town of **Parker ❽**, headquarters of the **Colorado River Indian Reservation**, which extends about 40 miles (64km) south to **Ehrenberg** and across the border into California. The reservation is unusual in that it is open not only to those whose ancestors (mainly the Mohave and Chemehuevi) lived here traditionally but to members of other tribes

whose homelands are hundreds of miles away. A complicated legal history has also resulted in a number of non-Indians owning land and living on the reservation. Residents derive much of their income either from farming or by catering to tourists attracted to **Lake Moovalya**, a reservoir below Parker Dam. Crowds here are smaller than those at Lake Havasu and Lake Mead but increase dramatically during spring break.

Parker is home to the **Colorado River Indian Tribes Museum** (Second and Mohave streets, open Mon–Fri 8am–5pm; Sat 10 am–3 pm; tel: 928-669-9211, ext 1335; donation), a terrific place to learn about the indigenous people who have made this part of Arizona their home. The museum displays an impressive collection of baskets, pottery, jewelry, and historical artifacts. There's a craft shop, and a casino dominates the adjacent shopping center.

State Route 95 veers east of the river south of Parker and, 35 miles (56km) later, intersects Interstate 10 at **Quartzsite ❾**. This scruffy, unincorporated hamlet is home to about 2,000 year-round residents and 200,000 snowbirds,

Recommended Restaurants on page 225

who migrate from the cold north in their RVs and mobile homes during the winter months. Most of these sun-worshippers alight in the surrounding desert, which is public land.

Rock show

Throughout the winter, Quartzsite's single main street is an amazing flea market, where a motley crew of vendors hawks everything from anvils to zithers. The season's biggest events, however, are the week-long **Quartzsite Powwow Rock & Mineral Show** (tel: 928-927-6325; free) and a series of smaller gem fairs which draw as many as a million visitors during January and February. Sellers offer precious or collectible stones of every size, shape, and description. Concurrent events include a rodeo, parade, and camel and ostrich races. Despite their quirky independence, the encamped snowbirds organize themselves well enough to hold dances, hoedowns, and potluck dinners to which the public is invited.

Continuing south on State Route 95, the remote **Kofa** and **Castle Dome** ranges loom as jagged escarpments to the east. Much of this pristine desert is protected by 665,400-acre (269,000-hectare) **Kofa National Wildlife Refuge ⑩** (tel: 928-783-7861), accessible via dirt roads and unimproved trails. Campers and backcountry hikers face primitive conditions and rough, waterless terrain but may be rewarded with a glimpse of some of the state's few remaining desert bighorn sheep. Rare California palm trees – the only palms native to Arizona – are found in the refuge's rugged, secluded canyons. Some botanists speculate that the palms were stranded here at the end of the last Ice Age.

Bordering the refuge is the military's **Yuma Proving Ground**. Secondary roads cross through this restricted area into **Cíbola** (tel: 928-857-3253) and **Imperial National Wildlife Refuges ⑪** (tel: 928-783-3371), which protect wetlands along the Colorado River north of Imperial Dam and Martínez Lake, offering birding, hiking, boating, fishing, hunting, and camping.

A sense of Yuma

State Route 95 returns to the Colorado at **Yuma ⑫**, a farming and military com-

The thermometer failed to show the true heat because the mercury dried up. Everything dries; wagons dry; men dry; chickens dry; there is no juice left in anything, living or dead

– J. R. Browne, 1864, on summer in Yuma

LEFT: Hopi girl at the Colorado River Indian Reservation.
BELOW: a desolate stretch of highway winds through the desert.

POISONOUS SNAKES AND INSECTS INHABIT THE AREA

Hikers need to keep an eye open for snakes and scorpions.

munity of about 65,000 where an important ford has existed since long before Europeans first visited. The Spanish presence here was brief, terminated by an uprising of the native Quechan in 1781. A riverside fort on the California bank, now run as **Fort Yuma Quechan Museum** (open Mon–Fri 8am–5pm, Sat 10am–4pm; tel: 619-572-0213; admission charge) by the Quechan Tribe, was built to protect travelers five years before the area fell under United States control under the terms of the 1854 Gadsden Purchase.

This was followed by construction of the penitentiary that is now **Yuma Territorial Prison State Historic Park** (Prison Hill Road; open daily 8am–5pm; tel: 928-783-4771; admission charge). Known as the Hell Hole, the prison housed 3,069 convicts before its closure in 1909. Its best-known resident was Pearl Hart, the prison's only female inmate, sentenced to five years for robbery. She was released two years early when it was learned that she was pregnant, presumably by one of her guards.

Other attractions include **Yuma Quartermaster Depot State Historic Park** (201 N. 4th Avenue, Yuma; open daily 9am–5pm; tel: 928-329-0471; admission charge), which preserves the original ford and quartermaster depot. Living-history demonstrations are offered by docents, recalling the bygone era when paddle-wheel steamers plied the Colorado.

Ride the rails

Day-trip options include boat rides, date farm and camel ranch tours, and the **Yuma Valley Railway** excursion train (1pm Sat, Sun Jan–Mar, 1pm Sun only Apr–May, Oct–Dec; tel: 928-782-9629; charge), a narrated, two-hour excursion in a 1922 Pullman coach featured in the film *Judge Roy Bean* that follows a 22-mile (35-km) route downriver. Not a restaurant but a recreation site, **Betty's Kitchen** (past Laguna Dam, 14 miles/23km north of Yuma) offers hiking, birding, picnicking and fishing in a lush, shady spot. A word of warning: this part of the Sonoran Desert is uncomfortably hot in summer, and many tourist businesses close – wisely – until relatively cooler weather returns in autumn. ❑

RESTAURANTS

Prices for a three-course dinner per person, excluding tax, tip, and beverages:
$ = under $20
$$ = $20–45
$$$ = $45–60
$$$$ = over $60

Beale Street Brews
18 E. Beale Street, Kingman
Open: B, L, D daily **$**
The Beale Street Brews coffeehouse is a lovely, airy space, just perfect for a quick pick-me-up when you're passing through. They serve specialty coffee drinks, healthy fruit smoothies, teas, and homemade pastries from 6am to 6pm. Enjoy live music on Friday nights and an open-mic evening. On either side is an art gallery and the Cellar Door Wine Bar (see below), Kingman's first wine bar.

Big John's Steak and Pub
717 N. Lake Havasu Avenue, Lake Havasu City
Tel: (928) 453-5858
Open: B, L, D daily **$**
A long-time local favorite for its certified Angus beef burgers and lively sports-bar atmosphere. Try the burgers or surf 'n' turf specials.

Cellar Door Wine Bar
414 E. Beale Street, Kingman
Tel: (928) 753-3885
Open: Wed–Thur 4pm–10pm, Fri 4pm–midnight, Sat 2pm–midnight **$**
Owned by the superbly bearded Scott Rhoades and his wife Nancy, both longtime teachers (hence the limited opening hours), the Cellar Door

occupies an attractive space in historic downtown Kingman and has been greeted with wholehearted enthusiasm by residents since it opened in 2008. The food as yet is strictly nibbles, but the gourmet cheeses and locally made bread are winners. The wine list showcases 45 reasonably priced, mostly Californian, wines, several premium beers, and non-alcoholic wines. They may also be purchased in the bottle shop. Entertainment includes live folk and bluegrass music, Saturday afternoon chess sessions, and wine tastings.

Chretin's Mexican Food
485 S. 15th Avenue, Yuma
Tel: (928) 782-1291
Open: L, D daily **$**
Filling, homemade Mexican specialties are the attraction at this no-frills restaurant, a favorite with locals for more than five decades.

Copper Cart Restaurant
103 W. Chino Avenue, Seligman
Tel: (928) 422-3241
Open: B, L daily **$**
A reliable bet in this neon-lit classic Route 66 town, the Copper Cart is a diner with a lot of old-fashioned atmosphere. The Mexican food and seafood specials are good bets.

Garden Cafe
250 Madison Avenue, Yuma
Tel: (928) 783-1491
Open: B, L only daily **$**
Birdsong and the scent of

lemon trees delight customers at this leafy oasis, which serves a delectable assortment of pancakes, quiches, salads, and tempting desserts.

Hubb's Bistro
315 E. Andy Devine Blvd, Kingman
Tel: (928) 718-1800
Open: D daily **$$**
Owners Jason and Jennifer Pfaff are restaurateurs with long experience in the hospitality industry who left Mississippi following Hurricane Katrina. They took over the 1909 Hotel Brunswick in 2006 and are slowly remodeling the historic lodging. The main reason to stop by is the bistro, which offers elegant Continental cuisine and has many fans.

Javelina Cantina
1420 McCulloch Blvd, Lake Havasu City
Tel: (928) 855-0220
Open: L, D daily **$–$$**
Expect a party atmosphere at this lively Mexican eatery, located near the London Bridge. Its spacious bar and patio are open year-round and popular for drinks. Margaritas are the main draw, along with an extensive tequila menu. Soak it all up with fish tacos or a cool salad featuring exotic fruits and seafood.

Mr D'Z Route 66 Diner
105 E. Andy Devine Avenue, Kingman
Tel: (928) 718-0066
Open: B, L, D daily **$**
Flamboyant colors, doo-wop tunes, and lots of formica and chrome give this diner lots of kitsch

appeal. The atmosphere is strictly cornball, but it's a good place for root beer, burgers, and fries.

OK Saloon and Road Kill Cafe
502 Route 66, Seligman
Tel: (928) 422-3554
Open: L, D daily **$**
Friendly local café with added personality: there's a carved naked lady bar post, and they collect dollar bills. The name is misleading: all the meat is fresh here. They make a mean barbecue sandwich.

River City Grill
600 W. Third Street, Yuma
Tel: (928) 782-7988
Open: L Mon–Fri, D nightly **$$–$$$**
Global fusion cuisine using natural and grass-fed meat, wild seafood, and organic produce are hardly mainstream in Yuma, but this neighborhood bistro has made converts from far and wide. The menu offers great seafood specials, such as crab cakes, tequila snapper, seafood gumbo, and sushi; you'll also find burgers, steaks, salads and pastas.

Shugrue's
1425 McCulloch Blvd, Lake Havasu City
Tel: (928) 453-1400
Open: L, D daily **$$**
Diners enjoy a view of London Bridge as they chow down on pasta, seafood, steak, and sandwiches. Food and service are consistently satisfying, and families appreciate the special children's menu.

Recommended Restaurants on page 239

SEDONA AND THE VERDE VALLEY

Spectacular red-rock formations surround this
popular getaway town, known for its dining,
shopping, and New Age vibrations

In 1996, a Northern Arizona University study found that 64 percent of visitors coming to **Sedona** ❶ were seeking a "spiritual experience." Of those, 43 percent specifically mentioned the area's male and female "vortexes," unusual power points in the earth where energy flows freely, affecting living things with their vibrations.

In case you haven't heard, the New Age is big business in this community of 11,000 in west-central Arizona's Red Rock Country. You can take Jeep tours to vortex sites, read all about the latest local UFO sightings and abductions, experience a sweat lodge with a genuine Native American healer, have your aura tuned, your chakras aligned, crystals placed on your body, be rebirthed, cover yourself from head to toe in the sacred healing mud of Sedona, even buy a T-shirt hand-dyed with Sedona Red Dirt "believed to bring good luck to the wearer." And still have time to shop at Sedona's faux Mexican marketplace, **Tlaquepaque**, before sunset sets the rocks afire.

It would be easy to write off Sedona as Arizona's answer to Santa Fe. But what both places have in common, beyond their sometimes wacky offerings, is a stunning natural setting and a quality sought after by all the weary urban refugees, wealthy retirees, artists, and spiritual seekers who have moved here since the 1980s: inspiration. They seem to find it. The Cowboy Artists of America was established in Sedona, and today,

more than 50 galleries offer some of the most sophisticated art in the Southwest. The town is home to an array of world-class artists, writers, photographers, musicians, and others who ensure that Sedona maintains a jam-packed cultural calendar.

Natural splendor

But the main reason to visit Sedona is to get outdoors and enjoy the scenery. At this 4,000-ft (1,200-meter) elevation, temperatures stay above freezing year-round. Summer months see 90°F (32°C) days at low elevations, but relief is

Main attractions

OAK CREEK CANYON
SLIDE ROCK STATE PARK
RED ROCK-SECRET
  MOUNTAIN WILDERNESS
TUZIGOOT NATIONAL
  MONUMENT
JEROME
PRESCOTT
ARCOSANTI
CHAPEL OF THE HOLY CROSS
PALATKI AND HONANKI

PRECEDING PAGES:
red rocks. **LEFT:**
Slide Rock State
Park. **BELOW:** a
Sedona psychic.

TIP

Sedona's dramatic set-
ting and artsy atmos-
phere lend themselves
to a schedule of special
events, including the
Sedona International
Film Festival in March,
the Chamber Music Fes-
tival in May, and Jazz on
the Rocks in September.

BELOW: yucca
blossoms amid red-
rock formations
outside Sedona.

always just a hike away in thousands of
acres of cool, high-elevation national forest. Spring arrives early, with newly
leafed cottonwoods and wave after wave
of poppies, lupines, and other wildflowers on the desert floor. Summer brings
drenching monsoon rains and ephemeral
waterfalls in the canyons. By October,
fall leaves in **Oak Creek Canyon ❷** are
peaking. In January, the **Mogollon Rim**
is dusted with snow, but down in the valley the crowds have evaporated and
locals have taken back the trails. The best
remedy for cabin fever, say residents of
Flagstaff, 30 miles (48km) to the north, is
a drive to Sedona.

The route of choice from Flagstaff is
spectacular **Highway 89A**, which spirals down off the ponderosa-pine-clad
Colorado Plateau into Oak Creek
Canyon. The road descends stratum by
stratum from pale Kaibab Limestone
into the variegated Supai Group, the
Hermit Formation, and the Schnebly
Hill Formation. Differential erosion has
carved a fantasyland of rock formations
here: alcoves, arches, hoodoos, buttes,
and mesas with anthropomorphic
names such as Cathedral Rock, Coffee

Pot Rock, Bell Rock, and Vultee Arch.

Oak Creek Vista is a good place to
stop and get a first look at the canyon
described by Zane Grey in *The Call of
the Canyon* as "a gigantic burrow for
beasts, perhaps for outlawed men – not
for a civilized person." Civilization, for
better or worse, finds its way into the
canyon regularly now: an astounding 4
million visitors a year make the drive.
But before Arizona's first designated
scenic highway was built in the 1940s,
early residents remember Oak Creek
Canyon as a gloomy, isolated place,
home to deer, elk, bobcats, black bear,
and at one time grizzlies.

The first permanent homesteader in
the canyon was Irishman Jim Thompson
who, in 1876, built a log cabin at Indian
Gardens, where Tonto Apaches had only
recently been raising corn, squash, and
beans. Homegrown produce is still one
of the main attractions at **Garland's Oak
Creek Lodge** (open Apr–mid-Nov; tel:
928-282-3343), a 1930s cabin resort
located 7½ miles (12km) north of
Sedona. It's almost impossible to get a
room reservation here, but don't miss a
stroll in the gardens (a popular wedding

Map on page 230

Recommended Restaurants on page 239

venue) and one of the lodge's famous dinners, a chef's choice of whatever is fresh that day, served family style, in a warm, friendly atmosphere.

Two miles (3km) south of Garlands, is 55-acre (22-hectare) **Slide Rock State Park ❸** (8am–7pm summer, to 6pm spring/fall, 5pm winter; tel: 928-282-3034; admission charge). In 1907, Frank Pendley built a home and planted an apple orchard in the meadow above Slide Rock that is still producing today. *Life* magazine named Slide Rock one of the top 10 swimming holes in the United States, and the park attracts some 1,600 bathers on a typical hot July day.

But even if you don't want to whoosh down the natural rock chute (it's hard on the rear), stop here for a stroll along the creek, which is home to more than 20 species of fish.

Red-rock trails

Slide Rock may also be your best bet for trailhead parking during peak seasons. Several spectacular hikes – including the 3-mile (5-km) **West Fork of Oak Creek Trail**, which follows the creek through a narrow slot canyon – take off near here

into the 44,000-acre (17,800-hectare) **Red Rock–Secret Mountain Wilderness ❹**. It's easier to find solitude in the backcountry. Better still, connecting trails allow you to begin in Oak Creek Canyon and end up in **West Sedona**. One possibility is **Sterling Pass Trail**, which connects with **Vultee Arch Trail** for a 4-mile (6-km) one-way hike. Inexpensive **Sedona Redrock Passes** are required to park and hike in the area and are available from area businesses, at trailheads, and from the Red Rock Ranger

The iconic profile of Cathedral Rock peaks over the treeline.

BELOW: shops on Highway 89A in Sedona.

Oak Creek.

BELOW RIGHT:
Chapel of the
Holy Cross.

District of Coconino National Forest (open Mon–Fri 8am–4:30pm; tel: 928-203-7500, 928-203-2900), on Highway 179, just south of the Village of Oak Creek. Five small campgrounds line Highway 89A in Oak Creek Canyon (one is closed seasonally); they fill quickly and reservations are essential.

Sedona has suffered from a very visible, unregulated real-estate boom, which, to its present regret, allowed runaway development and over-scaled homes to blight its famous red-rock vistas. Since then, new zoning has led to environmentally sensitive, smaller-scale public buildings like the attractive little Sedona Library. Outside the library is an engaging bronze statue of Sedona's founder, Sedona Schnebly, a Missouri pioneer who with her husband T. C. began farming 80 acres (32

hectares) on the west bank of Oak Creek in 1902. Some of the most spectacular vistas in Sedona lie along **Schnebly Hill Road**, a dirt road that winds onto **Munds Mountain**. It's closed in winter, but for careful drivers this makes a scenic alternative to Interstate 17.

House of worship

For many spiritual seekers, Sedona's breathtaking setting is all the proof they need that God exists. In 1932, architect and sculptor Marguerite Bruswig Staude, a student of Frank Lloyd Wright, conceived the idea for a Catholic church literally rising up from the symbolic cross at the center of the Christian faith. She went around the world searching for the right location and found it in Sedona. Built on one of Sedona's famous vortexes, or power centers, on forest service land outside downtown Sedona, the **Chapel of the Holy Cross** (Chapel Road, off US 179, tel: 928-282-4069; open daily 9am–5pm; free) was a remarkable achievement in 1956, when it was completed. Its soaring angled glass facade framing an oversized cross is snugged between two 250-ft (76-meter) redrock

The First Lady of Arizona Letters

The rancher and writer Sharlot M. Hall was "a genuine young frontierswoman," wrote Charles F. Lummis, her editor and friend. "Not of the cheap drama and Sunday-edition counterfeits, but a fine, quiet, loveable woman made strong and wise and sweet by life in the unbuilded spaces."

This love of "unbuilded spaces" began early. The first white child born in Kansas, in 1870, Sharlot and her family traveled west along the Santa Fe Trail in 1882 and built up a ranch on Lynx Creek near Prescott, which Sharlot continued to run until 1928, when she began her museum. She retained a love of adventure, the outdoors, and free-spirited living until her death in 1943.

In 1906, she helped defeat a congressional bill to make New Mexico and Arizona a single state by using her epic poem *Arizona* to sway the US Congress. In July 1911, while serving as territorial historian (the first woman to serve in the territorial government), she and famed guide Al Doyle spent 10 weeks journeying by wagon through the remote Arizona Strip. Her glowing accounts of the trip led Congress to include the area when statehood was granted in 1912.

She wrote 10 books and more than 500 articles, stories, and poems and was the first woman to be inducted into Arizona's Hall of Fame.

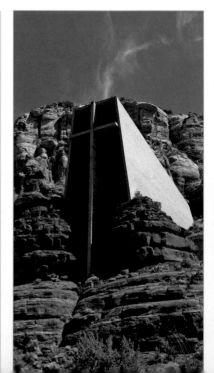

Recommended Restaurants on page 239

pinnacles with a 1,000-ft (300-meter) cliff for a backdrop and seems to have arisen spontaneously from the redrocks themselves. One of the main attractions in Sedona, it was voted one of Arizona's Seven Man-Made Wonders in 2007.

For lessons in how to live harmoniously with the environment, look no farther than the Sinagua Indians who lived in Sedona a thousand years ago. They farmed along Oak Creek and built warm, south-facing cliff-side pueblos in the red rocks that blend seamlessly with their surroundings.

Hundreds of ruins are secreted away in the red rocks, but the easiest to visit are **Palatki** and **Honanki** ❺ on the north side of the valley. To reach them, drive Highway 89A west 9½ miles (15km) from the Y intersection with Highway 179. Turn right on FR 525, drive 6 miles (10km) to where FR 795 branches to the right, and take FR 795 2 miles (3km) to a dead end. For Honanki, continue on FR 525 another 3¼ miles (5km) beyond the intersection with FR 795. Forest Service rangers offer tours daily.

Reservations are required to visit Palatki. Call Palatki (office open daily 9.30 am–3.30 pm; tel: 928-282-3854). Honanki is open daily 10 am–6 pm. No reservations required, but please call Palatki or the Red Rock Ranger District (928-282-4119) before going.

Ancient crossroads

The Verde River Valley is increasingly a bedroom community for those who'd rather live in Sedona but can't afford the rent. One such town is **Cottonwood** ❻, 17 miles (27 kim) southwest of Sedona. Picnicking, camping, canoeing, and fishing for trout, bass, and catfish are available at 320-acre (130-hectare) **Dead Horse Ranch State Park** (open daily 8am–5pm; tel: 928-634-5283; admission charge). Nearby is **Tuzigoot National Monument** ❼ (open daily 8am–6pm summer, to 5pm winter; tel: 928-634-5564; admission charge), a large Sinagua pueblo built on a high ridge above the **Verde River**. Begun as a small pueblo in AD 1000, Tuzigoot grew to 110 rooms in the 1200s, as Sinagua refugees from drought-stricken northern areas moved

Sedona is a center of New Age culture.

BELOW: at its height in the late 1300s, Tuzigoot had more than 100 rooms and perhaps 225 residents.

Remnants of the Verde Valley's mining boom clutter a yard near Cottonwood.

BELOW: a view of Jerome from the site of the former Little Daisy Mine.

south. The fertile, well-watered Verde Valley became an important prehistoric crossroads for traders, but eventually over-population, diminishing natural resources, and epidemics seem to have taken a toll. The pueblo took on a defensive appearance and began to store more food. By 1425, all the residents had moved away.

Tuzigoot is a Tonto Apache word meaning "crooked water," a reference to a cres-cent-shaped lake near the monument. The Apache are still a strong presence in the Verde Valley, where they have intermarried with Yavapai Indians to such a degree that the two groups have merged into the Yavapai–Apache Nation. They live together on three separate tracts of land on the 560-acre (225-hectare) **Yavapai–Apache Reservation** and operate the successful **Cliff Castle Casino** (Montezuma Castle exit 289, off Interstate 17; tel: 800-381-SLOT) in **Camp Verde**, now the Verde Valley's main employer. Even if you don't

gamble, stop at this casino for a look at the tribe's administrative offices, which were designed by Hopi architect Dennis Mumkena in the shape of a kiva. The inte-rior (not open to the public) is decorated with symbols connected to Hopi legends.

Before Tuzigoot National Monument was deeded to the National Park Service, in 1939, it was the property of the United Verde Copper Company, the Verde Val-ley's primary industry, from 1882 to 1953. Two miles (3km) northwest of Cottonwood is the old smelter town of **Clarkdale ⑧**, which is sputtering back to life with the revival of the historic **Verde Valley Railroad** (once-daily after-noon excursions 1pm–5 pm, summer 9am, 2.30pm departures; tel: 800-320-0718, www.verdecanyonrr.com; reservations required).

The Verde Valley Railroad carried ore and passengers – the Verde Mix, it was called. Today, it's strictly tourists, with about 60,000 passengers a year boarding the old locomotive for the four-hour, 40-mile (64-km) round-trip from **Clarkdale** to **Perkinsville**. With its bright blue engines and obvious family appeal, the railroad is a pleasant way to spend an

Recommended Restaurants on page 239

afternoon. It also offers one of the easiest ways to view **Sycamore Canyon Wilderness**, a 21-mile-long (34-km) gash in the earth, with 700-ft-high (215-meter) red cliffs, huge cottonwoods, endangered wildlife, and bald and golden eagles in winter.

Sin City

The Verde Valley Railroad was financed by Senator William A. Clark, owner of the United Verde Mine in **Jerome ❾**. Jerome began life as a mining camp in 1876 and eventually yielded $1 billion of copper, gold, silver, zinc, and lead during its 77 years of operation. Seeming to defy gravity as it clings to the side of 7,743-ft (2,360-meter) **Mingus Mountain**, quaint little Jerome could be a miniature Bisbee, with its stacked Victorian "painted ladies," narrow streets, and innovative art galleries. But it beats it hands down for breathtaking scenery, with vertiginous views of the Verde Valley all the way north to the San Francisco Peaks.

Entranced by such beauty, it's easy to forget the reality. Between 1895 and 1935, 150 miners lost their lives in the 4,650-ft-deep (1,420-meter) shaft. Even in the 1940s, the son of a mine executive recalls, "the miners were in rubber boots, working in water about a foot deep. It was humid, and very, very hot … They could work only 20 minutes without rest."

Despite this sad history, by 1900 Jerome had 2,681 residents, making it the fifth-largest town in Arizona Territory. Americans and immigrants from Mexico, Spain, Italy, Austria, Ireland, and Eastern Europe vied for lodging, often having to bunk in shifts. Prostitution was so common it was intermittently legalized. Saloons, opium dens, and gambling houses did a roaring trade, leading the *New York Sun*, in 1903, to dub Jerome "the Wickedest Town in the West" and to express the opinion that "the best thing that could happen to Jerome would be a nice, big, citywide fire."

Mud slides, floods, and devastating blazes did destroy much of the town between 1894 and 1925, but somehow it has never given up the ghost. A handful of artists, retirees, and others looking for cheap digs began restoring individual buildings in the 1960s, and now the whole town is listed on the National Register of Historic Places. Jerome's inter-

During one of three fires that swept through Jerome in the late 1890s, Jennie Banters, a local madam, encouraged firemen to save her bordello by offering her services for free.

BELOW: the Spirit Room saloon in Jerome.

Arcosanti

The focus here is putting into practice the communitarian ideas of one visionary on how we should live with nature and each other

U nless we reinvent the American dream in terms of the physiology of it, then it's not going to be a dream, it's going to be doomsday," Italian-born architect Paolo Soleri told an interviewer in 1995. Soleri was talking about the pollution, congestion, social isolation, and enormous waste of resources caused by Americans' pursuit of the good life at the expense of the rest of the planet. Furthermore, states Soleri, "We would be in need of 40 planets by the year 2050, if the American dream becomes the planetary dream."

Soleri's solution? Arcosanti, an experimental city on 25 acres in the high country of Cordes Junction, 70 miles (115km) north of Phoenix. Since 1970, Soleri's Cosanti Foundation has been building the new community, which incorporates large, siltcast, concrete structures, and solar greenhouses. It is a strange vision in the midst of sweeping grasslands surrounded by mountains,

prompting everything from praise for its far-reaching vision to horror from one critic who labeled it "a social experiment that has more to do with totalitarianism than harmonious living."

When complete, Arcosanti will soar 25 stories high, house 7,000 people, and include apartments, businesses, studios, and performance venues in an urban setting that emphasizes privacy linked to accessible public spaces. The complex is designed in accordance with the concept of "arcology" (architecture+ecology) developed by Soleri. In such a system, artificial structures and living things interact as organs do in the human body, with efficient circulation of people and resources, and solar orientation for lighting, heating, and cooling.

Soleri began developing his arcological concepts after spending 18 months studying with famed architect Frank Lloyd Wright at Taliesen West in Scottsdale and Taliesen East in Wisconsin. Taking to heart the famous edict, "Form ever follows function," he returned to Italy and began building large ceramics, using processes that led to the award-winning windbells of ceramic and bronze that are sold to support his experimental work, as well as the siltcast architectural structures at Arcosanti. Soleri returned to Arizona and began constructing his first experimental village, Cosanti, in Paradise Valley in 1956, which remains his permanent home today.

Volunteers and students from around the world, many with no previous design experience, undertake a five-week workshop that teaches building techniques and arcological philosophy, while continuing the city's construction. Residents are workshop alumni who continue the work of planning, construction, and teaching. They produce the world-famous Soleri Bells as well as host 50,000 tourists each year. Daily tours ($6 fee) introduce visitors to the site, and concerts and other events are held regularly in the Colly Soleri Music Center, named for Soleri's late wife. Shows include dinner and are often followed by a light show on the opposite mesa. Tours of Cosanti in Paradise Valley are also available. ❏

● *For more information, contact Arcosanti at 928-632-7135 or www.arcosanti.org.*

LEFT AND ABOVE: Arcosanti reflects the "arcological" philosophy of its founder, architect Paolo Soleri.

Recommended Restaurants on page 239

esting art galleries are its best feature today. **Jerome State Historical Park** (open daily 8am–5pm; tel: 928-634-5381; admission charge), located in the 8,000-sq-ft (750-sq-meter) 1916 home of "Rawhide Jimmy" Douglas above his Little Daisy Mine, has a model of the mines, an assay office, old photos, mining tools, and mineral displays.

Capital idea

By contrast, upstanding Victorian values seem to ooze out of **Prescott** ❿ (pronounced PRES-cut), a tidy little town cradled in a forested basin beneath the **Bradshaw Mountains**, south of Jerome. Prescott itself has a population of over 41,500, but mushrooming subdivisions in neighboring Prescott Valley have pushed the total population over 122,000, making it one of Arizona's fastest-growing areas. Tree-shaded streets, solid Victorian buildings, and an elegant courthouse make Prescott's town center a delightful place to linger on a sleepy summer afternoon. Several historic hotels offer lodging, including the 1927 **Hassayampa Inn**, a gorgeous grande dame in the old style, recently renovated and

featuring antiques, painted ceilings, and plush furnishings.

Prescott had noble aspirations from the get-go. When President Lincoln made Arizona a territory in 1863, Governor John Goodwin and other appointed officials toured the territory for three months, looking for a site for the new capital that had lands rich in mineral wealth and grazing but was relatively free of Confederate sympathies. The party based itself at Fort Whipple and chose gold-rich Granite Creek for the new settlement, which they named Prescott, after the historian noted for his work on Mexico. Government buildings were built in 1864, at the height of the campaign against the Tonto Apache and Yavapai Indians. As with the Verde Valley, the shoe is on the other foot these days. **Bucky's Casino**, operated by the small Yavapai Indian tribe, is one of Prescott's booming new businesses.

Prescott lost the capital to Tucson in 1867 (it eventually ended up in Phoenix), but quickly consoled itself with gold mining and large cattle-ranching opera-

Signs warn visitors of the dangers of open mine shafts.

BELOW: houses cling to Jerome's Cleopatra Hill.

Bull riding at the Prescott Frontier Days rodeo.

BELOW: Watson Lake near Prescott.

tions on the surrounding grasslands. The town became legendary as a hard-drinking haven for cowboys spending their pay on a Saturday night. By the early 1900s, 40 saloons lined Montezuma Street, or **Whiskey Row**, as it was known. Working cowboys from surrounding ranches are still very much in evidence and have been known to down a whiskey or two at the **Palace Saloon**, one of the last honky-tonks on Whiskey Row. What's billed as "the world's oldest rodeo" takes place in early July (Payson also claims that honor). And the popular Arizona **Cowboy Poets Gathering** (www.sharlot.org) attracts several hundred saddlestruck bards to the town in August.

Western visions

Six miles (10km) north of Prescott, just north of Highway 89A, the **Phippen Museum of Western Art** (open Tue–Sat 10am–4pm, Sun 1–4pm; tel: 928-778-1385; admission charge) honors western artist George Phippen, founder of the Cowboy Artists of America. The museum has a good selection of paintings, sketches, and bronzes by up-and-coming as well as established Western

artists. Arizona's territorial history is beautifully told at the **Sharlot Hall Museum** (open Mon–Sat 10am–5pm, Sun noon–4pm; tel: 928-445-3122; donation; admission charge), housed in the 1864 Governor's Mansion and 11 other buildings. It was founded in 1928 by former territorial historian Sharlot Hall, a pioneer Prescott rancher, travel writer and, not incidentally, cowgirl poet.

Trails lace **Prescott National Forest** ⓫. One of the most popular is 1.7-mile (3-km) **Thumb Butte Loop Trail**, which winds through ponderosa pine, then crosses pinyon-juniper and oak forest for good views of Prescott and the surrounding countryside. **Granite Mountain Wilderness** is also popular with hikers and rock climbers. For information, contact Prescott National Forest (tel: 928-443-8000). A beautiful drive north through the grasslands of **Chino Valley** takes you to Ash Fork and Interstate 40. Highway 69 heads south past dirt roads leading to old mines and historic ranches before connecting with Interstate 17 at **Cordes Junction**, the turnoff for **Arcosanti** ⓬, the futuristic concrete city founded by visionary architect Paolo Soleri. ❑

Rᴇsᴛᴀᴜʀᴀɴᴛs

Prices for a three-course dinner per person, excluding tax, tip, and beverages:
$ = under $20
$$ = $20–40
$$$ = $40–60
$$$$ = over $60

The Asylum Restaurant
Jerome Grand Hotel,
200 Hill Street, Jerome
Tel: (928) 639-3197
Open: L, D daily $$–$$$
For assured yet unpretentious New Southwest cuisine and awesome views on a par with anything in Sedona, don't miss this restaurant in a former hospital atop Cleopatra Hill in Jerome. At dinner, choose among lobster tail, shrimp skewers, Sonoran spiced chicken pasta, achiote-rubbed pork tenderloin, mesquite-bacon-wrapped filet mignon, and veggie specials.

Coffee Pot Restaurant
2050 W. Highway 89A,
Sedona
Tel: (928) 282-1118
Open: B, L daily $
A legend since the 1950s, the Coffee Pot is a down-home diner famous for its 101 omelettes.

Cowboy Club
241 Highway 89A, Sedona
Tel: (928) 282-4200
Open: L, D daily $$
Cowboy cuisine takes a Sedona twist at this stylish eatery adorned with spurs, boots, lariats, and other buckaroo gear. Ribs, meat loaf, and beef are given gourmet treatment. Don't pass up oddities like fried cactus, rattlesnake, and bison.

Desert Flour Bakery and Bistro
Castle Rock Plaza, 6446
Highway 179, Oak Creek
Tel: (928) 284-4633
Open: B, L daily, D Wed–Sat $
A casual spot that bakes its own bread, pastries, and wood-fired pizzas, plus an array of sandwiches, salads, and more substantial fare such as steak and fish.

Garland's Oak Creek Lodge
Highway 89A, Sedona
Tel: (928) 282-3343
Open: D Mon–Sat, closed
Nov–Mar $$
Four-course prix-fixe dinners are served in a relaxed dining room, family style, at this resort in Oak Creek Canyon. Guests have first preference, but there are sometimes reservations available for non-guests, so check for cancellations. It's well worth the effort because the country-style cuisine leans heavily on the resort's organic produce.

Heartline Cafe
1610 Highway 89A, Sedona
Tel: (928) 282-0785
Open: L, D daily $$
An eclectic mix of flavors emanates seductively from the kitchen of Charlie Kline, a classically trained chef with creativity to burn. Among the entrees are smoked mozzarella ravioli, pecan-crusted trout, and chicken with prickly-pear sauce.

L'Auberge de Sedona
301 L'Auberge Lane, Sedona
Tel: (928) 282-1667
Open: B, L, D daily $$$$

This enchanting resort restaurant offers prix-fixe, six-course French dinners right beside Oak Creek. The menu changes nightly to reflect what's seasonal.

Oak Creek Brewery and Grill
2050 Yavapai Drive,
West Sedona
Tel: (928) 204-1300
Open: L, D daily $–$$
This popular microbrewery is a good place to sample seriously good ale in a relaxed atmosphere. The grill offers pub food, including wood-fired pizza; spicey Sonoran-style meat and fish dishes; and locally made Bratwurst.

The Palace
120 S. Montezuma, Prescott
Tel: (928) 541-1996
Open: L, D daily $$
An historic saloon on Prescott's infamous Whiskey Row, the Palace has been splendidly restored to its former splendor. It now serves up a meat-heavy menu of ribs, steaks, chops, and a memorable corn chowder.

Pietro's
2445 Highway 89A, Sedona
Tel: (928) 282-2525
Open: L, D daily $$
Praised as one of the finest Italian restaurants in the state, Pietro's brings style and imagination to even its most traditional offerings. Options include grilled eggplant rolled with goat cheese and sweet-pepper sauce, red-pepper ravioli filled with smoked mozzarella, and filet mignon grilled in a wine-shiitake mushroom sauce.

Prescott Brewing Company
130 W. Gurley Street, Prescott
Tel: (928) 771-2795
Open: L, D daily $
The beer is good, the crowd is spirited, and the food is cheap and filling at this popular brewpub, housed in an old mercantile building in downtown Prescott.

Reds Restaurant
Sedona Rouge Hotel and Spa, 2250 W. Highway 89A
Tel: (928) 203-4111
Open: B, L, D daily $$–$$$$
This resort restaurant offers relaxed dining and updated comfort-food classics. Many dishes are cooked in the wood-fired oven, a central feature of the open-plan kitchen.

Rene at Tlaquepaque
Highway 179, Sedona
Tel: (928) 282-9225
Open: L, D daily $$$–$$$$
One of Sedona's favorite special-occasion restaurants, Rene's offers a beautiful French Provincial dining room in the midst of the Mexican marketplace of Tlaquepaque.

Wildflower Bread Company
The Shops at Piñon Pointe,
Highways 179 & 89A, Sedona
Tel: (928) 204-2223
Open: B, L daily $
All the bread and pastries are homebaked at this fragrant little bakery in the back of an upscale shopping center. At breakfast, there are lemon-ricotta pancakes. At lunch, there's a variety of sandwiches on healthy whole-wheat and other breads.

BIRD-WATCHING

Varied biogeographical regions allow birders to experience a wide range of species, including subtropical birds not seen elsewhere in the US

Of the 23 documented species of hummingbirds in the US, 18 visit southern Arizona. Add to that the 10,000 sandhill cranes, snow geese, and other waterfowl that descend on flooded Willcox Playa in winter and the 4–10 million birds that migrate along the San Pedro River flyway, and it's clear why Arizona is one of the nation's top birding spots.

Hummers enchant visitors at bed-and-breakfasts in Ramsey and Miller Canyons in the Huachucas, Patagonia in the Patagonia Mountains, Madera Canyon in the Santa Ritas, and Cave Creek Canyon in the Chiricahuas. The latter is also popular for its summer populations of rare elegant trogons, a relative of Mexico's immortal quetzal bird, and other subtropical species such as sulphur-bellied flycatchers, red-faced warblers, and painted redstarts.

The densely vegetated banks of the Colorado River in the Grand Canyon are used by endangered Southwest willow flycatchers, a drab bird whose numbers are dwindling as native willows are replaced by exotic tamarisk. Bald and golden eagles are seen at Nankoweap Canyon in the Grand in winter and along the Verde River in Sycamore Canyon in central Arizona. Growing numbers of California condors are also seen soaring over the Grand Canyon alongside other carrion-eaters like turkey vultures and enormous desert ravens.

In the low desert, birds thrive in inventive ways. White-winged doves and cactus wrens feed on the nectar and succulent fruit of the saguaro. This signature cactus of the Sonoran Desert provides food, shelter, and moisture for many birds, including cute elf owls, which breed in nests pecked into saguaro trunks by Gila woodpeckers and declining populations of gilded flickers, while red-tailed and Harris hawks, and curve-billed thrashers build nests cradled by the cactus's spiny arms.

LEFT: commonly seen throughout the West, the Swainson's hawk migrates some 6,000 miles (10,000km) from Alaska to South America.

ABOVE: a Gila woodpecker perches on a giant saguaro blossom. The birds have distinctive coloring – black and white stripes on the back and flashing white wing patches. Adult males have a red cap.

ABOVE: a bird photographer waits for a shot at the Arizona-Sonora Desert Museum. Bird-watchers will find an abundance of guided tours, workshops, festivals, and organizations devoted to Arizona birds.
BELOW: hummingbirds use slender beaks and long, flicking tongues to sip nectar from flowers. Arizona has 18 species of hummingbirds; they are especially attracted to red blossoms.

TOP BIRDING ACTIVITIES

Birders will want to remember two important southern Arizona birding events: the Southeast Wings Birding Festival in mid-August and the Wings Over Willcox Sandhill Crane Celebration in January, when more than 10,000 cranes over-winter on the marshes and fields around Willcox Plaza.

● Southeastern Arizona Bird Observatory (tel. 520-432-1388; www.sabo.org) has information on local birding events. In spring and summer, participate in band-ing hummingbirds at San Pedro House, the visitor center and gift shop at San Pedro Riparian Area; guided river and canyon walks; owl excursions; and workshops on neotropical migrants like trogons and parrots. In fall and winter, SABO offers tours of top migratory waterfowl areas such as Sulphur Springs Valley and Whitewater Draw.

● Tucson Audubon Society (tel. 520-629-0510; www. tucsonaudubon.org) has free guided birding hikes, talks, and workshops and allows you to participate in local Christmas bird counts. Seven Audubon chapters through-out Arizona offer regional programs, including Yuma, where the California black rail, a small bird that lives among the marshes of the lower Colorado and Gila rivers, is one of five Arizona birds on Audubon's Watchlist of birds in peril. The others are California condors, Southwest willow flycatchers, Mexican spotted owls, and gilded flickers.

● Grand Canyon National Park Condor Ranger Talk: Wings Over the Canyon. Learn about the important condor rein-troduction program at the Grand Canyon and Vermilion Cliffs, one of three breeding populations in the world, through twice-daily talks in front of Kolb Studio at the South Rim's Grand Canyon Village. Summer only.

TOP: a Mexican jay at the northernmost extent of its range in Arizona. **BELOW:** a cactus wren alights on a cholla cactus; the birds often nest in cactus, using the needles to protect themselves from predators.

ABOVE: an elf owl nests in a saguaro cactus. Among the smallest owl species, the elf is found in Mexico and adjoining areas of the US. They feed on crickets, scorpions, centipedes, beetles, and other invertebrates and can be identified by a series of yipping, doglike calls.

Recommended Restaurants on page 249

MOGOLLON RIM AND TONTO BASIN

Once roamed by the Apache, this land of rugged
beauty encompasses ancient pueblos, historic
forts, and reminders of a violent past

Captain John G. Bourke, an Apache fighter under the command of General George Crook in the 1880s, described the **Mogollon Rim** as "a strange upheaval, a strange freak of nature, a mountain canted up on one side. One rides along the edge and looks down two and three thousand feet into what is termed the 'Tonto Basin,' a scene of grandeur and rugged beauty."

Bourke was equally impressed by the way the Apache lived so harmoniously with this rugged terrain. "The Apache was a hard foe to subdue, not because he was full of wiles and tricks and experienced in all that pertains to the art of war, but because he had so few artificial wants and depended almost absolutely upon what his great mother – Nature – stood ready to supply."

But the lessons of the Apache, brave fighters whom Bourke and Crook admired, were mostly lost on the white settlers whose lands they were charged with defending. Attracted initially by gold, then by timber, rivers, and rich lands that could sustain ranches and farms, those who came to the Mogollon Rim and **Tonto Basin** found themselves locked in an epic struggle of possession – with nature and their fellow men. Nowhere in Arizona saw more bloody battles between Indians and white men, ranchers and rustlers, homesteaders and rogue wild animals.

It was this authentic Wild West quality that led western novelist Zane Grey to fall in love with the area in the early 1900s. "For wild, rugged beauty, I had not seen its equal," he wrote. Grey built a hunting lodge near Payson and returned year after year to hunt bear and mountain lion with local guides like Babe Haught and Al Doyle. More than half of Grey's novels are set in the Tonto Basin, earning the area the official moniker Zane Grey Country.

Early inhabitants

This tour begins at **Camp Verde ❶**, off Interstate 17, where the **Verde River** meanders through the stark Verde Valley

Main attractions

MONTEZUMA WELL
MONTEZUMA CASTLE
   NATIONAL MONUMENT
FORT VERDE STATE
   HISTORIC PARK
WET BEAVER WILDERNESS
TONTO NATIONAL FOREST
PAYSON
TONTO NATURAL BRIDGE
   STATE PARK
MAZATZAL DIVIDE TRAIL

LEFT: hikers on the Mogollon Rim, Apache-Sitgreaves National Forest.
BELOW: fallen agave.

Agave is adapted to arid desert conditions, blooming only once in its lifetime.

BELOW RIGHT: Montezuma Castle National Monument.

basin. Farmers from the Prescott area founded the first Anglo settlement here in 1865, but 1,000 years earlier prehistoric farmers were raising corn, beans, squash, cotton, and other crops on these riverbanks, using technology perfected by the Hohokam to the south. A rare 12th-century Hohokam-style pithouse can be viewed at **Montezuma Well ❷**, 11 miles (18km) north of Camp Verde, along with irrigation ditches and pueblos built by the northern Sinagua culture. The Sinagua were adept dry-land farmers who moved into the Verde Valley from the Flagstaff area in the 1100s, following the eruptions of Sunset Crater Volcano.

Montezuma Well is a detached unit of **Montezuma Castle National Monument ❸** (open daily, 8am–6pm in summer, 8am–5pm rest of year; tel: 928-567-3322; admission charge). The "castle" is really a beautifully preserved five-story, 13th-century Sinagua cliff dwelling above Beaver Creek. It so impressed early settlers they erroneously thought it the palace of Aztec leader Montezuma. An adjoining pueblo, Castle A, has collapsed, but most of Montezuma Castle's

limestone walls and 20 rooms have survived, protected in an alcove high in the cliffs. Visitors may view the dwelling from a trail below but aren't permitted to enter.

By the time Spaniard Antonio de Espejo rode through the Verde Valley in 1583, these early farming cultures had disappeared. Strong but inconclusive evidence indicates the Sinagua may have moved back north into the Hopi and Zuñi pueblos in the 1400s. In their place were hunter-gatherer Yavapai Indians, related to the Havasupai and Hualapai of the Grand Canyon, and small bands of Tonto Apache. The latter proved so troublesome during an 1863 gold rush on the Hassayampa River and the subsequent settlement of the Verde Valley that the US Army was dispatched to build Fort Lincoln, later called Fort Verde.

Apache campaign

The fort became a staging area for General Crook (known as "Gray Eyes" by the Apache) and his army's successful Tonto campaign, which resulted in the defeat of Chief Chalipan and 2,300 Tonto Apache in the winter of 1872–73. As part

Writer of the Purple Sage

Pearl "Zane" Grey was born in Zanesville, Ohio, in 1872 and trained as a dentist before finding his calling as a self-taught Western writer and avid outdoorsman. Between 1903 and his death in 1939, Grey wrote 56 Western romances, 13 outdoor books, seven juvenile stories, three historical novels, a novel set in Ohio, one set in Tahiti, two screenplays and numerous short stories and nonfiction articles collected in some 20 anthologies.

Sales of his novels have exceeded 100 million copies, and at least 100 of his books and stories have been adapted to film. Much of their appeal lies in the portrayal of simpler times, authentic settings, and classic characters like the lone gunman Lassiter of *Riders of the Purple Sage*, a rugged individual who achieves redemption by wrestling with the ghosts of his past. Almost all of his tales reveal a West where man is engaged in an epic struggle with his environment and is either redeemed or destroyed by it.

Although Grey loved Arizona, he, wife Dolly and their children moved to Altadena, California, in 1918. Dolly handled her husband's business deals, freeing Grey to write, scout movie locations, and take extended hunting and fishing trips every fall using as a base his cabin in Payson, Arizona.

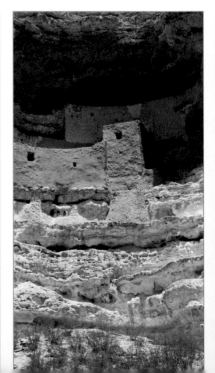

Recommended Restaurants on page 249

of the peace agreement with the Tonto Apache, the honorable Crook promised to provide jobs, farmland, and a police force and immediately had the Indian workers dig a 5-mile-long (8-km) irrigation ditch, planting 57 acres (23 hectares) of crops. **Fort Verde State Historic Park** ❹ (open daily 8am–5pm; tel: 928-567-3275; admission charge) preserves four surviving fort buildings, including General Crook's adobe headquarters. Exhibits include 1880s-era furnishings, old saddles, Indian crafts, letters, and uniforms belonging to cavalry, infantry, and the Apache scouts Crook used to understand and outmaneuver his opponents.

Forest trails

North of Camp Verde, hiking and swimming are popular activities at 6,700-acre (2,700-hectare) **Wet Beaver Wilderness** ❺, a lush oasis with sycamore-, cottonwood-, and ash-lined riverbanks. Trails follow the river and climb the 2,000-ft-high (610-meter) Mogollon Rim above. This is a popular area in summer, with swimming holes that provide respite from temperatures in the 90s°F (30s°C). The Red Rock Ranger District of the

Coconino National Forest (Hwy 179, just south of the Village of Oak Creek, near Sedona; tel: 928-282-4119 or 928-203-7500) has information on trails throughout the Mogollon Rim area.

The **General George Crook Trail**, which starts in **Dewey** ❻, near Prescott, proceeds east through Camp Verde, up along the Mogollon Rim, and finally ends at Cottonwood Wash near **Pinedale** ❼, is an Arizona State Historic Trail that passes through three national forests – Prescott, Coconino, and Apache-Sitgreaves – over its 138-mile (222-km) length. The trail was blazed in 1871 by Crook and his men and used for 22 years to patrol the northern boundary of the Apache Reservation. Connecting trails at the west end join the **Highline Trail** at the base of the Mogollon Rim in **Tonto National Forest**, allowing you to hike from desert scrub to pine fir forest. The Crook Trail is best hiked in spring or fall; portions are open for cross-country skiing in winter.

To access the eastern section of the trail, drive east on Highway 260 from Camp Verde, turn north on Highway 87, then east on unpaved Forest Road 300,

Surgical instruments from the 19th century are displayed in Fort Verde's infirmary.

BELOW: llamas are used for pack trips in Tonto National Forest.

Air-traffic control in Payson.

the 1928 logging road that parallels the Crook Trail for 42 miles (68km) along the forested rim. Views are breathtaking from this perched route, with range after range of hazy mountains, emerald forest basins and valleys, and heart-stopping drops below limestone outcrops. All is not beauty and light, however. The remains of the devastating 1990 Dude Fire, which blackened 24,000 acres (9,700 hectares) and killed six firefighters, can still be seen.

Also along the road are monuments to the major conflicts of the Apache campaign: the Battle of Skull Cave (1872), the Battle of Turret Butte (1873), and the final showdown, the Battle of Dry Wash (1873), which resulted in the deaths of 22 Apaches and the flight of the remainder, clearing the rim country for white settlers.

Rim country

BELOW: horseback riding is the best way to travel the remote reaches of the Mazatzal Mountains.

Scenic Highway 87 drops down from the Mogollon Rim into the heart of the Tonto Basin. Historic homes, antique shops, and galleries line the main street of the little Mormon settlement of **Pine ❽**, while nearby **Strawberry** (named for the

wild strawberries that used to grow here) preserves Arizona's oldest one room log schoolhouse. Built in 1885, it is open on summer weekends and by appointment (call Strawberry Lodge at 928-476-3333 for information).

Busy little **Payson ❾** started out as a gold-mining camp in 1881 but is now more popular as a shopping center, a getaway destination for Phoenicians, and a base for exploring the cliffs of the Mogollon Rim, which loom majestically over the town. Limestone deposited at the bottom of an ancient ocean forms the cliffs surrounding the Tonto Basin. Mineral springs at **Pine Creek**, northwest of Payson, have carved the rock into the world's longest natural bridge, preserved at **Tonto Natural Bridge State Park ❿** (open daily Memorial Day to Labor Day 8am–7pm, Apr, Sept, Oct to 6pm, Nov–Apr to 5pm; tel: 928-476-4202; admission charge). At 400ft (120 meters) wide, with many limestone formations similar to those found in caves farther to the south, the bridge is a beautiful little oasis off the main highway and a bonus on any trip into the rim country.

Recommended Restaurants on page 249

Forest trails

What is advertised as the West's oldest rodeo (begun in 1884) takes place in Payson every August. Get in the saddle yourself or hike a trail in some of the state's most glorious forests. Tonto National Forest's **Payson Ranger District** (1009 E. Hwy 260, Payson) has information on hiking, horseback riding, and camping in the surrounding forest and the 252,000-acre (102,000-hectare) **Mazatzal Wilderness ⓫**, whose highest point, 7,894-ft (2,406-meter) **Mazatzal Peak**, dominates the southern skyline. You can arrange private horse-packing trips into the Mazatzals (pronounced MAT-a-zals) at the Forest Service office.

One of the most popular entry points into these steep, rocky mountains is the 6¼-mile (10-km) **Barnhardt Trail**, near the little town of **Rye**. The trail joins the 29-mile (47-km) **Mazatzal Divide Trail**, which runs along the crest of the Mazatzals and features stunning views of the Sierra Ancha Wilderness to the south and the San Francisco Peaks near Flagstaff to the north.

On the western side of the range is the 28-mile (45-km) **Verde River Trail**, which follows a wild and scenic stretch of the **Verde River**. Float trips are possible on the river, though water levels vary considerably depending on spring runoff and summer rains and, in some years, may not be high enough to use a boat. However you choose to explore the Mazatzals – on foot, on horseback, or by boat – be prepared for a hot, dry, rough country. Bring plenty of water, food and appropriate clothing.

Long pack trips were a mainstay of life in the Tonto Basin for Zane Grey, who made the Payson area his base. In 1921, his long-time guide Babe Haught, scion of Payson's first pioneer family, sold Grey several acres of land and built him a hunting cabin.

The Zane Grey Lodge burned to the ground in the 1990 Dude Fire, but you'll find a replica at the Gila County Historical Society's sweet little **Rim Country Museum** (open Wed–Mon 10am–4pm; tel: 928-474-3483 admission charge) on Main Street. The museum, housed in a 1907 forest ranger's house, has a marvelous display of Grey memorabilia that survived the fire (including the author's

BELOW: Apache men, *c.*1906.

> **TIP**
>
> The Mazatzal Divide Trail has been incorporated into the Arizona Trail, which will eventually stretch the length of the state from Mexico to the Utah border.

Tonto Natural Bridge State Park.

BELOW: the Verde River supports a rich growth of riparian vegetation such as cottonwood and willow.

tooled leather saddlebags, first editions of several of his books, and an embroidered waistcoat) as well as exhibits on the area's forests and Indians. The town has 800 residents, half of them retirees.

Family feud

Grey visited the Tonto Basin every fall, hunting and fishing with Haught and writing detailed notes about the landscape, the people, and the historic events that have given the rim country its unique character. No event has had more impact than the 1887 Pleasant Valley War, one of the most bloody and violent range wars of the frontier era, which pitted the Tewksbury family against the Graham family. Details vary, but the feud was between sheepmen and cattlemen and the Grahams' cattle-rustling activities. Adding fuel to the fire was the presence of cowboys from the Hashknife outfit who had been chased out of the Holbrook area. By the time the smoke cleared five years later, 30 people were

dead, including 12 Grahams and three Tewksburys. And residents of rim country weren't talking – even to famous authors.

Grey's novel, *To the Last Man*, wove fact with fiction. To try to uncover more of the truth, history buffs won't want to miss visiting **Pleasant Valley**, located between the rim country and the remote little settlement of **Young** ⓬. Hard to reach over rough dirt roads (turn off Highway 260 at Milepost 284, about 33 miles/53km east of Payson), Young is one of Arizona's last cow towns. In keeping with a long tradition of feistiness, local folks are independent types with little use for authority or development. Check out the **Antlers Bar and Café** (open daily; tel: 928-462-3265), which serves three squares daily and has walls displaying everything from old saddles and mining gear to dusty stuffed bears.

The first victim of the Pleasant Valley War, a Navajo sheepherder, is buried 5 miles (8km) north of Young. A white cross and sign mark the spot on Forest Route 200, a mile (1.6km) west of the road. ❏

RESTAURANTS

Prices for a three-course dinner per person, excluding tax, tip, and beverages:

$ = under $20
$$ = $20–45
$$$ = $45–60
$$$$ = over $60

Beeline Cafe
815 S. Beeline Highway, Payson
Tel: (928) 474-9960
Open: B, L, D daily **$**
This old-fashioned diner serves tasty all-American food and is a favorite of locals and weekenders, who drive up for breakfast then head into the forest to walk it off.

Cedar Ridge Restaurant
Mazatzal Hotel & Casino, Highway 87 (Mile Marker 251), Payson
Tel: (928) 474-6044
Open: B, L, D daily **$–$$**
In the casino on the south edge of Payson, this restaurant serves good food at reasonable prices. There's a buffet and early-bird special. The specialty of the house is slow-roasted prime rib.

Creekside Steakhouse
Christopher Creek
Tel: (928) 478-4557
Open: B, L, D daily **$–$$$**
East of Payson, in Christopher Creek, this steakhouse has a good selection of ranch country steaks, seafood, fresh trout, and one or two vegetarian dishes.

Cucina Paradiso
512 N. Beeline Highway, Payson
Tel: (928) 468-6500
Open: L, D daily **$–$$**

This casual Italian restaurant serves what is arguably the best food in town. The specialty is calamari, cooked several ways, including an unusual Caesar salad. Make reservations on Friday and Saturday, as Payson is a popular getaway for Phoenicians.

Fiesta Mexicana
911 S. Beeline Highway, Payson
Tel: (928) 468-0709
Open: L, D daily **$**
Filling, inexpensive Mexican food hits the mark at this local joint, one of two great little Mexican places in Payson (see review below). You'll find all the usual combinations of burritos, enchiladas, tacos, and meat and seafood dishes.

Fireside Espresso
614 N. Beeline Highway, Payson
Tel: (928) 474-8200
Open: B, L daily **$**
A great spot to get off the highway and fill up your go-cup with excellent java.

La Sierra Mexicana Restaurant
800 N. Beeline Highway, Payson
Tel: (928) 468-6711
Open: L, D daily **$**
This is a local favorite for Mexican food. The portions are large and reminiscent of what everyone's *mamacita* makes back in the old country. Try the *sopa de albondigas* (meatball soup), tamales, and fajitas, all of it accompanied by homemade chips and

salsa. Leave room for *flan* or *churros* for dessert. Service can be slow when they're busy, but always friendly.

Pine Deli
6240 Hardscrabble Mesa Road, Pine
Tel: (928) 476-3536
Open: B, L daily **$**
Locals love the pizza at this place. It's one of the few eateries in Pine.

The Red Elephant Bakery
1101 S. Beeline Highway, Payson
Tel: (928) 468-6202
Open: B, L daily **$**
Feather-light cakes and cookies from old family recipes are the stars at this wonderful little bakery. At lunch, there are hearty soups, quiches, and sandwiches. They also do afternoon tea and finger sandwiches. An unexpectedly civilized pleasure in rural Arizona.

Rimside Grill
Rimside Grill and Cabins, 3270 N. Highway 87 (mile marker 267), Pine
Tel: (928) 476-3349
Open: B, L, D Wed–Sun (call for winter hours) **$–$$**
This homey cabin resort north of Payson is owned by an enthusiastic young couple who have created a friendly, relaxed resort in the pines. The restaurant has a mellow ambience and dishes up excellent food. Specials change daily and might include chef's pasta, a seafood dish such as ahi tuna or salmon with dill sauce, a

Friday night fish fry and lunchtime fish and chips, prime rib on Saturdays, and yummy homemade desserts.

The Small Cafe
512 S. Beeline Highway #5, Payson
Tel: (928) 474-4209
Open: B daily **$**
Tucked away in a shopping center near the intersection of Highways 87 and 260, this friendly café specializes in breakfast. It has fresh-squeezed juice, egg dishes, pancakes, and almond-crusted French toast. Open until 2pm daily.

Strawberry Lodge
Highway 87, Strawberry
Tel: (928) 476-3333
Open: B, L, D daily **$**
The menu at this historic lodge is mainstream and comprehensive, so there should be something for everyone. Look for daily specials, and don't miss their homemade pies.

Zane Grey Dining Room
Kohl's Ranch Lodge, Highway 260, Payson
Tel: (928) 478-4211
Open: B, L, D daily **$–$$**
Hearty Western fare is offered at this mountain lodge. Choices range from a buttery filet mignon and barbecued baby-back ribs to rainbow trout with pinyon-nut crust. You'll find an assortment of good pastas and salads and specials such as Cajun-style catfish and hush puppies. Don't expect fast service at this tourist-oriented spot.

WHITE MOUNTAINS AND EAST CENTRAL ARIZONA

Forest-clad slopes offer stunning mountain drives, an abundance of recreational opportunities, and welcome relief from desert heat

I n his classic *A Sand County Almanac*, naturalist Aldo Leopold describes the **White Mountains** in the early 1900s as "the exclusive domain of the mounted man: mounted cowman, mounted sheepman, mounted forest officer, mounted trapper, and those unclassified mounted men of unknown origin and uncertain destination always found on frontiers."

A century later, rugged individualism is still a way of life in the White Mountains, but ever since Arizona's oldest roadway, Route 666, linked "the palms to the pines" along the Arizona–New Mexico border in 1926, isolation has been more a matter of choice than necessity. Newer paved highways have shrunk the time it takes to reach the White Mountains. As a result, carloads of overheated city slickers now make the pilgrimage on summer weekends, and almost every sleepy town is happy to host them, offering the gamut from rustic lakeside cabins, historic inns and homegrown museums to roundups, rodeos and hands-on archaeological digs.

Laid-back lifestyle

Visitors are lured to these skyscraping peaks, sapphire lakes and ice-melt streams by a laid-back western lifestyle, temperatures in the 70s°F (20s°C), and some of the Southwest's best trout fishing, winter sports, and mountain biking. Arizona's second- and third-highest mountains are found here – 11,403-ft (3,476-meter) **Baldy Peak**, sacred to the White Mountain Apache on whose reservation it lies,

and 10,912-ft (3,326-meter) **Escudilla Mountain**, on the adjoining 2-million-acre (809,000-hectare) **Apache–Sitgreaves National Forest**.

Silent Indian ruins are reminders that east-central Arizona also sits on a cultural frontier – a frontier breached by US Army soldiers sent to quell the Apache in the 1870s but never entirely subdued, as can be seen in the spirit of self-determination displayed on the San Carlos and White Mountain Apache Reservations today. Equally strong are the Mormon communities founded dur-

Main attractions
PAINTED DESERT
PETRIFIED FOREST
  NATIONAL PARK
MOGOLLON RIM OVERLOOK
SUNRISE SKI AREA
CASA MALPAIS NATIONAL
  HISTORIC LANDMARK
SPRINGERVILLE TO CLIFTON
  HIGHWAY
MOUNT GRAHAM
SALT RIVER CANYON

LEFT: White Mountain Apache Gaan dancer.
BELOW: cowboy, Whiteriver Rodeo.

Backpackers enjoy the view from the Mogollon Rim.

BELOW: the Long Logs section of Petrified Forest National Park.

ing the same period, which prospered by trading meat and vegetables with the troops at Fort Apache. Descendants of pioneer families still work the land, trade with travelers, and exert political clout from their mountain stronghold.

King cattle

Holbrook ⓭, 92 miles (148km) east of Flagstaff on Interstate 40, is a convenient place to start your explorations. Founded as a railroad town in 1881, the vast surrounding grasslands quickly attracted cattlemen, and the town became a major ranching center. The Hashknife outfit was one of the most famous cattle companies, running 60,000 cattle on a million acres (405,000 hectares) and becoming the third-largest cattle empire in the United States. Rustling and poor management eventually shut down the ranch in 1900, but not before Hashknife cowboys had become celebrated for their whoop-'em-up Saturday-night ways in upstanding Mormon towns to the south.

Situated near the Navajo, Hopi, and Apache reservations, Holbrook is a good place to pick up silver-and-turquoise jewelry, pottery, and Apache baskets at a local trading post or attend Indian dances held nightly on the lawn next to the old courthouse in summer. In January or February, you can post a letter via Hashknife Pony Express, which carries the mail on horseback from Holbrook to Scottsdale.

Trees of stone

The town is surrounded by the **Painted Desert**, a highly atmospheric backdrop of buttes, mesas, and banded pink, gray, brown, and purple badlands that have an unearthly glow at sunset or after a heavy rain. To explore this evocative landscape, drive southeast of Holbrook on Highway 180 to the south entrance of 147-sq-mile (381-sq-km) **Petrified Forest National Park** ⓮ (daily 7am–7pm summer, 8am–5pm winter; tel: 928-524-6228; charge), set aside in 1906 to protect one of the world's most abundant deposits of petrified wood. The southern section of the park contains the best examples of these highly prized gems. Resist the temptation to slip a few samples into

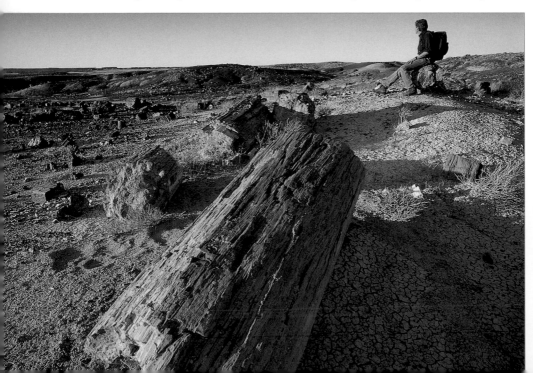

Recommended Restaurants on page 265

your pocket. Regulations strictly prohibit rock collecting in the park and, anyway, petrified wood is sold for pennies outside the park.

Exhibits in the **Rainbow Forest Museum** explain that petrified wood began forming 225 million years ago, when North America was about where West Africa is today. The warm tropical climate sustained enormous reptiles and amphibians (look for the fearsome crocodile-like phytosaur and "Gertie," a dinosaur found here in 1984), cycad ferns, and conifers up to 200ft (60 meters) tall. When these trees toppled into rivers, they were washed in logjams into swamps, then buried by silt and ash from volcanoes to the south. Silicates gradually mixed with groundwater and replaced woody cells with the jasper, amethyst, and smoky quartz so prized today.

A 27-mile (44-km) scenic drive, accessed at either end of the park, has pullouts, interpretive trails and picnic areas. The middle section contains a number of Ancestral Pueblo ruins, including **Agate House**, an unusual 900-year-old structure made of petrified

wood, and the 100-room **Puerco Pueblo**, occupied around AD 1400. Look for the spectacular petroglyphs here, one of which marks the summer solstice. The **Painted Desert Inn** (daily 9am–5pm), built in 1924 as a lodging, is now a national historic landmark and has exhibits and a bookstore. There are no campgrounds, but you may hike and camp by permit in the park's 43,020-acre (17,410-hectare) **Painted Desert Wilderness** and 7,240-acre (2,930-hectare) **Rainbow Forest Wilderness**.

Living wood becomes petrified when cellulose is gradually replaced with silica.

BELOW: a view of the Painted Desert from Whipple Point in Petrified Forest National Park.

White Mountain Apache men pose for a picture in 1909.

BELOW RIGHT: a princess is crowned at the Apache Tribal Fair in Whiteriver.

Bring a hat and plenty of water, food and sunscreen; summer is hotter than Hades in this relatively undeveloped park.

Along the rim

Highway 77, south of Holbrook, passes through a pair of oddly named Mormon towns. **Snowflake** ⓯ isn't named after the winter storms that occasionally blow through town but the combined surnames of Mormon elders William J. Flake and Erastus Snow who, in the 1870s, escaped government persecution of polygamists in Utah and headed south to Arizona to settle and convert Indians. About 19 miles (31km) to the south is **Show Low** ⓰, a small commercial center on the edge of the White Mountains, at the junction of Highways 77, 260, and 60. Show Low's strange name apparently dates from 1870, when the legendary Corydon Cooley, a former fur trader and Indian scout at nearby Fort Apache, challenged Marion Clark, his business partner, to a card game to settle differences over the ranch they co-owned. "Show low and you win," Clark reputedly said. Obligingly, Cooley pulled out an unbeatable deuce of clubs and won the ranch. Ironically, the gaming site (Cooley's kitchen) eventually became the town's Mormon Church. Its main street is called the Deuce of Clubs, where you'll find the town's motels, restaurants, and gas stations.

Stop between mileposts 347 and 348, 7 miles (11km) southeast of Show Low on Highway 260, to get your first look at the Mogollon Rim, the escarpment that sharply divides the Gila–Salt River watersheds and the mile-high Colorado Plateau. Stroll along the mile-long **Mogollon Rim Overlook** and **Nature Trail** for scenic vistas of forested peaks and shadowy valleys. Signs offer information on the ponderosa and pinyon pine, Douglas fir, three types of juniper, and Gambel and scrub oak that make up the forest.

Rodeo-Chediski Fire

The whole place looks like death," said a Show Low resident surveying the charred remains of her home. The house was one of 400 buildings destroyed by the Rodeo-Chediski Fire of 2002, the biggest in Arizona history.

Actually, the fire began as two separate blazes that merged into one monster conflagration. The first was started by a part-time firefighter hoping for work, the other by a lost hiker signaling for help.

Fueled by a buildup of deadwood and fanned by warm, gusty winds, the 15-day fire consumed nearly half a million acres (200,000 hectares) in Apache-Sitgreaves National Forest and the White Mountain Apache Reservation and forced the evacuation of more than 30,000 people from 10 towns, including Show Low and Pinedale.

Among the hardest hit, in addition to those whose homes and businesses were burned, was the White Mountain Apache Tribe, which lost more than 700 million ft (200 million meters) of timber, one of the reservation's main resources. Evidence of the fire will be visible for years in the charred landscape around Cibecue, site of the tribe's principal mill, but the economic fallout will last even longer. "This devastation will affect our kids for two or three generations," said tribal president Lorin Henry.

Recommended Restaurants on page 265

Lakeside–Pinetop **⑰**, 8 miles (13km) southeast of Show Low, is the largest resort area in the White Mountains, with a wide range of developed lodgings and restaurants. Lakeside (elevation 6,745 ft/2,056 meters), founded by Mormons in 1880, was originally called Fairview but changed its name to reflect its abundance of lakes. Soldiers laboring up the Mogollon Rim from Fort Apache often stopped to rest at Pinetop (elevation 7,279 ft/2,219 meters) and gave the town its name. All around are forest roads, hiking and horseback trails, and lakes and streams stocked with trout. The community was also voted the third-best mountain biking town in the country. Forest Route 300, a dirt logging road, begins here and heads west along the Mogollon Rim for nearly 200 miles (320km). It's impassable in winter.

For information on trail and road conditions, contact the **US Forest Service Lakeside Ranger District** (2022 W. White Mountain Blvd; tel: 928-368-5111) and, if you're planning on spending a day or two here, borrow the two cassette-tape audio tours interpreting the area's forest, wildlife, geology, and history.

Apache homeland

Just south of Lakeside–Pinetop is the 1.6-million-acre (650,000-hectare) **White Mountain Apache Reservation ⑱** (877-338-9628; www.wmat.nsn.us). An abundance of outdoor activities is available on the reservation, which offers a quiet, natural, and very spiritual setting for those wanting to get away from the all-American ambiance of adjoining areas. Permits for outdoor sports and visiting Indian ruins on tribal land are available at **Hon Dah** ("Be My Guest" in Apache) at the junction of Highways 260 and 73 about 5 miles (8km) south of Pinetop-Lakeside, an attractive roadside complex with a log motel and restaurant, casino, grocery store, and gas station. Or you can drive south on Highway 73 to the Game and Fish Department (tel: 928-338-4385 or 338-4386) at tribal headquarters in **Whiteriver ⑲**, where you'll find a motel, trading post, restaurants, a shopping center, hospital, and tribal offices.

While you're in Whiteriver, be sure to visit **Fort Apache**, the former US Army post built in 1870 as a supply base for soldiers sent to keep an eye on the White

TIP

Anglers will find lots of rainbow, brown, and brook trout as well as an occasional Apache trout and Arctic grayling in the lakes and streams of the White Mountains. A tribal fishing license is required for the White Mountain Apache Reservation.

BELOW: an Apache rodeo cowboy limbers up before competing.

TIP

Hikers and mountain bikers can hitch a ride up the mountain at Sunrise Ski Resort in the off-season. Chair-lifts run on weekends from late May to mid-October.

BELOW RIGHT: snow-covered forest near Greer.

Mountain Apache and prevent white settlers from encroaching on Indian land. The fort was later used as a staging area for campaigns against the Tonto and Chiricahua Apache. The army relied on friendly Apache scouts, of whom the most famous was Alchesay, who assisted Indian fighter par-excellence General George Crook in making peace with Geronimo in 1886. The commanding officer's quarters, adjutant's office, and officers' row still stand. Exhibits and photographs of the old fort are on display at the **Apache Cultural Center** (open Mon–Fri 8am–5pm, extended summer hours; tel: 928-338-4625; charge), 4 miles (6.4km) southwest of Whiteriver.

Snow trails

The White Mountain Apache also own and operate the popular **Sunrise Ski Area ㉒**, 20 miles (32km) east of Hon Dah, on 10,700-ft (3,260-meter) **Mount Ord**, which has three peaks – Sunrise, Apache, and Cyclone Circle – with 11 lifts and 65 ski runs. For diehard powder bunnies, there's an onsite hotel, restaurant, marina, and sports center offering ski, snowshoe, and mountain bike rentals.

A quieter option is to stay in the tiny community of **Greer ㉑** (pop. 100), 15 miles (24km) east as the crow flies. It's hardly a straight shot for drivers: continue on Highway 260 for 10 miles (16km), then drop south on Highway 373 for 5 miles (8km) until it dead-ends in the village. But Greer, nestled at an elevation of 8,500ft (2,600 meters) in a beautiful valley at the headwaters of the Little Colorado River, is worth the trip. It's the kind of stopped-in-time place with local characters and friendly innkeepers that seems to have stepped right out of the mythical Brigadoon.

Small-town memories

Greer was originally called Lee Valley after Mormon pioneer Willard Lee, who founded the town as a farming community in 1879. The name was changed in 1898, at the request of the post office, to honor America Vespucius Greer, a prominent Mormon. It was the generous hospitality and good cooking of townspeople like Molly Butler, however, that attracted famous guests like President Theodore Roosevelt and writer Zane Grey, who spent days hunting cougar and

Father and Son Team

"Civilization? I have always avoided it whenever possible." So said explorer, naturalist, and writer James Willard Schultz, author of 37 books, who, in 1914, moved into a cabin in Greer, where he wrote, among other books, *In the Great Apache Forest: The Story of a Lone Boy Scout*, a tale inspired by the World War I adventures of Molly Butler's children, George and Hannah Crosby.

Schultz, a refugee from a wealthy East Coast family, moved out west as a young man and had lived for many years among the Blackfoot Tribe in Montana, the subject of his first book, *My Life as an Indian* (1907). He dubbed his new home Apuni Oyis (Butterfly Lodge) and was soon joined by his half-Blackfoot son, Hart Merriam, or Lone Wolf, a popular American Indian artist.

Lone Wolf found inspiration here for paintings and sculptures of Western scenes, purchased by such luminaries as Herbert Hoover and Mrs. Calvin Coolidge. Lone Wolf inherited the cabin in the mid-1920s and lived here on and off until his death in 1970. Butterfly Lodge is now on the National Register of Historic Places and has been converted into a museum (open summer weekends only; tel: 928-735-7514) containing Schultz's writing desk, Lone Wolf's paintings and other memorabilia.

Recommended Restaurants on page 265

bear in the backcountry guided by Molly's husband John. True, the 1908 **Molly Butler Lodge** hasn't been quite the same since Aunt Molly died, although new owners are trying to breathe some life into the aging hostelry. But no matter. You can have a fish fry or a steak here for old times' sake and stay at one of the other lodges in the valley. Your best bet for consistently good food and lodging in Greer is the privately owned **Greer Lodge Resort** (tel: 928-735-7216; www.greerlodgeaz.com), which offers a woodsy central lodge and rooms, rustic and luxury cabins, the award-winning Red Setter bed-and-breakfast inn, and two attractive restaurants overlooking the meadows.

The down-home **White Mountain Lodge** is a good choice. It's housed in the 1892 Lund Home, Greer's oldest residence, and offers guest rooms and modern log cabins on the edge of a beautiful riverside meadow. **Greer Lakes Recreation Area**, which surrounds Greer, has cross-country skiing and hiking trails and four campgrounds with fishing.

Memories of John and Molly Butler remain strong for Wink Crigler, Molly's

granddaughter, who, with her sister Sug (short for Sugar), now operates the family's 1889 **X Diamond** and **MLY Ranch** over the hill from Greer. Flyfishing, horseback riding, roundups, and an archaeological dig and massage are offered on this 20,000-acre (8,100-hectare) working ranch, 7 miles (11km) west of **Eagar** ㉒, off Highway 260. Don't pass up a chance to visit **Wink's Little House Museum** (tours by reservation; tel: 928-333-2286; admission charge). Begun in 1990 as a memorial

The White Mountains are crisscrossed with Nordic skiing and snowshoeing trails.

BELOW: Lake of the Woods outside Pinetop-Lakeside.

Bold black-on-white designs are a common feature of Mogollon and Ancestral Puebloan pottery.

BELOW: Raven Site Ruin, a Mogollon pueblo above the Little Colorado River.

to her late husband Oscar, a rodeo champ, the museum's collection of finely tooled saddles and trophies has swelled to include pioneer tools, the buggy used in John Wayne's 1960 movie *The Alamo*, and vintage clothing. The *pièces de résistance*, however, are the antique music machines, including nickelodeons, pianolas, and one of only 700 violin "virtuosas" in the world, which Wink plugs in and brings to toe-tapping life during her two-hour tour. If the Smithsonian is America's Attic, the Little House Museum is surely Arizona's.

Mogollon ruins

The Little House Museum is one of the undiscovered delights of the White Mountains, and so is the large number of relatively unvisited prehistoric Mogollon Indian ruins throughout the mountains. The Mogollon culture originated in the mountains of southwestern New Mexico, where they lived on ridges and farmed corn, beans, and squash in the valleys, supplementing their diet with deer, antelope, rabbit, and other game.

They were the first people in the Southwest to make pottery, which they learned from their trading partners to the south. Beautiful black-on-white pottery decorated with images of lizards, traders, macaws, and other daily scenes characterize the Mimbres branch of the Mogollon culture and is highly prized among collectors today. After AD 1000, the Mogollon moved north to Arizona's east-central mountains, where they merged with the Ancestral Pueblo culture. Archaeologists can still identify their settlements by the presence of their signature pottery style and other cultural traits such as the construction of rectangular kivas, or ceremonial chambers.

Casa Malpais

Springerville in Round Valley is situated in the heart of Mogollon country, with one of the most important ruins, **Casa Malpais National Historic Landmark ㉓**, 2 miles (3km) north of downtown, perched on five basalt terraces above the Little Colorado River. The 14-

Recommended Restaurants on page 265

acre (6-hectare), two-story **House of the Badlands**, as it was called by 19th-century Spanish-speaking residents, is one of the most complex Mogollon communities yet discovered and caused excitement in the archaeological world when excavations began there in the 1940s. The site was occupied between AD 1266 and the late 1400s by an estimated 300 people. Unusual features include a large rectangular kiva, evidence that sacred ceremonies and burials took place in natural fissures throughout the site, and a solar calendar.

Tours of the pueblo are conducted daily (weather permitting) and begin at **Casa Malpais Museum and Visitor Center** on Main Street (open daily 8am–4pm; tel: 928-333-5375; call for reservations; admission charge), which has exhibits on Casa Malpais and Springerville, a film about excavations at the pueblo, and information on the area.

Wildlife lovers won't want to miss the relatively unpublicized 1,362-acre (551-hectare) **Sipe White Mountain Wildlife Area** ㉔ (open daily, tel: 928-367-4281; free), 2 miles (3km) south of Springerville. Administered by Arizona Game and

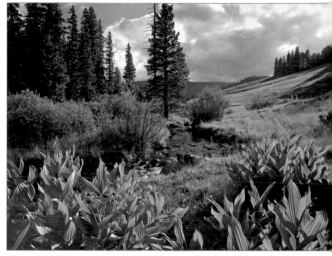

Fish, Sipe Ranch is an old ranch homestead that was purchased to protect the threatened Little Colorado spinedace, a tiny native fish. It also provides winter range for up to 800 elk and 175 acres (70 hectares) of wetlands used by hundreds of bird species, including migratory avocets, sandpipers, white-faced ibis, and other waterfowl. Ask for information on how to reach the Mogollon petroglyph panel near the old homestead.

Corn lilies and sneezeweed grow along a brook near the headwaters of the Little Colorado River.

BELOW: 11th-century pueblo ruins

Cooling off in a mountain stream.

The source of the basalts used in construction of Casa Malpais is obvious when you stand atop the pueblo and look south. The **Springerville Volcanic Field**, the third-largest volcanic field in the continental United States, covers 1,158 sq miles (3,000 sq km) and contains 405 vents, craters and shield volcanoes, which began erupting 3 million years ago. To the south of Greer is the older **White Mountain Volcanic Field**, created by a different type of volcanism 8 million years ago. Baldy Peak, sacred to the Apache, is at its center. The youngest lava flows are from Twin Knolls, northwest of Springerville, a double volcano that erupted twice.

The **Renée Cushman Art Collection Museum** ㉕ (150 N. Aldrice Burk, Springerville; tel: 928-333-4514; tours by appointment year-round) can be found in the town of **Springerville**. Renee Cushman was the daughter of a prominent

European artist. Her family traveled extensively around the world. After marrying for a second time, she moved to the White Mountain Hereford Ranch in Springerville. When she died in 1969, she left her entire art collection to the Church of Jesus Christ of Latter-day Saints. The museum is in one wing of the LDS Meeting House in Springerville. The building is appropriately designed to show her treasured pieces, which include three ink drawings by Tiepolo, a complete set of Austrian china, a priceless drawing by Rembrandt, and a single piece by Sir Godfrey Kneller. Many of the pieces range from the Renaissance period to the 20th century.

This is another unique White Mountains museum, not least for its charming tour guide L. D. Austin, an elderly Mormon whose knowledge of this extraordinary world-class art collection is seemingly limitless.

The roads less traveled

Two breathtaking but white-knuckle drives wind precipitously from the mountains to the low desert. The first, the 123-mile (198-km) **Springerville to**

Recommended Restaurants on page 265

Clifton Highway (Route 666/191), follows the eastern edge of Apache-Sitgreaves National Forest and the Arizona–New Mexico border. It reaches an elevation of 9,000ft (2,700 meters) at Hannagan Meadow, then drops into the copper mining towns of Morenci and Clifton – a plummet of 5,000ft (1,525 meters). The route, one of the country's first federal road projects, opened in 1926, with 5,000 dignitaries puttering into the high country in their Model T Fords for the ribbon-cutting festivities, which included barbecued bear. Things have quieted down considerably since then. This is now one of the state's most beautiful but lonesome highways, driven only by a handful of motorists each day.

The road has long been promoted as the route that Spanish conquistador Francisco Vásquez de Coronado took through the mountains into New Mexico in 1540. Some historians now dispute that, including former Interior Secretary Stewart Udall, who grew up in St. Johns and is an authority on Coronado's route through the Southwest. Udall believes the Coronado expedition took a route 40 miles to the west, in the gentler topography of the Natanes Plateau.

Check road conditions before starting out. Snow may make sections of the road impassable in winter. The road leaves Springerville and heads south through **Nutrioso** ㉖, another odd local name derived from the Spanish words for beaver (*nutri*) and bear (*oso*). It was home to Arizona's first forest ranger at the turn of the century, when Apache National Forest was part of Black Mesa Forest Reserve.

The next community is 8,050-ft (2,450-meter) **Alpine** ㉗, originally known as Bush Valley, near the headwaters of the San Francisco River, where Escudilla Mountain, which features prominently in Aldo Leopold's writings, dominates the horizon. There is good camping at **Luna Lake**, a wildlife refuge where you can see bald and golden eagles and look for Luna agate. Dog sled races are held here in January.

The road's halfway point is **Hannagan Meadow** ㉘, named for Robert Hannagan, a Nevada miner who had a cattle ranch here in the 1870s. Legend has it that Hannagan racked up $1,200 in debt to some neighbors, who chained him to a tree until his son arrived from New Mexico to bail him out.

Hannagan Meadow Lodge (tel: 928-339-4370; www.hannaganmeadow.com), renovated in 1996, was built at the same time as the road for travelers making the two day trip into the high country; it's still a logical place to gas up, stop for lunch, or spend the night in one of the rustic cabins. **Hannagan Meadow Cross-Country Ski Trail** starts nearby and has 12 miles (19km) of backcountry paths.

Dangerous curves

South of Hannagan Meadow, the road begins to live up to its reputation as one of the best "serious-drivers' roads in America," with sharp hairpins that make a slalom course look straight. Step out of the car for some calming breaths at the Blue Vista overlook, on the edge of the 2,000-ft (600-meter) Mogollon Rim, and look down into the pinyon-juniper forests and savannah

> *We abuse land because we regard it as a commodity belonging to us. When we see land as a community to which we belong, we may begin to use it with love and respect.*
>
> —Aldo Leopold

BELOW: a scenic road winds through Apache-Sitgreaves National Forest.

The Salt River forms a natural boundary between the San Carlos and White Mountain Apache reservations.

BELOW:
Aravaipa Canyon.

grasslands of the upper Sonoran ecosystem, 4,000ft (1,200 meters) below.

To the east are the **Blue Range Mountains**, where, since 1997, several packs of Mexican wolves have been released. The Blues contain the last designated primitive area in the National Forest System and are a fine place to lose yourself for a while on foot. Simply turn off, park, and start walking. Perhaps you'll get lucky and hear a wolf howl, glimpse one of the resident herds of Rocky Mountain bighorn sheep, or surprise a blue heron on a creek.

Copper country

Twelve miles (19km) farther and the road drops below the Mogollon Rim into copper country. **Morenci ㉙** is a mining town owned by the Phelps Dodge company (free tours are given on weekdays by appointment). Arizona isn't called the

Copper State for nothing, and Morenci is the leading copper producer in the USA. But at a cost. The open-pit mine, built in 1937, gradually swallowed the old town of Morenci; today's community is a modern replacement. **Clifton ㉚**, on the other hand, retains much of its historic charm. Nestled in a rugged canyon carved by the San Francisco River, the former copper-mining town still has a number of historic buildings, including the 1912 Southern Pacific Depot, Clifton Jail (which was blasted from a cliff face), and the Chase Creek Historic District with its outstanding Territorial architecture.

From Clifton, continue south to the junction with Highway 70 and head west through the cotton-growing town of **Safford ㉛**. Looming more than 8,000ft (2,400 meters) above Safford is 10,720-ft (3,270-meter) **Mount Graham ㉜**, home of **Mount Graham International Observatory** (Fri–Sat 6pm–10pm). This University of Arizona observatory houses several huge telescopes and has been controversial from the start because it impinges on the habitat of the Mount Graham red squirrel. Safford's science, culture, and education center – **Discov-**

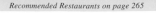
Recommended Restaurants on page 265

ery Park – has a 12-passenger spaceship simulator that gives visitors a virtual tour of the solar system and a 20-inch telescope. Mount Graham visitor center is in Discovery Park (open to the public Fri 6pm–10pm, Sat 4pm–10pm; tours of the observatory May–Nov by reservation; tel: 928-428-6260; admission charge). The 35-mile (56-km) **Swift Trail Parkway** ascends the mountain; camping, hiking, and fishing are available in Coronado National Forest until snow halts access.

North of Safford is an unpaved road leading west into **Aravaipa Canyon Wilderness Preserve ㉝** (open daily; tel: 928-828-3443). The Nature Conservancy protects 7,000 acres (2,800 hectares) of this magical 10-mile-long (16-km) canyon, where author Ed Abbey wrote movingly of encountering a mountain lion along Aravaipa Creek at dusk.

You can hope for a precious encounter with one of the big cats or perhaps a less intimidating bobcat, a rare bighorn sheep or more than 200 bird species. Camping and hiking are only allowed throughout this remote canyon with a permit from the Bureau of Land Management in Safford (tel: 928-348-4400).

Globe and the Salt River

Highway 70 continues to **Globe ㉞**, the site of enormous silver and copper deposits, which led to boom growth between 1870 and 1920 and the success of the Old Dominion Copper Company, one of the world's largest copper-mining operations. You won't miss the enormous man-made terraces on the north side of town; they look almost extraterrestrial.

Globe's name came from the extraction of a large, orb-shaped piece of silver with what appeared to be a rough outline of the continents upon it.

Downtown Globe retains a 19th-century feel, and you can take a historic walking tour of 25 buildings ranging from the 1906 Gila County Courthouse (now the Cobre Valley Center for the Arts) to the "Oldest Woolworths in the West" (1916). Homey Globe was one of contrarian Ed Abbey's favorite Arizona towns. The main reason

The Salt River Canyon.

BELOW: the Large Binocular Telescope, one of the world's largest, at Mount Graham

Besh-Ba-Gowah ruins have been partially restored.

BELOW:
the Salt River
Canyon Bridge.

to stop in Globe is to view the large Salado ruin known by the Apache name **Besh-Ba-Gowah**, or House of Metal, for the abundance of precious metals that attracted newcomers in the late 1800s. Besh-Ba-Gowah was begun in 1225 and abandoned around 1400.

The 200-room pueblo was first excavated in the 1930s, but excavation has been sporadic ever since. Now partially stabilized, the ruin is still revealing its secrets. Large quantities of beautiful polychrome pottery have been uncovered at the site and are on display in the small museum.

North of Globe, Highway 60 skirts the **San Carlos Apache Reservation ㉟**. Globe was originally part of the reservation, but when silver was found there in 1870 the boundaries were redrawn, causing prolonged bitterness with the San Carlos Apache, who allied themselves with Geronimo and other warring Apache leaders. The San Carlos Apache now hold

the popular **Apache Days** in Globe in October and one of Arizona's best rodeos in November in San Carlos. **San Carlos Apache Culture Center** (US 70, milepost 272, Mon–Fri 9am–5pm; tel: 928 475-2894; www.sancarlosapache.com) has a special exhibit, "Window on Apache Culture," which describes the Apache's spiritual beginnings and important ceremonies such as that of Changing Woman, an ancient female puberty ritual.

Highway 60 follows a dramatic twist-and-turn route through the **Salt River Canyon ㊱**. The Jesuit missionary Padre Eusebio Francisco Kino visited this canyon in 1698, naming it Salado for the salt springs in the area (eventually that name would also be applied to the prehistoric people who once lived here).

The bridge over the Salt River and the beginning of the climb into the White Mountains marks the boundary between the San Carlos Apache Reservation and White Mountain Apache Reservation, which lies to the north. This is the second of the beautiful scenic byways on this tour and a perfect sunset drive, when lengthening shadows in the canyon deepen the drama of the colorful formations. ❑

RESTAURANTS

Prices for a three-course dinner per person, excluding tax, tip, and beverages:

$ = under $20
$$ = $20–45
$$$ = $45–60
$$$$ = over $60

373 Bar and Grill Restaurant

Greer Lodge, 44 Main Street, Greer
Tel: (928) 735-7216
Open: B, L, D daily year round **$–$$**
This attractive custom-built log restaurant is the hub of Greer Lodge and Greer's most pleasant rendezvous. It has a stone fireplace, huge windows, a wraparound deck, and stunning views across the meadows to the Little Colorado River. Stick with the award-winning hourly ranch style cuisine and you won't be disappointed. Steak, prime rib, and fish dishes such as salmon, halibut, and trout almondine shine here. Breakfast includes egg dishes, pancakes, waffles, and lighter options. The chef uses organic produce whenever possible.

Amberian Peaks Lodge and Restaurant

One Main Street, Greer
Tel: (928) 735-9977
Open: B, L, D daily, summer only **$–$$**
An elegant bed-and-breakfast lodge in Greer, Amberian has a romantic bistro that's just the thing for a quiet dinner. The chef has a way with buffalo and salmon. The focus is specialty pizzas in the casual

Cantina, a bar with a huge log deck. Take-out pizza is available.

Booga Reds

521 E. Main Street, Springerville
Tel: (928) 333-2640
Open: B, L, D daily **$**
Hungry travelers stop here for comfort food – roast beef, mashed potatoes and gravy, pancakes, homemade pie – as well as a selection of Mexican dishes.

Christmas Tree

453 N. Woodland Road, Pinetop
Tel: (928) 367-3107
Open: L, D daily **$$**
Who could resist a steaming bowl of chicken and dumplings? That's the specialty of this out-of-the-way country restaurant, which also offers such satisfying entrees as beef stroganoff, lamb chops, roasted honey duck, New York strip steak, and barbecued ribs.

Corky's BBQ Hamburgers & Ice

580 W. Cleveland Street, St Johns
Tel: (928) 337-2388 **$**
Under new ownership, this burger place in St Johns is popular with the locals.

Hannagan Meadow Lodge

Highway 191 22 miles (35km) south of Alpine
Tel: (928) 339-4370
Open: B, L, D daily **$–$$**
Diners can watch deer and elk browse in the meadow around this rustic lodge's restaurant, a lovely room with wood beams and

linen-covered tables. The menu offers a choice of hearty steaks, burgers, and chops, as well as trout, grilled salmon, jumbo fried shrimp, and baked chicken with lime-butter sauce.

Mesa Italiana Restaurant

2318 E. Navajo Boulevard, Holbrook
Tel: (928) 524-6696
Open: L, D daily **$–$$**
The best Italian restaurant in Holbrook offers some great entrees. Try baked ziti or the chicken Jerusalem, a delicious melange of chicken breast sauteed with butter, garlic, artichoke hearts, mushrooms, and shrimp and covered in a white-wine and lemon sauce.

Molly Butler Lodge

109 Main Street, Greer
Tel: (928) 735-7226
Open: L, D daily **$–$$**
Mormon pioneers Molly and John Butler built their early 1900s homestead in Greer, a tiny forested community next to the Apache reservation. While John served as hunting guide to Theodore Roosevelt and writer Zane Grey, Molly was famous for her home cooking. The food here is still worth an overnight trip to one of Greer's bed-and-breakfasts or the Greer Lodge cabin resort. Try the aged steaks, prime rib, and perfectly cooked halibut. There's usually a fish fry on Friday night. All dishes are accompanied by baked potato, salad, fresh veggies, and warm bread.

Licaro's

571 W. Deuce of Clubs, Show Low
Tel: (928) 537-8220
Open: B, L, D daily **$**
Generous portions of Mexican food, steak, seafood, pasta, and salad are the formula at this Western-style restaurant.

Pasta House

2188 E. White Mountain Boulevard, Pinetop
Tel: (928) 367-2782
Open: L, D daily **$–$$**
Homemade pasta is the cornerstone of the menu, though you will also find veal, chicken, and fish.

Turquoise Room

La Posada Hotel, 303 E. 2nd Street, Winslow
Tel: (928) 289-2888
Open: B, L, D daily **$–$$$**
Classically trained English chef John Sharpe creates food worthy of a last meal on earth at his excellent restaurant inside Winslow's restored La Posada, originally designed by architect Mary Colter for railroad concessionaire Fred Harvey. Sharpe's award-winning Southwestern food is a homage to local, sustainably produced foods and native cultures as well as the glory days of Harvey House restaurants and, not incidentally, his English roots. Among the winners are a yin-yang corn and black-bean soup, a hearty Native American cassoulet, piki bread with Hopi hummus, a classic prime rib au jus, Navajo churro lamb, and elk medallions. Save room for bread pudding, gelato, and flaky pies.

Recommended Restaurants on pages 283–5

PHOENIX AND ENVIRONS

Summer heat can purge the mind of lucidity, but air conditioning – and a strong economy – made the Valley of the Sun one of America's fastest-growing metropolitan areas

Widespread irrigation and post-World War II air-conditioning were primarily responsible for the growth of the modern metropolis of **Phoenix ③**, which now has 3.6 million people, making it the US's sixth largest city. With the long-overdue arrival of the first 20 miles (32km) of METRO light rail service connecting communities throughout the Valley of the Sun in December 2008, and 37 miles (60km) of extensions already approved, inroads are being made into Phoenix's near-total dependence on automobiles and its accompanying traffic headaches and smog.

Solar power, alternative fuels, and green building have become a cause celebre for the city and some private developers. A citywide water conservation education program has reduced water usage by 20 percent in the past 20 years. Today, Phoenix uses just 3 percent groundwater from its aquifers – down from a high of 35 percent in the profligate 1980s; 90 percent of water greening up Phoenix's 200-plus golf courses, irrigating crops, and used in award-winning riparian habitat restoration projects is reclaimed. Drought-tolerant xeriscaping and water-catchment devices are, finally, the height of fashion.

Risen from the ashes

Long ago there existed here a civilization adapted to the harsh conditions of the Salt River Valley. As early as 500 BC, the Hohokam people developed an intricate system of canals for irrigating fields of corn, beans, squash, and cotton. Remains of that ancient system were absorbed and expanded in 1868 by the Swilling Irrigation Canal Co., the first Anglo organization to stake claims in the long-deserted valley. The following year, their settlement was named Phoenix by an Englishman who saw a new civilization rising like the mythical bird from the ashes of the vanished Hohokam.

What rose from the ashes was an aggressive ranching community that catered to miners and military outposts.

Main attractions
HERITAGE SQUARE
PHOENIX ART MUSEUM
HEARD MUSEUM
ARIZONA BILTMORE HOTEL
COSANTI
PUEBLO GRANDE
TALIESIN WEST
APACHE TRAIL

PRECEDING PAGES: Superstition Mountains. **LEFT:** teeing off at a Scottsdale resort. **BELOW:** mini mariachi.

Frank Lloyd Wright left an indelible mark on the Phoenix cityscape.

Canals were extended through the alluvial valley, watering fields of cotton and alfalfa, pastures for cattle, and rows of citrus to the horizon's edge. Water storage began on a grand scale with construction of Roosevelt Dam, dedicated in 1911 and still the world's largest masonry dam, on the Salt River some 90 miles (145km) upstream from Phoenix.

Three more dams on the Salt, and two on its major tributary, the Verde, allowed agriculturalists to send water where they liked. The Salt River itself became the driest place in the region.

Residents with long memories recall the 1930s as a Phoenician golden age. Those who couldn't afford the Arizona Biltmore Hotel found it too snobbish anyway and frequented a lively downtown that still retained a Spanish-American flavor. In summer, when temperatures often exceeded 110°F (43°C) and daytime highs did not dip below the hundreds for months, locals complained less about the heat than they boasted of tricks to stay cool. It was common sport

to be pulled on an aquaplane along the canals, holding a rope from a car.

Phoenix was transformed forever by World War II. The open desert was ideal for aviation training, and much of Phoenix became something of an extension of nearby Luke Air Force Base. Aviation equipment companies moved into the valley and even the cotton fields turned out silk for parachutes. It is less known that Phoenix had internment camps for German prisoners of war, and many of the prisoners, as susceptible to the desert's allure as anyone else, remained in the area after the war to become a part of the community.

The military revolutionized Phoenician life with a device called air-conditioning. The city had previously seen use of the evaporative or "swamp" cooler, but now there was genuine refrigeration. Suddenly Phoenix was a year-round possibility for those who couldn't stand the heat. The great migration was on. Camelback Mountain, at whose feet lay the most elegant dude ranches, was engulfed by suburbia. To the east, greater Phoenix swallowed up the once-isolated communities of Scottsdale, Tempe, Mesa, and

Apache Junction. Golf courses replaced dude ranches and resorts sprouted like desert flowers after a thunderstorm.

The stereotypical newcomer over the past decades has been the snowbelt retiree living in rule-bound planned communities of upscale houses or proletarian acres of mobile homes. But the more recent influx of career-oriented young people in high-tech industries has so altered the population in the past couple of decades that the average resident within city limits, contrary to popular belief, is younger than the national average.

Downtown Phoenix

The geographical setting of Phoenix is impressive. To the east soar the massive Four Peaks and the flank of the Superstition Mountains, while the Sierra Estrella, sacred to the Gila and Salt River tribes, rides the southwest horizon in dorsales of blue silk. Hemming in the city north and south are lower ranges of Precambrian gneiss and schist, framing the Phoenix trademark peak of Camelback Mountain, a freestanding, rosy, recumbent dromedary with a sedimentary head and granitic hump, and recently renamed Piestewa

Peak, a landmark that now honors fallen Iraq war hero Lori Piestewa, the first Indian woman to die in a US conflict.

And what of the city itself? Even by US standards, Phoenix is a young city and, like others of its age, lacks a strong personality, seeming at times to be rather sterile, especially when many of its residents retreat into the air conditioning in summer. But downtown Phoenix has blossomed into an impressive cultural center with an array of performing-arts venues and expansions of the top-rated Heard and Phoenix art museums, displaying a new maturity in this young city.

Heritage Square Ⓐ (115 N. Sixth Street; tel: 602-262-5029; free), a block east of the **Civic Plaza**, is what remains of the city's Victorian heritage and is part of downtown's Copper Square and **Heritage and Science Park**. Most striking of Heritage Square's 11 buildings – some of them, like the Lath House Pavilion, quite modern – is the **Rosson House** (Wed–Sat 10am–3.30pm, Sun noon–3.30pm; closed mid-Aug through Labor Day; tel: 602-262-5029; charge), built in 1895 and once one of the most prominent homes in Phoenix. Some of the other houses here,

Temperatures in the Phoenix area exceed 100°F (37.8°C) on more than 90 days a year, with an average scorching high in July of 106°F (41°C).

BELOW: Rosson House, Heritage Square

Arizona Science Center.

BELOW:
Redevelopment of downtown Phoenix has given the city much-needed venues for sporting events and the arts.

Several multimillion-dollar expansions since 1997 have created a funhouse of hands-on science. The center has 300 exhibits in five themed galleries on four floors, where kids can explore inside the human body, understand networks and the digital world, experiment with solar power, and otherwise be "dazzled by science." There is an immersion theater that offers a thrilling virtual experience of different weather conditions and a flight simulator in an exhibit on aviation. Arizona's dominance as a center for astronomy is highlighted in the planetarium and a recently installed IMAX theater has been a bit with kids.

dating from the early 1900s, were moved from other locations to save them from demolition. Also part of downtown's Copper Square and Heritage and Science Park are the **Phoenix Museum of History** (open Tue–Sat 10am–5pm; tel: 602-253-2734; admission charge), with interactive exhibits of the city's development, and the **Arizona Science Center** (open daily 10am–5pm; tel: 602-716-2000; charge), housed in a beautiful $50 million building designed by famed architect Antoine Predock.

The center hosted two wildly popular traveling exhibitions in 2008. One on Human and Animal Grossology focused on the slimey, oozy, and stinky bodily functions about which kids love to ask. The other, *Narnia*, allowed visitors to enter and imagine themselves part of the two current films in the *Chronicles of Narnia* series through elaborate sets, props, and costumes. Two new IMAX films in the theater are also guaranteed hits with kids: *Deep Sea 3D* and *The Polar Express*.

Seat of government

Arizona's modest state capitol building lies 1½ miles (2.4km) to the west of downtown, along Washington Street. The **Arizona State Capitol Museum** Ⓑ (Mon–Fri 8am–5pm, Sat 11am–2pm; tel: 602-926-3620; free) uncovers some of the building's secrets. The capitol was constructed in 1899 to house the territorial government; its dome was covered in 1976 with 15 tons of copper donated by the state's mining interests. Atop the dome is *Winged Victory*, a quarter-ton

statue dating from 1899 that turns with the wind. Much of today's governing is done in adjacent modern structures, but the restored Senate and House of Representatives chambers are open to visitors. Furnishings and ornamentation throughout the building date from 1912, when Arizona became a state.

The classy **Phoenix Art Museum** Ⓒ (Tue 10am–9pm, Wed–Sun 10am–5pm, free admission Tue; tel: 602-257-1880, www.phxart.org; charge) at Central Avenue and McDowell Road, a mile (1.6km)

In addition to art exhibits, the Phoenix Art Museum presents films, lectures, workshops, and children's activities.

Paintings by Salomon de Bray (right) and Dante Gabriel Rossetti (above) at the Phoenix Art Museum's "Passport to Europe."

BELOW: Allan Houser's *Earth Song*, 1978, at the Heard Museum.

north of Heritage Park, has just completed a huge $50 million expansion that has created an entirely new four-level wing to accommodate international shows, a new lobby, and a sculpture garden. Galleries display some 17,000 individual art works by American and Asian artists, Southwest painters from the Taos School, and recent Mexican artworks. Art of the American West includes works of Thomas Moran and Frederic Remington.

The **Heard Museum** ❶ (daily 9.30am–5pm; tel: 602-252-8848; www.

heard.org; admission charge) is one of the must-sees in Phoenix, even for those travelers who aren't particularly fond of museums. It was founded in 1929 to house the Heard family's collection of American Indian art and artifacts, and it remains an exceptional collection. Two huge expansions in 1999 and 2004–5 have enhanced the visitor experience, giving the museum a major presence on Central Avenue, a few blocks north of the Phoenix Art Museum.

The museum's signature exhibit, *Home: Native People in the Southwest*, tells the story of Arizona's Indian tribes through multimedia. On the ground floor, the Crossroads Gallery and adjoining Lorena Ohl Gallery have revolving exhibits of cutting-edge Indian artists. Some 250 historic *kachina* dolls are on display in the Lincoln Gallery, along with other masterworks by native peoples of the Southwest, and two galleries on the South Courtyard Balcony level have permanent exhibits on Indian boarding schools and pottery. The Sandra Day O'Connor Gallery has displays about the museum's founders and its permanent collection.

The restaurant (there is one run by the same company in the Phoenix Art Museum), specializes in reasonably priced dishes made from all-organic produce. Phoenix feels positively European as sidewalk cafés such as these take advantage of the warm weather and Spanish courtyard ambiance.

Smaller branches of the Heard can be found in two far-flung locations in Greater Phoenix. The **Heard North** (tel: 480-488-9817) is located in an attractive building in a small shopping center, just south of Carefree. The permanent exhibit *Choices and Change: American Indian Artists in the Southwest* is well worth the drive north of downtown Scottsdale; an adjoining gallery has revolving exhibits.There is an Arcadia Farms restaurant onsite, a large gift shop, and a Sculpture and Native Plants Garden.

The **Heard West** (tel: 623-344-2200),

affiliated with the City of Surprise, is more of an educational facility but it, too, has 400 items from the Heard's permanent collections and is worth a look if you are in this neck of the woods.

A great monument to another period is the **Arizona Biltmore Hotel Resort and Spa E** (tel: 602-955-6600), 5 miles (8km) northeast of downtown and Heritage Park. With a slack economy to begin with, Phoenix hardly noticed the Great Depression of the early 1930s, living off its own agriculture and catering in

Contemporary art at a Scottsdale gallery.

BELOW LEFT: a Wright mosaic design at the Arizona Biltmore

Frank Lloyd Wright

When Frank Lloyd Wright (1869–1959) was in his sixties, an age when other men are retiring, he was designing buildings that continued to revolutionize architecture, dismissing the stagnation found in much architectural design. Indeed, the older he got, the more innovative and revolutionary his designs became. His unique Guggenheim Museum in New York City, for example, was completed in 1959, the year he died at the age of 90. From his earliest days as an architectural student in the Chicago area in the 1890s, Wright remained true to his philosophy of "organic architecture," which stated that a building should be an integral part of its natural surroundings.

"We must recognize the creative architect as poet and interpreter of life," he wrote. "This enrichment of life is the cause of architecture, as I see it." The historian Lewis Mumford wrote in 1929: "Wright has embodied in his work two qualities which will never permanently leave it – a sense of place and a rich feeling for materials." Wright's works in Phoenix, including Taliesin West and the Arizona Biltmore Hotel, on which he served as a consultant, revealed his belief that architecture should enhance both person and environment. Taliesin West, Wright's winter home and studio from 1937 to 1959, remains a school that encourages experimentation.

An oasis at the Desert Botanical Garden.

BELOW:
guests at the
Arizona Biltmore
relax in the pool.

fine style to those tourists who managed to keep their money. Built just before the crash of 1929, the Biltmore sailed in splendor through the bleakest of times. It is to the Biltmore that Phoenix owes the arrival of Frank Lloyd Wright. The hotel was originally designed by Albert Chase McArthur, a former student of Wright, who summoned the master for help. Wright came, and then stayed to create Taliesin West.

Wright probably gave more help than required, for the result was a masterpiece of textile block construction and is a delight for the eye – geometrically tidy, quietly whimsical, and aesthetically inspiring. Gutted by fire in 1973, the interior was refurnished with furniture and textile designs from all periods of Wright's career. The visitor who enters no other building in Phoenix should make it to 24th Street and Missouri to inspect the Arizona Biltmore.

A contemporary architect today who has caught worldwide attention is Paolo Soleri, an Italian who has lived in Arizona since 1956. In Scottsdale, Soleri's **Cosanti G** (open Mon–Sat 9am–5pm, Sun 11am–5pm; tel: 480-948-6145; donations accepted) offers a broad-brush overview of Soleri's architectural philosophy and of a grander site 65 miles (105km) north of Phoenix, Arcosanti. Cactus and olive trees are scattered amid Cosanti's earth-formed concrete structures, designed to maximize both ecological efficiency and use of space.

Pueblo Grande Museum and Archaeological Park G (Mon–Sat 9am–4.45pm, Sun 1pm–4.45pm, free admission Sun; tel: 602-495-0901; charge) is sited just outside the central city, wedged in between an interstate highway and the international airport. It is a confounding juxtaposition, but this ancient pueblo site is worth a look. A wheelchair-accessible trail, just over half a mile long, encircles the ruins and has numerous, well-written interpretive displays. The visitor center has artifacts from the Hohokam culture and this pueblo site.

The Hohokam people lived in southern Arizona until around AD 1450.

Experts at cultivation, the Hohokam developed a complex system of irrigation canals extending hundreds of miles; some of these canals remain today. It is conjectured that bad weather, internal conflicts, and salinization of farmland from over-irrigation may have contributed to the abandonment of the Salt River Valley in the 1400s.

The Pueblo Grande mound is actually two smaller mounds dating from around AD 1150. Less than 200 years later, the two mounds were combined into a mound the size of a football field and about 30ft (9 meters) high. Many of the buildings once on top of the mound were probably used for other purposes, including ceremonial. Immediately north of the mound, accessible by a walkway, is an excavated ball court similar to those found at ancient Maya sites in Mexico.

Beyond downtown

To the east of downtown, increasingly surrounded by the expansion of greater metropolitan Phoenix, the **Desert Botanical Garden** ❶ (open daily 8am–8pm, from 7am in summer; tel: 480-941-1225; admission charge) is located on 50 acres (20

hectares) within Papago Park. It is home to 139 rare, threatened, and endangered species of plants from around the world as well as the Sonoran Desert and is said to be the world's largest collection of desert plants living in a natural environment. Several trails lead through the plants, displays, and balmy air. The garden emphasizes, as one might expect, the Sonoran Desert of southern Arizona.

Not far away on the same road, the **Phoenix Zoo** ❶ (open daily 8am–5pm, 7am–2pm in summer; tel: 602-273-1341; admission charge) was voted the top kid-friendly destination in Phoenix in an *Arizona Republic* poll in May 2008. It has 1,200 animals housed on 125 acres (50 hectares) and 2½ miles (4km) of walking trails. The Arizona Trail features the flora and fauna of the Southwest.

Taliesin West ❶ (open daily for

Visitors explore the Phoenix Zoo on four trails: the Africa, Tropics, Arizona, and Children's Trails.

BELOW: Taliesin West was the school and winter residence of architect Frank Lloyd Wright.

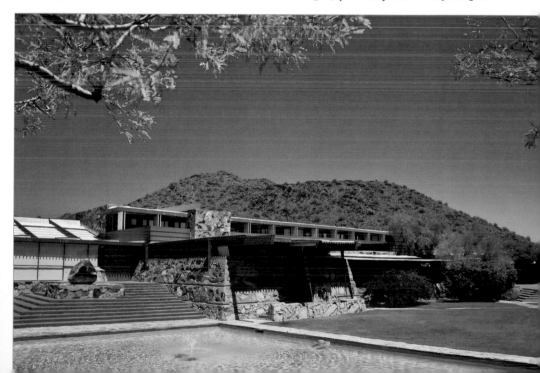

BELOW: Wright continually redesigned the interior of Taliesin West, using it as a laboratory for testing new ideas.

guided tours 9am–4pm, gift shop and grounds close at 6pm, special evening tours available at certain times of year; tel: 480-860-2700; charge), in the foothills of northeastern Scottsdale, was Frank Lloyd Wright's personal residence and architectural school.

In fact, most of the buildings and facilities continue to be an ongoing, hands-on educational exercise for architectural students. New techniques in the use of natural materials were developed here, often after the many failures that Wright considered part of the educational process. Rocks from the desert and sand from dry washes were melded into foundations, walls, and walkways, all the while following geo-metrical proportions that stayed con-stant from the smallest ornamental detail to the dimensions of the build-ings themselves.

Some of Wright's trademark tech-niques, such as the squeeze-and-release of a cramped entranceway opening into an expansive room, are apparent here. But from a distance, the buildings merge so beautifully with the landscape, they almost disappear.

Around Phoenix

Development leaped to the northwest when **Sun City**, America's first fully planned retirement community, was pitched by the Del Webb Corporation in 1960. More recently, cactus forests to the north of Phoenix have been bulldozed for a realty bonanza, and Phoenix and Scottsdale have competed in annexing the area under the pretext that they are trying only to control development. Expansion has taken such forms as trailer parks to the east, tract housing to the west, and walled-in mazes of simulated adobe ranchettes in the newly populated areas to the northeast. For those prefer-ring humanity untrammeled by nature, there are the sumptuous resorts north of Scottsdale (itself rich with resorts), three mountainside Pointe resorts on the north and south edges of Phoenix, and the ele-gant new Sheraton Wild Horse Pass Resort on the Gila River Indian Reserva-tion adjoining Chandler, southwest of Tempe. Gone is any pretense of the dude-ranch culture common before World War II, and the only reference to cactus may be worked into the macrame in the lobby. Offering golf, tennis, spas,

Recommended Restaurants on pages 283–5

pools with underwater bar stools, gourmet restaurants, nightclubs, discos, refrigerated suites, and a clientele armored in platinum credit cards, these are not desert hideaways but total-concept luxury resort complexes.

Apache Trail

Of the desert drives outside Phoenix, the most spectacular is the **Apache Trail ❸**. As an Arizona initiation rite, locals like to take visiting friends out for a drive along the curvy route. During this desert ritual, in-the-know motorists will turn to passengers just before a series of steep, hairpin turns and hoarsely whisper something to the effect that the brakes are out. If you can avoid having a local jokester at the wheel, a drive along the Apache Trail is a day well spent. Most of the chills and thrills come from the spectacular scenery along the way, including mountains, sheer cliffs, canyons, and a series of large lakes. The 45-mile-long (72-km) trail – actually a section of State Highway 88 – snakes its way past the **Superstition Mountains** and along the edge of the **Four Peaks Wilderness** in **Tonto National Forest**, just east of metro Phoenix.

The Apache Trail's moniker reflects its Native American history. Attracted by the availability of water from the Salt River and Tonto Creek, the Salado people inhabited the area as early as AD 1150. Many farmed along the flat land on the water's edge and built cliff dwellings in the mountainous terrain. Later, nomadic Apache and Yavapai Indians found sanctuary in the canyon lands.

By the 1860s, Anglo-European traders and prospectors drifted into the mountains. One such entrepreneur was German-born Jacob Waltz, who periodically came into the fledgling community of Phoenix with sacks of gold nuggets that he claimed were from his secret mine in the Superstition Mountains. Waltz died without revealing the location of his mine, and the enduring legend of the Lost Dutchman Mine

Scottsdale is known for its high-end spas and resorts.

BELOW: Pueblo style building at the Phoenician resort in Scottsdale.

A "sheriff" lays down the law in Goldfield Ghost Town.

BELOW: the Apache Trail winds along the edge of Apache Lake.

worked its way into local folklore. (Back then, apparently, nobody knew the difference between Dutch and Deutsch).

By the early 20th century, Phoenix's influential farmers and ranchers saw gold in the form of a steady water supply at the confluence of the Salt River and Tonto Creek. The federal government agreed, and the site was chosen to be one of the first major reclamation projects in the West. Funds for **Theodore Roosevelt Dam** ㊴ were approved in 1903 – as was money for the construction of a roadway linking the outskirts of Phoenix to the dam site. The roadway, of course, was the Apache Trail, which followed portions of the old Indian pathway. By the time the dam was completed in 1911 (and dedicated by its namesake), millions of pounds of freight had been hauled up the road by mule teams and wagons, and tourists, too, had gotten their first glimpses of the wild and beautiful landscape of the Superstition Mountains.

No need to worry about encountering mule teams today, although you might pass some grazing cattle or wildlife, including coyotes, rattlesnakes, various bird species, and even elusive bighorn sheep. The plant life includes the usual suspects of the upper Sonoran Desert – saguaro, prickly pear, and cholla cactus – as well as striking century plants. Look for pockets of deciduous trees along the washes and creek beds; in spring, after a rainy winter, roadsides are ablaze with lupines, Mexican gold poppies, owl's clover, and other wildflowers.

Coming from Phoenix, most visitors drive the Apache Trail south to north, picking up State Highway 88 off U.S. 60 in **Apache Junction**, a suburban community (this is a good place to get gas – there aren't any service stations along the scenic part of the road). The scenery starts just outside Apache Junction, where the road is flanked on one side by **Goldfield Ghost Town** (daily 10am–5pm, saloon to 8pm; tel: 480-983-0333; charge) and on the other by **Lost Dutchman State Park** (daily sunrise–10pm; tel: 480-982-4485; charge). The ghost town – once a mining hamlet – has been

Recommended Restaurants on pages 283–5

recreated as an Old West town, complete with shootouts, a narrow-gauge railroad, shops, and a restaurant, while the park offers hiking and trails, ranger-led programs, picnic areas, and campsites.

About 7 miles (11km) from the park is an overlook for **Canyon Lake**, the first of the three lakes created by the Roosevelt and other dams. The lake is visually striking but often crowded on warm weekends. You can rent a boat from the marina, cruise the lake aboard a steamboat, or hike one of several trails.

Tortilla Flat and beyond

A few miles beyond Canyon Lake is **Tortilla Flat**, once a rest stop for freight operators and construction workers traveling to Roosevelt Dam. Today, it's a series of false-front buildings that lures tourists with burgers and chili, drinks served in mason jars, and a gift shop stuffed with souvenirs. For good luck, pin a dollar bill to the wall of the restaurant or gift shop (the walls sport thousands) and buy a T-shirt that begs the question, "Where the hell is Tortilla Flat?"

At this point, many travelers turn back, but the most beautiful scenery begins beyond Tortilla Flat. A few miles up, the pavement ends, but the gravel road is well maintained (watch for flash flooding during heavy rains) and suitable for all vehicles except RVs and cars pulling trailers. Here, the road begins its precipitous descent into **Fish Creek Canyon**, the scenic high point of the drive and the spot where the no-brakes story usually unfolds. As the road twists downward, cliffs, mountains, and the creekbed (usually dry) become visible. Parking areas and hiking trails are at the bottom of the hill.

About 5 miles (8km) farther, you will get your first glimpse of **Apache Lake**, the most remote of the man-made lakes, hence the quietest and, some say, the loveliest. Against painted cliffs, the lake is 17 miles (27km) long and rather narrow. You can take a boat almost to the foot of Roosevelt Dam at the lake's eastern end. A small marina offers boat rentals, bait, supplies, and light meals.

At the end of the Apache Trail is the mighty Roosevelt Dam, which, at 280ft (85 meters), is the highest masonry dam in the world. There are several points from which to view the dam and **Roo-**

The Hohokam raised corn, squash, beans, and cotton by creating a flood irrigation system with over 1,000 miles (1,600km) of canals.

BELOW: the Apache Trail leads into the Superstition Mountains outside Apache Junction

Salado ruins at Tonto National Monument.

BELOW: Casa Grande Ruins National Monument.

sevelt Lake (visitor center open daily 7.45am–4.30pm; free), the largest man-made lake in central Arizona; a visitor center, boat ramps, and campgrounds are on the lakeshore.

Closing the circle

At this point, you have several choices. You can return the way you came, head back to Phoenix via Highways 188 and 87, or make a full loop around the Superstition Mountains by continuing southeast on Highway 88 and then west on U.S. 60. The latter option offers the most attractions, including **Tonto National Monument** ⑩ (open daily 8am–5pm; tel: 928-467-2241; admission charge), site of well-preserved cliff dwellings occupied by the Salado from the 13th to early 15th century. Set in natural limestone alcoves, the apartment-like structures were built of rough quartzite crudely mortared with mud. These were topped with mud-and-wood roofs, many of which can still be seen, as can the ghostly handprints of the

workers in the mud. Examples of fine Salado pottery and woven textiles are exhibited in the visitor center.

It's a scenic drive around the eastern side of the mountains through the little mining towns of **Miami** and **Superior** to the **Boyce Thompson Arboretum** ㊶ (open Sept–Apr 8am–4pm; May–Aug 6am–4pm; charge), a showplace for desert plants and wildlife founded in the 1920s by mining magnate William Boyce Thompson. Self-guiding trails wind through 35 acres (14 hectare) of beautifully landscaped grounds. A stone house listed on the National Register of Historic Places serves as an interpretive center.

A 25-mile (40-km) detour on highways 79 and 287 leads to **Casa Grande Ruins National Monument** ㊷ (open daily 8am–5pm; tel: 520-723-3172; admission charge), a prehistoric village occupied by the Hohokam until about AD 1450. The central structure is a four-story "great house" (now protected by a modern roof). Though its function remains a mystery, the presence of holes aligned with the sun on the equinox and solstices suggest that it may have been used as an observatory. ❑

RESTAURANTS

Prices for a three-course dinner per person, excluding tax, tip, and beverages:

$ = under $20
$$ = $20–45
$$$ = $45–60
$$$$ = over $60

Arcadia Farms at the Heard Museum
2301 N. Central Avenue, Phoenix
Tel: (602) 251-0204
Open: B, L daily **$–$$**
The popular Arcadia Farms franchise at the Heard Museum and nearby Phoenix Art Museum marries sophisticated, European-style museum dining with locally raised ingredients inspired by the indigenous foods of the Southwest. Reasonably priced and carefully presented artisanal salads, sandwiches, and hot specials lure both local businesspeople and museum visitors. Try wild salmon salad with cactus-pear glaze, sweet corn succotash on local greens with prickly-pear vinaigrette, chicken tamale tart, or rosemary roasted ham baguette.

Christopher's Fermier Brasserie
Biltmore Fashion Park, 2584 E. Camelback Road, Phoenix
Tel: (602) 522-2344
Open: L, D daily **$$–$$$**
Contemporary French-inspired cuisine is beautifully presented at this lively four-in-one location – a restaurant, wine bar, brewery, and cigar lounge. Highlights include the wild mushroom and foie gras soup, risotto,

and seafood cooked in a wood-burning oven. Leave room for such gloriously indulgent desserts as chocolate bread pudding.

Cowboy Ciao
7133 E. Stetson Drive, Scottsdale
Tel: (480) 946-3111
Open: L, D daily **$$–$$$**
This quirky contemporary eatery brings new meaning to the term "spaghetti Western," with playful culinary pairings such as porcini-mushroom-crusted ribeye steak, pesto-crusted elk loin, and smoked pork in chipotle balsamic barbecue sauce atop soft polenta. Sounds odd, perhaps, but the chefs manage to pull it off with an infectious sense of fun and daring.

Ed Debevic's Short Order Deluxe
2102 E. Highland Avenue, Phoenix
Tel: (602) 956-2760
Open: B, L, D daily **$**
This frenetic, old-fashioned diner has a mini-jukebox in every booth, loads of retro charm (harassed waitresses notwithstanding) and a choice of familiar, almost-like-mom's fare – burgers, fries, meatloaf, malteds, and much more.

Hap's Real Pit BBQ
101 S. 24th Street, Phoenix
Tel: (602) 267-0181
Open: L, D daily **$**
Forget the low-rent atmosphere and dig into some of the best barbecued spare ribs in the Phoenix area.

House of Tricks
114 E. Seventh Street, Tempe
Tel: (480) 968-1114
Open: L, D daily **$$**
Ask for a table on the leafy covered patio, order a round from the open-air bar, then prepare to enjoy such tasty and creative dishes as pork rack with jalapeño-orange marmalade, grilled Middle Eastern spiced salmon, or grilled Angus sirloin with mashed potatoes and shiitake mushroom gravy. A fireplace keeps patrons toasty on the rare chilly nights in winter. A winning marriage of cuisine and atmosphere.

Joe's Farm Grill
3000 E. Ray Road, Gilbert
Tel: (480) 563-4745
Open: L, D Sun–Thur **$**
The Johnston family who have created this New American restaurant in their old farmhouse have a winner here. From pesto-topped burgers and sweet potato fries to salads made with organic greens grown just a few feet away, there's something here for the whole family. Find a picnic table under the trees and kick back. There's also a coffee shop and farm stand.

Kai
Sheraton Wild Horse Pass Resort and Spa, Gila Indian Reservation, 5994 W. Wild Horse Pass Boulevard, Chandler
Tel: (602) 225-0100
Open: D Tue–Sat **$$$**
The heart and soul of Indian country beat strongly at Kai, one of Phoenix's most lauded

and reliably excellent restaurants. Executive chef Michael O'Dowd and Native American chef de cuisine Jack Strong, along with consulting chef Janos Wilder, have concocted a unique menu that pays homage to indigenous foods of the desert and beyond. Hearty Western dishes showcase produce raised by reservation school children, Sea of Cortez shrimp, tepary beans and rare seeds from the Sonoran Desert; buffalo raised by the Cheyenne Tribe; and Colorado lamb. Reserve a table on the balcony overlooking the Estrella Mountains for a great sunset.

La Hacienda
Scottsdale Princess Resort, 7575 E. Princess Drive, Scottsdale, AZ
Tel: (480) 585-4848
Open: L, D daily **$$–$$$**
Fabulous gourmet Mexican food shines at this resort restaurant. Try the *cochinillo asado*, barbecued suckling pig marinated in bitter orange, pepper, and tamarind, or *costillas de cordero*, a charbroiled rack of lamb with pumpkin-seed crust and chili plum sauce. And don't forget the margaritas!

Lon's at the Hermosa
Hermosa Inn, 5532 N. Palo Cristi Road, Paradise Valley
Tel: (602) 955-7878
Open: L, D nightly **$$$–$$$$**
This gorgeous art-filled Southwest restaurant, housed in artist Lon Megargee's old home, is a truly special place for a

romantic night out. The award-winning New American menu includes beautifully conceived meat, seafood, and pasta dishes such as pecan crusted pork, free-range chicken with goat-cheese gnocchi, and grilled filet of salmon with blackberry shellac, baby cabbages, marbled potatoes, corn, and fire-roasted tomatillo sauce. Everything on the menu is natural, organic, or sustainably sourced, and many of the greens and grains are grown by the chef on the grounds. There's a multicourse prix-fixe dinner monthly to highlight what's in season. They do a lovely brunch on Sundays.

Matt's Big Breakfast
801 North First Street, Phoenix
Tel: (602) 254-1074
Open: B, L Tue–Sun $
Fresh local food has created a big buzz at this sweet little retro diner in

an historic brick building on the corner of First and McKinley in downtown Phoenix. Chef Matt Pool uses organic produce, honey, cage-free eggs, and hormone-free meats to create healthy comfort food, such as eggs and thick-sliced bacon, stacked pancakes, cobb salad, salami scramble, omelettes, chili, burgers, juicy chicken sandwiches, and rosemary fries. Get here early to snag a seat. It closes at 2.30pm.

Palatte
606 N. Fourth Avenue, Phoenix
Tel: (602) 462-9400
Open: B, L Tue–Sun $
This shabby-chic restaurant is set in a 1914 home in downtown Phoenix, one of a new breed of nostalgia-provoking, inexpensive diners that Phoenicians are flocking to these days. Breakfast is the main reason to go. Try

roasted sweet potato pancakes topped with spiced mascarpone and toasted pecans or one of the "mishmashes," eggs fried with an assortment of ingredients. The beef sandwich (slow-braised, grass-fed beef with mashed white beans and olive gremolata on focaccia) is popular at lunchtime.

Pane Bianco
4404 N. Central Avenue, Phoenix
Tel: (602) 234-2100
Open: Tue–Sat 11am–3pm $
When local foods booster Chris Bianco is not cooking pizza in his popular dinner pizzeria in downtown Phoenix, you'll find him over at his new bakery on Central, selling rustic sandwiches made on his own hearty bread to the lunchtime crowd. Take-out only.

Pho Dinh Restaurant
2025 N. Dobson Road, Chandler
Tel: (480) 812-1877
Open: L, D daily $
Set in a corner of a large Asian marketplace known as Lee Lee, this casual Vietnamese restaurant serves authentic and reasonably priced food. Sample such specialties as barbecued pork with char-broiled ground shrimp; spicy salt-and-pepper squid; rice noodles tossed with shrimp, beef, pork, and chicken; and sizzling clay hot pots loaded with meat, shrimp, and veggies atop rice.

Pizzeria Bianco
623 E. Adams Street, Phoenix
Tel: (602) 258-8300
Open: Tue–Sat 5pm–10pm $$
Chef-owner Chris Bianco

helped found the Phoenix branch of Slow Food. In his charming but very tiny pizzeria, in an old brick home in historic Heritage Square, he conjures Phoenix's most authentic Neapolitan pizza, such as the Margherita, using fresh-tasting sauces made from heirloom organic tomatoes, homemade mozzarella, and other local organic ingredients.. Only reservations for large groups are taken, but Bianco has a method in his madness. He owns a wine bar next door, where patrons relax with a glass of wine and get to know their neighbors, thereby building community in this sprawling metropolis.

Quiessence Restaurant and Wine Bar
The Farm at South Mountain, 6106 S. 32nd Street, Phoenix
Tel: (602) 276-6360
Open: D only Tue–Sun (closed July) $$–$$$
The lovely rural setting – on a 12-acre (5-hectare) organic farm south of Phoenix – makes this wonderful restaurant inside a historic farmhouse unique in bland Phoenix. But it's the amazing food – all of it fresh, organic, and sustainably sourced – that takes Quiessence to the next level. Everything is simply prepared, with an eye to marrying flavors and textures, allowing the ingredients to step forward and shine. The menu changes daily, reflecting what's available. One signature dish is braised lamb with roasted vegetables, procured from a local sheep farmer. Six-course sampling menus are reasonably priced. Reservations

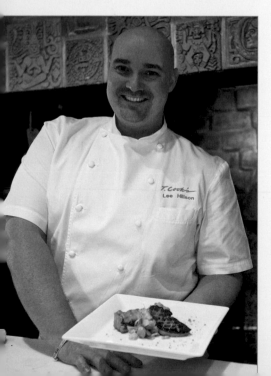

LEFT AND TOP RIGHT: resorts like the Royal Palms in Scottsdale serve both classic and cutting-edge cuisine.

are strongly suggested. If you're here between September and April, come early and enjoy visiting South Mountains organic gardens, shops, and two other cafés. They are closed in summer.

RadioMILANO
3950 E. Campbell, Phoenix
Tel: (602) 956-6600
Open: D only daily $–$$
All tables are shared, European-style, at this neighborhood hangout. The Italian menu includes deviled eggs with bacon and chives, risotto, roast chicken, an assortment of pastas, and wild mushroom meat loaf. Spaghetti and meatballs, buttered noodles, and pizzeta are free for kids if they eat before 7pm. They serve interesting cocktails and many wines and beers by the glass.

RoxSand
Biltmore Fashion Park, 2594 E. Camelback Road, Phoenix
Tel: (602) 381-0444
Open: L, D daily $$–$$$
The owner of this slick contemporary restaurant is a proponent of "fusion cuisine," a cross-cultural approach to combining flavors and ingredients. It's not unusual to open the meal with a Middle Eastern braised curried chicken, rice tamale with Thai peanut sauce, or short ribs with Korean soy and honey marinade, then move to air-dried duck with buckwheat crepes and pistachio-onion marmalade, or chicken breast with Louisiana étouffée sauce. Leave the jeans at home.

The Stockyards
5001 E. Washington Street, Phoenix
Tel: (602) 273-7378

Open: L, D daily $–$$
Steakhouse with 19th-century decor and Old West specialties like Rocky Mountain oysters (the tender bits you remove to make a bull into a steer) and hand-cut beef.

San Carlos Bay Seafood Restaurant
1901 E. McDowell Restaurant, Phoenix
Tel: (602) 340-0892
Open: L, D daily $
Mexican seafood is the bill of fare here. Highlights include a tender octopus cocktail; fiery shrimp *endiablados*; a rich "seven-seas" stew stocked with crab, cockles, shrimp, and squid; shrimp with tangy green-chili sauce; and *pescado a la Veracruzana* (grilled snapper with olives, tomatoes, onions, and peppers).

T. Cook's
Royal Palms Resort, 5200 E. Camelback Road, Phoenix
Tel: (602) 808-0766
Open: L, D daily $$–$$$
This Mediterranean-style restaurant drips romance. It's hard to go wrong here. Poultry, beef, and pork cooked in a wood-burning oven are popular, although other dishes such as paella and sauteed lobster are equally tempting. Chocoholics may want to skip dinner and move directly to the heavenly chocolate sampler.

Taggia
Fire and Sky Resort, 4925 N. Scottsdale Road, Scottsdale
Tel: (480)-424-6095
Open: B, L, D daily $$–$$$$
Situated inside a dramatically remodeled motel, this Italian restaurant is a foodie haven. Italian chef Claudio Urchiuoli, a proponent of Phoenix's

Slow Food movement, creates authentic coastal Italian seafood using ingredients sourced locally and from sustainable fisheries worldwide. The result is unpretentious rustic Italian cuisine that celebrates both ingredients and flavor. Urchiuoli isn't afraid to use unusual fish like bream. Other winners are hearty sausage dishes and pasta favorites like pumpkin ravioli with sage butter. For dessert, there are sinful, authentically Italian cakes handmade by Urchiuoli himself.

Wright's at the Biltmore
Arizona Biltmore Hotel, 2400 E. Missouri Avenue, Phoenix
Tel: (602) 381-7632
Open: D nightly $$–$$$$
This fine-dining restaurant in Phoenix's historic Arizona Biltmore Hotel is a treat you'll long remember. The Continental cuisine has recently been taken up a notch by the resort's new executive chef, who has created a fresh, regionally inspired menu that uses ingredients sourced at boutique farms across the country. You'll find dishes showcasing Maui goat cheese, Colorado lamb, elk from Wyoming, wild salmon from Alaska, and snails from Oregon, in addition to wild boar

medallions, buffalo tenderloin, and filet mignon. It all works beautifully, bringing back echoes of grand dining at this historic western resort in the 1920s. A feather-light soufflé flavored with chocolate, Grand Marnier, and butterscotch is a specialty. Order them at the start of the meal due to preparation time.

Zinc Bistro
15034 N. Scottsdale Road, Suite 140, Scottsdale
Tel: (480) 603-0922
Open: L, D daily $$$
In the center of the popular new Kierland Commons development on the Phoenix-Scottsdale border, this top-rated French haute-cuisine restaurant is a perfect choice for an elegant lunch or dinner. Chef-owner Matt Carter knows how to please the most refined sensibilities. The basil chicken, creamy risotto, and filet mignon are all winners. Made-to-order chocolate soufflé with Grand Marnier-infused chocolate sauce are a specialty and must be ordered at the start of the meal.

Prices for a three-course dinner per person, excluding tax, tip, and beverages:
$ = under $20
$$ = $20–45
$$$ = $45–60
$$$$ = over $60

THE HEARD MUSEUM

This remarkable museum is devoted to the heritage and living cultures and arts of Native people, with an emphasis on those of the Southwest

The museum, based in Phoenix, was founded by Maie Bartlett Heard in 1929, soon after her husband Dwight died, to house the couple's art collection. Much of the archaeological material came from La Ciudad Indian ruin, at 19th and Polk streets, which the Heards bought in 1926.

For 20 years, Mrs. Heard served as director of what was then a small family museum in a dusty one-horse western town. When she died, in 1951, the Heard grew into Arizona's premier cultural museum, adding a museum store selling authenticated Indian arts and crafts and an annual Indian Market and Fair. Following a multimillion-dollar expansion, it now has 10 galleries.

The museum's main interpretive exhibit, "HOME: Native People in the Southwest," is the best exhibit on southwestern Indian tribes in the state. Highlights include a multiscreen film; quotes and interviews from community members on the importance of family, culture, land, and languages; full-size Indian dwellings; and the Barry Goldwater and Fred Harvey collection of historic katsina, or kachina, dolls.

Other permanent exhibits include "Remembering Our Indian School Days," a poignant look at Indian boarding schools; "Around the World," featuring the Heard's global collection; and "Every Picture Tells a Story," an examination of symbols in Indian art. Changing exhibits focus on contemporary arts and crafts, such as jewelry and fashion design.

Two small satellite branches – in Scottsdale and Surprise – have permanent exhibits displaying items from the Heard collection and interesting temporary exhibits. Like the main museum, the Scottsdale branch has a store and excellent organic dining. The Surprise branch emphasizes educational workshops.

ABOVE: *Awatovi Prayers*, 2003, by Michael Kabotie, Hopi. The Heard exhibits both traditional and modern art.
RIGHT: *Niman katsina*, *c.*1983, by Hopi artist Tino Youvella. Kachina "dolls" – religious icons originally made for children – depict the ceremonial dancers who represent Hopi spirits.

ABOVE: a third phase chief's blanket by Navajo weaver Rene Begay. This style was developed in the early 1860s during the "classical" period of Navajo weaving before the Long Walk – the expulsion of the Navajo to Bosque Redondo in New Mexico. The style has been revived and refined by modern weavers.

THE INDIAN FAIR AND MARKET

Rivaling July's Santa Fe Indian Market in size and prestige, the Heard Guild's annual Indian Fair and Market, held every March on the beautiful grounds of the museum, attracts Indian vendors and art collectors from around the country and is Arizona's biggest Indian arts and crafts gathering. A total of 650 outstanding Indian artists display and sell their work at this juried show, which highlights exceptional pottery, basketry, sculpture, jewelry, paintings, weavings, and other arts by America's best Indian artists. Among the scheduled events are Indian dancing and storytelling in the amphitheater. Traditional Indian foods like Navajo fry bread and Hopi piki bread are on sale in the food booths. Every year, one outstanding Southwest artist is honored at the market.

Museum members gain early admission and purchasing privileges the first morning of the show. The new Phoenix Metro Light Rail stops at the Heard Museum, which is located at 2301 N. Central Avenue, Phoenix, a block away from the Phoenix Art Museum. The Heard is also host to a Spanish Market, held each November, devoted to the Southwest's Hispanic art and culture. For information about opening hours, exhibits, and special events, call the Heard Museum general line at (602) 252-8840 or log on to www.heard.org.

ABOVE: lectures, performances, and other special events are held at the museum's Steele Auditorium. **TOP RIGHT** a basket from the Heard family's original collection. **BELOW:** visitors can browse and purchase fine works by contemporary Native artists at the museum's Berlin Gallery.

RIGHT: a pitcher by celebrated Acoma potter Lucy M. Lewis, who revived ancient black-on-white pottery styles.
FAR RIGHT: a Hopi dancer performs at the Heard Guild Indian Fair and Market. The annual event attracts nearly 20,000 visitors and 650 artists.

SOUTHERN ARIZONA

Successive cultures – Indian, Hispanic, Anglo –
have left their mark on the region's desert
landscapes and quirky small towns

Tucson, Arizona's second-largest city and the focal point of the southern tier of the state, has a maverick streak that's characteristic of the region as a whole. Tucsonans value individuality. They tend to be politically more liberal and culturally more daring than their conservative neighbors, and, as a community, identify themselves more closely with the city's Hispanic roots.

They also share an awareness of the environment. Ringed by mountain peaks and bracketed by parklands, Tucson embraces its desert setting. A short drive from downtown leads into Tucson Mountain Park or Saguaro National Park. A bit farther on are the breezy heights of Mount Lemmon and the Santa Catalina Mountains.

An independent spirit is evident elsewhere in the south. In the old mining town of Bisbee, a coalition of artists and entrepreneurs have transformed decaying saloons into shops and restaurants and have breathed new life into the "painted ladies" once occupied by the town's thriving middle class. A similar revival occurred in Tubac, the state's oldest European settlement, founded about 1723. Had it not been for the vision of various artists and business people, the village – now a popular arts colony – might have been left to the elements. The atmosphere in Tombstone is far more commercial but no less vital. The "town too tough to die" has capitalized on Wyatt Earp's fateful encounter at the OK Corral, with staged shootouts, stagecoach rides, and an entertaining, if hokey, Old West ambience.

But the towns of southern Arizona are merely grace notes to the landscape. The Sonoran Desert is the dominant presence. Sky islands like the Chiricahua Mountains offer relief from the sere lowlands. The lush grasslands that so

enticed Spanish *rancheros* now support Arizona's small but scenic "wine country," and wetlands ranging from desert springs to the San Pedro River sustain a profusion of plant and animal life, including the thousands of migratory waterbirds that flock to the seasonal marshes of Willcox Playa.

The population grows thinner and the landscape more austere west of Tucson, where dark volcanic mountains jostle the sky. This is the homeland of the Tohono O'odham, the Desert People, whose descendants were the original masters of drawing life from this unforgiving land. ❑

PRECEDING PAGES: Presidio Historic District, Tucson. **LEFT:** Seven Falls in Bear Canyon. **TOP:** Cinco de Mayo celebration. **ABOVE LEFT:** Tempe City Hall.

Recommended Restaurants on pages 306–7

TUCSON AND ENVIRONS

Smaller and more liberal than Phoenix, with
a streak of feisty independence, Arizona's
"Old Pueblo" embraces its Hispanic roots
and scenic desert setting

Tucson ❶, or the Old Pueblo, as it's
known locally, is a modern metropolis of some 946,000 souls that has
insinuated itself across 500 sq miles
(1,300 sq km) of southern Arizona's
Sonoran Desert between five encircling
mountain ranges. Warm winters, low
year-round humidity, an unbeatable desert
setting, hundred-mile vistas, and perhaps
the easiest access to hiking, biking, camping, horseback riding, rock climbing, and
skiing of any city in the nation have lured
visitors for decades. Four-star resorts,
spas, dude ranches, historic inns, and
gourmet restaurants nudge up against
nature parks, Wild West towns, Indian
reservations, and Mexican border towns.

To get oriented and enjoy a killer sunset
view, drive up **Sentinel Peak Ⓐ**, the dark
volcanic hill west of downtown Tucson
with the whitewashed "A" (the work of
University of Arizona students since
1915). Used as a lookout by Mexican soldiers between 1821 and 1853 (hence the
name), the peak now known as "A"
Mountain offers sweeping views of the
burgeoning city, nearby mountains, and
the basin-and-range topography all the
way into Mexico, 65 miles (105km) away.

Long before Spanish, Mexican, and
Anglo settlers arrived, the Sonoran
Desert was home to the Hohokam Indians, irrigation farmers who left behind
pecked petroglyphs on basaltic boulders,
such as those at Signal Hill in Saguaro
National Park West. By the time of the
Spanish conquest, in 1540, the Hohokam
had been replaced by ancestors of

today's Tohono O'odham ("People of the
Desert," formerly known as Papago) and
Akimel O'odham ("People of the Water,"
also known as Pima) tribes, whose modern reservations adjoin Tucson. O'odham
people lived in a *rancheria*, a scattering
of huts built from mesquite limbs,
saguaro ribs and thorny ocotillo, along
the now-dry Santa Cruz River at the base
of "A" Mountain.

A rough beginning

The O'odham referred to their village as
Stjukshon (*stjuk* means "black"; *shon,*

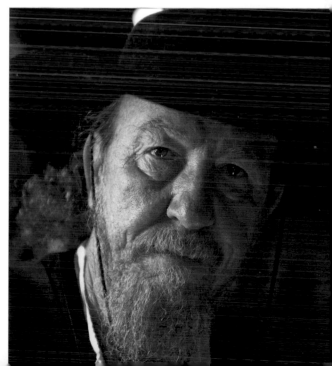

Main attractions
PRESIDIO HISTORIC DISTRICT
TUCSON MUSEUM OF ART
BARRIO HISTORIC DISTRICT
ARIZONA STATE MUSEUM
FLANDREAU SCIENCE CENTER
SAGUARO NATIONAL PARK
ARIZONA-SONORA DESERT
    MUSEUM
OLD TUCSON STUDIOS
TITAN MISSILE MUSEUM
BIOSPHERE 2

LEFT: St Augustine
Cathedral.
BELOW: an
"outlaw" at Old
Tucson Studios.

A mural by David Tineo adorns the exterior of the Tucson Museum of Art.

"hill"). This word was roughly transliterated to "Tucson" by Colonel Hugo O'Conor, an Irishman in the service of the Spanish Crown, when he was ordered to build a new garrison to protect nearby San Xavier Mission. The Tucson presidio replaced the one at Tubac in 1775, after its former commander, Juan Bautista de Anza, left to find an overland route to Alta California.

El Presidio de San Agustín del Tucson, just east of "A" Mountain, was heavily fortified with adobe walls 12ft (4 meters) high and 750ft (230 meters)

long, but soldiers found little protection here and complained that they spent more time making adobes than in military pursuits. Mexican tenure did little to improve a situation where settlers were at the mercy of Apache raiders. Even after it became American territory, Tucson remained essentially a Mexican town of miners, ranchers, and merchants. To Anglo traveler J. Ross Browne, it seemed "a city of mud boxes, dingy and delapidated, cracked and baked into a composite of dust and filth." Only with the coming of the railroad in the 1880s, linking markets across the country, did Tucson evolve from a rough Wild West outpost to a booming frontier trading center.

The old Presidio

Portions of the original Presidio wall are preserved in downtown's **Presidio Historic District ⓑ**, a good place to get a feel for Tucson's Spanish, Mexican, and Anglo heritage. Begin your historic walking tour at the **Tucson Museum of Art** (open Tue–Sat 10am–4pm, Sun noon–4pm; tel: 520-624-2333; admission charge) on the corner of Alameda and

Main Streets. Noted for its Spanish colonial paintings and furnishings, pre-Columbian artifacts from Latin America, pleasant courtyard and café (often frequented by downtown office workers), the museum's most interesting feature is the five historic houses incorporated into its layout (all open during museum hours).

La Casa Cordova, built in 1848, is Tucson's oldest home. A classic Mexican adobe with traditional saguaro rib ceiling latillas and dirt floors, it has a central courtyard and dark interior rooms that have been restored to reflect early life in the Old Pueblo, complete with beds, cribs and furnishings. One room has exhibits that trace the Presidio's history; an adjoining room contains, from November to March, the Nacimiento, a traditional Mexican nativity installation that changes yearly and uses more than 200 hand-painted figurines to create tableaux depicting the life of Christ.

In the museum's southwestern corner, two adjoining houses – the **Stevens/Duffield House**, also known as the Palice Pavilion, and the 1868 **Edward Nye Fish House**, constructed on the site of an old Mexican barracks with 15 ft (4½-

meter) ceilings and adobe walls more than 2ft (60 cm) thick – were built by wealthy merchants and were the center of social life in Tucson. The Fish House is now home to the **John K. Goodman Pavilion of Western Art**. On the other side of the museum, the 1860 **Romero House**, used by the Tucson Museum of Art School, and the **Corbett House**, a 1906 brick-and-stucco building on Main Street, incorporate the northern boundary walls of the Presidio. Privately owned **Old Town Artisans** carries arts and crafts by more than 150 Western, Indian, and Mexican artists and occupies an adobe, parts of which date to between 1862 and 1875.

Distinguished architecture

Stroll along Main and Court Streets to view other houses in **Snob Hollow**, as it was called, including the 1886 American Territorial-style **Julius Kruttschnidt House**, now El Presidio Bed and Breakfast Inn (297 N. Main); the **Owl's Club Mansion** (378 N. Main), a men's club with an ornate façade, and nearby **Steinfeld House** (300 N. Main), both designed

A resident of Pascua, a Yaqui Indian village annexed by Tucson in 1952.

BELOW: Presidio Historic District.

Restored adobes bring color and whimsy to the Barrio Historic District.

BELOW: Pima County Courthouse.

by renowned architect Henry Trost in the Spanish Mission style at the turn of the century. **El Charro Restaurant** (311 N. Court), which claims to be the oldest Mexican restaurant in the United States, occupies the 1900 **Jules Flein House**, built of Sentinel Peak basalt by a French stone mason who worked on St. Augustine Cathedral.

To see more of the Presidio, cross Alameda and enter 10-acre (4-hectare) **Presidio Park**. **Pima County Courthouse** (115 N. Church), a building that combines Spanish and Southwestern architectural styles in its columns, arches, decorated façade, tiled dome, interior courtyard and fountain, has a portion of the original Presidio wall inside. **St Augustine Cathedral** (192 S. Stone) was begun in 1896, though by the 1930s it had fallen on hard times and was subsequently used as a whorehouse, garage, bootlegger warehouse, and boxing arena. Completely refurbished in 1967, today it is noted for its magnificent 1922 carved sandstone façade, modeled after the Cathedral of Queretaro in Mexico, which depicts yucca, saguaros, and horned toads.

The bronze statue of Tucson's patron saint, St Augustine, above the entry is dramatically floodlit at night.

El Barrio

South of the **Tucson Convention Center** (260 S. Church) is the 13-block **Barrio Historic District** ⊙, where crumbling adobes with unusual metal flared roof drains, or *canales*, Territorial-style brick homes and skinny row houses have been lovingly restored by Bohemians, architects, and business people. The *barrio libre*, "the neighborhood where anything goes," is, according to writer

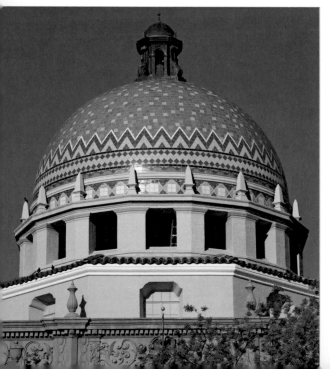

Recommended Restaurants on pages 306–7

Lawrence Cheek, "a lesson in urban living – courtyards instead of lawns, pastel colors that seem to drink the sunlight instead of fighting it." On a forgotten street, you'll come across entwined cacti blocking the entry to an old building or glimpse a Mexican tin hand of fate over an altar in an artist's compound. A Mexican factory (corner of Simpson and S. Main) turns out fresh tortillas daily. Opposite is **El Tiradito**, the **Outcast's Wishing Shrine**, the legendary unconsecrated burial place of a young man killed in a love triangle and the only national historical landmark dedicated to a sinner.

Adjoining El Tiraditio is **La Pilita Museum** (420 S. Main St; Aug–June Mon–Fri 11am–2pm, weekends by appointment; tel: 520-882-7454; donation), a charming community museum whose mission is to restore and preserve the La Pilita site. Affiliated with nearby Carrillo School, the research center and museum is run by volunteer educators well versed in the neighborhood. It has revolving art exhibits, award-winning after-school classes, and a fascinating collection of historic photos showing two

popular early Tucson pleasure parks – Elysian Grove and Carrillo Gardens – which occupied the site in Victorian times.

The Arizona Historical Society offers frequent guided walking tours of the historic downtown by reservation, leaving from the **Sosa-Carrillo-Fremont House** (151 S. Granada; Wed–Sat 10am–4pm; tel. 520-622-0946; charge), on the grounds of the Tucson Convention Center. This historic house was rented in 1881 to the daughter of the fifth territorial governor, famed explorer John C. Frémont. Admission is free the first Saturday of the month.

Museum row

East of downtown is a glut of worthwhile museums. The **Arizona Historical Society Museum** 🄳 (949 E. 2nd; open Mon–Sat 10am–4pm; tel: 520-628-5774; charge) is the place to bone up on Arizona's colorful history, including 1870s Tucson, and transportation and mining, with a full replica of an underground copper mine. Other museums can be

Outdoor art adorns the University of Arizona campus.

BELOW: El Charro, established in 1922, claims to be the country's oldest Mexican restaurant,

TIP

In October El Presidio is host to the Tucson Heritage Experience Festival, a melange of food, dance, and music. Scottish highland dancers follow old-time fiddlers; Burmese performers are sand-wiched between a *mariachi* band and Polish singers.

BELOW RIGHT:
Pueblo pottery collection at the Arizona State Museum.

found across the street on the **University of Arizona ⓔ** campus, founded by the territorial legislature in 1891 (in Old Main, the campus' oldest building) on land donated by a saloonkeeper and two gamblers. The University of Arizona was Tucson's consolation prize after it lost its bid to host the state capitol and the state insane asylum – both of which went to Phoenix – and today most Tucsonans agree they got the better deal.

First stop should be the **Arizona State Museum** (Park and University; open Mon–Sat 10am–5pm, Sun noon–5pm; tel: 520-621-6302; free), which occupies two buildings inside the west entrance. It was founded in 1893 to collect and preserve materials related to the native cultures of the Southwest and is the region's oldest anthropological and archaeology museum. An award-winning multimedia exhibit, *Paths of Life*, traces the origins, history, and contemporary life of the Seri, Tarahumara, Yaqui, O'odham, Colorado River Yumans, Southern Paiute, Pai, Western Apache, Navajo, and Hopi cultures.

Exhibits include a video and full-scale diorama of the Pascua Yaqui Deer

Dance, which is performed every Easter by residents of a Yaqui Indian village in the heart of Tucson. Displays on the long-vanished Hohokam, whose major community, Snaketown, was excavated by the university's Dr. Emil Haury, are found in the South Building.

The museum's newly opened Pottery Project displays some of the 20,000-plus Indian pots in ASM's collection, the largest and most comprehensive in the world, along with a state-of-the-art conservation laboratory and a new interpretive gallery featuring a multimedia Virtual Vault, video interviews with archaeologists and Indian potters, and hands-on experiences.

Photo feature

No one interested in photography should miss the **Center for Creative Photography** (open Mon–Fri 9am–5pm, Sat–Sun noon–5pm; tel: 520-621-7968; free), a world-class exhibit and research center with more than 50,000 photographs by leading 20th-century photographers such as Paul Strand, Edward Weston, and Alfred Stieglitz. It was conceived as a repository for the archive of

---

The Cactus League

Tolerable desert temperatures and wildflower blooms are two great reasons to travel to southern Arizona in February, March, and April. Another is to get an advance preview of the upcoming major league baseball season during spring training – an annual ritual that offers fans a chance to see teams like the Arizona Diamondbacks and Chicago White Sox compete in the Cactus League.

Most teams begin their workouts in mid-February, then play around 15 games in March and the first week of April. Games are held at popular venues like Electric Park in Tucson and Bank One Ballpark in Phoenix, which also offer special events such as fireworks nights, bat and T-shirt giveaways, and visiting sports mascots. The athletes often come over and meet fans after the games – an extra thrill for autograph-seeking kids.

Tickets go on sale as early as December and range from $5 for bleacher

seats to $15 for reserved seats. Lawn seating is available at most venues, making picnics a popular option for those not enamored of hot dogs, barbecue, and other stadium fare. Ticket information and game schedules can be obtained by calling the team's Arizona venue or by visiting www.arizonaguide.com or www.cactus-league.com.

Recommended Restaurants on pages 306–7

master landscape photographer Ansel Adams, and one of the best reasons to stop here is to make an appointment to view Adams's soul-stirring black-and-white photos of Yosemite and other western parks. Exhibitions of the center's holdings are held year-round.

On the other end of campus, **Flandrau: The UA Science Center, Planetarium, and Mineral Museum** (science center and planetarium open Thu–Fri 9am–3pm and 6pm–9pm, Sat noon–9pm, Sun noon–5 pm; observatory open Thu–Sat 7pm–10pm; tel: 520-621-STAR; charge) is out-of-this-world fun for kids and adults alike, with hands-on exhibits, night-sky viewing through a 16-inch telescope, star shows that include an introduction to Arizona skies, Native American skylore, and the demise of the dinosaurs, as well as evening laser light shows in the planetarium.

Look for exhibits and updates about the Phoenix Mars Mission, launched in 2007 to investigate water quality and habitability potential on the planet Mars. UA is the first public university to partner with NASA on this exciting mission, which landed on Mars in May 2008. For

more information, call 520-626-1974.

Those in town for Tucson's **Rock and Mineral Show** in February (the largest in the world) should check out the museum's large mineral collection and exhibit of global meteorites, one of which, the 1,400-pound (635-kg) Tucson Ring, was used as an anvil in the 1860s.

Urban oases

Escape the dust and artificial hush of the indoors and head north of downtown to **Tohono Chul Park** (7366 N. Paseo del Norte; open daily 8am–5pm; tel: 520-742-6455; admission charge). "Desert

The University of Arizona is a hub of art, science, and culture.

BELOW: Arizona State Museum,

Fairs and Fiestas

Whatever the occasion or the season, folks in southern Arizona like to get together for food, music, and good times

Perhaps it's the Mexican influence, but people in southern Arizona know how to have a good time. The annual calendar is jam-packed with parades, rodeos, fairs, and festivals featuring everything from bird-watching to chile tasting.

Fiestas celebrating Arizona's Mexican heritage are among the most popular and are held in every community with a sizeable Mexican-American population. Cinco de Mayo commemorates Mexico's victory over the French at Puebla on May 5, 1862, and is celebrated with spicy Mexican food, music and dance. Mexican Independence Day, September 16, is cause for even more celebration. Phoenix's Civic Plaza holds one of the biggest parties. Booths sell *carne asada*, or flame-broiled beef, and small Mexican flags, while mariachi bands and *ballet folklorico* take the stage, along with speakers reciting the call to arms that started the revolution in 1810.

Mariachi music, a style that traces its roots to 18th-century Spain, has become synonymous with Mexican fiestas. Some of the best bands in America can be heard every April in Tucson at the International Mariachi Conference and at the Christmas Mariachi Concert in Phoenix.

El Día de los Muertos, the Day of the Dead, is commemorated on All Souls Day, November 1–2. Family members decorate the graves of departed loved ones with marigold flowers, candles, and sugar skulls bearing the names of the deceased, then picnic at graveside. The historic Sosa-Carillo-Fremont House in downtown Tucson exhibits traditional *nichos*, flowered wreaths, and candles.

Christmas is a magical time in southern Arizona. El Centro de Las Americas in Tucson holds a month-long celebration of Mexican Christmas traditions called the Ferías Navideñas and Nacimiento Tour. Events include Las Posadas, a traditional dramatization of Jesus's birth. Tucson and Phoenix Botanical Gardens have elaborate displays of *luminarias* (lit candles in brown paper bags). The Tucson Museum of Art installs an elaborate nativity scene, or *nacimiento*, involving hundreds of figurines, in Casa Cordova, the work of a mother and daughter from a northern Mexican village.

Easter has special meaning for the Pascua Yaqui Indians of Tucson, whose Lenten ceremonies include traditional rituals like the Deer Dance. Native festivals occur throughout the year. The normally private Tohono O'odham Nation throws a lively three-day celebration with a powwow and rodeo every February in Sells, southwest of Tucson. The tribe also holds the Wa:k Powwow at Mission San Xavier del Bac in March. The Waila Festival, featuring O'odham "chicken scratch" music, is held at the Arizona Historical Society in Tucson in May.

Cowboys and rodeos are the focal point of the world's longest nonmotorized parade, which takes place at Tucson's La Fiesta de los Vaqueros, a huge outdoor rodeo, in February. Winter also brings the Gem, Mineral, and Fossil Showcase at venues around Tucson. Birders won't want to miss Wings Over Willcox, *the* big birding event in southeastern Arizona. It's held in January at Willcox Playa, winter home of thousands of migratory fowl. ❑

ABOVE: Cinco de Mayo celebration, Scottsdale.
LEFT: Mariachi Festival, Tucson.

Corner" in the Tohono O'odham language, the 49-acre (20-hectare) park was created to promote conservation of arid lands. It has nature trails and 500 plants from Sonora and the Southwest arranged by genus. Picnic here or have afternoon tea in the popular Tea Room. Closer to downtown, **Tucson Botanical Gardens** **G** (2150 N. Alvernon Way; open daily 8.30am–4.30pm; tel: 520-326-9686; admission charge) is in bloom all year. Of particular interest is the Native Seeds/SEARCH Ethnobotanical Garden, which cultivates native desert crops in its demonstration garden and has banked some 1,800 heritage seeds in an effort to preserve native foods. (Gardeners can buy these at the garden or by mail order.)

When temperatures top 100°F (38°C) in May and June, before the summer "monsoon" thunderstorms arrive, locals give up saying "but it's a dry heat" and head into the mountains surrounding the city. Trails abound in **Coronado National Forest** atop the rugged **Santa Catalina** and **Rincon Mountains**, northeast and east of town, respectively. A 40-mile (64-km) scenic drive into the Santa Catalinas (named by Jesuit missionary Padre Euse bio Francisco Kino in 1697) leads to the summit of 9,157-ft (2,791-meter) **Mount Lemmon** **H**, the highest peak in the area. Motorists pass through five distinct life zones before reaching the top, where temperatures are about 20 degrees cooler than at the base. **Mount Lemmon Ski Valley** (open year-round 9am–4pm; tel: 520-576-1400; charge), the southernmost ski resort in the United States, is a popular winter destination and offers fabulous chairlift views of the Tucson area on its Sky Ride the rest of the year. The town of Summer Haven suffered a devastating wildfire in 2003 but has now been rebuilt and offers food and lodging.

Cactus rustling was a serious problem in the 1970s and '80s as homeowners uprooted saguaros for their own yards. Saguaros are now protected by law.

Natural treasures

At the base of Mount Lemmon is **Sabino Canyon State Park** (open daily 8am–4.30pm; tel: 520-749-8700; fees for tram and parking), a lush canyon supporting cottonwood and willow bosque, deer, coyotes, javelinas, and numerous birds. One of the most heavily patronized day-use areas in Tucson, this historic canyon has seen mammoths, Hohokam irrigation ditches, and pony soldiers from the now-ruined Fort Lowell, who used to horse-

BELOW: a view of Tucson from Sentinel Peak.

A barrel cactus blooms at the Arizona-Sonora Desert Museum.

BELOW: Tucson Mountain District of Saguaro National Park.

back ride to the "ol' swimming hole." The visitor center has exhibits on the natural and cultural history of the mountains, a butterfly and hummingbird sanctuary, a self-guided nature trail starting behind the building, and daily naturalist-led walks.

From here, you can either hike, horseback ride or take one of the regular narrated shuttle tours (bicycles are allowed on some days) up the 3¾-mile (6.1-km) road that winds through the canyon. Popular trails include 5½-mile (9-km) round-trip **Seven Falls**, which follows the flat floor of **Bear Canyon** (14 stream crossings are necessary during snow-melt periods) to a waterfall, a welcome sight in this arid land. Allow at least half a day here.

Bike riders will particularly enjoy the two units of 87,000-acre (35,000-hectare) **Saguaro National Park** that bookend the city. The **Rincon Mountain District** (park open daily 7am–sunset, visitor center open daily 9am–5pm; tel: 520-733-5153; charge), off Old Spanish Trail in the 8,400-ft (2,560-meter) Rincons, preserves older stands of the multi-armed cactus.

If you choose only one section, though, make it the **Tucson Mountain District ❶** (park open daily 7am–sunset, Red Hills Visitor Center open daily 9am–5pm; tel: 520-733-5158), located west of the **Tucson Mountains**, which may be entered on the north from the West Ina Road exit off Interstate 19 or from downtown on Speedway via Gates Pass. The graded, 6-mile (10-km) **Bajada Loop Drive** passes through vigorous stands of young saguaro that march across the south-facing *bajadas*, or slopes, in Jolly Green Giant armies.

Surrounding them is typical Sonoran Desert Arizona Upland vegetation of yellow-blossomed paloverde trees, flame-tipped ocotillo, mesquite, and ironwood frequented by roadrunners, Harris's hawks, gila woodpeckers and other birds. Rangers at **Red Hills Visitor Center** on Kinney Road offer orientations and can tell you how to find Hohokam petroglyphs at the **Signal Hill** picnic area.

Desert flora and fauna

Desert animals are largely nocturnal, keeping cool in burrows or beneath rocks or shrubs during the day. Your best

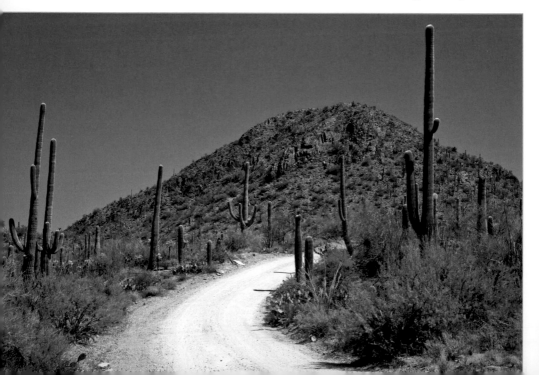

Recommended Restaurants on pages 306–7

chance of seeing and learning about Sonoran Desert flora and fauna is to visit the world-famous **Arizona-Sonora Desert Museum** ● (2021 N. Kinney Road; open daily 7.30am–5pm in summer, 8.30am–5pm rest of year; tel: 520-883-2702; charge) in adjoining **Tucson Mountain Park**. This isn't a museum at all but a large outdoor zoo, botanical garden, and nature trail that so effectively recreates the Sonoran Desert, the 299 species of native animals and 1,400 species of native plants that live here are fooled into thinking they never left home.

You'll need good walking shoes, a hat, sunscreen, and at least half a day to see all the exhibits, which include wild cats such as mountain lions, bobcats and jaguarundi; bighorn sheep; Mexican wolves; coyotes, and delightful furballs known as coatis, a relative of the ringtail, which snooze in the trees. Beautifully landscaped paths wander through a wildflower and cactus garden.

In the walk-in **Hummingbird Aviary**, hummers divebomb feeders and buzz loudly in the mesquite trees. An engaging **Life Underground** exhibit allows you to observe kit foxes, kangaroo rats, tarun

tulas, and other nocturnal animals asleep in their underground burrows. If you want to understand how elevation affects temperature and moisture for desert plants, check out the **Life Zones** exhibit, which takes you through five

The Life Zones exhibit at the Arizona Sonora Desert Museum explores ecological diversity within desert environments.

life zones – the equivalent of journeying from Mexico to Canada in just a few short steps. A new raptor presentation by naturalists, featuring free-flying hawks, is very popular; check for times at the entrance.

After visiting this museum, you'll never look at the desert with the same eyes again. There is an international food court offering excellent and interesting meals and a pleasant restaurant. An art gallery shows temporary exhibits, and a well-stocked gift shop sells books and many unique items.

Not far from the Arizona Sonora Desert Museum, the **International Wildlife Museum** ● (4800 W. Gates Pass; open Mon–Fri 9am–5pm, Sat–Sun 9am–6pm; tel: 520-629-0100; admission charge) features dioramas with more than

BELOW: a rock climber scales Windy Point in the Santa Catalina Mountains.

A Titan II missile rests in its silo at the Titan Missile Museum. It's the last of more than 50 such missiles in Arizona and elsewhere in the western US.

BELOW: three amigos entertain an audience at Old Tucson Studios.

400 mammal, bird, and insect species from all over the world, as well as interactive exhibits and wildlife films. The museum is an educational program of the Safari Club International Foundation. The displays are quite elaborate and informative, but the Safari Club's conservation message has a distinctly hollow ring considering that the animals on display were hunted and taxidermed; there are no living creatures at this facility at all.

Strike the set

There's more fakery at the **Old Tucson Studios** Ⓛ (201 S. Kinney Rd; open daily 10am–4pm; tel: 520-883-0100; admission charge), one of the most visited attractions in Arizona after the Grand Canyon. Originally constructed in 1939 as a set for the movie *Arizona* (and reconstructed after a major fire in 1995), more than 300 movies and TV shows have been filmed here, including the John Wayne movie *Rio Lobo* and *Tombstone*, starring Kurt Russell. Highlights at this family theme park include gunfights, saloon shows, musicals, Native American storytelling, games, rides, and a Town Hall Museum.

Air and space

Davis-Monthan Air Force Base "Aircraft Boneyard" Ⓜ (Kolb Road; open for bus tours 9am–5pm; tel: 520-228-8448 or 520-574-0462 for tour reservations; admission charge), east of Tucson, was dedicated by Charles Lindbergh in 1927. During World War II, it was a training ground for B-17 bombers and still trains pilots in combat aircraft. One of the base's tenants is the **Aerospace Maintenance and Regeneration Center**, where the U.S. military takes advantage of the dry climate and hard ground surface to mothball an extraordinary 5,000 planes and helicopters before they go to the great Junkyard in the Sky.

Nearby, the **Pima Air and Space Museum** Ⓝ (6000 E. Valencia Rd; daily 9am–5pm; tel: 520-574-0462; admission charge) has more than 275 air- and spacecraft – the world's largest private aircraft collection. Exhibits include a replica of the Wright Brothers' *Kitty Hawk* and President John F. Kennedy's *Air Force One*. A Space Gallery looks at the history of space exploration. Children like the **Challenger Learning Center**, housed in the **Aerospace Exploratorium**, which has a mis-

Recommended Restaurants on pages 306–7

sion briefing room, transportation room, mission control area and space station.

Two other museums on the outskirts of Tucson offer entirely different visions of a space-age future. The **Titan Missile Museum ❷** (1580 W. Duval Mine Rd, Sahuarita; open daily 8:45am–5pm; tel: 520-625-7736; charge), 20 miles (32km) south of Tucson off Interstate 19, is a sobering reminder of Cold War politics and the only site in the United States with a disarmed US intercontinental ballistic missile (ICBM) still on its underground launch pad.

One-hour tours of this declassified subterranean museum allow visitors to hear a tape of an Air Force crew preparing to launch a nuclear missile, then see the missile itself – a 110-ft-tall (34-meter), 170-ton (when fully loaded) monster contained behind 6,000-pound (2,700-kg) blast doors. Not recommended for the squeamish.

A far more positive experience awaits visitors at **Biosphere 2 ❸** (open daily 9am–4pm; tel: 520-838-6200; admission charge) in the town of **Oracle** 30 miles (48km) north of Tucson. Basically a 3-acre (1-hectare), glass-enclosed terrar-

ium designed to support the four men and four women who sealed themselves inside the facility for two years in 1991, Biosphere 2 was a grand, private experiment that went awry.

Amid accusations of hype, New Age cultism, poor science, and failed systems that endangered the health of the "bionauts," Biosphere 2 started down the long road to credibility in 1996, when Columbia University's Lamont-Doherty Earth Observatory took over its management. The University of Arizona took over in 2007, with a three-year lease. The agreement to pay a $100 annual fee to owners CDO Ranching and Development may extend to 10 years. A $30 million gift from the Philecology Foundation, founded by Edward P. Bass, funds Biosphere 2's operations and some research projects. Other grants and awards, primarily from the National Science Foundation, also support research activities.

It's the sort of comeback that, according to some Tucsonans, can happen only in the Southwest – a place, as writer Barbara Kingsolver liked to say, "where mountain lions make bets with rabbits, and rabbits can win."   ❑

Despite a rocky start, Biosphere 2 is now utilized for research and education.

BELOW: Biosphere 2's rainforest is one of several environments contained within the 3-acre glass structure.

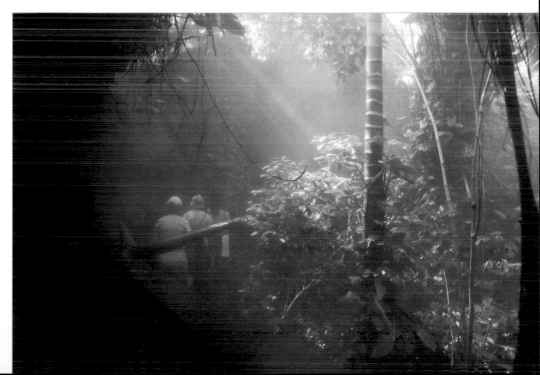

RESTAURANTS

Beyond Bread
Campbell Village, 3055 North Campbell Street
Tel: (520) 322-9965
Open: Mon-Fri 6.30am–8pm, Sat 7am–8pm, Sun 7am–6pm **$**
What could be simpler or more delicious for breakfast than a loaf of bread still warm from the oven and a steaming cup of coffee? You'll find more than 20 varieties of bread as well as thick sandwiches, salads, pastries, and cakes at this friendly and aromatic bakery and café.

Blue Fin Seafood Bistro
7053 N. Oracle Road
Tel: (520) 531-8500
Open: L, D Mon–Sat **$$–$$$**
This hip restaurant has the most varied piscine menu in town. Blue Fin has a bar downstairs with live music on weekends. Upstairs there are cozy booths. Service is friendly, fast, and efficient. If you're in the mood for fish, this is the place.

Café Poca Cosa
88 E. Adway Boulevard
Tel: (520) 622-6400
Open: L, D Tue–Sat **$**
Chef and owner Susana Davila serves innovative Sonoran cuisine with daily specials listed on a chalkboard, from *carne asado* to chicken cooked several ways, bathed in fresh herbs

and sauces and served with home-made tortillas. Her daughter runs a second, smaller restaurant nearby serving tamales with unusual nouveau Mexican fillings and sauces.

Café Terra Cotta
3500 Sunrise Drive
Tel: (520) 577-8100
Open: D daily **$–$$**
This Tucson favorite produces crowd-pleasing dishes on the creative edge of contemporary Southwestern cuisine. Don't pass up the garlic custard or one of a half-dozen wood-fired pizzas as a starter for the table. A few notable entrées include rack of lamb with chile bread pudding; duck carnitas spring roll; prawns stuffed with herbed goat cheese; and salmon crusted with sunflower seeds served on masa corncakes. There's a second restaurant in Phoenix.

Cup Café
The Hotel Congress, 311 E. Congress Street
Tel: (520) 622-8848
Open: B, LK, D daily **$$**
You'll find a little slice of Bohemia at this café in the historic Hotel Congress, which serves a hearty breakfast, a variety of thick lunch sandwiches, and an eclectic dinner menu with Italian and Southwestern touches.

Dakota Café
6541 E. Tanque Verde Road
Tel: (520) 298-7188
Open: L, D Mon–Sat **$–$$**
Set in a complex of faux Old West buildings known as Trail Dust Town, the restaurant has won kudos for its healthful and imaginative cooking. The menu ranges from meat loaf sandwiches, burgers, and several vegetarian dishes to specials like chicken enchiladas, braised pork tacos, and tempura shrimp. Patio dining is available.

El Charro Mexican Café
311 N. Court Avenue
Tel: (520) 622-1922
Open: L, D daily **$**
A venerable stone building in the Presidio Historic District houses what claims to be the oldest family-operated Mexican restaurant in the United States. Tasty Sonoran-style food is the bill of fare here, including spinach enchiladas, chimichangas, tamales, and carne seca (dried beef), a house specialty. Satellite restaurants are located at El Mercado (Broadway and Wilmot) and Tucson International Airport.

Elle: A Wine Country Restaurant
3048 E. Broadway Boulevard
Tel: (520) 327-0500
Open: L, D Mon–Sat, D Sun **$–$$**
Italian-inspired dishes

LEFT: traditional Mexican fare at El Charro.
RIGHT: the Gold Room delights diners with creative and contemporary Southwestern dishes.

are refreshing in their simplicity yet intriguingly creative. Clear, natural flavors add nuance to entrées such as risotto with butternut squash, balsamic-roasted onion and sage, or a simple capellini with tomatoes, basil, and garlic. True to its name, the restaurant offers a selection of more than 40 wines by the glass.

El Minuto
354 S. Main Avenue
Tel: (520) 882-4145
Open: L, D Mon–Sat $
Spicy and filling Mexican food are served at this stripped-down cantina near El Tiradito shrine. The place is popular with locals and tourists, so expect a lively crowd.

Gold Room
Westward Look Resort and Spa, 245 E. Ina Road
Tel: (520) 297-1151
Open: B, D daily, L Mon–Sat, Br Sun $$$
Fabulous food dreamed up by award-winning executive chef Jamie West and a panoramic view of Tucson from the foothills of the Catalina Mountains. Dishes include melt-in-the-mouth seared ahi tuna, vodka-infused smoked salmon, and toast points, Asian-inspired pan-seared salmon with wasabi potatoes, bok choi and ginger sauce, and a Sonoran "surf 'n' turf" featuring cowboy steak, lobster mac and cheese, and tumbleweed potatoes. West grows all his produce and herbs in an on-site organic garden. Tours are offered on Saturday mornings.

Janos
3770 E. Sunrise Drive
Tel: (520) 615-6100
Open: D Mon–Sat $$$

Ensconced in elegant digs at the Westin La Paloma hotel, the celebrated Janos continues its tradition of blending French and Southwestern influences to produce one of Tucson's most rewarding gastronomic experiences. The menu changes often, but a sampler menu (a series of small courses each accompanied by a different wine) could include lobster and brie relleno, cognac-scented beef tenderloin, and lamb sirloin marinated in lemon, basil, garlic and olive oil. The desserts are equally entrancing, and a wine cellar with 700 selections (20 are offered each night) will keep oenophiles happy on return visits. The more casual J Bar next door is a less expensive alternative. Chef Janos is also executive chef of Kai at the Wild Horse Pass Resort in Phoenix.

Lovin' Spoonfuls
2000 N. Campbell Avenue
Tel. (520) 323-7700
Open: B, L daily, D Mon–Sat $
Healthy eaters will be thrilled by this vegetarian and vegan restaurant, which has been winning raves for such meat- and dairy-free dishes as adzuki-bean burgers, soy bacon cheeseburger, veggie chili dogs, and country fried "chicken." There's a gluten-free menu, too, as well as organic wine and beer.

Sachiko Sushi Restaurant
1101 N. Wilmot Rd
Tel: (520) 886-7000
Open: L Mon–Sat, D daily $–$$
When you grow tired of tacos and enchiladas,

drop by this highly regarded sushi restaurant, known for authentic preparations and reasonable prices. The menu of hot dishes, including tempura, teriyaki, and noodles, is also quite good.

Tohono Chul
7366 N. Paseo del Norte
Tel: (520) 797-1222
Open: 8am–5pm daily $
It's difficult to imagine a more peaceful spot than the patio at this restaurant in Tohono Chul Park. Watch humming birds in the garden as you enjoy a breakfast of English scones, buttermilk pancakes or huevos rancheros. The lunch menu offers raspberry chipotle chicken, spinach fettuccine alfredo, grilled salmon, and large salads, among quite a few other choices. Come for the famous afternoon tea. You can browse the gift shop after your meal, or burn off a few calories

by strolling through the desert park.

Wildflower
7037 N. Oracle Road
Tel: 520-219-4230
Open: L Mon–Sat, D daily $$
This classy, contemporary bistro has a knack for pleasing patrons with a worldly mix of American, Asian, and European cuisines. Clear, earthy flavors are artfully assembled in such dishes as roasted rack of lamb with Dijon crust, Tuscan white-bean ravioli with wood-grilled chicken, and meatloaf with whipped potatoes.

Zinburger
1865 E. River Road
Tel: (520) 299-7799
Open: L, D daily $–$$
Burgers get high-class treatment at this mod spot, which also has tasty, creative appetizers (try the truffle fries), thick milkshakes, pie, and, interestingly, a small but thoughtful choice of wines.

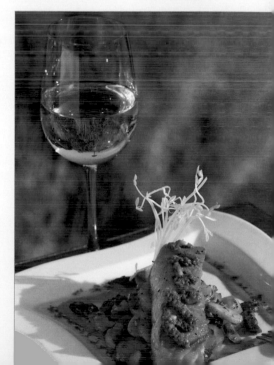

WINE COUNTRY

This may come as news to most Arizonans, but not to the White House, which has been serving fine Arizona wines since 1989

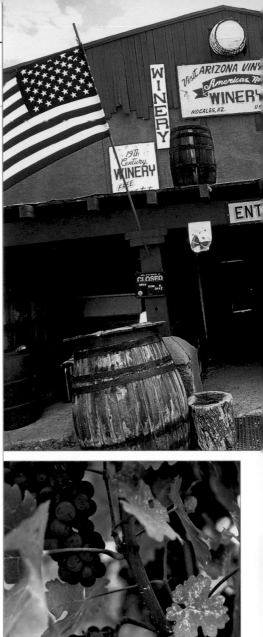

What is the common Arizona link between a Hollywood filmmaker and the lead singer of the band Tool? Answer: They are the latest wine enthusiasts to experiment with boutique wine making in Arizona, increasingly tipped as the next great wine region in the US.

Oenophiles enjoy spending long weekends touring the state's three main wine-growing regions – southeastern Arizona, the Sonoita/Elgin area, and northern Arizona – and discovered the many inventive ways that food, wine, and tourism are interweaving to create a new cultural experience along Arizona's backcountry highways.

Spanish monks raised vines in Arizona in the 17th century, but it wasn't until 1973 that a retired soil scientist planted the first vines in the Sonoita region, whose rich red soils, 5,000-ft (1,500-meter) elevation, oak-dotted grasslands, and ideal climate soon lured others. There are now 50 small vineyards in Arizona. A variety of grapes are grown, including Mediterrean grape varietals such as Petite Verdot, Petite Syrah, Tempranillo, Mourvedre, and Grenache. The state's first all-organic winery, Granite Creek, recently produced its first wines in northern Arizona's Chino Valley. Some wineries, such as Dos Cabezas, under new ownership and recently relocated to Sonoita, are pairing with neighboring fine-dining restaurants to promote their wines, or, like Kokopelli Winery in Chandler, creating their own wine bar to promote their wines.

Visitors are taking notice. Arizona wineries receive more than 30,000 visitors a year, bringing dividends

for those whose passion for *terroir* (a region's unique wine character) led them to try their luck in these laid-back rural Arizona destinations. For further information on visiting Arizona Wine Country, visit www.arizona vinesandwines.com.

LEFT: a selection of red wines from Callaghan Vineyards.
RIGHT: ripe Cabernet grapes ready for harvest.

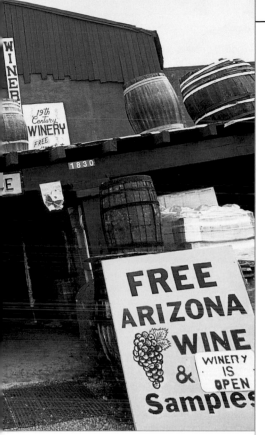

ABOVE: situated outside Nogales on scenic Route 82 near the Mexican border, Arizona Vineyards has a tasting room packed with sculptures, paintings, casks, and other wine-related artifacts.

BELOW: a variety of wines from Sonoita Vineyards; the vineyard grows Chardonnay, Sauvignon Blanc, Cabernet Sauvignon, Merlot, Pinot Noir, and Mission grapes.

VISITING THE WINERIES

The eight wineries in Elgin/Sonoita, Arizona's oldest wine-growing region, offer an excellent general introduction to Arizona's vineyards and winemaking.

Award-winning **Callaghan Winery** now produces a new generation of exciting wines from Mediterranean grapes. Nearby **Village of Elgin Winery** uses Sauvignon Blanc, Cabernet Sauvignon, and Sangiovese single varietals to create award-winning small-batch wines and has a harvest food-and-wine festival in September. **Dos Cabezas,** bought by winemaker Todd Bostock in 2006, saw its Viognier white and El Norte red win Governors Awards for Best in Arizona the following year. The tasting room is next to Canela Bistro on Highway 82. All are only open on weekends.

Nearby Willcox Plaza has six small family-run wineries but is best known as a grape-growing region. Musician Maynard Keenan, owner of Caduceus, the label under which he produces wines from his northern Arizona Merkin Vineyard, now co-owns the most famous of its wineries, Dos Cabezas, since renamed **Arizona Stronghold**. Film producer Sam Pillsbury, former owner of Dos Cabezas, has begun **Pillsbury Wine Company**, where he has returned to basics and is playing with new grape blends.

Among the few places selling Keenan and Pillsbury's wines is **Page Springs Cellars** (open daily) in northern Arizona's Verde Valley. Owner and winemaker Eric Glomski co-owns Arizona Stronghold and Pillsbury Wine Company, and offers tastings of their wines alongside his own Rhone-style wines. Using Sedona as a base, you can visit eight wineries. Near Prescott, **Granite Creek**, the state's first organic winery, is a wonderful place for a picnic and to hear live music on weekend afternoons.

ABOVE: Kent Callaghan of Callaghan Vineyards pours a sample of red wine. Callaghan specializes in Mediterranean and Spanish varietals.

BORDER COUNTRY

Ghost towns, Spanish missions, Old West history,
and entrancing desert landscapes lure travelers to
"la frontera" – Arizona's colorful borderlands

E dge places: those no-man's lands where foreign entities rub up against each other, boundaries blur, and something entirely new emerges. Arizona's border with the Mexican states of Sonora and Chihuahua is one such frontier, a geographical crossroads that has witnessed cultural confluence and collision for centuries.

The recipe begins geographically with the convergence of both the **Chihuahuan** and **Sonoran Deserts** and the **Rocky Mountains** and **Sierra Madre**. Fold in a huge expanse of volcanic basin-and-range topography rising in elevation from just over 1,000ft (300 meters) in the west to nearly 10,000ft (93,000 meters) in the east, and pierce it with one of the last free-flowing rivers in the country, the San Pedro. Then mix in half a dozen Indian cultures, 18th-century Spanish missions, 19th-century American forts and mining towns, modern retirement communities, state-of-the-art astronomical observatories, and twin border towns where cultures constantly meet and merge, and you have a unique salsa – one of the fieriest in the West.

Ecological crossroads

Begin this tour from Interstate 10, just over the New Mexico line. Drop south and west on Highway 80 into the **Chiricahua Mountains** via **Portal**. These high peaks are made of uplifted rhyolite, fused ash from an explosion in nearby Turkey Caldera 25 million years ago. Erosion by rainfall has created an extra-ordinary rockscape preserved in 17-sq-mile (44-sq-km) **Chiricahua National Monument** ❹ (visitor center open daily 8am–4.30pm; tel: 520-824-3560; admission charge), on the western side of the Chiricahuas, south of Willcox.

To view the rocks, follow the 6 mile (10-km) **Bonita Canyon Drive,** which climbs from the visitor center through lush **Bonita Canyon** to **Massai Point,** the starting point for a short nature trail and day hikes among the rocks. Rocky Mountain and Sierra Madrean wildlife mingle in these mountains via a natural

Main attractions

CHIRICAHUA MOUNTAINS
FORT BOWIE
BISBEE
TOMBSTONE
KARTCHNER CAVERNS
RAMSEY CANYON
TUMACACORI
SAN XAVIER DEL BAC
KITT PEAK
ORGAN PIPE CACTUS
  NATIONAL MONUMENT

LEFT: an O'odham girl shows her handiwork.
BELOW: Coronado National Memorial

Geronimo, posing with his wife, at Fort Sill, Oklahoma, where he remained until his death in 1909.

corridor running through the Chiricahuas to Mexico. Mexican plants and animals such as rare Apache fox squirrels and Chihuahua and Apache pines live side by side with species more commonly found north of the border. Of particular interest are the birds that summer in the Cave Creek area. Top of the list is the trogon, a Mexican native with a long, coppery tail and bright feathers, sulphur-bellied flycatchers, tanagers, chickadees, warblers, and a variety of hummingbirds. Surrounding the monument is **Coronado National Forest** (tel: 520-388-8300) and **Chiricahua Wilderness**, which contain 100 miles (160km) of hiking trails and many delightful camping spots. A rough forest road traverses the mountains, but is closed by snow in winter. Check the weather forecast before starting out.

On the trail of the Apache

To the Chiricahua Apache Indians, this was the "Land of Standing Up Rocks." Led by Cochise, Victorio, and Geronimo, they successfully evaded capture by US Army troops during the 1860s and 70s, when settlers began encroaching on Apache territory, but they were eventually forced to surrender. Massai Point provides a view of **Cochise Head**, said to be the profile of the old Apache warrior. To learn more about the Apache Wars, visit nearby **Fort Bowie National Historic Site** ❺ (visitor center open daily 8am–4.30pm; tel: 520-847-2500). This ruined adobe outpost once consisted of barracks, officers' quarters, storehouses, a trader's store, and a hospital. It was built to protect the Butterfield Overland Mail Stage and local residents. A 1½-mile (2½-km) self-guided trail to the ruins leaves from Apache Pass Road.

Highway 80 continues south to the 1902 copper-smelting town of **Douglas** ❻ past guest ranches, heart-lifting views of the **Peloncillo Mountains**, and a roadside plaque near **Skeleton Canyon** at the spot where Geronimo surrendered in 1886. The five-story **Gadsden Hotel** (built 1907) is a faded beauty that bills itself as "the last of the grand hotels." Once host to Theodore Roosevelt, its main attraction now is the lobby, which contains massive marble columns decorated with 14-karat gold leaf supporting a

Recommended Restaurants on pages 323–5

vaulted ceiling with stained-glass panels.

About 15 miles (24km) east of Douglas is the 93,000-acre (38,000-hectare) **John Slaughter Ranch Museum ⑦** (open Wed–Sun 10am–3pm; tel: 520-558-2474; admission charge), once owned by former Texas Ranger and Cochise County sheriff John Slaughter. His 1890s house, corral, and other buildings have been restored as examples of ranch life during Arizona's territorial years. A 2,330-acre (940-hectare) section is now protected as **San Bernardino National Wildlife Refuge**.

Copper Queen

Douglas served the old copper mining town of **Bisbee ⑧**, which spreads for 3 steep miles (5km) across **Mule Pass Gulch** and **Tombstone Canyon** in the 5,000-ft (1,500-meter) **Mule Mountains**, just west of Douglas. Starting out as a rowdy, cosmopolitan mining camp in 1877, early mining claims were won and lost at the faro table by hard-drinking miners and ex-soldiers. The first major mining operation began when Judge Dewitt Bisbee (who never saw the town named for him) and other San Francisco business-men bought the **Copper Queen Mine** in 1880. But with underground copper seams running for miles into other claims, cooperation proved the only way for everyone to get rich, and the still-powerful Phelps Dodge corporation was born.

Bisbee's colorful history – lynchings, murders, miners, working girls, and hopeful immigrants – is showcased in clever, interactive exhibits at the **Bisbee Mining and Historical Museum** (open daily 10am–4pm; tel: 520-432-7071; admission charge), housed in the 1897 **Phelps Dodge General Office Building**. Now a satellite of the Smithsonian Institution, this museum is one of the Southwest's true gems. A standout is the depiction of the Bisbee Deportation of 1917, when 1,000 striking miners were loaded at gunpoint into boxcars and expelled from the state for "anti-government" activities.

Down and dirty

The other unmissable attraction in Bisbee is the **Queen Mine Tour** (daily tours 9am–3.30pm; call for reservations, tel: 520-432-2071 or 866-432-2071; admission charge). Visitors are equipped with yellow slickers and miner's helmets and

Bisbee – the city of foul odors and sickening smells.

—Editor of the *Tucson Citizen*, circa 1900

Guides at the Queen Mine – former miners themselves – lead visitors on a subterranean tour.

lamps, and sit astride an old mine train for the chilly trip down the shaft with a flinty ex-miner – himself a mine of information about drilling, blasting, mining etiquette, and the cushy life of a sanitary engineer, or "shit nipper."

After yielding 8 billion pounds (3.6 billion kg) of copper, Bisbee's 33 mines (and an astonishing 2,500 miles/4,000km of tunnels) were all closed by 1975, including the yawning abyss of the **Lavender Open Pit Mine**, on the edge of downtown, which long ago swallowed a whole mountain.

Some of the Southwest's funkiest art galleries, museums and offbeat lodgings are housed in historic buildings downtown (including the OK Jail and miners' boarding houses. Many are on a popular self-guided historic walking tour of downtown's steep hills – you'll soon understand why postal workers in Bisbee refuse to home-deliver mail.

View the 1939 **Phelps Dodge Mer-**

cantile, 1906 **Post Office and Library**, the 1880s **Miners Hotel** in Brewery Gulch, and the 1902 four-story, red-roofed **Copper Queen Hotel,** where you can sleep in the Theodore Roosevelt Suite, John Wayne Room (a straight shot for the Duke after a night in the adjoining saloon bar), or, if you're male, take your chances with the spectral Julia, the "soiled dove" who haunts the Ghost Room on the third floor.

Tough towns

A highway tunnel through the Mule Mountains opens onto the limestone **Chihuahuan Desert** terrain of creosote, yucca, ocotillo, and sweeping vistas of the alluring **Dragoon Mountains** to the northwest, where you can hike and camp at **Cochise Stronghold ❾**, the warrior's hideout. Immediately ahead is the "Town too Tough to Die": **Tombstone ❿** (tel: 888-457-3929). The old mining town was the setting of the infamous OK Corral gunfight in 1881, which pitted US Marshal Wyatt Earp, his brothers Morgan and Virgil, and "Doc" Holliday against the Clanton and McLaury boys, ranchers whose extracurricular activities included cattle rustling and harboring stagecoach robbers. Unless you're in the mood for stage-set Wild West artifice, avoid the costumed cowboys, mock gunfights, and tourist traps, though you may get a kick out of the old **Bird Cage Theater,** where working girls plied their trade in 14 "cages" or "cribs" suspended from the ceiling.

Instead, take a walk over to the 1882 Victorian red-brick **Tombstone Courthouse State Historic Park** (open daily 8am–5pm; tel: 520-457-3311; admission charge) to view the original courthouse setup and a reconstructed gallows. Diagrammed exhibits offer two theories about what happened during the 30-second OK Corral gunfight, in which Virgil and Morgan Earp were wounded and three members of the Clanton gang killed. The Clantons and other victims of frontier justice are buried in **Boothill Cemetery**, one of the tackiest graveyards you will ever visit – so kitsch that it's a must-see – complete with fake-looking headstones, cute epitaphs, and piped-in Willie Nelson music.

Tombstone's eateries also veer toward the hokey, but worth a look is a joint called the **Nellie Cashman Restaurant**

and Pie Salon, which was once a hospital run by an Irish mining camp follower known as "the Angel of Tombstone."

Tombstone and Bisbee are resurrected mining towns. To see what happens when boom leads to bust, drive a dirt road east from Tombstone to the ghost mining towns of **Gleeson**, **Courtland**, and **Pearce ⑪**. Pearce hosted an 1894 gold rush and is now the only site with sizeable ruins (a two-story corner mercantile store, a post office, and the jail)

A Bisbee art gallery; the former mining town has a thriving art scene.

BELOW: the weathered ruins of the guardhouse at Fort Bowie, built in 1862 to protect the Apache Pass.

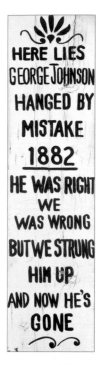

HERE LIES
GEORGE JOHNSON
HANGED BY
MISTAKE
1882
HE WAS RIGHT
WE
WAS WRONG
BUT WE STRUNG
HIM UP
AND NOW HE'S
GONE

ABOVE: Boothill grave marker.
BELOW: Tombstone "gunfighters."

From Pearce, paved Highway 191 heads north to Interstate 10, past **Willcox Playa** ⑫, which floods in winter to form a wetland that attracts, along with nearby **White Water Draw**, more than 10,000 sandhill cranes, Canada and snow geese, and an array of other waterfowl.

Located between Willcox and Benson is the fabulous **Amerind Foundation and Museum** ⑬ (open Tue–Sun 10am–4pm; tel: 520-586-3666; admission charge). This is one of the Southwest's premier private archaeological and ethnographic collections. The dream of the amateur archaeologist William Fulton, who built this lovely hacienda-style ranch in 1937 to show off his artifacts, it should not be missed by archaeology buffs. There are excellent exhibits on the native peoples of the Americas and contemporary exhibits by some of the state's most talented native artists. This is an active research center. Important archaeological studies are co-published with the University of Arizona.

Some of those books may be found at **The Singing Wind Bookshop** (open 9am–5pm daily; tel: 520-586-2425), exit 304 near **Benson** ⑭. This unique bookstore is located in Win Bundy's ranch house, and is known for its wide range of books on the Southwest. An annual Thanksgiving fiesta attracts hundreds of book-lovers to hear authors read, and to enjoy the live music and food.

Subterranean world

From Benson, follow Highway 90 south for 9 miles (14km) to Arizona's most exciting new attraction: **Kartchner Caverns State Park** ⑮ (open daily 7.30am–6pm; tel: 520-586-CAVE for reservations, 520-586-4100 for info; no admission fee with cave tour). Kartchner is a rare "wet cave," with more than 90 percent of its colorful Escabrosa limestone decorations still growing. It was discovered in 1974 by cavers Randy Tufts and Gary Tenen beneath the **Whetstone Mountains** and Kartchner Ranch. The 2½-mile (4-km) cave was kept secret for 14 years while the cavers, the Kartchner family, and state officials debated how best to develop the caverns without destroying their delicate ecosystem.

State-of-the-art technology includes misting systems in the caves, double-lock doors to seal in moisture, and spe-

Recommended Restaurants on pages 323–5

cially blasted entrance tunnels. The new owners, Arizona State Parks, spared no expense in doing the job right, opening the caves in 1999.

Tours leave every 20 minutes from the **Discovery Center**, xeriscaped with interpretive nature trails of varying lengths. Inside, view a 15-minute multimedia film and interactive exhibits that include a simulated cave crawl-through and virtual cave tour. Book ahead; this is currently Arizona's hottest ticket. Or arrive by 7.30am to try for one of 100 tickets released daily on a first-come, first-served basis (hint: stay in the park's 60-site campground to ensure first dibs).

Rangers offer entertaining and informative talks on the porch before accompanying the tram to the cave entrance. Inside, in the **Rotunda** and **Throne Rooms** and the recently opened **Big Room**, the temperature is a steady, steamy 68°F (20°C), with paved, barrier-free walkways leading past deep mud flats and unusual formations, such as colorful shields, streaky "bacon," "fried eggs," flowing draperies, "cave popcorn," wavy helectites, ceiling-hanging stalactites and floor-growing stalagmites.

Record-breakers here are the 58-ft-high (18-meter) Kubla Khan column and a 21-ft-long (6-meter) soda straw, the longest in the United States. Both the caves and the strong conservation message being promoted are impressive. Note: Big Room tours are only available Oct 15–April 15.

Birding hot spots

Running parallel to Highway 90 is another impressive natural attraction. **San Pedro Riparian National Conservation Area ⑯** (visitor center open daily 9.30am–4.30pm; tel: 520-459-2555) preserves cottonwood-willow *bosque* along the **San Pedro River** for 100 miles (160km) between St. David and the Mexican border. Named a Globally Important Bird Area by the American Bird Conservancy, this perennial waterway supports more than 80 species of mammals, 45 reptile and amphibian species, 100 species of breeding birds, and 250 species of migrant and wintering birds. An astonishing 4–10 million migratory birds lay over every year.

Bird lovers can help **Southern Arizona Bird Observatory** (tel: 520-432-

BELOW LEFT AND RIGHT: once a wild and woolly mining town, Tombstone is now dedicated to rehashing its Old West history for the tourist trade.

A Bisbee sculptor at work in his studio.

1388) tag hummingbirds at **San Pedro House** near Sierra Vista in summer, or visit the Nature Conservancy's 300-acre (120-hectare) **Ramsey Canyon Preserve** ⓱ (open daily 8am–5pm Feb–Oct, Thur–Sun 9am–4pm Nov–Jan; tel: 520-378-2785; admission charge). A wonderful little nature center contains exhibits on the San Pedro and Ramsey Canyon ecosystem and a gift store; guided tours are offered Mar–Oct on Tue, Thur and Sat at 9am. In August, avian migrants from Mexico, attracted by the warm Sierra Madrean environment of the **Huachuca Mountains**, include painted redstarts, eared and elegant trogons, clouds of butterflies, bats, and 14 hummingbird species, flocking in the huge sycamores and at porch feeders.

Coronado's quest

The Huachucas (highest point, **Miller Peak**, at 9,466ft/2,885 meters) are a blessing during the 100°F (38°C) heat of summer, offering breathtaking drives with views into Mexico, camping in **Coronado National Forest**, and hiking. The 2,880-acre (1,160-hectare) **Coronado National Memorial** ⓲ (visitor center

open daily 9am–4pm; tel: 520-366-5515; admission charge) commemorates the location of what is thought to have been the first Spanish *entrada* into North America by Don Francisco Vásquez de Coronado, in 1540. Going on information from the advance party of Padre Marcos de Niza and the Moorish slave Esteban in the 1530s, the charismatic 30-year-old Spaniard financed his own expedition from Mexico City, following old Indian trails north across torrid desert and probably passing near 6,844-ft (2,086-meter) **Coronado Peak**. After months of fruitless travel, Coronado's search for gold and glory was deemed a failure, but it set the stage for what would later become a massive colonization effort by Spain.

In 1877, after the Southwest had become American territory, the US Army built **Fort Huachuca** ⓳ as part of its campaign against the Apache. Of the many soldiers who fought during the Apache Wars, none was more respected for its bravery than the fort's black troops, known to the Apache as Buffalo Soldiers. A room in the **Fort Huachuca Historical Museum** (open Mon–Fri 9am–4pm, Sat–Sun 1pm–4pm; tel: 520-533-5736; free) tells their story through memorabilia, photos, Indian artifacts, and dioramas. It is well worth a stop in the military base town of **Sierra Vista** (you'll pass right by the fort, now a training center for military intelligence). Note: due to stepped-up homeland security, only US citizens may currently visit this museum. You'll need to show driver's license and proof of car insurance, if you drive into the compound.

North of Sierra Vista, turn west on Highway 82. Look for pronghorn as you drive through 66 sq miles (170 sq km) of native grasslands at **Las Cienegas National Conservation Area** ⓴ (tel: 520-258-7200) into expansive rolling ranch and wine country. If this area looks familiar, it may be because the 17,500-acre (7,100-hectare) **San Rafael Ranch**, southeast of **Patagonia**, doubled as Oklahoma during the shooting of the 1955 film of the Rodgers and Hammerstein musical. Here, it is apparent why south-

BELOW: grasslands flourish in the high valleys of desert mountain ranges.

Recommended Restaurants on pages 323–5

ern Arizona was named one of the Top Five Birding Spots in the Nation by *Birding* magazine. Riparian birds like vermilion flycatchers may be glimpsed in these 5,000-ft (1,500-meter) grasslands, and some 300 avian species frequent the Nature Conservancy-run **Patagonia-Sonoita Creek Preserve** (open Wed–Sun 6.30am–4pm Apr–Sept, 7.30am–4pm Oct–Mar, guided tours Sat 9am; tel: 520-394-2400; admission charge), which preserves cottonwood-willow habitat from Patagonia north through **Madera Canyon** in the **Santa Rita Mountains.**

Spanish Missions

Nogales ㉑, which sits astride the US–Mexico border at the junction of Highway 82 with Interstate 19, is where most Arizonans get their border-town fix. Shop 'til you drop, try Sonoran *ranchero*-style food, and, if you're in the mood for dancing, look for a bar playing lively Norteña music. **Northern Sonora** and the stretch of Interstate 19 between Nogales and Tucson that follows the beautiful Santa Cruz River Valley contains several 17th-century Indian missions founded by Italian Jesuit missionary

Padre Eusebio Francisco Kino during the early Spanish colonial era. **Tumacacori National Historical Park ㉒** (open daily 8am–5pm; tel: 520-398-2341; admission charge) preserves three mission churches built between 1691 and the early 1800s.

Tumacacori and its sister missions of **Guevavi** (11 miles/18km south) and **Calabazas** (15 miles/24km south) were abandoned in 1771, after Spain recalled its Jesuit missionaries and replaced them with Franciscans. The present church began construction in 1800, finishing just before Mexican independence in 1821. Apache raiding grew so bad on the unprotected Mexican northern frontier that, in 1848, the residents moved away and the mission fell into ruin. A peaceful self-guiding trail leads through the church, which remains a remarkable testimony to the skills of Indian craftsmen.

The 5-mile (8-km) **Juan Bautista de Anza National Historic Trail** along the Santa Cruz River connects Tumacacori to **Tubac Presidio State Historic Park ㉓** (open daily 8am–5pm; tel: 520-398-2252; admission charge), which preserves part of the fort that was erected by the Spanish in 1752 to protect their

Catholicism was brought to the region by Spanish missionaries in the late 17th-century and remains a vital cultural force.

BELOW: San José de Tumacacori, a mission church built by O'odham Indians, was abandoned in 1848 as a result of Apache raids.

An inquisitive road sign near the desert town of Why.

missions following the 1751 Pima Indian Revolt. Apache raiding and political turmoil caused the site to be abandoned, but the settlement was revived following the 1853 Gadsden Purchase. By 1859, Tubac had become a mining boomtown and home to Arizona's first newspaper, the *Weekly Arizonan*, now on display in the presidio museum. With the founding of an art school in 1948, it morphed into an art colony. Popular with day-trippers, Tubac has about 100 studios and galleries and features an annual Festival of the Arts every February.

When Tumacacori was abandoned in 1848, residents moved north to **San Xavier del Bac Mission ㉔** (open daily 8am–5pm; tel: 520-294-2624; free). The "White Dove of the Desert" is considered the most beautiful of all the Kino church missions, with its classic white plaster exterior and ornate facing. It was founded as a satellite, or *visita*, of Tumacacori in 1700 and built by Tohono O'odham Indians in the late 1700s under the direction of Franciscan priests. It is still the parish church for the San Xavier Reservation today. In the 1990s, the tribe and members of a local friends' group

worked with an international team to restore interior murals. Restoration of the exterior is now being undertaken.

Desert skies

The 2.8-million-acre (1.1-million-hectare) **Tohono O'odham Reservation ㉕** sprawls west of Tucson across a surprisingly verdant desert landscape. The Tohono O'odham Nation's new **Himdag Ki Cultural Center and Museum** (open Mon–Fri 10am–4pm; tel: 520-383-0201; free) opened in 2007. The $15.2 million facility is 7 miles (11km) southeast of Sells, in the village of Topawa, with sacred Baboquivari Peak as a backdrop. The center has a library, an archive, classrooms, and in-depth exhibits about Tohono O'Odham culture. The outer ring of the exhibit hall has special sections about government, language, land, and food. A revolving central exhibit area currently displays artwork by 10 contemporary tribal members. The central hallway has a permanent exhibit celebrating Indian veterans of various wars. Nature paths, shade ramadas, footbridges, and an outdoor amphitheater tie the landscape to the building.

The signature cactus of this desert, the

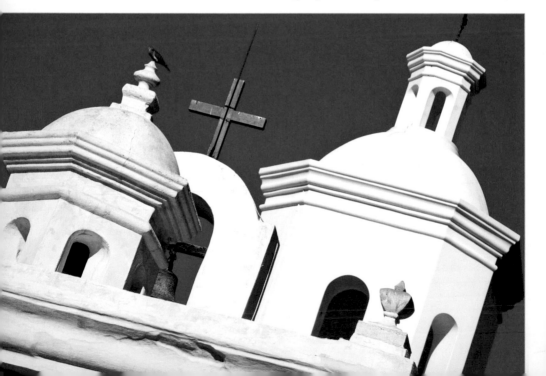

Recommended Restaurants on pages 323–5

delightfully anthropomorphic saguaro, can be found throughout the desert, and seems to wave its many arms in salutes, hugs, handshakes, and finger-pointing disapproval all along the two-lane **Ajo Highway** (Highway 86). Dramatically backlit mountains, huge desert basins, and storms can be seen hundreds of miles away across an almost hallucinogenic landscape.

A distinctive landmark near the US–Mexico border is 7,734-ft (2,357-meter) **Baboquivari Peak** ("narrow about the middle" in the Tohono O'odham language), a brooding volcanic neck believed by the "People of the Desert" to be the home of their creator god, I'itoi. The **Baboquivari Mountains** lie west of the border grasslands of 116,000-acre (47,000-hectare) **Buenos Aires National Wildlife Refuge** ㉖ (tel: 520-823-4251; visitor center open daily 7.30am–4pm, closed weekends June–Aug 15), which supports pronghorn and numerous bird species, including the endangered masked quail. Desert skies here are unbelievably clear, making southern Arizona a mecca for stargazers. **Kitt Peak National Observatory** ㉗ (open daily 9am–4pm and some nights; tel: 520-318-8726; admission

charge) has 22 telescopes of various sizes and types, including the huge McGath-Pierce Solar Telescope and the 4-meter Mayall Telescope for dark-sky viewing. A short self-guided tour takes you past the most state-of-the-art telescopes, and a visitor center offers exhibits that will keep you fascinated for hours.

The big empty

About three hours southwest of Tucson, drop south onto Highway 85 at **Why** (named for the Y in the road), and enter 516-sq-mile (1,336-sq-km) **Organ Pipe Cactus National Monument** ㉘ (open 24 hours; visitor center open daily 8am–5pm; tel: 520-387-6849; admission charge), which preserves cactus species mainly found south of the border. Remote and lightly visited, this national monument is nestled between the torqued and twisted volcanic **Ajo** and **Puerto Blanco Mountains** and is chock full of coyotes, desert tortoises, rattlers, kit foxes, and other rarely seen desert critters. After a rainfall, brittlebush, desert

Restoration of San Xavier del Bac has returned the interior to its original brilliance.

BELOW LEFT:
a bird-watcher
scans Buenos
Aires National
Wildlife Refuge.

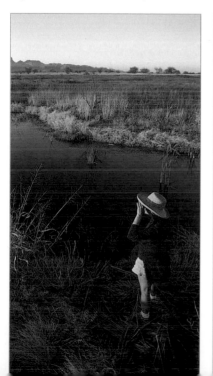

The Devil's Highway

El Camino Diablo, the Devil's Highway, is a rough, unpaved route from Carborca, Mexico, to Yuma, Arizona, across one of the most overheated and desolate landscapes in the Southwest. Prehistoric people used the route to transport shells and salt from the Gulf of California. Spanish soldiers led by Melchior Diaz were the first Europeans to travel the route in 1540. More than 150 years later, missionaries Padre Eusebio Kino and Padre Garces and explorer Juan de Anza also came this way.

After gold was discovered in California in 1849, thousands traveled the Devil's Highway. Between 400 and 2,000 people died of thirst on their way to the gold fields in the 1850s, making this the deadliest immigrant trail in the United States. Many of their graves, marked by heaps of stones and makeshift crosses, are still visible.

The road is best traveled in early spring or fall using a four-wheel-drive vehicle; summer temperatures reach 120°F (49°C), and winter nights can dip below freezing. There are no services or water. Carry one to two gallons (4–8 liters) of water per person per day and pack at least two days' extra water and food, as well as spare tires. Permits are required to enter the Barry Goldwater Bombing Range and Cabeza Prieta National Wildlife Refuge.

Illegal immigration is a long-standing and vexing problem along the border.

BELOW: Organ Pipe Cactus National Monument.

marigolds, poppies, lupines, and other wildflowers burst into bloom. Allow enough time to take the 56-mile (90-km) **Pueblo Blanco Scenic Drive** and 21-mile (34-km) **Ajo Scenic Drive** into the backcountry to view organ pipe cactus, rare Mexican elephant trees, limberbush, and senita cactus. Many dirt roads lead to historic ranches, mines, and prehistoric Indian sites; winter is the coolest time to visit.

Organ Pipe has been heavily used by illegal immigrants crossing from Central America into the US.

In 2006, the National Park Service completed a 23-mile (37-km) steel fence on its southern boundary, which has successfully prevented illegal vehicle crossings through the national monument. Border patrol and law enforcement officers patrol this area night and day, and you may encounter checkpoints. Overnight stays in the backcountry are no longer permitted. Carry identification.

Highway 85 leads south into **Sonora** and **Baja California,** via the border at **Lukeville ㉙**. If you go into Mexico only once on your travels, this may be the easiest place to do so (armed with Mexican car insurance and proof of citizenship). A few miles south of Lukeville is Mexico's **Parque Natural de Gran Desierto del Pinacate ㉚**, one of the world's truly extraordinary landscapes – an ebony-hued lava land topped incongruously by Sonoran Desert vegetation. Cool off at the seaside town of **Puerto Peñasco**, 65 miles (105km) south of Lukeville, where you can swim in the Gulf of California and enjoy endless sandy beaches.

Adjoining Organ Pipe Cactus is 86,000-acre (34,800-hectare) **Cabeza Prieta National Wildlife Refuge ㉛**, a sanctuary for desert bighorn sheep. Though beautiful, travel here is by permit only, due to the presence of the **Barry Goldwater Bombing Range** on the preserve's north side. In addition to these units, three new undeveloped national monuments have been set aside to protect the Sonoran Desert.

The 496,000-acre (200,724-hectare) **Sonoran Desert National Monument** (tel: 623-580-5500), 60 miles (100km) southwest of Phoenix, conserves a variety of habitats, from desert to montane, including wilderness areas, and may be accessed via Interstate 8 and AZ 238, east of the Gila Indian Reservation.

The 71,000-acre (28,732-hectare) **Agua Fria National Monument** (tel: 623-580-5500), 40 miles (65km) north of Phoenix, contains 450 prehistoric archaeological sites in scattered, remote locations around Agua Fria River Canyon. Access is via Interstate 17 at Badger Springs or Bloody Basin Road. Both monuments are managed by the BLM, Phoenix Field Office (tel: 623-580-5500).

The third unit is 129,000-acre (52,204-hectare) **Ironwood Forest National Monument** (tel: 520-258-7200), 25 miles (40km) northwest of Tucson, which protects a rich stand of rare ironwood trees, as well as three mountain ranges and three important archaeological districts on the National Register of Historic Places. There are two main points of entry: Avra Valley Road and Red Rock exits, from Interstate 10, then southwest on Sasco Road to Silverbell Road. ❑

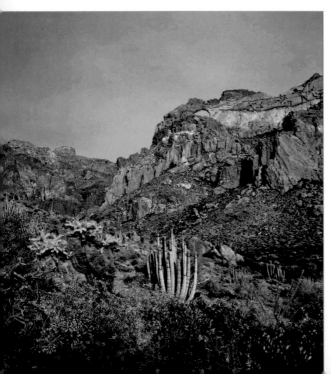

RESTAURANTS

Prices for a three-course dinner per person, excluding tax, tip, and beverages:

$ = under $20
$$ = $20–45
$$$ = $45–60
$$$$ = over $60

Adobe
5043 S Highway 92, Sierra Vista
Tel: (520) 378-2762
Open: L Mon–Fri, D Mon–Sat
$$$
The chef-owner of Sierra Vista's most popular fine-dining restaurant, Tucson native Donald Libasci, has impressive chops, having worked at Tucson's Canyon Ranch Spa and Ventana Canyon Resort. Elegant Southwestern and Latin American cuisine using market-fresh ingredients is the focus of his own establishment. Try the *poblano relleno*, a poblano pepper stuffed with goat cheese, as an appetizer, followed by entrées such as Yucatan free-range chicken, Maya mahi-mahi, or Argentine-style flat-iron steak. Desserts include *Panqueques de Manzana*, warm crepes filled with *dulce de leche*, spiced apples, and vanilla ice cream. The adjoining Lizard Lounge bar offers terrific margaritas, mojitos, and other Latin drinks.

Big Nose Kate's Saloon
417 E. Allen Street, Tombstone
Tel: (520) 457-3107
Open: L, D daily **$**

The food – mostly salads, sandwiches, and pizza – is nothing to write home about, but the decor is colorful in a vaguely Victorian way, the service (by waitresses in saloon-girl costumes) is generally attentive, and the live country music is entertaining. A reasonable choice in a town that caters mostly to the tourist trade.

Bisbee Breakfast Club
75A Erie Street, Bisbee
Tel: (520) 432-5885
Open: B, L daily **$**
Housed in a renovated former drug store in adjoining Lowell, this large, airy breakfast spot is the area's hottest ticket with the morning crowd. Retro without being pretentious, it serves up creative modern diner breakfasts and some interesting lunch selections, including a variety of unusual wraps, burgers, and salads.

Bisbee Coffee Company
2 Copper Queen Plaza, Bisbee
Tel: (520) 432-7879
Open: B, L daily **$**
A popular daily gathering spot in downtown Bisbee that serves good coffee, pastries, and quiches and has WiFi.

Bisbee Grille
Copper Queen Plaza, Bisbee
Tel: (520) 432-6788
Open: L, D daily **$–$$**
This central restaurant offers a range of grilled foods, including ribs,

burgers, and steaks. Seafood, pasta, meatloaf, and salads round out the menu.

Cafe Roka
35 Main Street, Bisbee
Tel: (520) 432-5153
Open: D daily (seasonal closings, check hours) **$$**
Chef Rod Kass has created an upscale, artsy environment in historic downtown Bisbee in which to present his creative brand of northern Italian cuisine. Four-course meals may include artichoke and portobello mushroom lasagna; scallops with spinach pasta; rack of lamb; roasted duck; or grilled salmon. The menu is not extensive, but it changes frequently. Reservations are sug-

gested, especially on weekends.

Cafe Sonoita
3280 Highway 82, Sonoita
Tel: (520) 455-5278
Open: L Tue–Sat, D Thur–Sat
$–$$
One of the few places in Sonoita with extensive lunch and dinner hours, this tiny restaurant inevitably gets lots of business. The attractive dining room in the Western-style building has tiled floors and white tablecloths, with brightly painted walls covered in art. At lunchtime, there is a large menu of soups, salads, burgers, and sandwiches as well as Southwest staples like quesadillas and burritos. At dinner, choose from hearty prime rib, steak

RIGHT: locally grown chiles add hot, earthy flavor to Southwestern cuisine.

Prices for a three-course dinner per person, excluding tax, tip, and beverages:
$ = under $20
$$ = $20–45
$$$ = $45–60
$$$$ = over $60

medallions, buffalo burgers, stuffed chicken dishes, and pasta.

Canela Southwestern Bistro

3252 Highway 82, Sonoita
Tel: (520) 455-5873
Open: D Thur–Sun; seasonal closings, check with restaurant $$$–$$$$
In 2007, husband-and-wife chef-owners John Hall and Joy Vargo returned to John's local ranch roots, bringing with them classical Cordon Bleu training and a passion for superbly prepared but accessible food. Many of the ingredients at this unexpectedly gourmet weekend dinner restaurant at the Sonoita–Patagonia crossroad are locally sourced,

and the couple grows their own organic greens, tomatoes, and herbs. The enormous steak-frites or pork tenderloin and mac 'n' cheese have a loyal local following, but this menu is so beautifully in tune with the seasons, it's worth savoring several things. Homemade soups are smooth, creamy, and vibrant, and mouth-watering Point Reyes blue cheese makes an appearance on one of the best artisanal cheese plates around. Simple entrées like seared wild ahi tuna over organic greens, goat cheese, and spring-pea ravioli, or glazed duck breast and tabbouleh, are spectacular without being showy. Desserts are perfectly sized for even dessert refuseniks and include a trio of homemade ice creams, pots de creme, and milk chocolate torte. Pair with a wine from neighboring

Dos Cabezas Winery or one of the other local Elgin wineries, and you have Wine Country cuisine at its finest. Reservations are advised.

Cantina Romantica

Rex Ranch, off Amado exit 48 on I-19, Tubac
Tel: (520) 398-2914
Open: daily L, D $$–$$$
The menu is not extensive at this rustic hacienda on the 4,000-acre (1,620-hectare) Rex Ranch north of Tubac, but in this case, small is beautiful. Grilled meats are the specialty, although you'll find a tasty selection of vegetarian dishes, including bountiful salads. Several varieties of chili are used to great advantage, as are tequila, citrus, and prickly pear. Highlights include a pecan-crusted pork roulade with chili sauce; grilled double-cut lamb chops with a port wine, cherry, and jalapeño jus; grilled citrus chicken and shrimp with tequila and prickly pear sauce; and wild mushroom and basil lasagna. There's no bridge across the Santa Cruz River to the ranch. You have to drive through the water.

Dot's Diner

Shady Dell RV Park,
1 Old Douglas Road,
Bisbee, AZ
Tel: (520) 432-1112
Open: B, L daily $
This 1957 Art Deco-style diner is the real deal. Diners like these have been manufactured by the Valentine Manufacturing Co. in Kansas since the 1930s. You'll have to wait for one of the 10

stools at the counter, but it's worth the time. A new owner is doing a good job of keeping up the authentic vintage atmosphere, friendly ambience, and great food for which the famous Dot, the previous owner, was famous.

Galleano's

601 W. 4th Street, Benson
Tel: (520) 586-3523
Open: L, D daily $
Benson's best restaurant is family owned and specializes in Italian cuisine. The food is fresh, prices are reasonable, and it's always busy.

Gathering Grounds

319 McKeown Avenue, Patagonia
Tel: (520) 394-2097
Open: B, L daily, D Thur–Sat $–$$
This wonderful coffeehouse and meeting place in the center of Patagonia serves fresh-tasting, locally sourced food at incredible prices. At breakfast, there's excellent organic Fair Trade coffee to accompany substantial egg dishes and unusual muffins and pastries. At lunch, choose from interesting quiches, salads, soups, wraps, and hot and cold sandwiches. Dinner entrées are geared to healthy ranch country appetites. They run the gamut of pork and prime ribs, ribeye and New York steak, all with interesting sauces, to lighter fare like grilled Alaskan cod with avocado butter, salmon with apricot and horseradish sauce, and portobello mushrooms stuffed with risotto. WiFi.

Grand Cafe and Gallery

1119 G Avenue, Douglas
Tel: (520) 364-2344
Open: B, L, D Mon–Sat **$–$$**
Choices are limited in
this border town, but
you'll find decent Mexi-
can and American food
at this eatery, whose
walls are covered in
images of Marilyn Mon-
roe. The usual choice of
burritos, flautas, fajitas,
steaks, and seafood are
on the menu.

The Grasslands Bakery & Cafe

3119 Highway 83, Sonoita
Tel: (520) 455-4770
Open: L Fri–Sun only **$**
This terrific little natural-
foods bakery and café
makes incredibly good
organic baked goods,
including croissants and
streusel kuchen and
deep-dish pies with spelt
flour crusts. The dining
room offers homemade
soups, salads, warm
pasta salads, hot and
cold sandwiches,
quiches, and excellent
desserts. Take note:
most of Sonoita's best
restaurants are open
only on weekends to
cater to day-trippers
from Tucson. Plan
accordingly.

High Desert Market and Cafe

203 Tombstone Canyon,
Bisbee
Tel: (520) 432-6775
Open: B, L, D daily **$**
Situated in the old Blue
Sky Cafe, this laid-back
spot is a combination
market, bakery, and
cafe with indoor and out-
door seating. They do
good coffee and a large
selection of baked
goods and interesting
dishes such as strata
savory bread pudding
with sausage and spring
rolls. There are also a
variety of salads and
sandwiches on organic
whole-wheat bread. It's
good for a quick, bud-
get-friendly meal.

Longhorn Restaurant

501 E. Allen Street,
Tombstone
Tel: (520) 457-3405
Open: L, D daily **$–$$**
Everything is super-sized
at this tourist-oriented
Western saloon and
restaurant, including the
humongous hot dogs
(the largest in Cochise
County), ribs, and
steaks. By most
accounts, the food and
service are good.

Melio's Trattoria

12 Plaza Road, Tubac
Tel: (520) 398-8494
Open: L, D daily **$–$$**
Familiar but well-done
Italian food in a cozy,
unpretentious setting.

Nellie Cashman Restaurant

117 S. 5th Street, Tombstone
Tel: (520) 457-2212
Open: B, L, D Mon–Sat **$–$$$**
Named for an angelic
mine camp follower, this
restaurant is in an 1879
building in Tombstone.
The food serves mainly
mainstream tourist fare –
silly-named egg dishes at
breakfast, burgers and
sandwiches at lunch, and
standard Western dishes
at dinner. Their pies are
the main draw.

OK Cafe

220 E. Allen St, Tombstone
Tel: (520) 457-3980
Open: B, L daily **$**
A decent choice for a
breakfast of pancakes,
steak and eggs, biscuits
with gravy, and other tra-
ditional American fare.
The lunch menu
includes bison, ostrich,
and emu burgers.

The Outside Inn

4907 S Highway 92,

Sierra Vista
Tel: (520) 378-4645
Open: L Mon–Fri, D Mon–Sat **$$**
A good choice for a
romantic dinner, the Out-
side Inn is quiet and
attractive. The seafood is
especially good. Patio
dining is available, but
the restaurant is small,
so reservations are rec-
ommended.

Rosa's Little Italy

7 Bisbee Road, Bisbee
Tel: (520) 432-1331
Open: D Wed–Sun **$$**
Rustic Sicilian and South-
ern Italian food is well
prepared at this small,
atmospheric trattoria in
Bisbee. There are numer-
ous classic dishes,
including veal piccata,
fettuccine Alfredo, and
tiramisu for dessert.

Tree of Life Cafe

Tree of Life Rejuvenation
Center, Patagonia
Tel: (866) 394-2520
Open: B, L, D daily **$–$$**
Non-guests at this pri-
vate residential retreat
center are welcome to
join residents for meals
that consist of creatively
prepared, beautifully
presented, low-glycemic,
vegetarian/vegan raw
foods. The menu is glob-
ally inspired, 100 per-
cent organic, and
seasonal. Produce is
grown on-site. Meals are
served at set times and
prix fixe. You must make
a reservation 48 hours
in advance to eat here.
The center offers an
interesting roster of spa
services, classes, work-
shops, treatments, and
retreats, if you decide to
check in. This is a fascinating and unexpected
bonus in Border Country
for travelers interested
in alternative health and
healing modalities.

Velvet Elvis

292 Highway 82, Patagonia
Tel: (520) 394-2102
Open: L, D daily **$**
An eccentric little place
in downtown Patagonia
that is known for its
thin crust, wood fired
pizza. You can get it with
a variety of toppings.
Wash it all down with a
choice of freshly
pressed juices, organic
wines, or microbrews.
Soups and salads are
also quite good.

Wagon Wheel Saloon

400 W. Naugle Avenue,
Patagonia
Tel: (520) 394-2433
Open: L, D daily **$**
This authentic cowboy
bar and restaurant has
been catering to local
buckaroos for more than
60 years and offers
exactly what you would
expect from a cowboy
joint – barbecued ribs,
steaks, burgers, and
plenty of ice-cold beer.

INSIGHT GUIDES

TRAVEL TIPS

ARIZONA & THE GRAND CANYON

The Guides That Are Streets Ahead

INSIGHT GUIDES

www.insightguides.com

Insight Guides to every major country are also available.

TRAVEL TIPS

TRANSPORTATION

GETTING THERE
AND GETTING AROUND

GETTING THERE

By Air

Phoenix Sky Harbor is Arizona's main airport. In 2006, more than 41 million passengers flew on 19 airlines to over 100 cities world-wide. Tucson International Airport is much smaller, with 12 airlines used by more than 4 million passengers a year. Among the carriers serving these airports are:

Air Canada: tel: (888) 247-2262; www.aircanada.com
ATA: tel: (800) 435-9282; www.ata.com
America West: tel: (800) 235-9292; www.americawest.com
American: tel: (800) 433-7300; www.aa.com
British Airways: tel: (800) 247-9297; www.british-airways.com
Continental: tel: (800) 525-0280; www.continental.com
Delta: tel: (800) 221-1212; www.delta-air.com
Northwest-KLM: tel: (800) 225-2525; www.nwa.com
United Airlines: tel: (800) 864-8331; www.ual.com
US Airways: tel: (800) 428-4322; www.usairways.com

The following commuter airlines offer service within the region, including Phoenix, Tucson, Flagstaff, Tusayan (Grand Canyon), Las Vegas, Los Angeles, Lake Havasu City, Kingman, Show Low, and Yuma:
Air Vegas: tel: (800) 255-7474
America West: tel: (800) 235-9292
Mesa: tel: (800) 637-2247
Scenic: tel: (800) 446-4584
Southwest: tel: (800) 435-9792
Sunrise: tel: (800) 347-3962

Important Note: Expect delays departing US airports due to new Homeland Security anti-terrorism rules. These are apt to change, so check before flying. Most important-ly, foreign visitors are now required to submit information about themselves online to Homeland Security and be preapproved for travel to the US at least three days before they travel instead of filling in green landing cards prior to landing in the United States and presenting them at US Passport Control. The new rules make it compulsory for short-term visitors to the US to register via the website of the Electronic System for Travel Authorization before boarding an aircraft. The site officially opened on August 1, 2008. The revamped system affects nations participating in the visa waiver program, which gives citizens from 27 countries the right to remain in the US for short periods of time without a visa. Those who fly across the Atlantic on a regular basis do stand to benefit, since an approved application remains valid for up to two years, or until the traveler's passport expires. It also entitles the holder to multiple entries into the US during this period.

While traveling, pack items in both carry-on and checked luggage in clear bags, leave gifts unwrapped, and take laptops out of bags for inspection by Transportation Security Administration (TSA) personnel. Consider wearing slip-on shoes as all footwear must be removed and scanned by X-ray machines. Passengers may carry *one* carry-on resealable 1 quart size clear plastic bag, which can contain liquids or gels in containers of 3 ounces of less. The contents in the plastic bag must fit comfortably and be completely closed/sealed and subjected to X-ray inspection separate from carry-on bag.

By Train

Amtrak offers more than 500 destinations across the US. The trains are comfortable and reliable, with lounges, dining cars, domed viewing cars, snack bars, and, in some cases, movies, live entertainment, and, on the Southwest Chief, interpretive talks about the Navajo and Hopi Indian reservations by local experts. Most routes offer sleeper cars with private cabins in addition to regular seating with pull-out foot rests that offer reclined sleeping.

Amtrak's Southwest Chief runs from Chicago to Los Angeles, across northern Arizona, with stops in Winslow, Flagstaff (bus service connects to the Grand Canyon), and Kingman, Arizona. The Sunset Limited runs from Miami to Los Angeles, across south-central Arizona, with stops at Tucson and Phoenix.

Ask about two- or three-stopover discounts, senior citizens' and children's discounts, and Amtrak's package tours. International travelers can buy a USA Railpass, good for 15 to 30 days of unlimited travel on Amtrak throughout the US.

Call **Amtrak** (tel: 800-872-7245; www.amtrak.com) for detailed scheduling.

By Bus

One of the least expensive ways to travel in America is by interstate bus. The largest national bus company is Greyhound (tel: 800-231-2222; www.greyhound.com). The company routinely offers unlimited travel for 7, 15, 30, or 60 days. Within Arizona, several shuttle companies offer service out of Phoenix Sky Harbor International Airport. They include Arizona Shuttle (tel: 800 888 2749; www.arizonashuttle.com), serving Phoenix and Tucson; Open Road Tours (tel: 800-766-7117; www.openroadtours.com), serving the South Rim of the Grand Canyon twice daily, connecting in Flagstaff; Flagstaff Express (tel: 928-225-2290; www.flagstaffexpresss.com) connecting Flagstaff and Phoenix; Shuttle "U" Prescott (tel: 800-304-6114; www.shuttleu.com), serving Prescott; and Sedona Phoenix Shuttle (tel: 800-448-7988; www.sedona-phoenix-shuttle.com), serving Sedona.

GETTING AROUND

Public Transportation

Light Rail

In December 2008, Phoenix inaugurates METRO light rail service, providing visitors with convenient access from Phoenix Sky Harbor International Airport to the downtown area, serving Tempe, Mesa, Glendale, and Phoenix. Trains run every 10 minutes during rush hour, every 20 minutes during off-peak periods. For more information, log on to www.valleymetro.org/metro_light_rail.

Buses

Greyhound bus service and shuttle buses (see above) link cities in Arizona. Once there, city bus lines can be an excellent and inexpensive way of getting around. Valley Metro (tel: 602-253-5000; www.valleymetro.org) provides public transportation in the Greater Phoenix Area. Sun Tran (tel: 520-792-9222) serves the metro Tucson area and has transit centers at major destinations throughout the city. The South Rim of Grand Canyon National Park provides free shuttle buses to attractions within the park with paid entrance. Scheduled shuttle bus service is also available between both rims and surrounding communities such as Tusayan and Flagstaff.

Private Transportation

By Car

Driving is by far the most convenient way to travel in Arizona, especially outside the major cities. Two east-west interstates – I-40 in the north and I-10 in the south-central region – traverse the state, the centrally located north-south Interstate 17

links Flagstaff with Phoenix, and there are a number of paved state highways linking towns throughout the state. Major roads are well maintained, although backcountry roads are frequently unpaved and some may be impassable using a regular passenger vehicle. If you plan on driving into remote areas or in heavy snow, mud, or severe weather, it's a good idea to rent a four-wheel-drive vehicle with good clearance.

Maps and Information

Your greatest asset as a driver is a good map. They can be obtained from tourism offices, filling stations, supermarkets, and convenience stores. If you're traveling across the Indian reservations in northern Arizona, purchase the top-rated Indian Country road map, which is so detailed it is used by local residents.

Maps of national parks, forests, and other natural areas are usually offered as part of your entrance fee. For hikers, topographical maps are available through Trails Illustrated (www.trailsillustrated.com); these maps are often in bookstores. The most detailed topographical maps are available from the US Geological Survey (www.usgs.gov/sales.html).

Although roads are maintained even in remote areas, it is advisable to listen to local radio stations and to check with police officers for the latest information on weather and road conditions, especially in winter or if planning to leave paved roads. The Arizona Department of Transportation offers the 511 Traveler Information Service, allowing you to get information about closures, construction, delays, public transit, weather, and more by dialing 511 or logging on to www.az511.gov.

Driving in Remote Areas

If you plan on driving in uninhabited areas, carry a spare tire and extra water – at least a gallon (4 L) per person per day. A cell phone is a good idea, too, although some areas will be out of range. Service stations can be few and far between. Not every town will have one, and many close early. It's always better to have more fuel than you think you'll need.

A word of caution: If your car breaks down on a back road, do not strike out on foot. A car is easier to spot than a person and provides shelter. If you don't have a cell phone or your phone doesn't work, sit tight and wait to be found. A compact disk may be used as a signaling device in place of a mirror. Keep cool, do not exert yourself, ration water prudently, and eat lightly.

Car Rental

Most rental agencies require you to be 21 years old or over (25 at some locations) and have a valid driver's license and a major credit card. Many take debit cards, too, and some will take cash in lieu of a credit card, but this might be as high as $500. Non-English speaking travelers must produce an international driver's license from their own country.

You will find rental car companies in most cities and airports. Rental vehicles range from economy cars to luxury convertibles, vans, and 4WD vehicles. Rates are cheap, and most companies offer unlimited mileage. But you should still shop around, preferably online, for the best rates and features. Local rental firms outside the airport are often less expensive than the national companies because they don't charge high airport fees.

It's cheaper to arrange car rental in advance. Check with your airline, rental agent, or the Internet for package deals that include a car: rental rates can be reduced by up to 50 percent if you buy a so-called "fly-drive" deal.

Go over the insurance coverage provisions carefully with the agent before signing the rental agreement. Loss Damage Waiver, or Collision Damage Waiver, is essential. Without it, you'll be liable for any damage done to your vehicle in the event of an accident. You are advised to pay for supplementary Liability Insurance on top of standard third-party insurance. Insurance and tax charges can add a lot to an otherwise inexpensive rental – assume about $15–25 per day.

Major rental car companies are:
Alamo: tel: (800) 327-9633
Avis: tel: (800) 331-1212
Budget: tel: (800) 527-0700
Dollar: tel: (800) 800-4000
Enterprise: tel: (800) 325-8007
Hertz: tel: (800) 654-3131
National: tel: (800) 227-7368
Thrifty: tel: (800) 367-2277

RV Rentals

No special license is necessary to operate a motor home (or recreational vehicle – RV for short) but they aren't cheap. When you add up the cost of rental fees, insurance, gas at today's exhorbitant prices, and campground fees, renting a car and staying in motels or camping may be less expensive. For additional information about RV rentals, call the Recreational Vehicle Association (tel: 800-336-0355; www.rvra.org).

A CCOMMODATIONS

HOTELS, YOUTH HOSTELS, BED & BREAKFASTS

CHOOSING LODGINGS

Reservations and Prices

Grand Canyon National Park

Grand Canyon's popular South Rim has a number of lodgings, but available rooms can be hard to find. Plan on reserving as far ahead as possible: Xanterra Parks and Resorts, the park concessionaire, allows you to reserve 13 months ahead, a good idea if you want to stay at the top lodgings. The rimside historic El Tovar, Bright Angel, and Grand Canyon Lodges on the South and North Rims are most popular, followed by the modern Thunderbird and Kachina Lodges between El Tovar and Bright Angel. The last to fill up are the Maswik and Yavapai Lodges, in the forest away from the rim. Last-minute cancellations do come up, so check the reservations line.

Tusayan, the gateway community to the park, has mainly chain motels with good amenities, such as breakfast buffet bars, in-room coffee-makers, and outdoor pools (the Grand Hotel also has an indoor pool). They are popular with tour buses that cannot be accommodated at the South Rim and with families who need distractions for the kids. They also fill fast, so booking ahead is necessary here, too.

All lodgings within the park may be booked through Xanterra Parks and Resorts, 6312 South Fiddlers Green Circle, Suite 600N, Greenwood Village, CO 80111; tel: toll-free within the United States (888) 297-2757, (303) 297 2757 outside the United States, fax: (303) 297-3175; www.grandcanyonlodges.com.

Chain Hotels and Motels

These are ubiquitous throughout the United States and have many fans. Some people dislike chains because they offer no variety, lack a personal touch, and are often located in the most commercial, nondescript areas of town next to busy highways. The advantage is that once you've been to a hotel run by a particular chain, even though these are usually a franchise, you can bank on certain facilities and a standard of service wherever you are in the US. For travelers wanting to focus on their vacation, this can be a boon.

Bed-and-Breakfasts

Bed-and-breakfasts vary greatly in terms of price and quality, but the one thing they have in common is that they are almost invariably in a private and/or historic home. Few have restaurants, and facilities will not be as extensive as in a regular hotel. Privacy can be an issue in older inns, but some have separate cottages with self-catering facilities, allowing you to come and go as you please. Hosts are usually a mine of information about local sights, and this can be a great way to make lifelong friends. For those travelers who enjoy the personal ambience – not to mention the afternoon teas, wine and cheese happy hours, and gourmet breakfasts found in many places – bed-and-breakfasts are a great choice.

Camping

Private Campgrounds

A nationwide network of private campgrounds, called Kampgrounds of America (KOA), has members in Arizona. They offer good-quality

RIGHT: Phoenician Resort, Scottsdale.

facilities, including swimming pool, restaurant, laundry, etc. Most accept reservations. Contact KOA at PO Box 30558, Billings, MT 59114-0558; tel: (406) 248-7444; www.koa.com.

Camping on Public Lands

Camping inside one of Arizona's world-class national, state, or tribal parks is a major attraction for many travelers. You'll find developed campgrounds with individual tent and RV sites that have an adjoining car parking spot, barbecue grills, picnic tables, and nearby flush toilets for about $10–25 per night – you can get more than one tent on a pitch. State park campgrounds are usually the best designed, and most have showers. Most campsites are on a first-come, first-served basis and fill by early afternoon at the most popular places (winter in the low desert and summer in the high desert mountains). Campsites in many national parks may now be reserved by calling (800) 365-CAMP or logging on to www.reservations.nps.gov. A number of federal and private campgrounds may be reserved by logging on to www.reserveamerica.com.

US Forest Service and Bureau of Land Management (BLM) camp-

grounds are usually "primitive," meaning they have designated sites and picnic tables, but usually only vault toilets. Many campgrounds have no water, so keep a 5-gallon (22-liter) water carrier in the car. The cost is low for these sites, making them an excellent budget option. Dispersed camping in nondesignated sites is allowed for free on national forest lands. Bring all you'll need and pack everything out when you leave.

Aside from food and water, the most useful items are moist babywipes for general hygiene, resealable plastic bags for trash, toilet paper, and a small trowel for digging a 6 inches (15cm) cat hole to bury human waste in the biological layer of the soil away from precious desert water sources. Treat, filter, or boil all water to avoid giardia, a nasty bug transmitted through contaminated water at campsites downstream from cattle grazing areas.

ACCOMMODATIONS LISTINGS

GRAND CANYON

Best Western Grand Canyon Squire Inn
Highway 64, Tusayan, AZ 86023
Tel: (928) 638-2681 or
toll free (800) 622-6966
Larger and better appointed than most properties in the Best Western chain, this hotel – on a commercial strip in Tusayan, just outside the national park – offers large rooms and a plethora of distractions, including a bowling alley and tennis courts. The restaurant is your best bet for a good steak and seafood dinner if South Rim restaurants are booked. Pool, restaurant, coffee shop, bar, exercise room, sauna, air conditioning, television. **$$–$$$**

Bright Angel Lodge & Cabins
West Rim Drive, Grand Canyon, AZ 86023
Tel: (928) 638-2631 or
(888) 297-2757 (reservations)
www.grandcanyonlodges.com
This rustic lodge was designed by Mary Jane Elizabeth Colter in 1935 and built on the site of Bright Angel Camp, the first tourist facility in the park. The historic turquoise-trimmed lobby features Indian motifs and a huge fireplace. There's a museum about the famous Harvey Girls in a side room as well as a fireplace made of all the rocks in the Grand Canyon. The accommodations range from dormitory-style rooms with shared baths to

private cabins with canyon views. Creature comforts are simple, but the location and price make the lodge a good value. Reservations for the rim cabins should be made at least a year in advance. Restaurant, coffee shop, ice cream parlor. **$$**

El Tovar Hotel
Grand Canyon, AZ 86023
Tel: (928) 638-2631 or
(888) 297-2757 (reservations)
www.grandcanyonlodges.com
This rustic European hunting lodge-style inn was built in 1905 of stone and Oregon pine. It offers a level of luxury not found elsewhere on the South Rim and is worth the splurge. Standard rooms tend to be small, although deluxe rooms and suites (which have terrace with spectacular views) are quite commodious. The dining room serves the best food on the South Rim. The lobby, with Mission-style furnishings, high ceilings, a fireplace, and assorted moose and antelope heads hanging from dark log walls, is worth seeing even if you're not spending the night. Restaurant, bar, gift shop, air conditioning, TV. **$$$$**

Grand Canyon Lodge
Bright Angel Point, AZ 86052
Tel: (928) 638-2611 or
(888) 297-2757 (reservations)
www.grandcanyonlodges.com
A log-and-limestone lodge with 50ft (15m) ceilings and a glass-walled sunroom overlooking the canyon is

the centerpiece of this historic complex – the only lodging inside the park's North Rim. A few motel-style rooms are available but lack the rustic charm of the small log cabins clustered around the main building. Cabins are available in four sizes, some better appointed than others. A few have canyon views but are usually booked a year or more in advance. The dining room is wrapped in windows, but the cuisine generally falls short of the setting. No matter. The views can't be beaten. Be sure to make dinner reservations several weeks before your arrival. Restaurant, cafeteria, bar, gift shop, horseback ride concession. **$$**

Grand Hotel
PO Box 3319, Tusayan, AZ 86023
Tel: (928) 638-3333 or
toll free (888) 634-7263
Large, comfortable, nicely appointed rooms, an airy lobby, and a dinner show featuring local Navajo dancers are among the attractions of this 127-room National Park Lodge-style motel on Highway 180/64 in Tusayan, just outside the national park. Restaurant, bar, indoor pool, fitness room, air conditioning, television. **$$**

Hualapai Lodge
Route 66, Peach Springs, AZ
Tel: (888) 255-9550
www.destinationgrandcanyon.com
Located in the Hualapai Indian tribal village of Peach Springs about 60

miles from the popular new Skywalk attraction in Grand Canyon West, this modern lodge is the only lodging on the reservation. There are 60 oversized, comfortable rooms with amenities. Book a room on the side away from the train tracks. A concessionaire offers river rafting and other activities. Restaurant, saltwater pool, spa, fitness center, gift shop. **$$**

Maswik Lodge
Grand Canyon, AZ 86023
Tel: (888) 297-2757 (reservations)
www.grandcanyonlodges.com
About 300 guest rooms and cabins are offered at this run-of-the-mill lodge, a 15-minute walk to the South Rim through the forest. The cabins tend to be a little rough around the edges. Ask for a room in Maswik North if you're concerned

PRICE CATEGORIES

Price categories are based on the cost of a double room for one night in the high season (January–April):
$ = less than $75
$$ = $75–150
$$$ = $150–200
$$$$ = more than $200

about comfort. Restaurant, bar, gift shop, television.

Phantom Ranch

Tel: (928) 638-2631 or (888) 297-2757 (reservations)
The only lodging in the bottom of the Grand Canyon offers basic log-and-stone cabins and single-sex dormitories. Make reservations as early as possible (Xanterra accepts bookings up to 13 months in advance). Meals at the dining hall are served family style and should be reserved ahead of time. Check the Bright Angel transportation desk (tel: 928-638-2631) for last-minute openings. Postcards mailed here are carried out of the canyon by mule. Restaurant. **$–$$**

Havasupai Lodge

Supai, AZ 86435
Tel: (928) 448-2111
Located down inside the western Grand Canyon, in the tiny Indian village of Havasupai, this 24-room motel can only be reached via the river or by hiking or riding a mule down into the canyon from the rim. All 24 rooms have two beds, private baths, and are air conditioned, nonsmoking. There are no phones or TVs. Strictly for the adventurous. **$$**

Thunderbird and Kachina Lodges

Grand Canyon, AZ 86023
Tel: (888) 297-2757 (reservations)
Sandwiched between El Tovar and Bright Angel Lodge, these low-slung

vintage motels are an unfortunate Sixties anachronism in the historic district. They do, however, have some modern amenities that are lacking in the rustic lodges. You'll get the best canyon views from Kachina Lodge's second-floor rooms. **$$**

Quality Inn and Suites Grand Canyon

PO Box 520, Tusayan, AZ 86023
Tel: (928) 638-2673 or toll free (800) 228-5151
Next to the IMAX theater in Tusayan, a short drive from the park entrance, this property is a cut above most chain hotels. The 232 rooms are large and comfortably furnished, the public spaces are airy and well maintained, and the suites are roomy

ABOVE: canyon view.

enough for families. Service here is very good, and the buffet is a firm local favorite. Restaurant, bar, outdoor pool, whirlpool, air conditioning, television. **$$–$$$**

PAGE AND THE ARIZONA STRIP

Best Western Arizona Inn

716 Rimview Drive, Page, AZ 86040
Tel: (928) 645-2466 or (800) 826-2718
This modern motel about a mile from downtown Page has 101 large rooms with queen-size beds and sweeping views of the desert. Outdoor pool, restaurant, bar, fitness room, air conditioning, television. **$$**

Canyon Colors Bed and Breakfast

225 South Navajo, Page, AZ 86040
Tel: (928) 645-5979 or (800) 536-2530
www.canyoncolors.com
Guests enjoy cheery, modern rooms at this house in a quiet residential area of Page. The two rooms, each able to accommodate four comfortably, have queen-size bed, futon, bath,

fireplace, television, VCR (access to an extensive video library). A full breakfast is included in the rate. Pool, television, air conditioning. **$$**

Courtyard by Marriott

600 Clubhouse Drive, Page, AZ 86040
Tel: (928) 645-5000 or (800) 851-3855
www.courtyard.com
This pleasant, Pueblo-style hotel offers comfortable, commodious lodging adjacent to the Lake Powell National Golf Course, one of the most scenic in the state. Restaurant, bar, laundry facilities, gift shop, outdoor pool, exercise room, air-con, TV. **$$**

Jacob Lake Inn

Highway 67 and 89A, Jacob Lake, AZ 86022
Tel: (928) 643-7232
www.jacoblake.com

This historic mountain inn is a welcome hub of activity in this sprawling, lonely country and the only lodging open year round. The thin-walled cabins and motel units have definitely seen betters days, but the coffee shop is lively, the tasty homemade pies and other fare are filling, and the milkshakes are justly renowned. Restaurant, gift shop, gas station. **$$**

Kaibab Lodge

HC 64, Box 64, Fredonia, AZ 86022
Tel: (928) 638-2389
Rooms at this mountain lodge, located on Highway 67 about 18 miles (29km) from the North Rim of the Grand Canyon, are tucked away in rustic cabins at the edge of a sweeping meadow. The main lodge, built in the 1920s, has an airy lobby with log beams, a big fireplace, Adirondack-style furniture, and television room (there are no televisions in guest rooms). Restaurant, gift shop. Open seasonally. **$$**

Lake Powell Resorts and Marinas

100 Lakeshore Drive, Page, AZ 86040
Tel: (928) 645-2433

LEFT: Lake Mead resort.

www.visitlakepowell.com
This former Wahweap Hotel is a large and busy hub for tourists exploring Lake Powell. All rooms have balconies or patios, but only about half overlook the lake. The Rainbow Room serves good American and Southwestern fare and has panoramic views of the lake. Rentals of power boats, houseboats, and other watercraft are available. Two pools, fitness room, restaurant, snack bar, lounge, air conditioning, television. **$$–$$$**

PRICE CATEGORIES

Price categories are based on the cost of a double room for one night in the high season (January–April):
$ = less than $75
$$= $75–150
$$$ = $150–200
$$$$ = more than $200

NAVAJO AND HOPI RESERVATIONS

Cameron Trading Post Motel
US 89, PO Box 339, Cameron, AZ 86020
Tel: (928) 679-2231 or (800) 338-7385
The motel adjoins a busy trading post built in the early 20th century and still serving the surrounding Navajo Nation and drivers on Highway 89. Rooms are comfortable and attractive, overlooking the scenic Little Colorado River canyon and bridge. But it's the trading post itself – and the treasures it contains, including a great little restaurant – that is the real attraction. Restaurant, gift shop, television, air conditioning, post office, gas station. **$$**

Goulding's Lodge
PO Box 3600001
Monument Valley, UT 84536
Tel: (435) 727-3231

www.gouldings.com
This former trading post, just outside the tribal park, has more than 60 motel-style rooms with Southwestern decor and balconies. The restaurant serves typical American dishes and has spectacular views. There's a great little museum with exhibits on all the movies shot in Monument Valley and the original owners. The hotel can arrange horseback riding and backcountry tours with Navajo guides. Restaurant, gift shop, indoor pool, tour desk, air conditioning, TV (with VCR and collection of Westerns shot in Monument Valley. **$$**

Holiday Inn Chinle – Garcia Trading Post
Navajo Route 7, Chinle, AZ 86503
Tel: (928) 674-5000
A good second choice if Thunderbird Lodge, inside

Canyon de Chelly National Monument, is full. The 108 room modern inn is half a mile from the park. Fitness center, outdoor pool, self-serve laundry. Park tours can be arranged. Air conditioning, TV, data ports, fridge, coffee-maker, hairdryer, and iron. Children under 19 stay free and eat free in the Mexican restaurant, located on the site of the old trading post. **$$**

Holiday Inn Kayenta
PO Box 307, Kayenta, AZ 86033
Tel: (928) 697-3221 or (800) 465-4329
A busy place with large and well-kept, if predictable, lodging. The hotel is at the intersection of US 160 and 163 about 24 miles (38km) from Monument Valley Navajo Tribal Park. The restaurant serves American and Navajo fare.

Restaurant, gift shop, outdoor pool, tour desk, air conditioning, TV. **$$**

View Hotel and Restaurant
Monument Valley, UT 84536
www.monumentvalleyview.com
In October 2008, the only hotel within Monument Valley Navajo Tribal Park will open to the public. Completely Navajo-owned and built in harmony with its surroundings, all the rooms in the hotel will have scenic views. The visitor center is next door. Online reservations are now being taken. **$$**

FLAGSTAFF AND ENVIRONS

Arizona Sled Dog Inn
10155 Mountainaire Road, Flagstaff, AZ 86001
Tel: (928) 525-6212 or (800) 754-0664
www.sleddoginn.com
Located on the edge of rustic Mountainaire, south of Flagstaff off Interstate 17, this modern lodge has seven tranquil rooms on the edge of the national forest. All have full baths, log furniture, down comforters, but no phones or TVs. There are two large living rooms with rock fireplaces, a hot tub, and sauna. Full breakfast includes homemade granola. The inn is home to dogs, horses, and other pets. **$$**

Fall Into Nature
4555 South Lake Mary Road, Flagstaff, AZ 86001
Tel: (928) 714-0237 or (888) 920-0237
www.fallintonature.com
This modern three-suite bed-and-breakfast is down a woodsy road just southeast of town. There's hiking, horseback riding,

and fishing on Upper Lake Mary. **$$**

Grand Canyon Railway Hotel and Resort
235 N. Grand Canyon Boulevard Williams, AZ 86046
Tel: (928) 635-4010 or (800) THE TRAIN
www.thetrain.com
A reconstruction of the 1908 Fray Marcos Hotel, this new 89-room hotel at the historic train depot mixes turn-of-the-20th-century ambiance with convenience. The Western-style lobby celebrates the art of Frederic Remington; a saloon has a player piano and a beautifully carved bar from a London pub. Restaurant, bar, air-con, TV, indoor pool. **$$**

Hilton Garden Inn Flagstaff
350 W. Forest Meadows Street, Flagstaff, AZ 86001
Tel: (928) 226-8888 or (800) 333-0785
www.flagstaff.gardeninn.com
Set on a busy commercial strip, a few minutes from downtown, this property – one of the newer hotels in town – delivers Hilton-style

efficient lodging. Pool, fitness room, whirlpool, air conditioning, TV.

Hotel Monte Vista
100 N. San Francisco Street, Flagstaff, AZ 86001
Tel: (928) 779-6971 or (800) 545-3068
Dark and a bit threadbare, this downtown landmark, opened in 1927, was once a favorite of celebrity guests such as John Wayne, Clark Gable, and Spencer Tracy. You can still find some old-time charm here, but the hotel is best suited for students, backpackers, and other budget travelers. Some rooms have shared baths. Restaurant, bar. **$**

The Inn at 410
410 N. Leroux Street, Flagstaff, AZ 86001
Tel: (928) 774-0088 or (800) 774-2008
www.inn410.com
This handsome wood-frame bed-and-breakfast set on a quiet downtown lot offers nine rooms and suites beautifully

decorated in styles ranging from Old West and Victorian to French Country, some with fireplace and Jacuzzi. An inviting living and dining room, big front porch and backyard garden give guests plenty of room to roam. Breakfasts are bountiful and expertly prepared. **$$–$$$**

La Posada
303 E. 2nd Street (Route 66), Winslow, AZ 86047
Tel: (928) 289-4366
Designed in the late 1920s by Mary Elizabeth Jane Colter, who considered it her masterpiece, this rambling hacienda-style hotel adjoining the train station was only open for

27 years before it was closed and later gutted. Restoration began in 1997, and the hotel now offers more than 20 guest rooms furnished in the spare but elegant style of the period. The hotel's grand open spaces, with their heavy beams and vaulted

ceilings, have been faithfully restored by private owners using Colter's original plans. There's a gourmet restaurant. This is a fascinating historic site and good value. Ask for a room on the other side of the hotel from the station. Restaurant, bar. **$$**

Radisson Woodlands Hotel Flagstaff
1175 W. Route 66, Flagstaff,
AZ 86001
Tel: (928) 773-8888 or
(888) 201-1718
www.radisson.com
A lobby with Italian marble floors, granite architectural details and plush

furnishings set the tone of this hotel, among the most sumptuous in town. Rooms are spacious and tasteful. A Japanese restaurant and sushi bar are a pleasant surprise. Two restaurants, outdoor pool, fitness center, air conditioning, TV. **$$**

ARIZONA'S WEST COAST

Havasu Springs Resort
2581 Highway 95, Parker,
AZ 85344
Tel: (928) 667-3361
www.havasusprings.com
This huge resort about 20 miles (32km) south of Lake Havasu City encompasses three motels, but the real attraction is houseboat rentals. The vessels sleep up to 12 people and have various features, but all are equipped with bathrooms and complete galleys.
$$$–$$$$
London Bridge Resort
1477 Queens Bay,
Lake Havasu City, AZ 86043
Tel: (928) 855-0888
www.londonbridgeresort.com

Part Tudor mansion, part southwestern oasis and part tropical getaway, the resort is popular with the party crowd who come more for the pools, water sports, and open-air night club than the large condominium-style guest quarters. The bridge itself is in the backyard. Expect a glut of revelers during spring break. Restaurant, night club, three pools, tennis courts, golf course, marina, boat rentals, air conditioning, TV. **$$–$$$$**
Shiloh Inn
1550 S. Castle Dome Avenue,
Yuma, AZ 85365
Tel: (928) 782-9511 or

(800) 222-2244
www.shilohinns.com
Spacious rooms with couches, microwaves, refrigerators, and patios or balconies are among the most comfortable in Yuma, and the well-maintained lawn is a welcome patch of green in an otherwise stark desert landscape. Suites with kitchenettes are also available. Pool, restaurant, bar, exercise room, TV, air conditioning. **$$–$$$**
Temple Bar Resort
Temple Bar, AZ 86643
Tel: (928) 767-3211 or
(800) 752-9669
www.sevencrown.com
This 18-unit motel is set on

the shore of Lake Mead surrounded by miles of open desert. A variety of watercraft, including ski boats, patio boats, fishing boats, and jet skis, are available for rent at a fully equipped marina. Restaurant, marina, RV facilities, TV, air-con. **$$**

SEDONA AND THE VERDE VALLEY

Amara Creekside Resort
310 N. Highway 89A, Sedona, AZ
Tel: (866) 455-6610
www.amararesort.com
This top-rated boutique hotel on the banks of Oak Creek has the feel of organic architect Frank Lloyd Wright's spectacular home and studio in Scottsdale but with a striking modern sensibility geared toward today's travelers. The low-profile hotel is the linchpin of Sedona Center, which includes two shopping centers and restaurants, all linked by a self-guided nature trail with exhibits developed by the Sedona-based Institute of EcoTourism. The resort has 100 tranquil rooms, including 24 suites with whirlpool tubs. All have pillowtop mattresses, walk-in closets, and Aveda bath

products; many overlook the creek or lawn and have patios. Creekside dining in three restaurants. Spa. Heated outdoor saltwater pool. Meeting rooms. WiFi throughout. **$$$–$$$$**
Briar Patch Inn
3190 N. Highway 89A, Sedona,
AZ 86336
Tel: (928) 282-2342 or
(888) 809-3030
www.briarpatchinn.com
Set on the banks of Oak Creek a few miles north of Sedona, this historic canyon hideaway offers 18 cozy cabins with stone-and-wood-panel walls, rustic furnishings, and Indian rugs; some cabins have decks and fireplaces. Complimentary full breakfast is served in an attractive dining room or on a terrace overlooking the creek in summer, often to the strains of live classical

musicians. Massage and wellness programs are available. **$$**
Cathedral Rock Lodge & Retreat Center
61 Los Amigos Lane, Sedona,
AZ 86336
Tel: (928) 282-7608 or
(800) 352-9149
www.cathedralrocklodge.com
The lodge has areas ideal for large groups or families: a suite, a cottage, and a two-bedroom house with views of gardens and Sedona's redrock scenery. TV, VCR. **$$**
Enchantment Resort
525 Boynton Canyon Road,
Sedona, AZ 86336
Tel: (928) 282-2900 or
(800) 826-4180
www.enchantmentresort.com
This famous resort has a glorious Boynton Canyon location with luxurious accommodations. Pueblo-style *casitas* have single

rooms as well as one- and two-bedroom suites, many with living rooms, fireplaces, and patios. All are decorated in a contemporary southwestern style,

PRICE CATEGORIES

Price categories are based on the cost of a double room for one night in the high season (January–April):
$ = less than $75
$$ = $75–150
$$$ = $150–200
$$$$ = more than $200

and the views are universally gorgeous. The Yavapai Dining Room specializes in fine southwestern and Continental cuisine and has panoramic views of the canyon. A second restaurant, Tii Gavo, offers a more casual atmosphere. A spa with a wide range of facilities and services is also on the grounds. Four pools, two restaurants, fitness center, pitch-and-putt golf course, nature walks, mountain bike rentals, tennis courts, meeting facilities, children's program, air conditioning, TV. **$$$–$$$$**
Garland's Oak Creek Lodge
PO Box 152, Oak Creek, AZ
Tel: (928) 282-3343
www.garlandslodge.com
A unique historic lodge on a wooded homestead next to

RIGHT: Enchantment Resort.

Oak Creek. With its roaring fires and porches with rocking chairs, the lodge offers a quintessential cabin-in-the-woods experience. Rustic but beautifully maintained, the 16 air-conditioned cabins have no phones or TVs and are surrounded by gardens. Full breakfasts, four-course dinners, and afternoon teas are included in the price and include organic fruits and vegetables grown onsite. Two-night minimum. Dinner, served family style in the cozy dining room, is open to a limited number of non-guests. Reserve well ahead; the lodge is often booked a year in advance. Dinner reservations here are like gold dust. Closed Nov–Mar and Sundays. **$$$$**

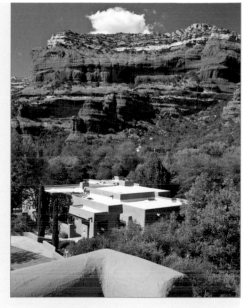

MOGOLLON RIM AND THE TONTO BASIN

Grey Hackle Lodge
PO Box 145, Payson, AZ 85541
Tel: (928) 478-4392
www.greyhacklelodge.com
Eleven log cabins set on 4 acres (1.6 hectares) just east of Payson. Some are one-room cabins with kitchenettes; others are two-story cabins with full kitchens and fireplaces. Simply furnished, the cabins are well maintained. Private baths, TV. **$$**
Majestic Mountain Inn
602 E. Highway 260, Payson, AZ 85541
Tel: (928) 474-0185 or (800) 408-2442
www.majesticmountaininn.com

Regular rooms at this attractive stone-and-timber lodge in Payson have the style and comfort of a standard motel unit. If you're looking for something more comfortable, the luxury rooms are larger and have Jacuzzi and gas fireplace. Pool, meeting facilities, TV, air conditioning. **$$**
Koh's Ranch Lodge
Highway 260, Payson, AZ 85541
Tel: (920) 478-4211 or (800) 521-3131
www.ilxresorts.com
Set on Tonto Creek in the ponderosa pine forest east of Payson, cabins are quite

roomy, with dining areas, kitchenettes, patios and fireplaces. Rooms in the main lodge are somewhat more modest, though several have fireplaces. All are furnished in contemporary style. Restaurant, cowboy bar, outdoor pool, horseback riding, mountain bike rentals, exercise room, putting green, playground, TV, air conditioning. **$$–$$$**
Mountain Meadows Cabins
HC 2, Box 162E, Payson, AZ 85541
Tel: (928) 478-4415
www.mountainmeadowscabins.com
Six cabins situated east of Payson under the

Mogollon Rim at an elevation of 6,400ft (1,950m). Each has a private bath, kitchen, and fireplace. Most of the land surrounding the cabins is part of a national forest. Kitchen, TV, VCR, barbecue grill. **$$**

WHITE MOUNTAINS

Greer Lodge
44 Main Street, Greer, AZ
Tel: (928) 735-7216
www.greerlodgeaz.com
This large resort on the south end of the little mountain community of Greer offers an assortment of comfortable cabins and luxurious rooms in its attractive log lodge overlooking the meadows

and the Little Colorado River. Freestanding cabins are dog and kid friendly; the upscale lodge is adult, pet-free only. Many free amenities, including fly-fishing lessons, use of mountain bikes, binoculars, and telescopes in summer, and snowshoes in winter. Onsite restaurant, air

conditioning, fireplaces, TVs. **$$–$$$**
Molly Butler Lodge
PO Box 134, Greer, AZ 85927
Tel: (928) 735-7226
The first lodging in Greer (1910) was run by Mormon pioneers Molly and John Butler. It is now rather run down but the bar is still a lively community gathering place at the end of the day

and the restaurant is popular for its fish fry,

steak, and beer on Friday nights. The 11 guest rooms are very bare bones but have a unique rural charm. **$**

Red Setter Inn
44 Main Street, Greer, AZ
Tel: (928) 735-7216
www.redsetterinn.com
Now owned by Greer Lodge but managed separately, this beautiful hunting lodge-style bed-and-breakfast is set on 10 acres (4 hectares) and is one of Arizona's loveliest

backwoods getaways. The inn has nine luxurious suites with four-poster and sleigh beds topped by cozy feather comforters. All rooms have baths or showers, TVs and phones and access to balconies or decks overlooking the river. A full breakfast is served in the dining room or guests may eat at the nearby Greer Lodge restaurant. There are three sitting rooms with fireplaces. The downstairs sitting room has

games, and a TV/DVD player with DVD library. Four differently sized log cabins, on the other side of the river, may be rented separately. Activities include private fishing and access to miles of national forest trails. Two-night minimum on weekends. Adults only. **$$$–$$$$**

White Mountain Lodge
140 Main Street, PO Box 143, Greer, AZ 85927
Tel: (928) 735-7568 or (888) 493-7568

www.wmlodge.com
Set in an 1892 log home overlooking Greer Meadow and the Little Colorado River, this welcoming family-run country inn has three suites with kitchenettes, sitting rooms, and TVs, as well as six log cabins with kitchens and fireplaces or wood-burning stoves; some cabins also have whirlpool tubs. On weekends, there's a two-night minimum stay. **$$–$$$**

PHOENIX

Arizona Biltmore Resort and Spa
24th Street and Missouri Avenue, Phoenix, AZ 85016
Tel: (602) 955-6600 or (800) 954-0086
www.arizonabiltmore.com
This grand hotel inspired by Frank Lloyd Wright (who acted as consultant on the project) is the last word in grace, dignity, and architectural distinction. Two 18-hole golf courses, full-service spa, fine dining in two restaurants, bars, five swimming pools, fitness center, biking, shops, business center, air conditioning, TV, valet parking. **$$$$**

El Rey Motel
121 E. Ash Street, Globe, AZ 85501

Tel: (928) 425-4427
A short drive east of Phoenix, and a world away, this vintage 1950s motor lodge is the real deal in the historic mining town of Globe. Classic desert roadside vernacular touches include individual carports, wagon wheels, and a communal barbecue and picnic area. The 23 rooms are nicely maintained, and all have baths and cable TV. An excellent choice for the nostalgic at heart and families looking for a good deal. **$–$$**

Embassy Suites Phoenix Airport
1515 N. 44th Street, Phoenix, AZ 85008
Tel: (602) 244-8800 or

(800) 447-8483
Just minutes from Sky Harbor International Airport, this all-suites hotel offers spacious accommodations with separate bedrooms and living rooms and contemporary furnishings. The high-rise surrounds a central courtyard with an outdoor pool. A good choice for business travelers who need extra room or for families with small children. Restaurant, bar, pool, exercise room, meeting facilities, airport shuttle, air conditioning, TV. **$$–$$$**

Fairmont Scottsdale Princess
7575 E. Princess Drive, Scottsdale, AZ 85255
Tel: (480) 585-4848
www.fairmont.com
This luxurious resort sprawls 450 acres (180 hectares) at the base of the McDowell Mountains north of Scottsdale. Spanish Colonial architecture, antique furnishings, fountains, generous patios, and immaculate landscaping create a rich and exotic ambiance. Spacious rooms and casitas are decorated in muted desert tones, with fine southwestern furnishings, large bathrooms and terraces. Seven restaurants serve Spanish and Mexican cuisine. Restaurants, bars,

two 18-hole golf courses, tennis courses, three pools, fitness center, spa services, shops, business center, meeting facilities, TV, air conditioning. **$$$$**

Hermosa Inn
5532 North Palo Cristi Road, Paradise Valley, AZ
Tel: (602) 955-8614 or (800) 241-1210
www.hermosainn.com
Centrally located in a residential area between Phoenix and Scottsdale, this quiet rustic historic inn includes restored portions of the original adobe home and studio of cowboy artist Lon Megargee in the 1930s, which he subsequently converted to a guest ranch and inn. Subsequent owners have added a swimming pool, tennis courts, casitas, and villas. This is an historic structure, so expect smaller rooms and bathrooms furnished with charming southwestern details. The onsite restaurant, Lon's, is top rated for its artisanal American cuisine. **$$$$**

Gainey Suites Hotel
7300 E. Gainey Suites Drive,

LEFT: Arizona Biltmore.

LEFT: Royal Palms Hotel.

Scottsdale, AZ 85258
Tel: (480) 922-6969 or
(800) 970-4666
www.gaineysuiteshotel.com
This independently owned, all-suites boutique hotel adjacent to Gainey Village development is a great budget option in upscale Scottsdale. The 162 attractively decorated suites range in size from studios to two-bedrooms, sleeping two to eight people. Pillow-top mattresses with take-home teddy bears, fully equipped kitchens, flat-screen LCD TVs with with on-demand movies, CDs, and games, and free Wi-Fi throughout. Pool, outdoor hot tub, laundry facilities, and continental breakfast. Golf tee times at over 50 local courses can be arranged through the hotel. **$$–$$$**

Hotel San Carlos
202 N Central Avenue, Phoenix, AZ 85004
Tel: (602) 253-6668
www.hotelsancarlos.com
Built in 1928, this multistory Italian Renaissance-style hotel was the first high rise, fully air-conditioned, luxury hotel in downtown Phoenix. After undergoing a recent million-dollar restoration, it is slowly returning to its former glory and is a member of the Historic Hotels of America. Many of the original fixtures and fittings are intact, especially in the grand lobby, which has chandeliers, a copper-doored elevator, decorative moldings, and other details. The 121 rooms, including 11 suites, are cramped by today's standards and at the mercy of ancient plumbing and thin walls. Still, all have attractive period features as well as Serta Sleeper mattresses, coffeemakers, cable TV, data ports, clock radios, ceiling fans, and irons. Rooftop pool, two restaurants, gift shop, barber shop. Staff are friendly and helpful, and the hotel is within walking distance of the Phoenix Art Museum and Heard Museum. **$$–$$$**

Maricopa Manor
15 W. Pasadena Avenue, Phoenix, AZ 85013
Tel: (602) 274-6302 or
(800) 292-6403
www.maricopamanor.com
When it was built in 1928, this hacienda-style bed-and-breakfast was in the countryside outside town. Now, it's in the heart of the city, a block from the busy Camelback corridor. An acre (0.4 hectare) of landscaped grounds shelter the property from the surrounding bustle. All seven rooms are suites with attractive, mostly contemporary Southwest furnishings. Four luxury suites have fireplaces and whirlpool tubs. Pool, air conditioning, TV, gardens, complimentary breakfast, Wi-Fi throughout. **$$–$$$**

The Phoenician
600 E. Camelback Road, Scottsdale, AZ 85251
Tel: (480) 941-8200 or
(800) 888-8234
www.thephoenician.com
No extravagance is overlooked at this landmark resort at the base of Camelback Mountain.

Guest rooms, suites, and casitas are lavishly furnished, with marble bathrooms, patios, Italian linens, and original art; some have travertine fireplaces. The grounds and public spaces are equally elaborate. The resort's 250 acres (100 hectares) encompass a world-class 27-hole golf course, nine pools (including a 165ft/50m water slide), manicured gardens, 11 tennis courts, a full-service spa, and an extensive art collection. The 11 restaurants and lounges range from Mary Elaine's, perhaps the finest French cuisine in the state, and the Praying Monk, set in a wine cellar with barrel-vaulted ceilings, brick archways and European antiques, to casual outdoor dining and an ice cream parlor. All this luxury doesn't come cheap, though you may be surprised at just how affordable a standard room can be during the sweltering summer off-season. Several bars, bike rentals, gift shops, children's program, meeting facilities, air conditioning, TV. **$$$–$$$$**

Pointe Hilton Squaw Peak Resort
7677 N. 16th Street, Phoenix, AZ 85020
Tel: (602) 997-2626 or
(800) 876-4683
www.hilton.com
With an elaborate water park and extensive children's program, this luxury resort is a hit with kids. Guest quarters are mostly two-room suites furnished in contemporary style with a few Spanish Colonial touches. Adults may prefer to avail themselves of the 18-hole golf course, full-service spa, tennis courts, or four pools. Jogging trails meander through immaculate grounds. Eight restaurants range from quick, casual eats to haute cuisine. Shops, air conditioning. **$$$–$$$$**

Ritz-Carlton Phoenix
2401 E Camelback Road, Phoenix, AZ 85016
Tel: (602) 468-0700 or
(800) 241-3333
www.ritzcarlton.com
This grand hotel across from the Biltmore Fashion Park shopping center offers impeccable service and elegant accommodations. Antique furnishings and paintings in public spaces lend an air of Old World sophistication. Guest quarters are furnished with reproductions and have marble bathrooms. Pool, fitness center, restaurants, bar, air conditioning, TV. **$$$–$$$$**

Royal Palms Hotel and Casitas
5200 E. Camelback Road, Phoenix, AZ 85018
Tel: (602) 840-3610 or
(800) 672-6011
www.royalpalmsresortandspa.com
You'll feel as if you've wandered into a Mediterranean villa at this recently renovated hotel, built in the 1940s. Walled courtyards with antique fountains, gardens, antique European furnishings, and beautifully restored architectural details create an atmosphere of romance and opulence. Each deluxe casita is designed in a distinctive style, ranging from Spanish Colonial to contemporary. Other rooms aren't quite so lavishly appointed. The restaurant, T. Cook's, is considered one of the finest in the city. Bar, pool, tennis court, fitness room, air conditioning, TV. **$$$$**

Sheraton Wild Horse Pass Resort and Spa
Gila River Indian Community, 5594 W. Wild Horse Pass Boulevard, Chandler, AZ 85226
Tel: (602) 225-0100 or
(888) 218-8989

www.wildhorsepassresort.com
The Pima (Akimel O'odham) and Maricopa (Pee Posh) tribes have been renowned hosts since the 19th century, and their heritage is woven into every detail of this luxury resort, just south of Phoenix. The sight and sound of water in the desert is the central motif throughout. A replica of the Gila River meanders through the grounds. A riverside pool with waterfalls replicates the Hohokam ruins of Casa Grande. A dramatic mural retells the tribes' history in the domed lobby – itself a spectacular reference to a traditional Pima roundhouse. Pima basketry and Maricopa pottery designs adorn the two large winds containing the guest rooms. Wild horses gallop into view while coyotes can be heard yipping at night. The 500 rooms have patios or balconies and views of the golf course, Estrella Mountains or the Gila River. All have minibars, safes, phones, bath and shower, and TVs. Amenities include a 36-hole golf course, a Native-inspired spa, horseback riding, a hiking trail system, two tribal museums, cultural tours, boat rides on the replica river, and a nearby casino. The resort's fabulous four-star dinner restaurant, Kai, showcases contemporary American Indian-inspired cuisine, using greens and other foods grown on the Gila Reservation and other Indian reservations in the US. **$$$$**

TUCSON

Adobe Rose Inn
940 N. Olsen Avenue, Tucson, AZ 85719
Tel: (520) 318-4644 or (800) 328-4122
www.aroseinn.com
Built in 1933 and enclosed by 1ft (30cm) thick pink adobe walls, this snug bed-and-breakfast is in a quiet residential neighborhood near the University of Arizona. The six rooms and cottages are furnished in a rustic southwestern style; one room has a corner kiva fireplace. A full breakfast is included. Pool, TV, air-con, and high-speed Internet connection. **$$**

Arizona Inn
2200 E Elm Street, Tucson, AZ 85719
Tel: (520) 325-1541 or (800) 933-1093
www.arizonainn.com
One of downtown Tucson's top lodgings, this elegant historic southwestern inn is just 5 minutes from the University of Arizona but feels like its own oasis. Guest rooms and suites are tastefully furnished with antiques and are mainly in casitas, with patios and fireplaces, amid 14 acres (6 hectares) of manicured grounds and gardens. Outdoor pool, tennis

courts, massage, exercise room, fine dining, bar, air conditioning, TV. Reserve well ahead. **$$$**

Clarion Hotel Randolph Park
102 N. Alvernon Way, Tucson, AZ 85711
Tel: (520) 795-0330
www.clarionhotel.com/hotel/az128
This comfortable chain hotel is within walking distance of shopping malls, theaters, and restaurants. The room rate includes a hot breakfast buffet. Whirlpool, in-room microwave, laundry service, air conditioning, TV. **$$–$$$**

El Presidio Bed and Breakfast
297 N. Main Avenue, Tucson, AZ 85701
Tel: (520) 623-6151
Since 1985, innkeeper Patti Toci has run an elegant award-winning bed-and-breakfast in this 1886 house, part of downtown El Presidio Historic District. Four comfortable suites (two with private entrances) are furnished with antiques. All have telephones, TVs, complimentary beverages, fruit and snacks. Guests enjoy a full gourmet breakfast around a single table in the sunny veranda room, which looks out onto a restful flowered courtyard with fountain. Two-night minimum. **$$–$$$**

Hotel Congress
311 E. Congress, Tucson, AZ 85701
Tel: (520) 622-8848 or (800) 722-8848
www.hotelcongress.com
John Dillinger and his gang stayed at this quirky 1919 hotel near the Amtrak station, though the clientele nowadays is mostly hip young backpackers and budget travelers. Rooms offer basis comforts, but the place has some interesting touches such as old-fashioned radios and telephones, an Internet cafe, a lively saloon and late-hours night club, and a great little coffee shop that has been featured on the Food Network. Idiosyncratic and inexpensive. Private and shared hostel rooms are available. Bar, nightclub, restaurant. **$**

Lazy K Bar Guest Ranch
8401 N. Scenic Drive, Tucson, AZ 85743
Tel: (520) 744-3050 or (800) 321-7018
www.lazykbar.com
The ranch's 24 adobe casitas are set in the Tucson Mountains overlooking the Santa Cruz Valley, about 16 miles (26km) northwest of Tucson. Recreational opportunities abound, with a riding program, spa, live entertainment, and cookouts. American Plan (all meals included), pool, hot tub, volleyball and basketball courts, ranch store, meeting facilities, air conditioning. **$$$–$$$$**

Lodge on the Desert
306 N. Alvernon Way, Tucson, AZ 85711
Tel: (520) 325-3366 or (800) 456-5634
www.lodgeonthedesert.com
Built in 1936 and thoroughly renovated, this

in-town resort consists of a compound of casitas amid well-tended gardens, cacti, and shady palms, with views of the Santa Catalina Mountains. Most rooms have patios and fireplaces; some have tiled floors and exposed beams. A restaurant, Cielos, is highly regarded. Pool, restaurant, air conditioning, TV. **$$–$$$**

Loews Ventana Canyon Restaurant
7000 N. Resort Drive, Tucson, AZ 85750
Tel: (520) 299-2020 or (800) 234-5117
www.loewshotels.com
Tucson's premier resort is an island of luxury and comfort in the desert outside the city. Rooms are large and beautifully furnished, each with a private balcony overlooking the city or Santa Catalina Mountains. The design of public spaces, including the terraces, meeting rooms, restaurants, and the lobby, offers an understated elegance in keeping with the desert setting. Diversions range from two world-class 18-hole golf courses, a complete spa, and one of the best restaurants in Tucson. Two pools, eight tennis courts, fitness

TRANSPORTATION

ACCOMMODATIONS

ACTIVITIES

A – Z

center, meeting facilities, restaurants and lounges, shops, bike rentals, air conditioning, TV. **$$$$**

Omni Tucson National Golf Resort and Spa
2727 W. Club Drive, Tucson, AZ 85742
Tel: (520) 297-2271 or (800) 528-4856
www.omnihotels.com
Golfers will think they have died and gone to heaven at this luxury resort in the foothills of the Santa Catalina Mountains, home of the annual PGA Tucson Open golf tournament. Rooms and suites are very large and furnished in a contemporary style, some with fireplaces and/or kitchenettes, many with patios and balconies. The real attraction, however, is the 27-hole golf course, one of the most beautiful and challenging in the region. Non-golfers can have themselves pampered at the full-service spa or lounge by one of the two pools. Two restaurants serve American and southwestern cuisine. Tennis courts, basketball courts, fitness center, nature trails, lounges, air conditioning, TV. **$$$–$$$$**

Tanque Verde Guest Ranch
14301 E. Speedway Boulevard, Tucson, AZ 85748
Tel: (520) 296-6275 or (800) 234-3833
www.tanqueverderanch.com
More of a spa resort than a

RIGHT: Westward Look Resort.

ranch, Tanque Verde is sandwiched between Saguaro National Park and Coronado National Forest at the base of the Rincon Mountains. More than 70 rooms and suits are simple and comfortable; many have fireplaces and/or patios. Casitas are large and sumptuous. The ranch is a destination in itself, and there's never a dull moment. Activities include trail rides, complimentary tennis lessons, nature hikes, lectures, live entertainment, and bountiful meals and cookouts, Spa, indoor and outdoor pools, horseback riding and lessons, tennis courts, fitness room, basketball and volleyball courts, children's program, airport shuttle, air conditioning. American Plan (all meals included). **$$$$**

Westward Look Resort
245 E. Ina Road, Tucson, AZ 85704
Tel: (520) 297-1151 or (800) 722-2500
www.westwardlook.com
Not just another elegant Tucson ranch resort, the superb Westward Look Resort has a long and interesting history. It was built around a 1912 hacienda on 80 acres (32 hectares) in the Santa Catalina Foothills. More than 200 guest rooms are all suite-sized, furnished in

luxurious southwestern style, and grouped in graceful casitas that ensure complete privacy (perfect for a retreat or to get that novel finished). Abundant wildlife makes this a great place for nature lovers. Opportunities for recreation and relaxation are numerous. Facilities include three pools and whirlpools, a fitness center, a superb spa specializing in authentic, hard-to-find East Indian Ayurvedic treatments professionally carried out by well-trained therapists, tennis courts, a Celestron 2000 telescope, hiking on the resort's extensive nature trails, horseback riding, mountain biking, and strolls through a variety of desert gardens. A fine restaurant, the Gold Room, overlooking the city has the best views in Tucson. It features delicious New Western cuisine by award-winning chef Jamie West, who showcases produce he grows in the property's organic garden (chef tours

available). Meeting facilities, air conditioning, TV. **$$$–$$$$**

White Stallion Ranch
9251 W. Twin Peaks Road, Tucson, AZ 85743
Tel: (520) 297-0252 or (888) 977-2624
Guests get an authentic taste of the Old West at this working cattle ranch on 3,000 acres (1,200 hectares) bordering Saguaro National Park. Accommodations range from snug, stripped-down single rooms to larger and more comfortable two-bedroom suites with living rooms. The emphasis is on horseback riding, but a variety of other activities, including nature hikes, tennis, swimming, hayrides, cookouts, and a weekly rodeo, provide plenty of other diversions. Kids enjoy the petting zoo. Meals are served family-style in the dining room. Stables and riding lessons, children's program, outdoor pool. American Plan (all meals included). **$$$$**

BORDER COUNTRY

Beatty's Miller Guest Ranch and Orchard
2173 E. Miller Canyon Road, Hereford, AZ 85615
Tel: (520) 378-2728
www.beattysguestranch.com
This all-nonsmoking, family-run backcountry retreat occupies an apple orchard adjacent to the Miller Peak Wilderness. Housekeeping units include two apartments and four cabins, each with a bedroom, sitting room and full kitchen. Visitors have access to the hummingbird and butterfly gardens.

Flame-colored tanagers and hummingbirds are the big draw for the serious birders who frequent this place. No meals served. **$$**

Birders Vista Bed and Breakfast
5147 South Kino Road, Sierra Vista, AZ
Tel: (520) 378-2493
www.birdersvista.com
This large, immaculately kept, modern stucco home is conveniently located 10 minutes from Sierra Vista, Ramsey Canyon, and the San Pedro River. It offers a friendly, European-style bed-

and-breakfast experience that will appeal to those who enjoy mingling with their hosts and other guests. Set on 4 acres (1.6 hectares) of open desert, and sheltered by a stand of mature pines, orchards, and landscaping that attract a variety of birds. Two bedrooms have sitting areas with private baths and entrances. A suite is available with two pretty bedrooms, sitting room, and private bath. A full breakfast is included with room rate, including

homemade organic plum jam from the onsite orchard; early birders can make arrangements for continental breakfast. Owners Johnnie and Audrey Eskue are avid and well-informed birders and extend a low-key, down-home Texan welcome and the run of their comfortable home. Amenities include TV, computor with Internet access, videos, games, and library. Johnnie's carved wood sculptures and many paintings by local artists adorn the walls and are for sale. **$$**

Bisbee Grand Hotel
61 Main Street, Bisbee, AZ 85603
Tel: (520) 432-5900
Elegantly restored Victorian bed-and-breakfast with period decor in the heart of downtown. A saloon on the ground floor evokes a spit-and-sawdust Old West atmosphere, and the theme is carried through 13 guest rooms. In some cases, private bathrooms are located down the hall. Billiard room, breakfast included. No in-room telephones or TVs. **$$**

Circle Z Ranch
PO Box 194, Patagonia, AZ 85624
Tel: (520) 394-2525 or (888) 854-2525
www.circlez.com
Accommodations range from individual rooms to suites or private cottages in several adobe buildings at the foot of the Santa Rita Mountains about 60 miles (100km) south of Tucson. The main activities are horseback riding, pack trips, and birding at the adjoining Nature Conservancy preserve. There is a three-day minimum stay. **$$**

Copper City Inn
99 Main Street, Bisbee, AZ 85624
Tel: (520) 432-1418 or 4254
www.coppercityinn.com
The three beautifully remodeled, Southwest-themed rooms in the Copper City Inn, a three-level duplex across from the theater on Bisbee's Main Street, are just the ticket for travelers looking for slightly more refined lodgings in funky, artsy Bisbee. All have secure, keyless entry, French windows and balconies, super-comfy queen beds, large closets and bathrooms with local toiletries, a wet bar with complimentary bottle of

wine (owner Fred Miller tends bar at the excellent Cafe Roka restaurant nearby) and bottled water, tea and coffee facilities, and cable TV, wireless Internet, and phones. A larger room downstairs has a full kitchen. Rear sun deck. Voucher for continental breakfast at nearby High Desert Market and Cafe included in room rate. Note: the inn, like much of Bisbee, is reached by climbing a flight of steep stairs. There is no disabled access. **$$**

Cross Creek Cottages
14 Cross Creek Road, Patagonia, AZ 85624
Tel: (520) 394-0054
www.patagoniaaz.com/lodging_crosscreek
This ranch in the countryside on the outskirts of Patagonia is a wonderful base for anyone on a budget wanting to make an extended exploration of the Border Country. The 20-acre ranch has two cozy one- and two-bed cottages and a studio apartment on Sonoita Creek. The ranch has rescue donkeys, llamas, and an alpaca and adjoins the Native Seeds/SEARCH research center. There are beautiful views and places to walk. The owner, Regina Medley, is an artist with a gallery in Patagonia, and the former owner of the Duquesne House Bed and Breakfast. Works of art and antiques decorate each cottage, which have full kitchens, living rooms with woodstoves, separate bathrooms, and porches; the pretty studio apartment adjoining the owner's house and pool has a wet bar with continental breakfast fixings, microwave, and coffeemaker. This authentic Patagonia lodging is a real find. No credit cards. Long-term rates available. **$$**

Cochise Hotel
PO Box 27, Cochise, AZ 85606
Tel: (520) 384-3156 or 3414
The quirky, one-story Cochise Hotel was built in 1882 to serve railroad workers and has been continuously operational in the ghost town of Cochise

ever since. The hotel has five guest rooms with private baths and antiques, and maintains a studied austerity (the hotel still advertises "honest beds" and a menu featuring "railroad steak, jackrabbit fodder, spuds, and pullman's biscuits" – translated, that means comfortably updated antique beds with quilts and dinner of ranch steak and all the fixin's) . Manager Carla Adams often greets guests in period costume with warm cookies and tells tales about Big Nose Kate, Doc Holliday's girlfriend, who waited tables at the hotel, and other tidbits of local lore. An authentic Wild West experience for ghost town fanatics and history buffs. Reservations must be made at least one week in advance. **$–$$**

Copper Queen Hotel
11 Howell Avenue, Bisbee, AZ 85603
Tel: (520) 432-2216
This turn-of-the-20th-century landmark built during the heyday of the Copper Queen Mine drips with Old West atmosphere; guests have included John Wayne and Teddy Roosevelt. Rooms vary in size, are furnished with antiques, and most have been recently renovated. Restaurant, saloon, pool, TV, air conditioning. **$$**

Duquesne House Bed and breakfast
357 Duquesne Avenue, Patagonia, AZ 85624
Tel: (520) 394-2732
This converted former miners' boarding house is located in the artist haven of Patagonia, 19 miles (30km) from the Mexican border. Each accommodation in the long, low adobe building is a separate apartment with pretty touches such as Mexican tiles and wooden dressers. Each unit has a private entrance, sitting room with day beds, bedroom, private bath and access to a large screened back porch and extensive gardens that attract

hummingbirds and many other birds at the foot of the Patagonia Mountains. A full breakfast is served family style in the open dining/living room of the main house. There's a nice balance of co-mingling and privacy here, and guests will find themselves wanting to linger and enjoy Patagonia's many charms, including art galleries, a healing center, local cafes, and dance concerts in a converted chapel. **$$**

George Walker House Bed and Breakfast
2225 W. George Walker Lane, Paradise, AZ 85632
Tel: (520) 558-2287
www.thegeorgewalkerhouse.com
Carefully restored 1902 pioneer home, 5.5 miles (9km) from Portal in the Chiricahua Mountains near the Mexican border. The large cabin has two bedrooms, one with a queen bed and the other with two double beds, and a shared bathroom. The large sitting/dining room has a woodstove, TV, extensive library, and games. The immaculate 1960s kitchen is fully stocked with food; you'll only need to bring fresh meats and produce. From May on, feeders attract Cave Creek's famous hummingbirds, and 140 of the 180 species of butterfly found in the Chiricahuas. The owners live in the cabin next door and are very knowledgeable about the natural and cultural history of the mining ghost town of Paradise and the Walker family.

Inn at Castle Rock Bed and Breakfast
112 Tombstone Canyon Road, PO Box 1161, Bisbee, AZ 85603
Tel: (520) 432-4449
www.theinn.org
This old two-story Victorian boarding house is a down-home, granny's-attic kind of place. Rooms are small but very authentic, and the location is advantageous for exploring Old Bisbee. Overall, the place is a bit funky, but where else will you find a flooded

TRANSPORTATION

mineshaft in the center of the breakfast room? **$$–$$$**

Portal Peak Lodge
PO Box 364, Portal, AZ 85632
Tel: (520) 558-2223
Adjoining Cave Creek, not far from Chiricahua National Monument, the lodge's 16 rooms are attractively furnished in southwestern style. Rooms open onto a long deck, with magnificent views of the mountains. A restaurant, grocery store, and gift shop are on the premises. **$$**

Ramsey Canyon Inn Bed and Breakfast
29 Ramsey Canyon Road, Hereford, AZ 85615
Tel: (520) 378-3010
www.ramseycanyoninn.com
This stone inn is adjacent to The Nature Conservancy's 380-acre (155 hectare) Ramsey Canyon Preserve. Six guest rooms, each with a private bath, and three apartments (across Ramsey Creek) with kitchens. A gourmet breakfast is included, served family style. There is organic shade-grown coffee and teas and choice of several amazing homemade pies made by innkeeper Shirlene DeSantis using fruit from the inn's organic orchards. There's usually a two-night minimum. The inn is very popular. Book well ahead. **$$–$$$**

Rancho De La Osa Guest Ranch
PO Box 1, Sasabe, AZ 85633
Tel: (520) 823-4257 or (800) 872-6240
This famous dude ranch sits on one of the last great Spanish land grant haciendas along the US-Mexico border, just southwest of Tucson. Developed by Navajo historian Louisa Wetherill in 1921, it has been used as a quiet desert getaway by many celebrities over the years, from US presidents to supreme court justices and well-known novelists. The Hacienda, built between the 1830s and 1860s, now houses two dining rooms and four sitting rooms. The Cantina

is reputed to be the oldest building in the state and has been occupied continuously since the early 1700s. It is used as a gathering place for cocktails, live music, and after-dinner relaxation. The Territorial-style ranch house has 21 adobe rooms furnished with Old Mexico antiques. All rooms are on the ground floor near the pool, hot tub, dining areas, and horse corrals and are nonsmoking. They have separate entrances, porches with stunning views, and most have a wood-burning fireplace. Activities include horseback riding, mountain biking, nature hikes, birdwatching, bocce ball, croquet. Themed weekends include cookouts, roundups, and other Western activities. American Plan (includes all meals and activities). **$$$–$$$$**

Rex Ranch Resort and Spa
131 Amado Montosa Road, Amado, AZ 85645-0636
Tel: (520) 308 2014 or (800) 547-2696
www.rexranch.com
Where do overworked southern Arizona innkeepers and restaurateurs go for a reasonably priced romantic getaway, a little pampering, and good food? Many say Rex Ranch, a beautiful historic ranch resort, across the Santa Cruz River just south of Tucson, where the rest of the world seems a long way away. There are 30 different types of pleasant Southwest-style rooms and suites at the ranch, occupying several houses, and two casitas. All have private or shared patios, coffeemakers and fridges, Wi-Fi (fee extra), and all but two have private bathrooms with baths or showers. Fine dining in the ranch's well-loved Cantina Romantica Wed-Sun in high season features Continental cuisine. Pool, hot tub, meeting rooms, spa, rose gardens, fountains, yoga, horseback riding, mountain biking, bird watching, hiking, volleyball,

games room. **$$–$$$**

San Pedro Bed and Breakfast
3123 Thistle Road, Sierra Vista, AZ 85636
Tel: (520) 458-6412
Set on 5 acres (2 hectares) in the San Pedro Riparian National Conservation Area. A suite in the ranch house has a sitting room, refrigerator, and balcony. A separate guest house offers a room with refrigerator. Guests are treated to a full southwestern breakfast. **$$**

San Pedro River Inn
8326 S. Hereford Road, Hereford, AZ 85615
Tel: (520) 365-5532
www.sanpedroriverinn.com
Four adobe guest houses are spread out on the inn's 20 acres (8 hectares), where cottonwood trees attract 261 species of birds. Each adobe has a living room, kitchen, and private bath; two- and three-bedroom units are available. A continental breakfast is served. The San Pedro Riparian National Conservation Area is a 5 minute walk away and birding tours are offered. Extensive natural history library and horse boarding facilities. **$$**

Shady Dell RV Park
1 Old Douglas Road, Bisbee, AZ 85603
Tel: (520) 432-3567
www.theshadydell.com
The restored vintage aluminum travel trailers aren't something you see every day, even in artsy Bisbee. You get to spend the night in a classic 1950s trailer, a mad-cap Polynesian-themed bus or dry-docked yacht. Each is comfortable and has a stove, fridge, percolator, dishes, linens, and cassette tapes of big band, early rhythm and blues, and favorite old radio programs played on reproduction vintage radios. Some also have old black-and-white TVs. Even if you don't stay in the RV park, don't miss eating at the onsite Dot's Diner, a minuscule 1957 10-stool diner. Restrooms

and showers are shared. **$–$$**

The Gardens at Mile High Ranch
901 Tombstone Canyon, Bisbee, AZ
Tel: (520) 432-3866
www.gardensatmilehighranch.com
Child- and pet-friendly 1920s travel motel that is a great budget option for tourists looking for a casual getaway in a quiet, natural setting, just a mile up Tombstone Canyon. The six nonsmoking apartments or guest rooms have been nicely restored with private baths, kitchenettes, pullout couches, cable TV, and Wi-Fi. There are 3 acres (1.2 hectares) of mature gardens, and a healthy continental breakfast is included. What really sets apart this homey place is the warm welcome sisters Maggie and Tara Kohanek extend to the guests and several retired miners who live here permanently, cared for by the sisters. Maggie and Tara are talented bodyworkers and offer massage, colon cleansing, detox, and other spa treatments in a separate healing center behind the main house backing onto the national forest. **$–$$**

Tombstone Boarding House and Bed and Breakfast
108 N. 4th Street, Box 906, Tombstone, AZ 85638
Tel: (520) 457-3716
Built in the 1880s, this cluster of adobes occupies a quiet spot one block from town. Seven guest rooms, each with private bath, are furnished with items associated with Tombstone's colorful Old West history. A small, two-room miner's cabin has a private bath. **$$**

PRICE CATEGORIES

Price categories are based on the cost of a double room for one night in the high season (January–April):
$ = less than $75
$$ = $75–150
$$$ = $150–200
$$$$ = more than $200

TRANSPORTATION ACCOMMODATIONS ACTIVITIES A – Z

A CTIVITIES

THE ARTS, FESTIVALS, SPORTS, SHOPPING, PARKS, AND HISTORIC SITES

THE ARTS

Theater, symphony, concerts, ballet, and art exhibitions can be found mainly in Phoenix and Tucson in central and southern Arizona, to a lesser extent in the northern Arizona communities of Flagstaff and Sedona and, seasonally, at the Grand Canyon, which hosts a popular Chamber Music Festival every September. Many of Arizona's pioneer communities and Indian reservations have seasonal festivals of the arts, however, where you'll find traditional cultural offerings. The University of Arizona in Tucson and Arizona State University in Phoenix are cultural hubs, including Frank Lloyd Wright's last major venue, Grady Gammage Memorial Auditiorium in Tempe and Centennial Hall on the UA campus in Tucson. Tempe, Mesa, Scottsdale, and Sedona all have well-subscribed centers for the arts. For more information, check in-chapter listings.

Buying Tickets

The easiest way to reserve and pay for tickets is simply to call up the relevant box office or go to the venue's Web site and pay by credit card. Sometimes, however, you will be required to make reservations through Ticketmaster, a ticket agency that runs a pay-by-phone operation and also has outlets in certain music and discount stores. Ticketmaster (tel: 480-784-4444) charges a commission fee of $20 or more above the normal cost of a ticket.

FESTIVALS

The following festivals and other events are listed by month, and then according to where they fall within that month. Sports events are listed separately.

January

First Peoples World's Fair and Powwow (Tucson). Tribes from all over the country converge on Tucson for this big powwow. Tel: (520) 622-4900.

Wings Over Willcox (Willcox). Birders flock to the flooded *playas* of southeastern Arizona, which attract thousands of migratory wading birds each winter for talks and events. Tel: (520) 384-2272.

February

Arizona Renaissance Festival (Apache Junction). Music, theater, crafts, games, and tournaments on weekends from February to early April. Tel: (480) 982-3141.

Festival of the Arts (Tubac): The oldest event of its kind in the Southwest, this six-day arts festival at the beginning of February showcases the work of hundreds of artists, craftspeople, and musicians in the tiny arts community of Tubac, just south of Tucson. Tel: (520) 398-2704.

Gold Rush Days (Wickenburg). A melodrama, shootouts on Frontier Street, a beard-growing contest, a rodeo, a parade, arts and crafts booths, and food celebrate the Old West over three days. Tel: (928) 684-5479.

Matsuri Japanese Festival (Phoenix): Heritage Arts and Science Park in downtown Phoenix is the venue for this weekend-long festival celebrating all-things Japanese in late February. Tel: (602) 262-5071.

O'odham Tash Indian – Casa Grande Indian Days (Casa Grande): Coinciding with the World Championship Hoop Dance Contest, this powwow includes Indian ceremonies, a rodeo, and an arts and crafts festival. Tel: (520) 836-4723.

Tucson Gem and Mineral Show (Tucson): The largest gathering of precious-stone fans in the world sells out every hotel in Tucson in February. Book ahead. Tel: (520) 322-5773

Quartzite Powwow Gem and Mineral Show (Quartzite): A popular gathering of gem fanatics in airstream trailers in this dusty Old West town, timed to coincide with the Tucson Gem and Mineral Show. Tel: (928) 927-6325.

Sedona International Film Festival (Sedona): A-list celebrities gather in Red Rock country for this increasingly popular independent film fest. Includes classic films, premieres, and workshops. Tel: (928) 282-1177

Winterfest (Flagstaff): This month-long celebration of winter includes a parade, Northern Arizona University sports, arts and crafts exhibits, sled-dog races, food events, Alpine and Nordic skiing, concerts, lectures, cultural happenings, plays, and family activities. Tel: (928) 774-4505

Winterfest Jamboree (Lake Havasu City): This winter desert festival includes street fairs and powerboat races on Lake Havasu. Tel: (928) 855-4115.

March

Bluegrass On the Beach (Lake Havasu City): This three-day celebration of bluegrass has moved from Parker to the shores of Lake Havasu City and features many top acts the first weekend in March. Tel: (209) 785-4693.

National Festival of the West (Scottsdale): This huge four-day western festival features a western music jamboree, concerts, a huge trade show, western film festival, the Cowboy Spirit Award, a cookout cookoff, mountain man rendezvous, cowboy mounted shooting, and Buffalo Soldiers reenactment. Tel: (602) 996-4387

Heard Museum Guild Indian Fair and Market (Phoenix): Some of the best Indian arts and crafts in the West are on sale at this annual event, which also features Indian food, music, and dance. Tel: (602) 252-8848.

Basha's Chandler Ostrich Festival (Chandler): Includes ostrich racing, music, a parade, art exhibits, carnival rides, and an auto show. Tel: (480) 963-4571.

Scottsdale Arts Festival (Scottsdale): This twice-yearly arts show features music and dance performances and crafts exhibitions. Tel: (480) 994-2787.

Territorial Days (Tombstone): The big deal is a reenactment of the events leading up to the gunfight at the OK Corral at this Tombstone Old West extravaganza. Tel: (520) 457-9317.

Wa:k Powwow (Tucson): San Xavier del Bac Mission, south of Tucson, is the host for this Tohono O'odham celebration of Indian culture. Includes intertribal dances, gourd dances, arts and crafts, food. Tel: (520) 294-5727.

April

Culinary Festival (Scottsdale): Food and music are the draw at this downtown Scottsdale celebration. Tel: (480) 945-7193.

Glendale Jazz and Blues Festival (Glendale): Glendale's longest running festival features national and local acts, artists-in-residence, arts and crafts, food, and wine tastings by local wineries. Tel: (623) 930-2299.

International Mariachi Conference (Tucson): A weeklong celebration of Mexican mariachi music, including workshops, concerts, an art exhibit, and a golf tournament. Tel: (520) 884-9920.

Maricopa County Fair (Phoenix): Entertainment, shopping, food booths, and a livestock fair are all part of the fun. Tel: (602) 252-0717.

Tucson Folk Festival (Tucson): Showcases national and regional musicians from Arizona and the Southwest and offers workshops, a gospel sing-along, a children's show, and food and craft booths.

Tel: (520) 792-6481.

Yaqui Easter (Tucson): Animistic beliefs and Christianity come together beautifully in this unique Easter celebration by Arizona's Yaqui Indian community, one of the not-to-be-missed events in the Indian year. Includes traditional Lent and Holy Week processions, reenactments, and ceremonies merged into the nature-based Yaqui culture over the centuries. Highlights include a lenten all-night fiesta featuring the Yaqui deer dancer and Holy Week ceremonies including matachine dancers and a maypole. Tel: (520) 791-4609.

May

Cinco de Mayo (Phoenix and Tucson): Commemorating a key historic battle in Mexico's history of independence, this colorful celebration is one of the Southwest's most popular events, featuring folkloric dancing, mariachis, norteno music, and great food. Tel: (602) 262-5025 (Phoenix); (520) 292-9326 (Tucson).

Mountain Man Rendezvous (Williams): One of the oldest mountain men get-togethers in the West features an encampment and traditional activities such as leatherwork, carving, and weaponry. Tel: (928) 635-1418.

Pine–Strawberry Arts & Crafts Festival (Pine): Down-home country crafts and community spirit are featured at this rural fest, with Navajo tacos served by the community center. Tel: (928) 476-4480.

Route 66 Fun Run Weekend (Seligman to Topock): Not a foot race but a classic car "run," with a festival in Kingman on Saturday that features Hualapai barbecue, booths, entertainment, and classic car judging, then a leisurely Sunday morning ride from Seligman to Topock on Route 66. Tel: (928) 753-5001.

Wyatt Earp Days (Tombstone): Gunfight reenactments are the highlight of this Memorial Day fest, along with Old West costumes and arts and crafts. Tel: (520) 457-3291.

June

Bluegrass Festival (Prescott): A summer solstice celebration of bluegrass featuring local bands. Tel: (928) 771-9274.

Folk Arts Fair (Prescott): Gold panning, candle making, toy making, and other kid-centered western arts and crafts at the Sharlott Hall Museum. Tel: (928) 445-3122.

Hon-Dah Powwow in the Pines (Whiteriver): Tribes from the US & Canada get together to compete in fancy dances and grass dances. Arts & crafts, food, and an Apache Sunrise dance. Tel: (928) 369-7568.

Juneteenth Festival (Tucson): Gospel, blues, and folk music, dance, and a fun run are on the agenda at this festival at the Kennedy Park Fiesta Area. Tel: (520) 225-2670.

Old Miners Day (Chloride): The highlight of the year in the almost ghost town of Chloride is an Old West festival featuring a large parade, mock gunfights, vendors, pie baking contests, a bake sale, raffle for door prizes, a 50-50, and food booths. Tel: (928) 565-2204.

July

Annual Hopi/Navajo Festivals of Arts and Culture (Flagstaff): The best of the best Indian artisans are featured in these popular juried shows at the Museum of Northern Arizona. Tel: (928) 774-5213.

Native American Arts & Crafts Festival (Pinetop-Lakeside): White Mountain Apache arts and crafts are featured. Tel: (928) 367-4290.

Pioneer Day Celebration (Snowflake): Snowflake's Mormon heritage is celebrated with arts and crafts and food booths. Tel: (928) 536-4331.

August

Arizona Cowboy Poets Gathering (Prescott): One of the biggest such gatherings in the West attracts the top cowboy poets in the nation. Tel: (928) 445-3122.

Fiesta de San Agustin (Tucson): A fiesta of live music, food, street dancing, and bullfighting honors Tucson's patron saint, Saint Augustine. Tel: (520) 624-1817.

Flagstaff Summerfest Festival in the Pines (Flagstaff): Ever-popular large festival at Fort Tuthill fairgrounds, just south of Flag, includes entertainment, 250 artisans, and children's activities. Tel: (928) 779-7611.

Southwest Wings Birding Festival (Bisbee): Arizona's longest running nature festival is an educational celebration of the diversity of birds, mammals, reptiles, and insects, in the sky islands of southern Arizona. Tel: (520) 803-7412.

Vigilante Days (Tombstone): A chilli cookoff, fun run, and street entertainment highlight this Old West festival sponsored by the Lions Club. Tel: (520) 457-3197.

Red Rocks Music Festival (Sedona):

Chamber music concerts and workshops are offered by internationally renowned musicians at this Labor Day event. Tel: (877) 733-7257

Old West Days (Holbrook): Old West reenactors, kids games, arts and crafts, food vendors, Bucket of Blood races, a 10K, 2-mile, and 20-mile bike race, a quilt show, and a talent contest take place in downtown Holbrook. Tel: (928) 524-6558.

September

Festival of Science (Flagstaff): A week of fascinating talks, presentations, and demonstrations by Flag's many scientists about topics from astronomy to geology and archaeology. Tel: (800) 842-7293.

Fiesta de Tlaquepaque (Sedona): Mariachis, folkloric dancing, food, and continuous entertainment highlight this fiesta at Sedona's main arts and crafts marketplace. Tel: (928) 282-4838.

Gold Camp Days (Oatman): Entertainments include the international burro bisket toss competition at this old mining community's annual celebration. Tel: (928) 768-6222.

Grand Canyon Music Festival (Grand Canyon): Internationally known classical musicians converge on the Grand Canyon for several weeks of chamber music concerts in the Shrine of the Ages Auditorium as well as blues concerts and an art show. Tel: (800) 997-8285.

Jazz on the Rocks (Sedona): Internationally known jazz musicians are the big draw at this popular annual Jazzfest in the red rocks. Tel: (928) 282-1985.

Navajo Nation Fair (Window Rock): The capital of the Navajo Nation is the location for the tribe's biggest fair of the year, including beauty pageant, a pro-rodeo, Indian dance competitions, food, arts and crafts. Tel: (928) 871-6478.

White Mountain Apache Tribal Fair & Rodeo (Whiteriver): A Labor Day rodeo and powwow event in the White Mountains featuring cowboy skills, dances, arts and crafts, food, and entertainment. Tel: (928) 338-4346.

October

Arizona State Fair (Phoenix): Fairground rides, concerts by big-name acts, livestock judging, food booths, and art shows are some of the attractions at this big fall month-long event. Tel: (602) 268-FAIR.

Helldorado Days (Tombstone): Music, arts and crafts, a parade, a fashion show, a carnival, and gunfight reenactments light up this Old West town. Tel: (520) 457-9317.

London Bridge Days (Lake Havasu City): This annual celebration commemorates the 1968 dedication of the bridge in the desert with a parade, costume competitions, live entertainment, and other fun sponsored by the Rotary Club. Tel: (928) 453-3444.

Norteño Music Festival and Street Fair (Tucson). One of the biggest music festivals in the Southwest celebrates northern Mexican music and rhythms. Tel: (520) 622-2801.

Prescott Folk Music Festival (Prescott): Fiddle, banjo, guitar, harmonica, mandolin, dulcimer, plus singers, songwriters, and storytellers are highlighted in concerts on six stages at the Sharlot Hall Museum. Tel: (928) 445-3122.

Rex Allen Days (Willcox): Cowboy movie star Allen is honored each year with this celebration featuring a fair, rodeo, art show, and cowboy dancing. Tel: (520) 384-2272.

Sedona Arts Festival (Sedona): A juried arts show among the red rocks. Tel: (928) 204-9456.

Thunderbird Balloon Classic (Glendale): A mass ascension of more than 150 balloons provides colorful skies above the American Graduate School for International Management. Tel: (623) 930-8400.

Tucson Heritage Experience Festival (Tucson): More than 50 heritage and cultural associations provide food in El Presidio Park, along with music, dance, storytelling, and entertainment. Tel: (520) 624-1817.

November

Western Music Festival (Tucson): Dedicated to preserving the ways of the old cowboys, this international music festival celebrates music of the Old West. Tel: (520) 743-9794.

December

Christmas Mariachi Festival (Phoenix): Held at the US Airways Center, this extravaganza of Mexican musicians is hugely popular for the holidays. Tel: (602) 379-7800.

Cowboy Christmas & Cowboy Poets Gathering (Wickenburg): Cowboy poets, musicians, singers, and others involved in the ranch community get together annually to celebrate their way of life in this charming event. Includes a chuckwagon breakfast and a cowboy mass. Tel: (928) 684-5479.

Festival of the Arts (Tempe): Mill Avenue and the area around Arizona State University is the venue for this top-rated juried art show around the holidays each year. Tel: (480) 967-4877.

La Fiesta de Tumacacori (Tumacacori): Apache and Tohono O'odham Indian dancers, Mexican folkloric dancing, mariachi music, arts and crafts, food booths, and other entertainments draw thousands to the old Spanish mission each Christmas. Tel: (520) 398-2341.

Pueblo Grande Indian Market (Phoenix): Pueblo Grande Museum hosts this annual gathering of 250 Native American artisans from more than 50 tribes at South Mountain Park. Also includes singers, dancers, food booths. Tel: (602) 495-0901.

SPORTS

Participant Sports

Hiking

It would be a shame to visit Arizona's stunning low- and high-desert country and not get out on a trail and hike, no matter your fitness level. Trails for all levels of walker can be found throughout the state, from strolls on urban trails, botanical gardens, and resort grounds in Tucson and Phoenix to challenging backcountry hiking in the Grand Canyon and other national, state, city, and tribal parks and national forests.

Ranger-led hikes on public lands are a great way to learn about the desert and stay safe in an unfamiliar landscape. The Sierra Club also offers guided hikes on weekends in many venues; contact their local chapter through their Web site to find out what is happening in your local area (www.sierraclub.org). Winter is the best time to hike in the low desert; summer in the high country.

Seasoned desert hikers hike in the cool post-dawn hours during the hot summer season and return by late morning; heat builds up in Arizona's rocks throughout the afternoon and continues to radiate into the surrounding landscape even after sunset, so evening hikes remain quite warm even though you are out of the direct sun.

Take precautions. Bring a liter of water for a short day hike, a gallon for a day out, and eat salty, high-energy snacks. Wear sturdy, supportive hiking shoes or sandals, a broad-brimmed hat, high SPF factor sunscreen, sunglasses, and breathable fabrics that can be rolled down to cover exposed skin.

Golf

There are scores of public and private golf courses as well as full-fledged golf resorts throughout the state. For a complete list, contact the Arizona Golf Association (7226 N. 16th Street, Suite 200, Phoenix, AZ 85020; tel: 602-944-3035; www.az golf.org) or pick up a copy of Golf Arizona (16446 Tombstone Drive, Fountain Hills, AZ 85268).

Tennis

There are public tennis courts in just about every city and large town in Arizona, though avid players may find it more convenient to stay in a hotel with courts. Contact the city or county Parks and Recreation Department for locations and hours. For information on tournaments, lessons, and leagues, contact the Arizona Tennis Association (7335 E. Indian Plaza, Suite 124, Scottsdale, AZ 85251; tel: 480-970-0599).

Cycling

Several organizations provide information on trails, races, group tours, and other events. The Greater Arizona Bicycling Association (www. sportsfun.com/gaba/index html) and the Arizona Bicycle Club (www.oneand zero.com/abccazb) have chapters throughout the state.

Fishing

Fishing licenses are required and can be obtained from the Arizona Game and Fish Department (2222 W. Greenway Road, Phoenix, AZ 85023; tel: 602-942-3000). Fishing on the White Mountain Apache Indian Reservation (Wildlife and Outdoor Recreation Division, PO Box 220, Whiteriver, AZ 85941; tel: 928-338-4385) and San Carlos Apache Indian Reservation (PO Box 0, San Carlos, AZ 85550; tel: 928-475-2361) require a tribal fishing license.

Kayaking, Canoeing, Rafting

Arizona offers an abundance of both whitewater and flatwater paddling. For information on routes and conditions, consult the agency that manages the river or lake. Other sources of information are paddling clubs and outdoor gear retailers. For more information, call the Prescott Paddle America Club (tel: 928-445-5480). For stream-flow conditions, check www.daztcn.wr.usgs.gov.

Skiing

Arizona has four downhill skiing areas but none with snowmaking capabilities (although that is on the agenda for the Arizona Snowbowl).

Arizona Snowbowl
PO Box 40, Flagstaff, AZ 86002
Tel: (928) 779-1951
Sunrise Park Resort
PO Box 217, McNary, AZ 85930
Tel: (928) 735-7669
Williams Ski Area
PO Box 953, Williams, AZ 86046
Tel: (928) 635-9330
Flagstaff Nordic Center (tel: 928-779-1951) has 25 miles (40 km) of groomed cross-country trails, instruction, and equipment rentals.

Spectator Sports

Professional and amateur football, baseball, golf, hockey, auto racing, and horse and dog racing take place exclusively in Phoenix and Tucson. The rest of the state is rural: spectator sports here are most likely to be exciting PRCA-rate pro rodeos. Details are noted below in the sporting event calendar and in a special box on Baseball Spring Training. For general information on Arizona sports news and schedules, log on to www.azcentral.com.

Sporting Events

January
Arizona and Livestock Show and Rodeo (Phoenix). The first rodeo of the season is one of the biggest. Tel: (602) 258-8568
Fiesta Bowl Football Classic (Tempe). A tradition in football circles. Tel: (480) 350-0911.
FBR Open Golf Tournament (Scottsdale). Played on picturesque TPC Golf Course in Scottsdale, this PGA golf tournament is one of the oldest and most revered. Tel: (602) 870-4431.

February
Arizona Diamondbacks (Phoenix): This major league baseball team plays home games at Bank One Ballpark from February to September. (602) 514-8400.
All-Arabian Horse Show (Scottsdale): Arabian horses strut their stuff at this event, the largest of its kind in the world. Tel: (480) 515-1500.
Parada del Sol and Rodeo (Scottsdale): A Jaycee fundraiser at WestWorld that includes a three-day PRCA-sanctioned rodeo with five performances. Tel: (480) 990-3179.
Scottish Highland Games (Mesa): The caber toss and other throwing athletic events, pipes and drums, dance, and other Celtic events highlight this popular event for kilt fans. Tel: (602) 432-0095.
Silver Spur Rodeo (Yuma): A PRCA pro-rodeo sponsored by the Jaycees,

followed by cowboy dancing. Tel: (928) 344-5451.
Tucson Rodeo – La Fiesta de los Vaqueros (Tucson): Bareback riding, steer wrestling, saddle bronc riding, tie-down roping, team roping, bull riding, and women's barrel racing are the highlights at this big winter rodeo. Tel: (520) 741-2233.

March
Cactus League Baseball Spring Training (various venues in southern Arizona). For information about teams and venues, see box. For information on current schedule, check with www.mlb.com or the stadiums.
Tucson Open: Held at the Omni Tucson National Golf Resort, this golf tourney attracts a high level of player. Tel: (800) 882-7660.
Standard Register PING LGPA Tournament (Phoenix): Women golfers compete at this tourney in the Phoenix area each spring. Tel: (602) 495-4653.
Welch's/Circle K LGPA Championship (Tucson): Women golfers compete at this championship in Tucson. Tel: (520) 791-5742.

April
La Vuelta de Bisbee Bicycle Race (Bisbee): Two road races and two time trials on Bisbee's hilly streets are the centerpiece of this bicycle extravaganza. Tel: (520) 432-5795.

May
Whiskey Row Marathon (Prescott): One of the toughest marathons in the US attracts runners from all over the country. Also includes a 10K, 10K racewalk, and 2-mile fun run. Tel: (928) 445-7221.

June
Grand Canyon State Summer Games (Phoenix): The Olympic-level multisport, multiage games attract athletes from throughout Arizona. Native American games take place at Fort McDowell. Tel: (480) 517-9700.
Pine Country Pro Rodeo (Flagstaff): A long-running event in northern Arizona's capital featuring rodeo events. Tel: (928) 526-1629.

July
Cowpunchers Reunion Rodeo (Williams): Real cowboys test their skills at this Old West rodeo event in the pines. Tel: (928) 635-1418.
Prescott Frontier Days Rodeo (Prescott): Considered the oldest rodeo in the West, this famous gathering draws cowboys from all over the country and also has fireworks, a parade, and a cowboy golf tournament. Tel: (928) 445-3103.

TRANSPORTATION ACCOMMODATIONS ACTIVITIES A – Z

Spring Training: Where to See Your Favorite Team

As many as 1.2 million fans have attended spring training games in southern Arizona in one season. Below is a list of where US baseball teams do their spring training. Locations do change periodically, so phone to check.

Chicago Cubs, Hohokam Park, Mesa; tel: (480) 964-4467
Anaheim Angels, Tempe Diablo Stadium, Tempe; tel: (480) 350-5205
Seattle Mariners, Peoria Sports Complex, tel: (623) 773-8720
San Diego Padres, Peoria Sports Complex, Phoenix; tel: (623) 773-8720
Milwaukee Brewers, Maryvale

Baseball Park, Phoenix; tel: (800) 933-7890
Colorado Rockies, Hi Corbett Field, Tucson; tel: (520) 327-WINS
Oakland Athletics, Phoenix Municipal Stadium; tel: (602) 392-0074
San Francisco Giants, Scottsdale Stadium; tel: (480) 312-2856
Kansas City Royals, Surprise Recreation Campus, Surprise; tel: (623) 222-2222
Texas Rangers, Surprise Recreation Campus, Surprise; tel: (623) 222-2222
Chicago White Sox, Tucson Electric Park; tel: (520) 434-1000
Arizona Diamondbacks, Tucson Electric Park; tel: (520) 434-1000

August

World's Oldest Continuous Rodeo (Payson): Another contender for world's oldest rodeo, Payson pulls out the stops for its biggest event of the year. Tel: (928) 474-4515.
Phoenix Amateur Golf Championship (Phoenix): A popular tourney among enthusiastic amateur golfers. Tel: (877) 988-4653.

September

Arizona Cardinals (Phoenix): This professional NFL football team plays home games at Sun Devil Stadium from September to January. The ASU varsity football team the Sun Devils also plays at this venue. Tel: (602) 379-0102.
University of Arizona Wildcats (Tucson): The UA varsity football team plays at Arizona Stadium on the UA campus. Tel: (520) 621-2287.
Phoenix Coyotes (Phoenix). This NHL hockey team plays at the America West Arena from September through April. Tel: (602) 252-WNBA.
Phoenix Greyhound Park (Phoenix): Located just north of Sky Harbor International Airport, this popular stadium offers nightly greyhound racing year round and betting from locations all over Phoenix. Fine dining and meeting rooms. Tel: (602) 273-7181.
Tucson Greyhound Park (Tucson): Year round greyhound racing and betting can be found in Tucson at this greyhound park. Tel: (520) 884-7576.

October

Phoenix Suns (Phoenix) This National Basketball Association team plays hard-hitting, fast-paced basketball games at America West Arena from October to April. The women's league team, the Phoenix Mercury, also

plays at this venue, as does an arena football team, the Arizona Rattlers, in the winter football season. Tel: (602) 379-7900.
Turf Paradise Race Course (Phoenix): Located just north of Sky Harbor International Airport, this horse racing venue has horse racing from 1pm to 6pm daily from October through May. Restaurant, sports bar, family picnic park. Tel: (602) 942-1101.

November

El Tour de Tucson Bicycle Race (Tucson): The largest perimeter bicycling event in the US, this charity fundraiser bike race is a very popular spectator event. Tel: (520) 745-2033.

December

Rillito Park (Tucson): Horse racing in Tucson takes place at this track on First Avenue throughout the winter season. Tel: (520) 293-5011.
Phoenix International Raceway (Phoenix): NASCAR, USAC, Indy, and Grand Am cars race at this auto raceway outside Phoenix. Tel: (602) 252-2227.

SHOPPING

What to Buy

You'll find both the most cutting-edge and the most traditional art in this diverse state, depending on your interests. Sedona is one of the four top art centers in the country (the others being Los Angeles, New York, and Santa Fe). There are numerous galleries showing sculpture, paintings, and other arts by nationally known artists in Red Rock

Country, and also in Phoenix suburb Scottsdale, well known for its galleries in Old Town. Traditional homespun pioneer arts are alive and well throughout the state, particularly in mountain towns, where women continue to practice the old-time crafts of quilting, spinning and weaving, pie making, and putting up preserves.

For most people, though, the main thrill is buying arts and crafts made by members of Arizona's Indian tribes. Each of the reservations offers places to pull off and buy locally made Indian handicrafts. Tribes specialize in different crafts, including woven rugs, sand paintings, kachinas, basketry, pottery, inlaid jewelry, beading, carving, and folk art from found materials. *(See pages 174–5 for more information.)*

The Phoenix area is well known, also, for winter production of citrus, as well as, increasingly, artisan foods such as locally raised and produced goat cheese, grass-fed beef, organically grown tomatoes, greens, and herbs. Wines from several up-and-coming vineyards in the Patagonia-Sonoita area, south of Tucson, also make excellent gifts.

Where to Shop

For sheer quantity and choice, Phoenix is still Arizona's top destination for shopping. You'll find the discount warehouse Costco in the north Valley, branches of gourmet grocer Trader Joe's, an IKEA furniture and household store in Tempe, and several excellent malls and shopping centers, where you can stroll and find unique designer clothing and gifts, stock up on basics, and even, at the internationally renowned Biltmore Fashion Park, enjoy a weekly farmers market. Scottsdale is well known for its Old West and contemporary art galleries as well as the state's largest concentration of shops. Tucson is the place for all things Mexican and has a popular arts cooperative in its El Presidio historic downtown area, where you can stroll through adobe buildings, just as in Old Mexico, and meet the artists. There are several popular outlet malls in Arizona, notably at Oak Creek in northern Arizona, famed retailer Nordstrom's Last Chance outlet in Phoenix, and Foothills Mall in Tucson.

In northern Arizona, Tlaquepaque Marketplace and galleries spread throughout Sedona specialize in contemporary southwestern art. You'll also find the state's largest collection of New Age items, such as crystals, guidebooks to local vortexes, and numerous alternative wellness services. T-shirts dyed in Sedona's red-rock mud are on sale in many commercial stores. In Flagstaff, contemporary pioneer- and Southwest-inspired creations such as split-twig figurine jewelery, innovative weavings, stained glass, and quilts can be found at The Artists Gallery on San Francisco Street. A branch of the excellent second-hand bookstore Bookman's adjoins Northern Arizona University, and there's a Borders Bookstore across the street. You're also close enough to the Navajo and Hopi Indian reservations here to find excellent katsinas, rugs, baskets, pots, and silver jewelry by Indian artists at several stores along Route 66 and on San Francisco Street.

Indian Arts

Wherever you are in Arizona, simply head out to the reservations to find historic trading posts, such as Cameron Trading Post, just north of Flagstaff on Highway 89; tribally owned arts cooperatives and roadside and in-home vendors of local Indian-made arts and crafts, such as those found across the Navajo Nation. Each of the Hopi mesas specializes in a different craft, which can be bought directly from the artisan, local stores, or the Hopi Cultural Center on Second Mesa. The White Mountain and San Carlos Apache of eastern Arizona are known for their leather work, beading, and basketry. The White Mountain Apache center of Whiteriver has arts and crafts for sale. In the Phoenix area, colorful pottery by the Maricopa may be found on the Gila Indian Reservation, at gift shops at Wild Horse Pass Resort in Chandler. In southern Arizona, fine Tohono

O'odham basketry is sold at the new Tohono O'odham cultural center, southwest of Tucson, and at the Arizona-Sonora Desert Museum in Tucson. If you're unable to visit the reservations, the Museum of Northern Arizona in Flagstaff and the Heard Museum in Phoenix and its branches are excellent places to buy authenticated Indian art pieces. Each museum has annual Indian marketplaces where you can buy juried pieces.

Souvenirs

Among Arizona's unique gifts are the copper bells designed by architect Paolo Soleri and manufactured and offered for sale at the experimental futuristic Soleri villages of Arcosanti and Cosanti. Gifts inspired by Prairie Architecture founder Frank Lloyd Wright can be purchased at his former home and school at Taliesin West in Scottsdale and Biltmore Fashion Park at the Arizona Biltmore Hotel on Camelback Road, which he helped design. Pottery made by Mark Arnegard can be purchased from Arne's pottery on Route 66, just west of downtown Flagstaff. You'll also find pottery aplenty in the former mining towns of Bisbee and Jerome, which have now been taken over by artists.

Food

Food lovers will want to bring home a taste of the Southwest. In southern Arizona, El Charro, the country's oldest Mexican restaurant, sells its salsas in jars, along with other chili-infused items. Pricklypear cactus jellies and syrups made by the Tohono O'odham Indians are on sale at the Arizona Sonora Desert Museum, which holds an annual Tohono O'odham fall harvest festival. At farmer's markets throughout the state and some delicatessens, you'll

find local goat cheese from Black Mesa Ranch in the White Mountains; olive oil from olives grown at Queen Creek Olive Farm and Mill, southeast of Phoenix; organic tomatoes raised near Bisbee; grass-fed beef from Date Creek Ranch, Wickenburg; eggs from EmmaEggs Family Farm outside Flagstaff; and fresh-pressed apple cider from Stout Mills in Willcox, among other "locavore" items. These make superb picnic fare while traveling or for a special Taste of Arizona carry-on meal on the plane ride home. Remember to eat them up before landing, though. Customs will require you to dispose of any fresh items.

Shopping Malls

Biltmore Fashion Park
2502 E. Camelback Road, Phoenix, AZ 85016
Tel: (602) 955-1963
Chandler Fashion Center
3111 W. Chandler Blvd, Chandler, AZ 85226
Tel: (480) 812-8488
Flagstaff Mall
4650 N. Highway 89, Flagstaff, AZ 86004
Tel: (928) 526-4827
Foothills Mall
7401 N. La Cholla Blvd, Tucson, AZ 85741
Tel: (520) 742-7191
Kierland Commons
15210 N. Scottsdale Road, Suite 250, Scottsdale, AZ 85254
Tel: (480) 348-1577
La Encantada
2905 E. Skyline Dr, Tucson, AZ 85718
Tel: (520) 299-3556
Mesa Riverview
1061 North Dobson Road, Mesa, AZ 85201
Tel: (480) 461-0050
Nordstrom Last Chance
1919 E. Camelback Road, Phoenix, AZ 85016
Tel: (602) 248-2843
Oak Creek Factory Outlet
6601 Highway 179, #A16, Sedona, AZ 86351
Tel: (928) 284-2150
Prescott Gateway
3250 Gateway Blvd, Prescott, AZ 86303
Tel: (928) 442-3684
Scottsdale Fashion Square
7014 E. Camelback Road, Suite 590 Scottsdale, AZ 85251
Tel: (480) 949-0202
Tempe Marketplace
2000 E. Rio Salado Pkwy, Tempe, AZ 85281
Tel: (480) 966-9338

LEFT: Arizona Diamondbacks.

Yuma Palms
1463 S. Yuma Palms Parkway, Yuma,
AZ 85365
Tel: (928) 329-4559

Museum Stores

Museum of Northern Arizona
3101 N. Ft. Valley Rd, Flagstaff,
AZ 86001
Tel: (928) 774-5213

Heard Museum
2301 N Central Avenue, Phoenix, AZ
Tel: (602) 252-8848

Phoenix Art Museum
1625 N. Central Avenue, Phoenix,
AZ 85004-1685
Tel: (602) 257-1222

Trading Posts

Cameron Trading Post
466 Highway 89, Cameron,
AZ 86020
Tel: (928) 679-2231

Hubbell Trading Post
PO Box 150, Ganado, Arizona 86505
Tel: (928) 755-3254

Artists' Cooperatives

The Art Barn
2330 North Fort Valley Road,
Flagstaff, AZ 86001
Tel: (928) 774-0822

The Artists Gallery
17 N. San Francisco Street,
Flagstaff, AZ 86001
Tel: (928) 773-0958

**Colorado River Indian Tribes
Library/Museum**
Rt. 1 Box 23-B, Parker, AZ 85344
Tel: (902) 669-9211, ext 335

D. Y. Begay's Weaving Studio
6929 East Jenan Drive, Scottsdale,
AZ 85254. By appointment only.
Tel: (602) 922-9232 or (520) 674-
3494

Gila River Arts and Crafts Center
Box 457, Sacaton, AZ 85247
Tel: (602) 963-3981

Hatathli Gallery
Navajo Community College, Tsaile,
AZ 86556
Tel: (520) 724-6650

**Hopi Arts and Crafts – Silvercraft
Cooperative Guild**
PO Box 37, Second Mesa, AZ 86043
Tel: (520) 734-2463

Jerome Artists Cooperative Gallery
502 North Main Street, Jerome,
AZ 86331
Tel: (928) 639-4276

Navajo Arts and Crafts Enterprise
PO Box 160, Window Rock,
AZ 86515
Tel: (520) 871-4090 or 871-4095

*Selected Stores and
Art Galleries*

Andrea Smith Galleries
Tlaquepaque Marketplace,
336 Hwy 179, Sedona, AZ 86336

Tel: (888) 399-5444

Arcosanti
HC 74, Box 4136, Mayer, AZ 86333
Tel: (928) 632-7135

Bookmans
1520 S. Riordan Ranch Road,
Flagstaff, AZ 86001
Tel: (928) 774-0005

DeGrazia Gallery in the Sun
6300 N. Swan Road, Tucson,
AZ 85718-3607
Tel: (520) 299-9191

Environmental Realists
Tlaquepaque Marketplace,
336 Hwy 179, Sedona, AZ 86336
Tel: (928) 282-4945

Garland's Navajo Rugs
PO Box 851, Sedona, AZ
Tel: (928) 282-4070

Poco Loco
81 Main Street, Bisbee, AZ
Tel: (520) 432-7020

Sedona Arts Center
15 Art Barn Road, Sedona,
AZ 86339
Tel: (928) 282-3809

Singing Wind Bookstore
West Singing Wind and North Ocotillo
Roads, off I-10, near Benson
Tel: (520) 586-2425

Spur Western Wear
509 East Allen Street, Tombstone, AZ
Tel: (520) 457-9000

Stout's Cider Mill
1510 North Circle 1 Road,
Willcox, AZ
Tel: (520) 384-2696

Tubac Center of the Arts
9 Plaza Road, PO Box 1911, Tubac,
AZ 85646
Tel: (520) 398-2371

Visions Fine Art
101 N. Hwy 89A, Suite E24, Sedona,
AZ 86336
Tel: (928) 203-0022

PARKS AND HISTORIC SITES

Northern Arizona

**Canyon de Chelly National
Monument**
PO Box 588, Chinle, AZ 86503
Tel: (928) 674-5500

Coconino National Forest
Supervisors Office,
2323 E. Greenlaw Lane, Flagstaff,
AZ 86004
Tel: (928) 527-3600

**Glen Canyon National Recreation
Area**
PO Box 1507, Page, AZ 86040
Tel: (928) 608-6404

Grand Canyon National Park
PO Box 129, Grand Canyon,
AZ 86023
Tel: (928) 638-7888

Grand Canyon–Parashant National

Monument
601 Nevada Highway, Boulder City,
NV 89005
Tel: (702) 293-8907

**Hubbell Trading Post National
Historic Site**
PO Box 150, Ganado, AZ 86505
Tel: (928) 755-3475

Kaibab National Forest
800 S 6th Street, Williams,
AZ 86046
Tel: (928) 635-8200

Monument Valley Navajo Tribal Park
Box 360289, Monument Valley,
UT 84536
Tel: (435) 727-5870

Navajo National Monument
HC 71, Box 3, Tonalea,
AZ 86044-9704
Tel: (928) 672-2700

Pipe Spring National Monument
HC 65, Box 5, Fredonia, AZ 7105

Riordan State Historic Park
1300 S. Riordan Ranch Street,
Flagstaff, AZ 86001
Tel: (928) 779-4395

Sunset Crater National Monument
Route 3, Box 149, Flagstaff,
AZ 86004
Tel: (928) 526-0502

Walnut Canyon National Monument
Walnut Canyon Road, Flagstaff,
AZ 86004-9705
Tel: (928) 526-3367

Wupatki National Monument
HC 33, Box 444A, Flagstaff,
AZ 86004
Tel: (928) 679-2365

Central Arizona

Apache–Sitgreaves National Forest
PO Box 640, Springerville, AZ 85938
Tel: (928) 333-4301

Buckskin Mountain State Park
5476 Hwy 95, Parker, AZ 85344
Tel: (928) 667-3231

Dead Horse Ranch State Park
675 Deadhorse Ranch Road,
Cottonwood, AZ 86326
Tel: (928) 634-5283

Fool Hollow Lake Recreation Area
off Highway 260, Show Low, AZ
Tel: (928) 537-3680

Fort Verde State Historic Park
PO Box 397, Camp Verde, AZ 86322
Tel: (928) 567-3275

Jerome State Historic Park
PO Box D, Jerome, AZ 86322
Tel: (928) 634-5381

Lake Havasu State Park
1801 Highway 95, Lake Havasu,
AZ 86406
Tel: (928) 855-2784

Lyman Lake State Park
US 191, Springerville, AZ
Tel: (928) 337-4441

**Montezuma Castle National
Monument**
PO Box 219, Camp Verde, AZ 86322

Tel: (928) 567-3322
Petrified Forest National Park
PO Box 2217, Petrified Forest,
AZ 86028
Tel: (928) 524-6228
Prescott National Forest
344 S. Cortez, Prescott, AZ 86302
Tel: (928) 443-8000
Red Rock State Park
4050 Lower Red Rock Loop Road,
Sedona, AZ
Tel: (928) 282-6907
Slide Rock State Park
Off SR 89A, Sedona, AZ
Tel: (928) 282-3034
Tonto Natural Bridge State Park
Off SR 87, Payson, AZ
Tel: (928) 476-4202
Tuzigoot National Monument
PO Box 68, Clarkdale, AZ 86324
Tel: (928) 634-5564

Southern Arizona

Agua Fria National Monument
222 N. Central Avenue, Suite 100,
Phoenix, AZ 85004
Tel: (602) 417-9200
Alamo Lake State Park
PO Box 38, Wenden, AZ 85356
Tel: (928) 669-2088
Boyce Thompson Arboretum State Park
37615 US 60, Superior, AZ
Tel: (520) 689-2723
Buenos Aires National Wildlife Refuge
PO Box 109, Sasabe, AZ 85633
Tel: (520) 823-4251
Cabeza Prieta National Wildlife Refuge
1611 N. Second Avenue, Ajo,
AZ 85321
Tel: (520) 387-6483
Casa Grande National Monument
1100 Ruins Drive, Coolidge,
AZ 85228

Tel: (520) 723-3172
Catalina State Park
11570 N. Oracle Road, Tucson,
AZ 85740
Tel: (520) 628-5798
Chiricahua National Monument
Dos Cabezas Route, Box 6500,
Willcox, AZ 85643
Coronado National Forest
Federal Building, 300 W. Congress,
Tucson, AZ 85701
Tel: (520) 670-4552
Coronado National Memorial
4101 E. Montezuma Canyon Road,
Hereford, AZ 85615
Tel: (520) 366-5515
Fort Bowie National Historic Site
PO Box 158, Bowie, AZ 85605
Tel: (520) 847-2500
Ironwood Forest National Monument
12661 E. Broadway, Tucson,
AZ 85748
Tel: (520) 722-4289
Kartchner Caverns State Park
179 W. Flint Street, Benson,
AZ 85602
Tel: (520) 586-CAVE
KOFA National Wildlife Refuge
356 W. First Street, Yuma, AZ 85366
Tel: (928) 783-7861
Lost Dutchman State Park
Apache Junction, AZ
Tel: (480) 982-4485
McFarland State Historic Park
Box 109, Florence, AZ 85232
Tel: (520) 868-5216
Organ Pipe Cactus National Monument
Route 1, Box 100, Ajo, AZ 85321
Tel: (520) 387-6849
Patagonia Lake State Park
PO Box 274, Patagonia, AZ 85624
Tel: (520) 287-6965
Picacho Peak State Park
PO Box 275, Picacho, AZ 85241
Tel: (520) 466-3183
Saguaro National Park
2693 S. Old Spanish Trail, Tucson,
AZ 85730
Tel: (520) 733-5153
Sonoran Desert National Monument
222 N. Central Avenue, Phoenix,
AZ 85004
Tel: (602) 417-9200
San Xavier del Bac Mission
1950 W. San Xavier, Tucson,
AZ 85706
Tel: (520) 294-2624
Tombstone Courthouse State Historic Park
219 Toughnut Street, Tombstone,
AZ 85638
Tel: (520) 457-3311
Tonto National Forest
2324 E. McDowell Road, Phoenix,
AZ 85545
Tel: (602) 225-5200

LEFT: San Xavier del Bac Mission,
south of Tucson.

National Park Passes

If you plan on visiting several parks on your vacation, consider buying a 12-month National Parks and Federal Recreational Lands Pass. The pass costs $80 and covers entrance fees to all federally managed parks (those managed by the National Park Service, the Bureau of Land Management, and the USDA Forest Service). It does not cover camping fees or other use fees, such as cave tours. Passes can be obtained at any park entrance station and one bonus is that fees will benefit the park where you purchase the pass. You may also purchase passes online by logging on to the USGS Web site at http://store.usgs.gov/pass. For more information, call 1-888-ASK-USGS.

Tonto National Monument
HC 02, Box 4602, Roosevelt,
AZ 85545
Tel: (928) 467-2241
Tubac Presidio State Park
1 Presidio Drive, Tubac, AZ 85646
Tel: (520) 398-2252
Tumacacori National Historical Park
PO Box 67, Tumacacori, AZ 85640
Tel: (520) 398-2341
Yuma Crossing State Historic Park
201 N. Fourth Avenue, Yuma,
AZ 85364
Tel: (928) 329-0471
Yuma Territorial Prison State Historic Park
PO Box 10792, Yuma, AZ 85366
Tel: (928) 783-4771

General Parks and Backcountry Information

Arizona State Parks Office
1300 W. Washington, Phoenix,
AZ 85007
Tel: (602) 542-4174
www.pr.state.az.us
Arizona Public Lands Information Center
Bureau of Land Management,
222 N. Central Avenue, Phoenix,
AZ 85004
Tel: (602) 417-9300
www.az.blm.gov/azso.htm
National Park Service
3115 N. 3rd Avenue, Suite 101,
Phoenix, AZ 85013
Tel: (602) 640-5250
www.nps.gov
USDA Forest Service
Southwest Regional Office,
517 Gold Avenue SW, Albuquerque,
NM 87102
Tel: (505) 842-3292
www.fs.fed.us

TRANSPORTATION

ACCOMMODATIONS

ACTIVITIES

A – Z

A – Z

A HANDY SUMMARY OF PRACTICAL INFORMATION, ARRANGED ALPHABETICALLY

A irport Taxes

Domestic flights include up to 20 percent in additional taxes to cover U.S. Excise Tax (7.5 percent), post-9/11 security costs, airport and facility fees, etc. Airlines include this in the final total for the plane fare.

B anks and ATMs

Foreign visitors are advised to take US dollar traveler's checks to Arizona since exchanging foreign currency – whether as cash or checks – can prove problematic. An increasing number of banks offer foreign exchange facilities, but this practice is not universal. Some department store chains offer foreign currency exchange. Most shops, restaurants, and other establishments accept traveler's check in US dollars and will give change in cash. Alternatively, checks can be converted into cash at the bank.

Credit cards are very much part of life in Arizona, as in other parts of the US. They can be used to pay for pretty much anything, and it is also common for car rental firms and hotels to take an imprint of your card as a deposit. Rental companies may oblige you to pay a large deposit in cash if you do not have a card.

You can also use your credit card to withdraw cash from ATMs (Automated Teller Machines). Before you leave home, make sure you know your PIN number and find out which ATM system will accept your card. The most widely accepted cards are Visa, American Express, MasterCard, Diners Club, Japanese Credit Bureau, and Discovery Card.

Budgeting for your Trip

There has never been a better time for overseas visitors to visit the United States. The dollar has plummeted to historic lows (more than 2:1 ratio) against the Euro and British pound, in particular, making the US an incredible bargain for European visitors. Allow $80–100/day for good-quality hotels for two people, although really memorable hotels and bed-and-breakfasts tend to run you closer to $150/night. At the other end of the spectrum, Arizona has attractive national forest, desert, and lakeside campgrounds with full facilities for about $16/night, and hostels and very barebones motel lodging can be found for less than $50. You can probably get away with $30/day per person for basic meals if you stick to diners, cafes, markets, and inexpensive restaurants and don't drink alcohol. Meals in better restaurants cost a lot more (see Restaurant sections at the end of relevant chapters for a guide) but if you're determined to visit that famous high-end establishment and don't have the cash, one insider trick is to eat lunch there: you'll find many of the items on the dinner menu at much lower prices and still get to say you've eaten at a hip eatery. Budget at least $4.50 per gallon for gas costs for your rental car; most economy vehicles get over 30 miles per gallon. Light rail, buses, and other public transportation in cities like Phoenix and Tucson are just a few dollars per ride, allowing you to get around for much less.

Business Hours

US stores are often open seven days a week and tend to stay open into the evening, especially in tourist areas. Government businesses are usually only open on weekdays from 8 or 9am to 4 or 5pm. US post offices are usually open at 8am and close around 5 or 5.30pm, open for more limited hours on Saturdays, and close on Sundays.

C limate

Temperature: Arizona spans half a dozen climate and life zones, but by and large, you will find sunny skies, low humidity, and limited precipitation. Climate varies widely with elevation. Climbing 1,000ft (300m) is equivalent to traveling 300 miles (500km) northward. In temperature, traveling from the lowest to the highest points in Arizona is like traveling from Mexico to the north of Hudson Bay in Canada. In Tucson, for example, it's possible to sun yourself at poolside in the morning and ski atop nearby Mount Lemmon in the afternoon.

The northern region averages around 73 percent sunshine; the southern part of the state averages around 90 percent. Yearly rainfall averages 12 inches (30cm); much of it falls in brief, intense thunderstorms during the summer "monsoon" season, when dry washes (arroyos) and narrow canyons are prone to flash floods and dangerous to travelers. Wind velocity in cities is under 8mph (13kph), although exposed and high-elevation areas tend to be gusty.

Average temperatures in low-elevation Phoenix and Tucson reach 100°F (38°C) in summer and fall but often soar to 110°F (43°C) or higher for long periods. Nights are warm and pleasant, usually ranging from 65°F (18°C) to 75°F (24°C). Winter and early spring are the ideal seasons to visit Phoenix and Tucson, with average daytime temperatures from 65°F (18°C) to 75°F (24°C); nighttime temperatures dip into the 30s°F. It's not unknown for southern Arizona to experience a frigid snap with snowfall in January. Come prepared. Phoenix gets about 7ins (18cm) of rain per year. Tucson, at a slightly higher elevation, gets 11ins (28cm).

It's a very different story in Flagstaff, capital of northern Arizona, 145 miles (230km) to the north at the base of the San Francisco Peaks, the highest mountains in the state. Temperatures here range from 75°F to 80°F (24°C to 27°C) in summer and fall to around 15°F (-10°C) in winter. Due to a long-running

CLIMATE CHART

Phoenix

■ Maximum temperature
□ Minimum temperature
— Rainfall

drought, annual precipitation in Flagstaff now averages 12.5ins (30cm), most of it falling in July, August, and January. Winter is very cold but generally sunny, with deep snows falling at times. Average snowfall at the Arizona Snowbowl in the San Francisco Peaks is 260ins (660cm). Spring is a mixed blessing in northern Arizona, bringing with it strong winds, as the jetstream changes direction from the northwest to the south, via the Gulf of California, the sources of those tropical storms in summer.

At its hottest, the South Rim of the Grand Canyon reaches 90°F. Temperatures run about 20°F (11°C) hotter at Phantom Ranch at the bottom of the gorge. Flash flooding is common during the monsoon season.

The weather is more comfortable and the crowds generally lighter in spring and fall, with average daytime highs from 65°F (18°C) to 75°F (24°C). Nights are chilly; be sure to bring a sweater or jacket.

Winter is quiet at the South Rim, although rooms may be hard to come by over the Christmas holiday, when El Tovar and other hotels put on special activities. Temperatures slip below freezing nightly, and snowstorms are common, although this can be a great time to do a river trip in the Grand Canyon, which stays relatively warm and mild. Expect icy conditions on roads and trails and occasional road closings due to snow.

The North Rim is about 1,000ft (300m) higher than the South Rim and is significantly cooler and breezier, with summer highs around 75°F (24°C). Evening and morning can be nippy, even in summer, so bring long pants and a sweater. The North Rim is blanketed with as much as 200 inches (510cm) of snow in

winter and is closed from mid-October to mid-May.

Crime and Safety

In general, Arizona is very safe. Be careful in backcountry areas, which occasionally have unbalanced individuals and antisocial survivalists. Avoid hiking and camping alone in remote areas, if you are a woman, and keep to yourself. There is some gang activity in Phoenix and Tucson, but most travelers should have little to worry about. While in the street, use your common sense: Don't carry around large sums of money or expensive video/camera equipment. Walk purposefully and don't make eye contact with unwelcome strangers or respond to come-ons. Don't travel alone at night. Ask the staff in your hotel for advice about areas that should be avoided.

Customs

You can bring into the US the following duty-free items: 1 liter of alcohol, if over 21 years of age; 200 cigarettes, 50 cigars (not Cuban), or 2kg of tobacco, if you're over 18; and gifts worth up to $100 ($800 for US citizens). Travelers with more than $10,000 in US or foreign currency, traveler's checks, or money orders

Safety Tips for Motorists

When you arrive, ask for advice from the car rental agent about the best route from the airport to your hotel. Better still, arrange to pick up your rental car from an agency near your hotel on the morning after you arrive, rather than tackle unfamiliar routes when very tired. Many car rental agencies will deliver your car to your hotel at no (or only a small) extra charge.

Use a map to plot out your route before you begin any journey, to stop you going astray.

Ignore any pedestrian or motorist who tries to stop you, for example by indicating some supposed fault on your vehicle or even by ramming your car from behind.

Always keep your car doors locked, windows closed, and valuables out of sight while driving.

Avoid taking short cuts in urban areas. If you get lost, drive to a well-lit and preferably busy area before stopping to look at your map.

TRANSPORTATION

ACCOMMODATIONS

ACTIVITIES

A – Z

must declare these upon entry. Meats, fruits, vegetables, seeds, or plants (and, note, even sealed prepared foods from them) are not permitted and must be disposed in the bins provided before entering. For more information, contact US Customs & Border Protection (tel: 877-227-5511; "Know Before You Go" document on www.cbp.gov).

Currency

American dollars come in bills of $1, $5, $10, $20, $50, and $100, all the same size. The dollar is divided into 100 cents. Coins come in 1 cent (penny), 5 cents (nickel), 10 cents (dime), 25 cents (quarter), 50 cents (half-dollar), and $1 denominations. There is no Value Added Tax (VAT) in the US but cities charge a sales tax, usually 7-8 percent of the sale. Car rental companies charge both sales tax and service fees.

D isabled Travelers

Under the Americans with Disabilities Act (ADA), accommodations built after January 26, 1995, and containing more than five rooms must be useable by persons with disabilities. Older and smaller inns and lodges are often wheelchair-accessible. For the sight-impaired, many hotels provide special alarm clocks, captioned television services, and security measures. To comply with ADA hearing-impaired requirements, hotels have begun to follow special procedures; local agencies may provide TTY and interpretation services. Check with the front desk when you make reservations to ascertain to what degree the hotel complies with ADA guidelines. Ask specific questions regarding bathroom facilities, bed height, wheelchair space, and availability of services. To find more about accommodations in where you can narrow your search to ADA-compliant properties. Restaurants and attractions are required to build ramps for those with limited mobility. Many major attractions have wheelchairs for loan or rent. Some provide menus, visitors guides, and interpreters for hearing- and seeing-impaired guests.

Paved trails suitable for use by travelers with disabilities can be found in many parks, including the Grand Canyon. Wheelchairs are available for temporary day use at Canyon View Information Plaza and Yavapai Observation Station at the South Rim. Wheelchair accessible

tours can be arranged through any lodge transportation desk (tel: 928-638-2631), and several whitewater rafting companies operating in the Grand Canyon offer rafting trips for people with disabilities with advance notice. Grand Canyon National Park publishes an Accessibility Guide, which has information on park facilities that are accessible to visitors with disabilities. It's available from NPS Information Centers, by writing to PO Box 129, Grand Canyon, AZ 86023, or online through the park's Web site: www.nps.gov/grca.

The Society for the Advancement of Travel for the Handicapped (tel: 212-447-7284; www.sath.org) publishes a quarterly magazine on travel for the disabled.

E lectricity

The United States uses 110 to 120 volts AC (60 cycles). If visiting from outside North America, you may require an electrical adapter for any electronics or appliances you want to bring. Las Vegas electrical outlets accept the standard North American plug with two flat parallel pins.

Embassies

Foreign embassies are all located in Washington, DC. Phone numbers include Britain (tel: 202-462-1340); Germany (tel: 202-298-4000); France (tel: 202-944-6000); and Australia (tel: 202-797-3000). Call directory enquiries for others.

Entry Regulations

Foreign travelers to the United States (including, as of January 2007, those from Canada and Mexico) must carry a valid passport; a visa is required for visits of more than 90 days. A return plane ticket is also normally required. Regulations have been changing (see note about bringing liquids on board planes in Airport Arrivals). For the most current information, contact the U.S. Department of Homeland Security at www.dhs.gov.

G ay and Lesbian Travelers

Phoenix is home to a large gay and lesbian community, and there's a growing number of gay-friendly stores and bars, nightclubs, and restaurants. You'll find news and entertainment listings for Phoenix in Echo Magazine, a free bi-weekly that is distributed in cafes, bookstores, and bars. For more information, write PO Box 16630, Phoenix, AZ 85011;

Emergency Numbers

In case of emergency, dial 911 to contact the police, fire, or ambulance service.

602-266-0550; tel: 888-324-6624; or log on to www.echomag.com. For information on virtually anything, from lodging to HIV/Aids resources in Phoenix, call **1N10** – a gay and lesbian community center – between 10am and 10pm seven days a week. Tel: 602-234-2752, 602-264-5436; www.1N10.org. The Tucson Weekly Observer (www.tucson observer.com) has information on the gay lifestyle in Tucson.

Traveling as a gay person in rural Arizona is likely to be more challenging. Lesbians, and to a lesser degree, gay men have a small presence in college and liberal arts towns like Flagstaff and Sedona, but are largely underground elsewhere, due to conservative attitudes. A helpful overview of gay resources throughout the state can be viewed at www.gayarizona.com.

H ealth

Health Insurance

It's vital to have medical insurance when traveling in the US. Although hospitals are obligated to provide emergency treatment to anyone who needs it whether or not they have insurance, you may have to prove you can pay for treatment of anything less than a life-threatening condition. Know what your policy covers and have proof of the policy with you at all times or be prepared to pay at the time service is rendered.

Health Hazards

Flash Floods
Sudden downpours – even those falling miles away from your location – can fill canyons and dry riverbeds with a deadly roaring torrent of water and mud that will sweep away everything in its path. Travelers should be especially careful during the summer monsoon season (July to September). Avoid hiking or driving in arroyos or narrow canyons, and never try to wade or drive across a flooded stream. If rain begins to fall, or you see rain clouds in the distance, move to higher ground. It's impossible to outrun or even outdrive a flash flood. Take action before water levels begin to rise.

Sunburn
Even a couple of hours outdoors can result in sunburn, so protect yourself

with a high-SPF sunscreen (be sure to put it on 15 minutes or so before going out in the sun) and polarized sunglasses and a broad-brimmed hat. The elderly and the ill, small children, and people with fair skin should be especially careful. Excessive pain, redness, blistering, or numbness mean you need professional attention. Minor sunburn can be soothed by taking a cold bath or using aloe vera gel.

Dehydration

Drink plenty of fluids and, if outdoors, carry bottles of water and a high-energy snack to eat. The rule of thumb is a gallon (4l) of water per person per day, and at least a liter for shorter walks. Don't wait to get thirsty; start drinking as soon as you set out. Dehydration and salt deficiency can lead to heat exhaustion, especially if you take medications, drink alcohol, or drink strong coffee. It's best to moderate or avoid alcohol and caffeine and drink plenty of water and take time to acclimatize to the heat if you are not accustomed to it. Also avoid the sun at its hottest: 2–4pm.

Drinking Water

All water from natural sources must be purified before drinking. Giardia is found throughout the West, even in crystal-clear water, and it can cause severe cramps and diarrhea. The most popular purification methods are tablets or filters (both available from camping stores) or by boiling water for at least 15 minutes. Drink only bottled water in Mexico and avoid ice cubes and salads.

Cactus

To avoid being pricked, stay on trails and wear long pants and sturdy boots. Some people may have allergies to the prickly varieties of these beautiful desert plants.

Heat Stroke

Long, uninterrupted periods of exposure to high temperatures can lead to heat stroke, which means that the body's core temperature rises to dangerous level and its normal cooling system – reddening and sweating – is overwhelmed. To head off problems, keep major arteries in your neck cool by wearing a wet bandanna or cotton shirt with a collar. If you start to feel dizzy and fuzzy-brained, feel muscle weakness and start to stumble, and your skin has become pale and dry rather than red and sweaty, immediately begin spraying yourself with water or, better yet, pour it on you. This creates

evaporative cooling and is the fastest way to recover. You can also lie down in a dark room with a wet sheet over you and the air-conditioning on. Whatever you do, don't jump into cold water in a pool: it can send your body into shock. Heat stroke is a common problem for light-eyed, light-haired Europeans from northern climates and is a potentially serious condition, so don't ignore the telltale signs.

Hypothermia

This occurs when the core body temperature falls below 95°F (35°C). At altitude, combinations of alcohol, cold, and thin air can produce hypothermia. Watch for drowsiness disorientation, and sometimes increased urination. If possible, get to a hospital, otherwise blankets and extra clothing should be piled on for warmth. If necessary, skin-to-skin contact is effective. Don't use hot water or electric heaters and don't rub the skin. The elderly should be careful in extremely cold weather.

Frostbite

Symptoms of frostbite, which occurs when living tissue freezes, include numbness, pain, blistering, and whitening of the skin. The most immediate remedy is to put frostbitten skin against warm skin. Simply holding your hands for several minutes over another person's frostbitten cheeks or nose may suffice. Otherwise, immerse frostbitten skin in warm (not hot) water. Refreezing will cause even more damage, so get the victim into a warm environment as quickly as possible. If one person is frostbitten, others may be, too.

Altitude Sickness

This is not a serious consideration in most parts of the state, although people traveling from sea level may feel uncharacteristically winded at elevations as low as 6,000 or 7,000ft (1,800–2,100m). The sensation usually passes after a few days. Symptoms, including nausea, headache, vomiting, extreme fatigue, light-headedness, and shortness of breath, intensify over 10,000ft (3,000m). Although the symptoms may be mild at first, they can develop into a serious illness. It's best to acclimate gradually when you are coming from sea level. Spend a few days at a lower elevation, then move higher.

Insects and Animals

Snakes
Arizona has two venomous snakes:

rattlesnakes and coral snakes. Only about three percent of people bitten by a rattlesnake die, and these are mainly very small children. Walk in the open, proceed with caution among rocks, avoid dark and overgrown places where snakes lurk, shake out bedding or clothing that has been lying on the ground, and wear sturdy hiking boots. Snakes often lie on roads at night because of the residual heat radiating from the pavement, so use a flashlight if walking on a paved road after dark. Most important: Keep your hands and feet where you can see them, and don't let children poke under rocks or logs.

Snakebite kits are good psychological protection but there is controversy over how effective they are. If bitten, first, stay calm, to avoid circulating the venom through your body more rapidly. Then apply a tourniquet lightly above the bite toward the heart. Try to identify the species and go immediately to the doctor.

Gila Monsters
North America's only venomous lizard, found in the Sonoran Desert, looks menacing but is easily recognized and rarely encountered.

Insects
Bees are abundant, which should concern only those allergic to bee stings. Carry an Epi pen to be safe when traveling. The kissing bug is an unusual-looking insect with an unpleasant bite. There are fire ants and some varieties of wasp. Their sting can be painful but isn't dangerous unless you're allergic to their venom. Cedar gnats, or no-see-ums, are one of the most annoying of bugs, starting in May when they, like many bugs, begin to hatch. They get into eyes, ears, noses, mouths, and hair and deliver a nasty bite that can swell and give flu-like symptoms. If camping or hiking among junipers (cedars, in pioneer slang), use fine-mesh netting and a tent with no-see-um-proof windows. Deer flies, a particularly large biting fly, may also be found in Four Corners locations and will present an annoyance to hikers.

The bite of a black widow spider and tarantula and the sting of a pale-colored desert scorpion's tail can pack a punch, but are rarely a serious health threat to adults. Scorpions are nocturnal, so use flashlights and never walk barefoot in the desert. They often hide in recesses, dark corners, and old wood piles and like to crawl into protected places, so shake out clothes or sleeping bags that have been on the ground and check your shoes before slipping into them in the morning.

Internet

The modems of many foreign laptops and handheld computers won't work in the US. You may need to purchase a global modem before leaving home or a local PC-card modem once you arrive in the US. For more details, log on to www.teleadapt.com. There are now numerous cyber cafes and business centers, such as Kinko's, in the US, where you can pick up email. Most charge a fee for Internet access, either on their computer or your laptop. At Starbucks coffee houses, for example, you must first purchase a T-Mobile Hot Spot pass (currently $9.95 day), before being able to log on; other coffeehouses and restaurants offer free Internet access as a customer incentive. You'll have fewer options in rural areas, but many lodgings offer dial-up high-speed (DSL) or Wireless Internet (WiFi) hot spots. Public libraries often have free WiFi.

Media

Television

All major cities have stations affiliated with major networks, local stations, and a vast number of cable hookups and satellite dish offerings. Hotel rooms usually have cable TV, but you often have to pay to watch movies (Pay Per View). Newspapers give daily and weekly information on TV and radio programs, and satellite TV programming has a program guide through the remote.

Newspapers and Magazines

Every city and most large towns have a local newspaper. For national and international news, along with local and regional events, check the following papers. Also available are the *New York Times*, *Los Angeles Times*, *Washington Post*, *USA Today*, and the *Wall Street Journal*. Forget about finding overseas newspapers, except in a few hotels and specialty bookstores. But most have a website these days, anyway, so if you have a laptop with you, you can read them online.

The state's largest newspaper is the *Arizona Republic* (200 E. Van Buren, Phoenix, AZ 85004; tel: 602-444-8000). Tucson's paper is the *Arizona Daily Star* (4850 S. Park Avenue, Tucson, AZ 85714; tel: 520-573-4220. The *Tucson Citizen* (4850

S. Park Avenue, Tucson, AZ 85714; tel: 520-573-4561) is a free weekly newspaper based in the same building as the *Daily Star* with information on what's happening and current events.

Northern Arizona's leading newspaper is the *Arizona Daily Sun* (1751 S. Thompson, Flagstaff, AZ 86001; tel: 928-282-3206), one of the oldest newspapers in the West. Indian news can be found in the *Navajo-Hopi Observer* (2224 E Cedar Avenue, Flagstaff, AZ 86001; tel: 928-226-9696) and the *Navajo Times* (Highway 264 & Route 12, Window Rock, AZ 86515; tel: 928-871-6642). The *Yuma Daily Sun* follows events in Yuma and may be reached at 2055 Arizona Avenue, Yuma, AZ 85364; tel: 928-783-3333. And the *Lake Powell Chronicle* has information on Lake Powell and Page and may be reached at 5 Elm Street, Page, AZ 86040; tel: 928-645-8888.

The following magazines feature profiles of interesting destinations and local people, as well as restaurant listings and a calendar of events: *Arizona Highways* (2039 W. Lewis Avenue, Phoenix, AZ 85009; tel: 800-543-5432; www.arizonahighways.com; and *Tucson Lifestyle* (7000 E. Tanque Verde Road, Suite 11, Tucson, AZ 85715; tel: 520-721-2929.

Post Offices and Postage

The opening hours of federal post offices vary between central, big-city branches, and those in smaller towns or suburbs; but all open Monday to Friday and some open also on Saturday mornings. Hotel or motel personnel will know the opening hours of the post office nearest you. Drugstores and hotels usually have a small selection of stamps. There are stamp-vending machines in the lobbies of most post offices as well as Automated Postal Centers that allow you to use a credit card to ship mail. ATM machines also usually sell stamps for domestic postage. As of May 12, 2008, first-class domestic rates are 42 cents for 1 oz with 17 cents for each additional ounce. Postcards are 27 cents each. Postage for oveseas letters is 94 cents for 1 oz; 72 cents to Mexico and Canada. Postage for overseas postcards is currently 75 cents; 55 cents to Canada and Mexico.

Large envelopes over 13 ounces must now be sent by two- to three-day Priority Mail in the US or Media Mail, if the envelope contains printed materials. The fastest service

offered by the post office is Express Mail, which guarantees next-day delivery to most destinations within the US, and delivery within two to three days to foreign destinations by Global Express Mail. Private courier services offering overnight and two-day delivery are usually the most reliable, although more expensive than the US Post Office. Ground delivery, taking an average of five days, is very popular. Telephone numbers for the main courier services are:
FedEx: (800) 238-5355
DHL: (800) 345-2727
UPS: (800) 742-5877

Public Holidays

Public holidays in the US include: New Year's Day (January 1), Martin Luther King's Birthday (January 15), Presidents Day (third Monday in February), Memorial Day (last Monday in May), Independence Day (July 4), Labor Day (first Monday in September), Columbus Day (second Monday in October), Veterans Day (November 11), Thanksgiving (fourth Thursday in November), and Christmas Day (December 25).

Telephones

In this era of cell phones, you'll find fewer public telephones in hotel lobbies, restaurants, drugstores, garages, roadside kiosks, convenience stores, and other locations throughout the state. The cost of making a local call from a pay phone for three minutes is 25–50 cents. To make a long-distance call from a pay phone, use either a prepaid calling card, available in airports, post offices, and a few other outlets, or your credit card, which you can use at any phone: dial 1-800-CALLATT, key in your credit card number, and wait to be connected. In many areas, locals calls have now changed to a 10-digit calling system, using the area code. Watch out for in-room connection charges in the more upmarket hotels: it's cheaper to use a pay phone in the lobby.

Cell phones: American cell phones use GSM 1900 or CDMA 800, a different frequency from other countries. Only foreign phones operating on GSM 1900 will work in the US. You may be able to take the SIM card from your home phone, install it in a rented cell phone in the US, and use it as if it's your own cell phone. Ask your wireless provider about this before leaving. Cell phones can be rented for about $45 a week in the US. Also available are

GSM 1900 compatible phones with prepaid calling time, such as those offered by T-Mobile (www.t-mobile.com). Be aware that you probably won't be able to pick up a signal in remote rural areas. Check the coverage before starting out.

Tipping

Service personnel expect tips in Arizona. The accepted rate for baggage handlers is $1 per bag. For others, including taxi drivers and waiters, 15–20 percent is the going rate, depending on the level and quality of service. Sometimes tips are included in restaurant bills for those dining in groups. Moderate hotel tipping is around 50 cents per bag or suitcase handled by porters and bellboys. A dollar or two for room service. You should tip a doorman if he holds your car or performs other services. It is not necessary to tip chambermaids unless you stay several days, then budget about $1 a day.

Visitor Information

Below is a list of tourist information offices in Arizona:
Arizona Office of Tourism
2702 N Third Street, Suite 4015, Phoenix, AZ 85004
Tel: (602) 364-3700 or (888) 520-3434
www.arizonaguide.com
Bisbee Chamber of Commerce
PO Box BA, Bisbee, AZ 85603
Tel: (520) 432 5421
www.bicbooarizona.com
Flagstaff Convention and Visitors Bureau
211 W. Aspen Avenue, Flagstaff, AZ 86001
Tel: (928) 779-7611 or (888) 788-FLAG
www.flagstaffarizona.org
Grand Canyon Chamber of Commerce
PO Box 3007, Grand Canyon, AZ 86023
Tel: (928) 638-2901
www.grandcanyonchamber.org
Greater Phoenix Convention and Visitors Bureau
400 E. Van Buren, Suite 600, Phoenix, AZ 85004
Tel: (602) 254-6500
www.visitphoenix.com
Lake Havasu City Convention and Visitors Bureau
Tel: (800) 242-8278
www.golakehavasu.com
Mesa Convention and Visitors Bureau
120 N. Center Street, Mesa, AZ 85201

Tel: (480) 827-4700
www.visitmesa.com
Navajoland Tourism Office
PO Box 663, Window Rock, AZ 86515
Tel: (928) 871-6436
www.discovernavajo.com
Nogales–Santa Cruz County Chamber of Commerce
123 W. Kino Park Way, Nogales, AZ 85621
Tel: (520) 287-3685
www.nogaleschamber.org
Page–Lake Powell Chamber of Commerce
644 N. Navajo Drive, Dam Plaza, Page, AZ 86040
Tel: 928) 645-2741 or (888) 261-7243
Parker Area Chamber of Commerce
1217 California Avenue, Parker, AZ 85344
Tel: (928) 669-2174
www.parkerareachamberofcommerce.com
Pinetop–Lakeside Chamber of Commerce
PO Box 4220, Pinetop, AZ 85935
Tel: (928) 367-4290 or (800) 573-4031
www.pinetoplakesidechamber.com
Prescott Chamber of Commerce
117 W. Goodwin Street, Prescott, AZ 86303
Tel: (928) 445-2000
www.visit-prescott.com
Rim Country Chamber of Commerce
100 W. Main Street, Payson, AZ 85547
Tel: (928) 474-4515 or (800) 672-9766
www.rimcountrychamber.com
Scottsdale Convention and Visitors Bureau
4343 N. Scottsdale Road, Suite 170, Scottsdale, AZ 85251
Tel: (480) 421-1004
www.scottsdalecvb.com
Sedona–Oak Creek Canyon Chamber of Commerce
PO Box 478, Sedona, AZ 86336
Tel: (928) 282-7722 or (800) 288-7336
www.visitsedona.com
Sierra Vista Convention and Visitors Bureau
21 E. Wilcox Drive, Sierra Vista, AZ 85635
Tel: (800) 288-3861
www.visitsierravista.com
Sonoita–Elgin Chamber of Commerce
PO Box 607, Sonoita, AZ 85637
Tel: (520) 455-5498
www.sonoitaelginchamber.org
Sonora Tourist Center
Tucson: (800) 470-6072
Sonora: (011) 52-631-314-4489
Tempe Convention and Visitors Bureau
51 W. 3rd Street, Suite 105, Tempe,

AZ 85281
Tel: (480) 894-8158
www.tempecvb.com
Tombstone Chamber of Commerce
PO Box 917, Tombstone, AZ 85638
Tel: (888) 457-3929
www.tombstone.org
Tonto Basin Chamber of Commerce
PO Box 687, Tonto Basin, AZ 85553
Tel: 800) 404-8923
Tubac Chamber of Commerce
PO Box 1866, Tubac, AZ 85646
Tel: (520) 398-2704
www.tubacaz.com
Tucson Convention and Visitors Bureau
100 S Church Avenue, Suite 7199, Tucson, AZ 85701
Tel: (520) 624-1817 or (800) 638-8350
www.visittucson.org
Williams–Grand Canyon Chamber of Commerce
200 W. Railroad Avenue, Williams, AZ 86046
Tel: (928) 635-1418
Yuma Convention and Visitors Bureau
202 S. 1st Avenue, Suite 202, Yuma, AZ 85364
Tel: (928) 376 0100
www.visityuma.com

What to Wear

Think cool and comfortable. With few exceptions, western dress is informal. A pair of jeans or slacks, a polo or button-down shirt, and boots or shoes are appropriate at all but the fanciest places and events. Shorts or capris and light shirts are suitable for most situations in the warmer months, although it's a good idea to have a sweater or jacket for evenings, high elevations, or overly air conditioned shops and restaurants.

Hot, jagged, uneven desert paths will quickly make mincemeat out of light sandals and tennis shoes. Be sure to bring a well-fitting, comfortable, and sturdy pair of hiking shoes or boots or outdoor sandals for outdoor activities. Try to break them in before a big hike. A thin, inner polypropolene sock and a thick, outer sock will help keep your feet dry and comfortable on long hikes. If blisters or sore spots develop, quickly cover them with moleskin or surgical tape, available at most pharmacies or camping supply stores.

A high-factor sunblock, wide-brimmed hat and sunglasses are essential, even if the day starts out cloudy. The sun is merciless, especially in the desert, where shade is scarce.

WHAT TO READ

Guides

Ancient Ruins of the Southwest: An Archaeological Guide, by David Grant Noble. Flagstaff: Northland Publishing, 2000.
The Architecture of the Southwest, by Trent Elwood Sanford. Tucson: University of Arizona Press, 1997.
Arizona's Ghost Towns and Mining Camps: A Travel Guide to History, by Philip Varney. Phoenix: Arizona Highways, 1998.
Cinema Southwest: An Illustrated Guide to the Movies and Their Locations, by John A. Murray. Flagstaff: Northland Publishing, 2000.
The Guide to National Parks of the Southwest, by Nicky Leach. Tucson: Southwest Parks & Monuments Association, 1992.

History and Culture

And Die in the West: The Story of the O.K. Corral Gunfight, by Paula Mitchell Marks. Norman: University of Oklahoma Press, 1996.
Arizona: A Cavalcade of History, by Marshall Trimble. Tucson: Treasure Chest Publications, 1989.
Arizona: A History, by Thomas E. Sheridan. Tucson: University of Arizona Press, 1995.
Beyond the Hundredth Meridian, by Wallace Stegner. New York: Penguin, 1953.
Book of the Hopi, by Frank Waters. New York: Penguin, 1963.
Book of the Navajo, by Raymond Locke. Los Angeles: Mankind Publishing, 1976.
The Exploration of the Colorado River and its Canyons, by John Wesley Powell. New York: Penguin, 1987.
Geronimo: The Man, His Time, His Place, by Angie Debo. Norman: University of Oklahoma, 1976.
Grand Canyon: An Anthology, by Bruce Babbitt. Flagstaff: Northland Press, 1978.
In the House of Stone and Light: A Human History of the Grand Canyon, by Donald J. Hughes.

Nature

Desert Notes: Reflections in the Eye of a Raven, by Barry Holstun Lopez.
New York: Avon, 1981.
The Desert Year, by Joseph W. Krutch. Tucson: University of Arizona, 1990.
Grand Canyon: Today and All Its Yesterdays, by Joseph Wood Krutch. Tucson: University of Arizona, 1989.
The Man Who Walked Through Time, by Colin Fletcher. New York: Random House, 1989.
Roadside Geology of Arizona, by Halka Chronic. Missoula: Mountain Press, 1983.

Fiction

The Bean Trees, by Barbara Kingsolver. New York: Harper, 1998.
Bisbee '17, by Robert Houston. Tucson: University of Arizona Press, 1999.
The Dance Hall of the Dead, by Tony Hillerman. New York: Harper & Row, 1973.
Days of Plenty, Days of Want, by Patricia Preciado Martin.

Send Us Your Thoughts

We do our best to ensure that the information in our books is as accurate and up-to-date as possible. The books are updated on a regular basis using local contacts, who painstakingly add, amend, and correct as required. However, some details (such as telephone numbers and opening times) are liable to change, and we are ultimately reliant on our readers to put us in the picture.

We welcome your feedback, especially your experience of using the book "on the road." Maybe we recommended a hotel that you liked (or another that you didn't), or you came across a great bar or new attraction we missed.

We will acknowledge all contributions, and we'll offer an Insight Guide to the best letters received.

Please write to us at:
Insight Guides
PO Box 7910
London SE1 1WE
Or email us at:
insight@apaguide.co.uk

Tucson: University of Arizona, 1999.
The Dark Wind, by Tony Hillerman. New York: Harper & Row, 1982.
Dead to Rights: A Joanna Brady Mystery, by J.A. Jance. New York: Avon Books, 1996.
Riders of the Purple Sage, by Zane Grey. New York: Penguin, 1990.
Skinwalkers, by Tony Hillerman. New York: Harper & Row, 1987.
Waiting to Exhale, by Terry McMillan. New York: Pocket Books, 1996.

Other Insight Guides

Companion **Insight Guide** titles cover every major travel destination in North America, from Alaska to Arizona. City titles include *Boston, New York, Philadelphia, Chicago, Orlando, Miami, San Francisco*, and *Washington DC*. Regional titles include *Colorado, New Mexico, New England, New York State, The New South, Texas* and *Utah*. A special title, *USA On the Road*, provides detailed itineraries for five tailor-made routes covering every region in the country.

These are complemented by a comprehensive range of easy-fold **Insight FlexiMaps**, laminated to make them durable and waterproof, and containing useful travel details. Local titles include *American Southwest, California, Florida, Florida's Gold Coast, Miami, Orlando* and *Phoenix*.

A special Insight Guide, *Cruising: All Questions Answered*, shows first-time cruisegoers how to pick the right ship and cruise for them.

Two new series provide detailed information to US destinations in compact form:
● **Insight Step by Step Guides** provide precise itineraries and recommendations from a local, expert writer for dining, lodgings and sightseeing; titles include *Las Vegas, New York* and *Orlando*.
● **Insight Smart Guides** are packed with information, arranged in a unique A–Z format that helps you find what you want quickly and simply. Titles include *Boston, Hawaii, Las Vegas, New York, Orlando*, and *San Francisco*.

ART & PHOTO CREDITS

Matt Abbe/iStockphoto 98L
Arizona Office of Tourism 4T, 129B,
140B, 156T, 206B, 207B, 224B,
238T, 238B, 256, 257T, 257B,
322B, 334T, 349
Doug Berry Photography/
iStockphoto 48B
Bisbee Mining and Historical
Museum 36–7, 68, 70
Ralf Broskvar/iStockphoto 253T
Nathan Chor/iStockphoto 168B
John Cordes/Icon SMI/Corbis
298BL
James Cowlin/Adstock Photos 72
Valerie Crafter/iStockphoto 248T
Richard Cummins 34, 73, 87R,
107, 237T, 245T, 280T, 288–9
Richard Cummins/Corbis 60B
David Elms, Jr/Adstock Photos
262B
epa/Corbis 263B
Paige Falk/iStockphoto 142T
Anton Foltin/iStockphoto 280B
Jill Fromer/iStockphoto 263I
Grand Canyon National Park 136B,
137T
Heard Museum Collection 9B,
190T, 274B
Loretta Hostettler/iStockphoto
88B
George H. H. Huey 16–7, 43, 50,
84, 95, 102, 106, 191B, 237B,
242, 244I, 252T, 252B, 282T,
303B, 314–5, 318B, 321B
George H. H. Huey/Corbis 259T
iStockphoto 85, 172, 244B
Kerrick James 1, 8D, 9L, 11B,
12–3, 14–5, 18, 21, 24, 33, 42,
67, 74–5, 78–9, 81, 88, 91, 92,
93, 97, 98R, 103, 104, 105, 108L,
108R, 109, 118–9, 120–1, 122–3,
130, 131, 134T, 134–5B, 141,
143B, 144T, 148–9, 150, 151,
152T, 152B, 153, 154, 155T,
155B, 157T, 157B, 159T, 160–1,
162, 169B, 185B, 186T, 207I,
212, 219, 220B, 221B, 245B,
246I, 246B, 258B, 259B, 260T,
264T, 272–3B, 290, 318T, 320T
Catherine Karnow 22–3, 29, 35,
56, 164T, 179, 180T, 184B, 187T,
229, 251, 255
Jim Kruger/iStockphoto 137B
Library of Congress 26L, 26R, 27,
32R, 38T, 38B, 39B, 40T, 40C,
40B, 41T, 46L, 46R, 54, 55, 58,
59, 60, 61, 62L, 62R, 62B, 63,
64–5, 66, 69, 71, 114, 185T,
186B, 195BL, 222T, 247, 254T,
270, 312

Saul Loeb/epa/Corbis 41B
Craig Lovell/Corbis 156B
Richard Maack/Adstock Photos
260B
Joe McDaniel/iStockphoto 253B
Morey Milbradt/Brand X/Corbis
261
Katherine Moffitt/iStockphoto
143T
NASA 195BR, 206T
Sarah Neal/iStockphoto 202B
Michelle Fay Nowitz 200, 217L
Richard Nowitz 2–3, 4B, 5B, 8T,
10T, 10B, 11T, 11C, 19T, 19B, 20T,
20B, 25, 34B, 38C, 47, 49, 51, 52,
53, 57, 80, 86L, 86R, 87L, 90, 94,
96, 110T, 110B, 112, 113, 116,
117, 125T, 125B, 129T, 135T,
136T, 138, 139T, 139B, 140T,
164B, 165T, 165B, 167T, 167B,
168T, 169T, 170, 171T, 173, 174T,
174B, 175T, 175B, 177, 178T,
178BL, 180B, 181T, 181B, 183T,
184T, 191T, 192, 193, 194T, 194B,
195T, 196T, 196B, 197T, 197B,
198T, 198B, 199B, 201T, 202T,
203B, 205, 208–9, 213, 215T,
215B, 216T, 216B, 217R, 218T,
218B, 220T, 221T, 223R, 224T,
226–7, 228, 230, 231T, 231B,
232T, 232R, 233T, 233B, 234T,
234B, 235, 236T, 236B, 268, 269,
271, 272T, 275T, 275B, 276T,
276B, 277T, 277B, 278, 279T,
279B, 282B, 284, 285, 291T,
291B, 292, 293, 294, 295B,
296TR, 296TC, 296TL, 296R, 297T,
297D, 298DR, 300T, 299B, 300T,
300D, 301, 302T, 302B, 303T,
304T, 304B, 305T, 305B, 306,
307, 311, 314T, 315T, 316T, 316B,
317L, 317R, 319T, 319B, 320B,
321T, 322T, 323, 324, 325, 326,
330, 332T, 332B, 334B, 337, 338,
339, 341, 344, 351, 352
Jay and Varina Patel/iStockphoto
144B
Mateo Pearson/iStockphoto 99
Phoenix Art Museum 273T, 274TL,
274TR
Larry Rice 222B
Dave Rock/iStockphoto 45
Alexander Rockwood/iStockphoto
281
John Sartin/iStockphoto 262T,
264B
Smithsonian Institution/National
Museum of American Art 39T
Marvin Sperlin/iStockphoto 248B
Alexey Stiop/iStockphoto 142B

Thomas Takacs/iStockphoto 171R
Kate Thompson/DB Studio 158B
Tom Till 48T, 76, 77, 82, 83, 89,
100, 101, 111, 124, 133, 182,
183B, 190B, 199T, 201B, 243,
266–7
Bill Timmerman/Phoenix Art
Museum 9T
Stephen Trimble 3B, 28, 30, 31,
32L, 115, 176, 178BR, 187B, 188,
189, 223L, 250, 254B, 258T,
295T, 310
Vlad Turchenko/iStockphoto 163
P. Wei/iStockphoto 203T
Wiley/Wales 158T, 159B

PICTURE SPREADS

6–7: Clockwise from bottom left:
Richard Nowitz (Monument Valley),
Kerrick James (Grand Canyon),
Richard Nowitz (resort), Richard
Nowitz (Sedona), Kerrick James (Lake
Powell), Arizona Office of Tourism
(Havasupai), Kerrick James (Colorado
River), Arizona Office of Tourism
(Canyon de Chelly), Heard Museum
Collection (Navajo blanket), Kerrick
James (bicycle)
146–7: Clockwise from bottom left:
Kerrick James (hikers), Arizona Office
of Tourism (condor), Arizona Office of
Tourism (bighorn sheep), Arizona
Office of Tourism (snow), Arizona
Office of Tourism (eagle), Kerrick
James (rattlesnake)
240–1: Clockwise from bottom left:
Steven Love/iStockphoto
(hummingbird), Yvonne
Smith/iStockphoto (hawk), Richard
Nowitz (bird-watcher), Frank
Leung/iStockphoto (woodpecker,
Mexican jay), James
Metcalf/iStockphoto (cactus wren),
George H. H. Huey (owl)
286–7: All photos Heard Museum
Collection, except 286–7T Richard
Nowitz
308–9: Clockwise from bottom left:
Roberto A. Sanchez/iStockphoto
(grapes), Kerrick James (two bottles),
Kerrick James (Arizona Vineyards),
Kirby Hamilton/iStockphoto
(corkscrew), Kerrick James (wine
tasting), Kerrick James (bottles)

Map Production:
Colourmap Scanning
© 2009 Apa Publications GmbH & Co.
Verlag KG (Singapore branch)